ADVERTISING AND CULTURAL POLITICS IN GLOBAL TIMES

This book is dedicated to my sister Violet Odih.
Her kindness and love have been an inspiration to me
and everyone that knows her.

Advertising and Cultural Politics in Global Times

PAMELA ODIH
Goldsmiths University of London, UK

Routledge
Taylor & Francis Group
LONDON AND NEW YORK

First published 2010 by Ashgate Publishing

2 Park Square, Milton Park, Abingdon, Oxfordshire OX14 4RN
52 Vanderbilt Avenue, New York, NY 10017

Routledge is an imprint of the Taylor & Francis Group, an informa business

First issued in paperback 2020

British Library Cataloguing in Publication Data
Odih, Pamela.
Advertising and cultural politics in global times.
1. Advertising--Social aspects. 2. Consumption (Economics)--Social aspects.
I. Title
659.1'042-dc22

Library of Congress Cataloging-in-Publication Data
Odih, Pamela.
Advertising and cultural politics in global times / by Pamela Odih.
p. cm.
Includes bibliographical references and index.
ISBN 978-0-7546-7711-6 (hardback)
1. Advertising. 2. Consumption (Economics)--Political aspects.
3. Social control. 4. Power (Social sciences) I. Title.

HF5823.O34 2010
302.23--dc22

2010004875

ISBN 978-0-7546-7711-6 (hbk)
ISBN 978-0-367-60272-7 (pbk)

Contents

List of Figures

Preface

Figure P.1 Advertising vistas and the cultural politics of representation

Source: Hovis 2008. Reproduced with kind permission of Premier Foods Group Limited.

Have you ever watched an advertisement and been amused by the creative ingenuity involved in transforming everyday relations into new social morphologies? Have you ever struggled with the application of rights and responsibilities to the marketized 'choices' for, ordinarily qualitatively valued services? During the 1990s Benetton astounded advertising conventions as its provocative 'hyper-ventilating realism' (Giroux 1993-1994) exploded onto the cultural political landscape. In more recent times, high-street brands have scaled extraordinary heights of corporate religiosity in their efforts to convince us of their commitment to ethical trading.

Have you ever wondered why advertising is so accomplished at replacing political conviction with the playful reverie of commodity culture? Indeed, what can sociology tell us about the transformation of political icons into floating signifiers? How many more simulations of political revolution, can advertising create before it reaches the limits of its transgressive aesthetics?

According to Meijer (1998:247) advertising's ability to construct uniquely revelatory stories about the contemporary world, should be greeted with optimism. This is because, advertising narratives, 'should be seen as part of the wide array of practices and technologies with which individuals nowadays have to constitute their sense of self as – among other things – citizens of ever expanding communities' (ibid). To this end, postmodern advertising aesthetics are transgressive. Examples of this transgressive aesthetic include the provocative narrative histories selectively drawn upon in advertising depictions of the politics of representation. Let us consider this issue with regards to an innovative advertising campaign launched in 2008, by the bread brand Hovis (Premier foods PLC). The campaign entitled *122 Years*, is a highly acclaimed, mammoth advertising venture. Filmed on an epic scale, the 122 seconds long advertisement selectively charts 122 years of the political history of Britain (BBC 2008a). The advertisement's visual imagery depicts major events, during this time frame, through the eyes of the Hovis boy, who picks up a loaf of bread in 1886 and subsequently time travels past legendry posters of the ill-fated Titanic and dramatic scenes of militant Suffragette protestors. Within a matter of seconds the Hovis boy is seen marching alongside his probable peers of young soldiers in World War I and sifting through the debris of World War II (see Figure P.1). The second assemblage of iconic scenes involves the Hovis boy in street party celebrations marking the coronation of Queen Elizabeth II in 1953. The visual imagery dazzles with enchantment as the Hovis boy travels through scenes depicting the vibrant youth culture of the swinging sixties and the cultural amour-propre of England's outstanding 1966 World Cup win. In the final episodes the Hovis boy is seen centre stage in a standoff between the police and striking miners in the 1980s. The film then fast forwards to London's spectacular fireworks display, which marked the dawn of the new Millennium. When, after a marathon 122 years of time travel, the Hovis boy arrives into 2008 and delivers the loaf of bread to his mum, the advertisement ends with the strapline 'As good today as it's always been'. Thus the advertisement equates the Hovis brand, from its inception in 1886 to its 122 year anniversary in 2008, with the most epic political events in Britain's history.

From Meijer's (1998) perspective, the cultural politics depicted in, for example, the Hovis *122 Years* campaign, is a creative feature of advertising visual culture. To this end, cultural politics refers to the crucial role, in an increasingly mediated world, that image plays in 'the multiple "maps of meaning" by which we make sense of the world and the unequal social relations of power that underlie all such cultural distinctions' (Jackson and Taylor 1996:357). Although advertising images may 'annoy us' or 'offend our fellow citizens', in so doing they may 'inspire new civil attitudes and lifestyles' (Meijer 1998:247). And this creative feature of advertising visual culture is particularly evident in postmodern aesthetic techniques that juxtapose unrelated or even oppositional visual metaphors, in such a manner that their collision generates new meaning (ibid).

Meijer (1998) makes the convincing argument that the creative propensities of advertising are extending into the civic realm and disrupting the modernist dichotomies separating consumer culture from politics. Thus, Meijer argues that rather than seeing advertising as 'the designer tools for daily spiritual deprivation' (1998:238), we should 'consider consumer culture instead as an as yet unmined source of civic capital' (ibid:247). While these observations are enlightening, one cannot but help feel that, Meijer's social constructivism insubstantially contends with the materiality of advertising technologies. This is because Meijer fails to apprehend visual culture in terms of the inextricable co-existence of objectifying powers and processes of subjectification, 'in relation to a field of power through which we constitute ourselves as subjects acting on others' (Foucault 1991:351). And this observation accords with Foucault's exploration of the possibilities for a formulation of the self by the self, based on a freedom from prescriptive rules of conduct. The possibility of freedom is 'centered on a problem of personal choice, of aesthetics of existence' (ibid:348).

'Aesthetics of existence' refers to a notion of morality oriented towards a mode of self-referential ethics rather than a set of external norms. The possibility of life as a tapestry for the application of artistic practice fascinated Foucault. Indeed, Foucault lamented the fact that 'art has become something which is related only to objects and not to individuals, or to life' (1991:350). In modern society aesthetic concerns have been sequestered to the province of creatives and artistic experts, they refer to interior decoration of our homes and are less relevant to 'the *techne* of life, the *techne tou biou*, how to live' (ibid:348). Foucault was passionately committed to resurrecting the art of existence, as is evident in the following statement:

> ...we should not have to refer the creative activity of somebody to the kind of relation he has to himself, but should relate the kind of relation one has to oneself to a creative activity. (ibid:351)

From the idea of aesthetics of existence, this book examines advertising as a 'technology of signs' intricately bound up with both the expansion of global networked capitalism, and the forms of cultural political resistance that globalization has precipitated. Foucault describes 'sign technologies' as formations of discourse and discursive practice, 'which permit us to use signs, meanings, symbols, signification' (1988:18). It is evidently clear that advertising as a form of 'civic capital' (Meijer 1998), encourages the production, by the consumer, of an aesthetics of self-forming ethical activities in, which the consumer makes 'a choice about existence' (Foucault 1991:361). But we all know that advertising is insatiable in its desire to inscribe our everyday world with social meaning. Thus, as part of 'making one's life into an object...for a *techne* – for an art' (ibid:362), the consumer becomes committed to the application of aesthetic values to 'one's life, one's existence' (ibid). And these processes of subjectification are even more remarkable when one considers the ability of advertising, in the 'network society' (Castells 1998, 2010), to amplify the global relationality of our local political actions.

Globalization refers to the intensification of worldwide processes integrating national economies through increasingly unfettered flows of commerce, and financial capital across national boundaries. The tendency for capitalist processes to converge in the production of a global market place is increasingly a consequence of the network society. Capitalism's historic post-1945 rapid decolonization, forced newly independent nations into a globally networked economic order in, which they were expected to adopt export-led trade as a primary vehicle of fiscal development. Thus capitalism has a legacy of global divisions of labour. Nevertheless, the deepening international connections of contemporary global processes, suggests that we are entering a new economic order driven by the powerful forces and the rapid diffusion of information technologies.

Alongside liberalization, and the growth of global corporations, has been an unprecedented advancement of counter globalization alternative trading networks. Flows of ethical commercial trade and ethical financial capital now circulate globally irrespective of national boundaries. And the velocity of circulation assumes unprecedented speed. Revolutions in advertising information technology and a dramatic restructuring of world capitalism have become integral to the political articulation of local crises of non-sustainable development. Of significance to this book, is the Fair Trade movement, and the role of multi-media advertising platforms as a mechanism for enrolling local groups into global supply chain sustainability. 'In this globalitarian conjuncture, the "advertising space" is no longer to be found in the breaks between films or the TV slots between programmers: it is now the real space-time of all communication' (Virillo 2005:113).

Acknowledgements

Professor David Knights (Keele University) has been, and continues to be, an inspiration to me. I would also like to pay tribute to Professor Barbara Adam (Cardiff University) and her ground breaking analyses into time and social theory. Professor Tim May (University of Salford) has also been an inspiration to me and I would to like to take this opportunity to say thank you.

My colleagues at Goldsmiths University of London, Sociology Department are dedicated and extraordinarily creative. I am very grateful for the opportunities and constant inspiration I gain from my colleagues. I would like to take this opportunity to say a particular thank you to Professor Celia Lury, Dr Brian Alleyne, Professor Vic Seidler and Professor Chetan Bhatt.

Neil Jordan has been a patient and very supportive commissioning editor. He kindly supported my initial book proposal and encouraged the development of my ideas into this book.

Friendships and family are so very important to me and I would like to say thank you to my lovely mother Mary, Louise (my niece) and Andre (my nephew). I would also like to take this opportunity to express a heartfelt thank you to my dearest friends Andrea Reay, Simon Meats and Ivalee Harris. Dr Richard Weight has been a delightful creative encouragement and kind friend.

Figure Acknowledgements

Book Cover: Trafalgar Square G20 Protest April 2009.
Source: Photographer Pamela Odih.

Figure P.1: Advertising vista and the cultural politics of representation, Hovis 2008.
Source: Reproduced with kind permission of Premier Foods Group Limited.

Part I: The Conservative Party, campaign poster 2004.
Source: Courtesy of the Advertising Archive. Reproduced with kind permission of The Conservative Party Archive.

Figure 3.1: Mon Bijou as Che Guevara.
Source: Reproduced with kind permission of Duailibi Petit Zaragoza Propaganda, São Paulo, Brazil.

Introduction
Liberal Vistas and the Political Economy of the Sign

The word 'democracy' has its origins in ancient Greece, where the concept emerged to describe a form of rule by the demos, which can be translated as a city state in which citizens governed. In this polis, human beings are essentially 'political animals', whose intellectual and moral capacities can only be attained by the uninhibited participation in democratic institutions structured to promote virtues in citizens. In comprehending, the relation between politics and virtue, Aristotle (384-322BC) pronounced that democracy was an educative phenomenon, which gives expression to the self-realization of human capacities stimulated by participating in political life. A principle feature of this operative conception of the virtuous individual as the good citizen, resides with the ability of education to actualize the intellectual, emotional and moral capacities, of an entire populous to their full potential. The nature of citizenship, Aristotle, declared in *Politics*, is reliant on cultivated self-knowledge. Thus, politics has aesthetic dimensions and '...if politics be an art, change must be necessary in this as in any other art' (Aristotle 2000:80).

Enlightenment discourse retained elements of Aristotle's concern to protect intrinsic rights through erudition, self-improvement and catechetic instruction. Nevertheless, a notable disjuncture appears in the seventeenth century, with the emergence of classical liberalism's 'possessive individualism' (Macpherson 1983). For Aristotle, 'political life must be seen as in large measure a means to the attainment of virtue understood as an end in itself' (Galston 1988:1280). Conversely, in the core components of 'possessive individualism', the Aristotelian 'relation of politics and virtue are reversed: virtue becomes the means, and the political community provides the ends' (ibid). The liberal economic market, of seventeenth century Europe, professed moral values and political ideals that emphasized the sovereignty of the individual. For, classical liberals 'what makes a man human is freedom from dependence on the wills of others' (Macpherson 1983:263). A liberal society is characterized by individuals that exist prior to social interaction and whose natural state is irrevocably a-social. The natural state of human nature is, therefore, 'atomistic' (i.e., isolated) and 'egoistic' (i.e., directed by self-interest). As Holton (1992:55) observes, classical liberalist human beings, 'represent self-contained atoms, whose objectives and strategies for action are formed without any necessary interaction with others'. Individual sovereignty is the natural predisposition of the human being, and thus to act, any differently, might be the result of the arbitrary coercion of some unnatural intervention. Suffice to say, that the individual is the definitive point of reference in liberal market society. In the sense that individuals are fundamentally atomistic, they possess a sense of their own self-interests, which motivate their human action and personal ambition. Thus the very humanity of human beings depends on, naturally ascribed desires and interests. And this suggests a further level of disassociation from a notion of collective will, i.e., the advocacy for self-reliance and a profound incredulity for unnecessary dependence on others. For, political life should assert the values of self-determination and 'freedom from any relation with others except those relations which the individual enters voluntarily with a view to his own interest' (Macpherson 1983:263).

This classical liberal account of individual sovereignty, informed a broad range of intrinsically educative practices, grounded in the assumption that, prior to entering social interaction, individuals articulate knowledge of their own objectives. Historically these, atomistic dispositions were regarded by economists as 'tastes', that is 'preferences analogous to the natural peculiarly personal requirements' of the individual (Holton 1992:56). Only individuals can fully discern their tastes, since these derive from the pre-social self rather than as a product of interaction with others. It is also taken as axiomatic that individuals are inherently rational and technically efficient in the satiation of their tastes. One consequence of this principle, is that classical liberalism is committed to an instrumental account of rationality 'where rational action is regarded as a characteristic of the way we choose means to reach a given end' (ibid:58). Economic liberals have traditionally bridged the pre-social dimensions of the individual and the necessity of social life, through the construct of private property and commitment to self-regulating markets (ibid).

Classical liberalism's overriding concept of market society fundamentally implies the cultivation of individual self-fulfillment and a 'commitment to developing the capacity of individuals...to pursue their own version of the "good life" for themselves, free from manipulation by others or from external pressures and constraints' (Carr and Harnett 2002:44). From this perspective, the task of actualizing classical liberalist virtues is axiomatic with the promotion of property rights, and the presumption that the possessive accumulation of material wealth is the principle vehicle through, which sovereign individuals can achieve their self-interests. The logical implication here is that sovereign individuals come to adopt a certain entrepreneurial form of practical relationship to their selves. Enterprise is represented here as playing a vital translating role, promising to align general political-ethical principles, with the goals of industry and the self-regulating activities of individuals (Miller and Rose 1993:100). Within this political-ethical environment, individuals are constituted as both objects of enterprise and instruments of enterprise as they make 'entrepreneurs of themselves, seeking to maximize their "quality of life" through the artful assembly of a "life-style" put together through the world of goods' (ibid:98). To this extent classical liberalism can be seen as a precursor to modern forms of governmental rationalities, which have become reliant upon the self-regulating capacities of subjects, configured and normalized by disciplinary technologies (ibid). Of significance here is the disciplinary affect of 'technologies of sign systems' (Foucault 1988).

Michel Foucault's accounts of disciplinary technologies, render intelligible liberal virtues in terms of very particular 'truth games related to specific techniques that human beings use to understand themselves' (ibid:18). 'Technologies of sign systems' reflect and reproduce 'a matrix of practical reason' (ibid). This book argues that sign technologies are both the medium, and outcome of liberal virtues. Indeed, liberalism's past, present and future need to be understood in relation to the disciplinary tactics of 'sign technologies'. In more specific terms, this book interrogates advertising as a 'sign technology', integral for the translation of global liberalized capitalism into geopolitical tactics.

Theoretical Frameworks: Liberalism and the Political Economy of the Sign

Foucault's (1982, 1991a) interrogation of the production of truth, examines liberalism in terms of practices concerned with the regulation of bodies in time/space, the government of conduct and the formulation of the self. Thus, Foucault is skeptical of the 'theme of liberation' in so far as it refers 'back to the idea that there does exist a nature or human foundation which…found itself concealed, alienated or imprisoned in and by some repressive mechanism' implying that 'it would suffice to unloosen these repressive locks so that man can be reconciled with himself' (1988a:2 cited in Simons 1995:47). For, 'the man described for us, whom we are invited to free, is already in himself the effect of a subjection much more profound than himself' (Foucault 1991a:30). In so far as power is embedded in the 'social nexus', subjectivity exists in reciprocal relation to power. Individual self consciousness is configured through the exercise of power within, which apprehensions of personal identity come to be engendered. As Foucault expresses it:

> …the individual is not a pre-given entity which is seized on by the exercise of power. The individual, with his [sic] identity and characteristics, is the product of a relation of power exercised over bodies, multiplicities, movements, desires and forces. (Foucault 1976, in (ed.) Gordon 1980:73-74)

Accepting that power is multiple and ubiquitous thus involves appreciating that there can be no 'true' essential subjectivity to be liberated from power. To this extent, power is positive in its existence and productive of self-identities along with their regimes of truth; rather than manifest in 'interdiction and operating by repression and deduction' (Dean 1994:156). Within the scope of this micro-physics of the self, Foucault depicts liberation movements, and their quest to emancipate subjects from the abuse of arbitrary power, as in fact bound up with disciplinary technologies directed at both constraining and enabling the power of subjection. For, it is evident that power/knowledge directly imply the preservation of the classical liberal autonomous self, against constraints that would undermine its sovereignty. Liberalism's propensity is not freedom but unfreedom as it binds us ever more 'tightly to our subjectivities through our efforts to liberate ourselves' (Simons 1995:47). Indeed, the historical emergence of classical liberalism, also marks the ascendency of disciplinary technologies that make possible the accumulation of capital and 'a political take-off as the traditional, ritual, costly, violent forms of power were superseded by a subtle, calculated technology of subjection' (Sheridan 1994:157).

Initially conceived, as a quest for the freedom of the sovereign individual from arbitrary power, the advancement of liberalism has been accompanied by the evolution of disciplinary technologies and normalization processes (Foucault 1982:213-4). The object of these technologies is the 'soul', to be understood as an entity, unlike in the Christian theological sense as a supernatural quality 'born in sin and subject to punishment' (Foucault 1991a:29). Rather, Foucault's account of the soul, regards it as a substantive category, 'born…out of methods of punishment, supervision and constraint' (ibid). As he expresses it:

> This real, non-corporal soul is not a substance; it is the element in which are articulated the effects of a certain type of power and the reference of a certain type of knowledge, the machinery by which the power relations give rise to a possible corpus of knowledge, and knowledge extends and reinforces the effects of this power. On this reality-reference, various concepts have been constructed and domains of analysis carved out: psyche, subjectivity, personality, consciousness, etc.; on it have been built scientific techniques and discourses, and the moral claims of humanism. (ibid:29-30)

It needs to be emphasized that Foucault is not assuming that the real human subject and, object of intellectual knowledge has been substituted for a non-corporal soul. The micro-physics of power permeates the entire society and operates through the soul on the body (Sheridan 1994). Thus 'a soul inhabits him and brings him to existence, which is itself a factor in the mastery that power exercises over the body. The soul is the effect and instrument of a political anatomy; the soul is the prison of the body' (Foucault 1991a:30). Suffice to say, that the soul is the product, and instrument, of technologies of: production; sign systems; power and the self. The raison d'étre connecting these technologies is the exercise of power upon the body, 'the body and its powers and capacities which are to be transformed in the processes of individualisation, and the body and its desires which are transformed in the construction of the self' (Marshall 1996:114).

There are historical reasons why our modern era is characterized by disciplinary technologies. The eighteenth century had witnessed a profound transition away from the spectacle of monarchical law, in which the body bore the inscription of monarchical sovereignty (Foucault 1991a). In the Ancien Régime's code of governance, transgression was punished by spectacular visual displays of violence against the body. Techniques of discipline assumed a certain art of inflicting pain on the body, '...tortured, dismembered, amputated...symbolically branded...exposed alive or dead to public view. The body [was] the major target of penal repression' (ibid:8). There is clearly an astonishing coincidence between 'the art of punishing' and the undertaking of 'technologies of sign systems'. In the Ancien Régime, criminality was conceived as transgressing the embodiment of the law, i.e., the absolute monarchy. Punishment had thus to assume a symmetry of vengeance, in which a complex theatrics of barbaric retaliation inflicted on the criminal's body, marked the re-instituted supremacy of the monarch's power. In the Ancien Régime 'the role of the criminal in punishment was to reintroduce, in the face of crime and the criminal code, the real presence of the signified – that is to say, of the penalty which, according to the terms of the code, must be infallibly associated with the offence' (ibid:128). The body thus bears on it the inscription of the monarch's power, and the obscene spectacle of punishment abundantly circulates the reinvigorated spectra of absolute power. Punishment is thus a 'technology of sign systems', an object of representation and the 'individual correction must, therefore, assure the process of redefining the individual as subject of law, through the reinforcement of the systems of signs and representations that they circulate' (ibid).

While it is the case that much of *Discipline and Punish* is preoccupied with the transition from the spectacle of punishment to the 'birth of the prison', the book is not merely a genealogy of the penal system. Rather, it is Foucault's observation that the technologies of discipline that emerged, in the context of the prison, later cascade into other contemporary institutions and are taken up by modern forms of governmental rationality. In this transformation two processes are in operation; the growth of liberal humanism and the displacement of the visceral body as a target for technologies of signs. And this association will become more evident when we reflect historically, on the transitional period of the Enlightenment. For, it was during this period that punishment is less prevalently a complex of signs marked onto the body of the criminal. The art of representation's punitive intervention is gradually driven asunder by the ineluctable march of a new juridical ethic that is predicated 'on a studied manipulation of the individual' (ibid:128). By the latter part of eighteenth and the beginning of the nineteenth century 'the representative, scenic, signifying, public model' of punishment is less prominent, as it comes to be replaced by a 'corporal, solitary, secret model of the power to punish' (ibid:131). The disappearing 'social play of the signs of punishment and the prolix festival that circulated them' marks not just a new orthodoxy in penal reform, but a transition in the modality of technologies of sign systems (ibid). The apparatus of corrective penalty, becomes less reliant on the improvised extravaganza of embellishments that pronounced the raison d'étre of sovereign power. The point of application is less inclined to be the symmetry of vengeance, but rather the 'transparency of the sign to that which it signifies' (ibid:106). What is necessitated is the establishment within 'the theatre of punishments, a relation that is immediately intelligible to the senses and on which a simple calculation may be based: a sort of reasonable aesthetic of punishment' (ibid). In short, the divergence from the inscription of marks on the criminal's body, is bound up with a new regime of penal power of 'exercises not signs: time-tables, compulsory movements, regular activities, solitary mediation, work in common, silence, application, respect, good habits' (ibid:128). Up until Foucault's analyses, historians tended to take for granted this transition from a punitive corporal action to the new juridical ethic and 'too readily' attributed it 'to a process of "humanization", thus dispensing with the need for further analysis' (ibid:7). Conversely, Foucault's intellectual skepticism ceaselessly interrogated the emergence of the liberal humanist penal reform. Foucault's observations lead him to argue that the 'birth of the prison' instituted a 'technique of coercion' that has as its objective not so much the creation of the judicial subject, but rather 'the obedient subject, the individual subjected to habits, rules, orders, an authority that is exercised continually around him and upon him, and which he must allow to function automatically in him' (ibid:129).

Axiomatic with this juridical ethic is a new modality of sign technologies. In the monarchical law of the Ancien Régime, punishment signifies absolute sovereignty; 'it uses the ritual marks of the vengeance that it applies to the body of the condemned man...and it deploys before the eyes of the spectators an effect of terror as intense as it is discontinuous, irregular and always above its own laws, the physical presence of the sovereign and of his power' (ibid:130). The reforming 'truth' of liberal humanism saw punishment as a means to rehabilitate 'individuals as subjects, as juridical subjects' (ibid). The 'birth of the prison' signifies the institutionalization of an advanced mode of sign technologies, which no longer 'marks' the body, but rather deploys signs as 'coded sets of representations' designed, in operation, to render intelligible 'a concerted orthopaedy applied to convicts in order to reclaim them individually' (ibid:130). Thus disciplinary technologies of sign systems coexist with 'a whole learned economy of publicity' (ibid:110). Where monarchical law was based on the mark of terror 'engraved on the memories of the spectators', with the birth of the prison, discipline 'is now based on the lesson, the discourse, the decipherable sign, the representation of public morality' (ibid). Signs operate to reinforce public cognizance of the link between the crime and the particularity of its punishment. In monarchical law, one witnessed in the penalty the metaphoric presence of the sovereign. Conversely, with the 'birth of the prison' one reads in the signs of punishment 'the laws themselves' (ibid:110). Moreover, the penalty is a sign economy of time 'as soon as the crime is committed, the punishment will follow at once, enacting the discourse of the law and showing that the code, which links ideas, also links realities' (ibid). Thus, 'posters, placards, signs, symbols must be distributed, so that everyone may learn their significations', and in so doing punishment assumes less the 'physical effect of terror' (ibid:111). In this promotional code of signifying practices punishment assumes the function of a school in, which the scope of the audience extends beyond the guilty person and is directed above all 'at others, at all the potentially guilty' (ibid:108).

It is within this positive mechanics of discipline that 'discourse will become the vehicle of the law; the constant principle of universal recoding' (ibid:112). For the birth of the prison, in actuality marks a more insidious sign of governance, discrete yet nonetheless capable of an effective inscription on the body and soul of individuals (Foucault 1991a). Much of the affect stems from liberal humanism's regalia of human rights and the growing belief, 'that to insist on the punishment exceeding the crime in savagery was, in a sense, to repeat the crime' (Sheridan 1994:137). This incredulity for the punishment-as-spectacle had the affect of transferring punishment further away from the domain of the everyday and into 'that of abstract consciousness' (Foucault 1991a:9). And in so doing the instructive mechanism of punishment alters its operation, for 'publicity has shifted to the trial, and to the sentence' (ibid). Within the liberal humanist regalia of human rights, 'the body now serves as an instrument or intermediary: if one intervenes upon it to imprison it, or to make it work, it is in order to deprive the individual of a liberty that is regarded both as a right and as property' (ibid:11). The body is now entangled within a castigating system of 'privations, obligations and prohibitions' (ibid). From being the object of unbearable physical pain, the punishment-body relation is transformed into the primary vehicle for 'an economy of suspended rights' (ibid). It is here that discourse unquestionably becomes a vehicle of the law. This is because the new humanist penal regime required 'a whole army of technicians' to take over from the key personnel, who were previously responsible for executing punishment-as-spectacle. As punishment begins to assume the much higher ambition of rehabilitating, 'curing' and reclaiming the criminal, there develops, exponentially, a new model army of 'warders, doctors, chaplains, psychiatrists, psychologists, educationalists' who 'by their presence near the prisoner, they sing the praises that the law needs; they reassure it that the body and pain are not the ultimate objects of its punitive action' (ibid:11). Thus, initially directed at the individual, the application of disciplinary sign technologies extends 'the whole length of the social network' so as to obfuscate a source of power and instead install the power to punish 'as an immediate reaction of all in relation to the individual' (ibid:130).

Discipline, then, will tend to become the most obscure dimension of the social order. In the milieu from, which the spectacle of monarchical law has disassociated from punishment, the process of discipline has 'taken to judging something other than crimes', namely, the soul of the individual. Indeed, now that 'the scandal and the light are to be distributed differently' (ibid:9), it is discourse that marks the social world with a litany of private rights, and judicial rituals to protect against the arbitrary infringement of these rights. Nowhere is this transition better illustrated than in the spectacular progression from the political order of neoliberalism, to global liberalism and the 'sign technologies' that are its condition and consequence.

Marketing the Soul

In the writings of Michel Foucault we are challenged to interrogate liberal humanist virtues. For more than twenty years of his academic career Foucault was concerned to trace a history of the manifold ways in Western culture 'that humans develop knowledge about themselves…' (1988:18). In an essay entitled *Technologies of the Self*, Foucault clarifies very important conceptual tools necessary for decoding liberal humanism as a system of knowledge with, 'specific "truth games" related to specific techniques that human beings use to understand themselves' (ibid). These techniques, assume four major forms of 'technologies' and each mode constitutes a vehicle of practical reason. The first is 'technologies of production', which permit the transformation of natural objects into resources for the mobilization of human interests. Foucault recognizes synergies here with dialectical materialism, 'for instance one sees the relation between manipulating things and domination in Karl Marx's *Capital*, where every technique of production requires modification of individual conduct-not only skills but also attitudes' (ibid). The theme of transformation is evident in, 'technologies of sign systems', the second mode of technology that humans use to organize social life and develop knowledge. Foucault describes this technology as modes of discourse and discursive practice, 'which permit us to use signs, meanings, symbols, signification' (ibid). In his book *Discipline and Punish*, technologies of sign systems enter into a matrix of practical reasoning that functions in a manner, which exceeds a positivistic ontology of the image as representing a mirror of the world that merely needs decoding. Instead, technologies of sign systems are integrated into penal practice and in so doing operate as modes of administration, regulation and discipline. Technologies of sign systems work in conjunction with the third specific technique that human beings have created to know themselves, i.e., 'technologies of power'. Foucault's focus here is premised on elucidating technologies that 'determine the conduct of individuals and submit them to certain ends or domination, an objectivizing of the subject' (ibid). These objectifying technologies form a recurrent theme in *Discipline and Punish.* And in his later work *Histories of Sexuality* technologies of power, are detailed in conjunction with the fourth of Foucault's technologies i.e., 'technologies of self'. These permit individuals to voluntarily carry out practices 'on their bodies and souls, thoughts, conduct, and way of being, so as transform themselves in order to attain a certain state of happiness, purity, wisdom, perfection or immortality' (ibid). According to Foucault, these four technologies often operate collaboratively, 'although each one of them is associated with a certain type of domination' (ibid). That is to say that each involves a regime of training and modification in the individual, directed not merely at the acquisition of skills but also in the development of attitudes. It is my intention to apply, Foucault's (1988) concept of technologies to render intelligible globalized liberal capitalism in terms of advertising sign-systems, concerned with the constitution of subjects, objects, regimes of 'truth' and subjugation.

The definition, here, of sign technologies draws attention to a genealogy of governance in terms of three operational axes of advertising sign-systems: (1) their propensity to substitute for political resistance the seductive enigmatic pleasure of things; (2) their capacity to inculcate humans into becoming subjects and objects of disciplinary technologies and (3) their capacity as a vehicle for governance at a distance. More specifically, my genealogy of governance examines advertising as a powerful inscriptive technology crucial to modern forms of governmental rationality. These issues raise, important concerns regarding the self-reflexive cultivation of political identity, in the context of an increasingly sophisticated genealogy of cultural politics articulated through advertising truths and the 'marketing of the soul' (Knights and Sturdy 1997). It is the central objective of this book to highlight and address these concerns.

Methodological Reflections

There are a number of methodological procedures operating in my intellectual examination of sign technologies and cultural politics, in the context of, global liberalized capitalism. Of significance is the abandoning of a whole epistemology of 'truth' that presupposes the objectivity of knowledge, and its premise on the ideal 'that knowledge can exist only where the power relations are suspended' (Foucault 1991a:27). In this epistemological tradition, the mechanism and modality of knowledge are presumed to reside outside the mobilization of power; shielded from powerful interests and demands. In contrast to the 'renunciation of power', as a primary condition of knowledge, Foucault convincingly impresses 'that power and knowledge directly imply one another' (ibid). As Foucault further expresses it 'there is no power relation without the correlative constitution of a field of knowledge, nor any knowledge that does not presuppose and constitute at the same time power relations' (ibid). A perhaps more revolutionary epistemological feature, of Foucault's power–knowledge couplet is the realization that 'the modalities of knowledge must be regarded as so many effects of these fundamental implications of power-knowledge and their historical transformation' (ibid:28). This has direct implications for the epistemological status of the Enlightenment's Cartesian subject. In Descartes *Cogito Ergo Sum*, it is the knowing subject 'that produces a corpus of knowledge, useful or resistant to power' (ibid). Conversely, Foucault's discursive examinations of the human sciences render intelligible, the subject of knowledge as inextricably tied to power-knowledge, 'the processes and struggles that traverse it and of which it is made up' (ibid). To this extent the system of power 'determines the forms and possible domains of knowledge' (ibid). Axiomatic with this account of knowledge is a conception of power, conceived not as a zero-sum property imposed on a powerless domain. Foucault's 'micro-physics' of power requires the abandoning of a conception of power seen as the possession of a privileged dominant entity. Rather than focusing on a source of power, Foucault urges that we decipher its exercise. In so doing, we are encouraged to appreciate power as a strategy.

The concept of power refers, here, to procedures and programmes, which operate 'in' and 'through' advertising net-works of social relations that are themselves perpetually in tension, in activity. And, this rhizomatous morphology intentionally presumes that power 'is manifested and sometimes extended by the position of those who are dominated' (ibid:27). In so far as, liberalism professes an inviolable sovereign self, whose freedom consists in the unrestrained, will to acquisitive materialism, it fails to appreciate that 'power is not exercised simply as an obligation or a prohibition on those who do not have it' (ibid). Rather the relations of power delve deep into the crevices of society and 'are not localized in the relation between the state and its citizens or on the frontier between classes' (ibid). This would require that we refrain from conflating politics with the materiality of a viable state in terms of its resources, personnel, institutions and citizens. Instead, we should be concerned with the 'body politic as a set of material elements and techniques that serve as weapons, relays, communication routes and supports for the power and knowledge relations that invest human bodies and subjugate them by turning them into objects of knowledge' (1991a:28). In this sense, liberalism is recognized 'less as a consequence of legal theorizes than as a chapter of political anatomy' (ibid). It is my intention here to demonstrate that, if it is to be accepted that power/knowledge relations invest the body politic, it is axiomatic that sign technologies, designed to liberate and preserve the autonomous self, are a spectacular practice of political anatomy.

Organization of this Book

This book traces brand 'new times' in cultural politics and global advertising media. In Part I, I examine the centrality of advertising to the new marketized governmental field of international corporate capitalism. Part I argues that, post-Fordist developments in the advertising industry coupled with the advent of postmodern visual cultures, during the 1990s, constituted a decisive transition in the governance of social life from 'biopower' to 'biopolitics'. According to Negri (2008:16), biopower is 'totalitarianism: the result of nineteenth and twentieth century struggles, the construction of welfare, the social dimension of consensus have all been absorbed by the totality of the state'. This definition of biopower is resonant with Foucault's (1977) account of modern power relations and the application of disciplinary technologies to individual bodies through processes of subjectification and objectification. It is evident that Foucault's genealogy of modern power traces the advent of governmental rationality in relation to a transition from biopower to 'biopolitics'. Foucault (1979) defines biopolitics as an insidious circulation of power through the social body so as to control populations by governing their humanity. In biopolitics, 'life now belongs to the field of power' (Negri 2008:31).

Part I: Governmentalization of Visual Culture

Drawing upon Foucauldian analytics, Part I of this book, argues that the rise of post-Fordist management practices in the 1990s extended 'reflexive accumulation' (Lash and Urry 1999) into the marketization of governmental practice. The primary intention of Chapters 1 and 2, of this book, is to critically analyse the integration of advertising into neoliberal market reforms of governmental practice. Chapter 1 provides the intellectual prologue to Chapter 2's comparative analysis of state healthcare market reforms in the United Kingdom (UK) and United States of America (US).

Chapter 2 is divided into four sections. Section one, entitled 'Signs of the Times: Neoliberalism and Aesthetic Accumulation'; examines the extraordinary prominence of advertising as an integral feature of neoliberal capitalist market reform. The central theme here is that axiomatic to market reform is the creation of 'market analogues', which take the form of advertising practice, and are directed at enabling market relations of competition and 'choice'. Section two entitled; 'Neoliberalism, Advertising and the Aestheticisation of Healthcare', demonstrates advertising as integral to market reforms of healthcare in the UK and US. Section three, entitled; 'DTCA and the Aestheticisation of Healthcare Services in Global Context', critically case studies the rise of Direct to Consumer Advertising (DTCA) in the UK and US healthcare service. This section uses document analysis to detail cultural politics directed at resisting the spread of advertising cultures in healthcare provision. Section four, entitled; 'Advertising Technologies and the Medicalization of Social Life', examines academic debates intent on criticizing the role of DTCA in the medicalization of social life. While detailed in their critique of DTCA, it is my contention that these studies fail to appreciate advertising's role in what Foucault (1990) describes as the 'cultivation of the self'. For, it is through the cultivation of the self, that 'the self-regulating capacities of subjects shaped and normalized in large part through' advertising cultures 'have become key resources for modern forms of government' (Miller and Rose 2008:26). It is my aim in Part I of this book, to deconstruct advertising technologies so as to reveal their political role in the support of a 'micro-physics' of power directed at the reflexive cultivation of a subject, self-disciplined into assuming individual responsibility for their present welfare and future healthcare; a process that Knights and Sturdy (1997) describe in the context of the UK financial services industry as the 'marketing of the soul'. It my intention to apply this concept, to the analysis of advertising, in the context of contemporary neoliberal market reforms of healthcare in the UK and US.

Part II: Postmodern-Political Caesura

Postmodern developments in advertising aesthetics have been integral to this extension of governmental rationalities, most especially the spectacular pervasion of commodity culture. Part II, of this book, argues that the 'biopolitical' regime that emerges with the advent of global liberalized capitalism corresponds, with a profound political caesura in modernist politics of representation. The emerging, postmodern visual culture provides individual subjects with a ceaseless array of social, familial and sexual lifestyles. Undoubtedly the cavalcades of signs and sounds that saturate our daily lives are splendid; indeed spectacular. In the shopping arcades of the Western metropolis the aesthetic of spectacle gathers momentum as fractal objects, and fractal forms bombard our senses with a single discernable oration 'I am therefore I shop'. But this seduction of the real is achieved through an abreaction. Postmodern advertising visual culture is a 'simplified operational mode…in which all particular contents are annulled at the very moment when they can be transcribed into each other' (Baudrillard 1994:87). It involves the negation of the core dichotomies of modernist thinking i.e. (i) the subversion of differences between real/imaginary, public/private and (ii) the dissolution of the classical modernist juxtaposition between subject and object. In modernity such binary modalities garnered 'weighty enunciations' as they protected 'articulated forms of meaning' from the superficialities of culture, and ensured 'that they cannot be translated into each other' (ibid). In postmodern advertising culture the modernist postulation of representation is displaced by the sheer contiguity, irony and hyper-reality of the postmodern sign. The effect of such a breakdown in the signifying chain is to subvert modernism's presumption that the 'meaning of truth preceded and determined the representations that communicated it' (Ryan 1988:559). In this sense, postmodern advertising culture proffers simultaneously the possibilities for the renascence of cultural politics and for its dissipation through indeterminacy.

Baudrillard argues that this phenomenon pre-stages a situation in which the social becomes overwhelmed by its solicitation and 'turns itself into advertising' (1994:88). According to Baudrillard this convergence between the social and political marks a society 'where the political economy, literally speaking is finally realized' (ibid). That is to say the political has become fully incorporated into commodity culture and predominated by the dynamics of exchange value. Baudrillard's startling visualization, anticipates an absolute solicitation of sociality realized through the permeation of advertising throughout everyday life. All distinction between the real and imaginary dissipates into 'a vestige of sociality hallucinated' everywhere and nowhere in particular (ibid). For Baudrillard, the omnipresence of advertising also precipitates its eventual demise. This is because the ephemerality of postmodern advertising has escaped any claim to advertising as informative communication. In so doing, advertising has forsaken 'the social and moral dramaturgy', crucial to its establishment as efficacious professional practice (ibid:89). For, Baudrillard, these conditions signify the death knell for advertising, not necessarily as a result of our apathy or even a disinclination to heed the clarion call of consumer culture. Baudrillard observes that today advertising is losing its power to another form of language even more adept at simplifying the social. The language, which mesmerizes Baudrillard, is the digitality of computer science. He observes that the micro-processing language of cybernetic systems is exceeding advertising's ability to reduce sociality into abstract self-referential signs. The digital language of micro-processing has overtaken advertising's ability to instantiate a 'rhetorical continuum' of sounds and signs; a three dimensional 'total environment' of simulacra (ibid:89). Baudrillard observes that 'the "thrill" of advertising has been displaced onto computers and onto the miniaturization of everyday life by computer science' (ibid). While Baudrillard's observations, concerning the figuration of sociality through digitalization, appear consistent with contemporary developments in media, his anticipation of the demise of advertising is misconceived. Indeed, the fascination of advertising still remains and this has been largely achieved by its integration into ethical trading networks, themselves configured by a revolutionary convergence of advertising with the micro-universe of digital communication technologies.

Part III: Geo-Political Caesura

Technological innovations in clothing production are integral to the proliferating fashion cycles, which have since the 1980s dictated women's fashion. It is evident that the prêt-a-porter glitz and short product cycles of women's fashion has disconcerting trajectories in the spatial disaggregation of global textile production. As Dicken (2003:329-330) expresses it:

> The highly concentrated purchasing power of the large retail chains gives them enormous leverage over textiles and garments manufacturers. When the market was dominated largely by the mass market retailers, demand was for long production runs of standardized garments at low cost. As the market has become more differentiated and more frequent fashion changes have become the rule, manufacturers are forced to respond far more rapidly to retailer demands and specifications. Under such circumstances, the time involved in meeting orders becomes as important as cost.

Advances in electronic communication enable manufacturers to map consumer preferences through Quick Response (QR) management systems. According to Cammett (2006:32), QR systems were first defined in 1985 and are so named because they dramatically accelerate the supply chain 'by speeding up order fulfilment and enabling retailers to respond quickly to shifting consumer tastes through improved information and merchandise flows'. Cammett suggests the emergence of QR, in the 1980s, coincided with an extended period of flagging sales and the imperative for retailers to stimulate consumer engagement in fashion. Formulating multiple fashion 'seasons', was a central marketing strategy, designed to invigorate relatively inelastic demand. It has been observed that 'by the mid-1980s, the standard six-month season was fragmented into at least six fashion cycles and many retailers began to offer about twelve distinct product lines annually' (ibid:31). Innovations in marketing management systems needed to be matched by retailers and their suppliers. It became imperative that retailers maintained perpetual turnover, limited costs, advanced forecasting and delivery reliability so as to curtail inventory risk. In and of themselves these innovations are insufficient without concomitant changes in manufacturing. Retailers needed suppliers that could keep pace with the relentless demands to replenish fast-selling stock. It has become increasingly evident that the manufacturing solution to accelerated apparel production cycles is, outsourcing. But to who's cost?

The rapid development of industrialization in developing countries, coupled with the liberalizing agenda of the World Trade Organization has encouraged many developing countries to become Export Processing Zones (EPZ). Analysts concur that clothing production within these EPZ is mostly carried out by females, indeed 80 per cent of workers within the industry are female and the vast proportion of this labour-force is unskilled or semi-skilled labour (Dicken 2007:256). The level of skill coupled with insidious gender divisions of labour often mean that 'such workers are easily hired and fired and have no protection over their working conditions' (ibid:258). It has been observed that a vast proportion of these workers are 'employed in contravention of government employment regulations' (ibid). Even where countries have a legal minimum wage 'in some case this is lower than a realistic minimum living wage' (Allwood et al 2006:x). Each month new and more sensational accounts of the 'sweatshop' working conditions experienced by women and children in EPZ are beamed into our lives. Global media diligently broadcast the disgraceful working conditions of unregulated sweatshops, where unions are prohibited and unscrupulous factory owners demand excessive working hours, with little regard for unions, health and safety protection or fair wage.

Global fashion labels exacerbate these conditions. This is because their histrionic public renunciation of 'sweatshop' practices contradicts their adoption of lean supply strategies that subject manufacturers and buyers to quality controls and insurmountable contracting delivery times. Consequently, while it might be the case that a global brand will stipulate the codes of practice to which its supplier must adhere, the constricting delivery times of global supply chains put pressure on suppliers to subcontract production. It is here that the clothing industry's low levels of capital investment attract small scale manufacturers producing garments in small plants with limited technology and high labour intensity. The labour force in these less regulated provinces of the global supply-chain is often poorly educated, unskilled women and children.

Fair Trade is a revolutionary geopolitical challenge to the exploitative relations of global capitalist accumulation. The Fair Trade movement supports sustainable and ethical relations of exchange and production, in countenance to the structural inequalities and economically destructive relations characteristic of global capitalist accumulation. Fair Trade emerged in the 1940s and 1950s as a form of fairer international system of goods exchange coincident with the development regime of the Bretton Woods era (Fridell 2006). Established in 1944, the Bretton Woods system inaugurated two international finance institutions, the International Monetary Fund (IMF) and the International Bank for Reconstruction and Development (eventually renamed the World Bank). Alongside these institutions was formulated a development regime orientated towards international market regulation as a primary means for the improvement of the economic plight of

Southern producers. Consequently economic development in this era focused on the imposition of international controls on capital flows and international market regulations of commodity production. For its part, the Fair Trade movement in its formative era (i.e., 1940s-1970s) fostered the re-embedding of international trade into a system of equitable economic trade-relations that benefited Southern producers (ibid:10). It was optimistically anticipated that Fair Trade networks would lay the foundations for a new trading system constituted by 'alternative trade organizations that would form part of a new international economic order based on strong state intervention at the national and international levels' (ibid). Although the Fair Trade movement remains committed to the alleviation of poverty and propagation of sustainable development, its strategic approach changed markedly in the 1980s in reaction to the spread of global neoliberalism (ibid). In the neo-liberalized markets and declining capital controls of international trade, it was no longer apposite to promote sustainable development in terms of the state regulation of international markets. In response the Fair Trade movement, introduced a new conception of alternative trade built on voluntaristic trading partnerships between producers and exporters. In place of the fetishized exploitative exchange relations of market capitalism, the Fair Trade movement prompts the achievement for providers of a fair price secured above the world's market's and protected against the market volatility that besets capitalist accumulation. Central to this alternative trade strategy is the inscription of products with labels designed to certify that the product accords with specified international labour standards and environmental sustainability conventions. The alternative trade labels also certify that the conditions of production are subject to regular inspection. Perhaps the most vital feature of the product labelling process is that the labels testify to the existence of 'long-term relations of solidarity between groups of producers, consumers and intermediaries committed to alternative trade networks' (Friedberg 2003:30). Part III of this book, extensively examines aesthetics, ethics and the political economy of Fair Trade citizen branding.

Chapter 6 provides the theoretical prologue to the empirical analyses in Chapter 7. Of particular concern to Chapter 7 is the possibility of an 'aesthetics of existence'. In its advocacy of a 'beautiful life' (Foucault 1991:349), advertising is promisingly relevant to the promotion of:

> a very strong structure of existence, without any relation with the juridical per se, with an authoritarian system, with a disciplinary structure. (Foucault 1991:348)

This is to envisage the possibilities of advertising beyond its conventional imbrications with the problem of discipline and the '*techne* of the self' (ibid). In a way it is to imaginatively conceive of advertising in terms of the '*techne* of life, the *techne tou biou*, how to live' (ibid). This, in turn, leads to an appreciation of advertising as belonging among the cultural inventions and 'treasury of devices, techniques, ideas, procedures, and so on, that cannot exactly be reactivated, but at least constitute, or help to constitute, a certain point of view which can be very useful as a tool for analyzing what's going on now – and to change it' (ibid:349-350). In many respects advertising, therefore, represents a modern secular ethics no longer grounded in externally imposed political, social and economic structures. Rather, advertising's celebration of a 'de-traditionalized' (Giddens 1993) postmodern consumer culture provides a novel source of encouragement for academic scholars, that seek to rid us of the idea 'of an analytical or necessary link between ethics and other social or economic or political structures' (Foucault 1991:350). It partially succeeds in this advocacy, most especially through its promotion of life as a tapestry for the application of art. In the resolve for a more beautiful life, advertising has clear resonances with Foucault's concept of 'the bios as a material for an aesthetic piece of art' (ibid:348). And this idea relates to the fact that the aesthetics of advertising visual cultures tend not to associate ethical problems with externally imposed quasi-juridical structures. Rather, in the advertising of Fairtrade labelled products the consumer is presented with what Foucault describes as the 'problem of personal choice, of aesthetics of existence' (ibid). In this articulation, ethics is transformed into a creative activity and ontologically bound up with the making of 'ourselves as a work of art' (ibid:351).

Advertising, in this sense forms part of the struggle against the production of ethics that attempt to normalize populations and governmentalize individuality. The kind of relationship that advertising invites us to have with ourselves calls upon an aesthetics of ethics 'which determines how the individual is supposed to constitute himself [sic] as a moral subject of his own actions' (ibid:352). And this implies a unique mode of subjectification, in which individuals are invited to recognize their moral obligations through commodity culture. So political power is exercised by the consumer through an aesthetics of, self-forming, ethical activities in, which the consumer applies deciphering techniques 'in a choice about existence' (ibid:361). As part of 'making one's life into an object…for a *techne* – for an art' (ibid:362), the consumer becomes committed to the application of aesthetic values to 'one's life, one's existences' (ibid). Chapter 7 asks important ethical questions about the outcomes of this mode of subjectification.

Part IV: Techno-Political Caesura

As dominant functions and processes in the informational age, become pervaded by networks, the greatest insecurity is to be 'invisible to the programs commanding the global networks of production, distribution and valuation' (Castells 2009:33). Indeed, the accentuation of the social and cultural exclusion, of vast segments of the world's population from the power centres of global networks, has become a formidable obstacle to sustainable development. It is the backlash of the alienated in the form of anti-globalization movements that constitutes the empirical focus of Chapter 8. On balance the rise of networked global capitalism has paralleled the development of geopolitical strategies organized in the form of global networks. Given that 'the specific structure of communication of a given society largely shapes social movements' (ibid:301), it is unsurprising that organized resistance to globalized market capitalism is increasingly structured around networks. However, what is uniquely interesting about, globally networked social movements is the integration of multimodal digital communication processing technologies, into geopolitical strategies. Part of the motivation fuelling this micro-electronic technological revolution can be explained in terms of global times, and the increasingly acute distinction between the 'space of flows' and the 'space of place'.

In traditional social theory, space provides a material context for enacting, simultaneously, shared social practices. To this end, 'space defines the time frame of social relationships' (Castells 2010:xxxi). Space in this sense is contiguous with the physicality of material place. And thus, the 'space of places' is 'the space of contiguity' (ibid). Advances in micro-electronically operated digital communication technologies have transformed the spatiality of social interaction by decoupling the contiguity of space-time, as a boundary to the communicative interaction of social actors. The emerging re-configured spatial context has been called 'the space of flows' (ibid:xxxii). This form of spatiality is defined as 'the material support of simultaneous social practices communicated at a distance' (ibid). It refers to a radical transformation in communication technologies and the new 'possibility of practicing simultaneity without contiguity' (Castells 2009:34). Given that the dominant logic of global capitalism is the relentless annihilation of space by time, alternative projects for the structuration of trade will involve an engagement with the fact that global capitalist accumulation is rapacious in its annihilation of the space of places. In global times, the disaffected are deeply fragmented by the double logic of their exploited inclusion and alienated exclusion from the space of flows. The resulting local demands for solutions to global problems, have directed the concerns of alternative trade initiatives. Organizations such as the Fair Trade movement directly challenge international commercial relations that operate around abstract market principles that devalue and exploit producers and the environment. In their endeavour to create a more socially and ecologically sustainable society, alternative trade initiatives are orientated towards the 'translation' of global political spaces into local political concerns.

It is precisely because, contemporary advertising technoscapes are multimodal using both convergent communication networks and mainstream advertising media, that they are able to translate the divergent interests of alternative trade networks and thus shape the process of global political change. Focusing on the network structure of the Fairtrade Foundation, Chapter 8 identifies advertising technoscapes as integral mechanisms, for the re-embedding of international commodity-chains into relations of solidarity between globally dispersed actor-networks committed to achieving sustainable development. And this integration of advertising into alternative trading networks has precipitated a systemic transformation in the global arena of cultural politics. Indeed, it is my contention that a profound techno-political caesura has precipitated a revolutionary convergence between the social and political, thus marking a new and exciting geo-political terrain for cultural politics in global times.

PART I
Governmentalization of Visual Culture

The Conservative Party, campaign poster 2004

Source: Courtesy of the Advertising Archive. Reproduced with kind permission of the Conservative Party Archive.

Chapter 1
Governing Neoliberal Vistas and the Cultural Politics of Economic Life

Michel Foucault's analysis of government, in sixteenth century political theory, provide the basis from, which to comprehend the exercise of power in modern society. Foucault argued that 'governmentality' is the foundation of modern political thought and practice. The notion of governmentality refers to an 'ensemble formed by the institutions, procedures, analyses and reflections, the calculations and tactics that allow the exercise of this very specific albeit complex form of power' (Foucault 1991b:102). In order to regulate individual conduct in accordance with the programme of broad economic vision, governmentality has as its strategic target population. And this constitutes 'its principal form of knowledge political economy and as its essential technical means of apparatuses of security' (ibid). For it is through, 'the shifting ambitions and concerns of all those social authorities that have sought to administer the lives of individuals and associations' that advanced liberal democracies govern (Miller and Rose 2008:26).

Governmentality in this sense is essentially concerned with the issue of population and the articulation of a kind of rationality that 'indirectly' mobilizes the possible field of action of others (ibid). The concept of 'indirect' mechanisms of governance is an important advance to Foucault's original conception of governmentality. Miller and Rose (2008) argue that the contemporary analysis of governance necessitates an appreciation of the multifarious modes through which subjective meanings, identities and actions are aligned with the political agenda of government. Axiomatic to this assertion is the persuasion that modern political power is exercised through an assemblage of officials, organizations and techniques many of which are only tangentially connected to the formal institutions of the state (ibid:26). For Miller and Rose (2008), this observation engenders a more prescient mode of governmental analysis, one that focuses on the evasive ambitions and relevancies of the multitude of social authorities that have sought to manage the everyday life of subjects and institutions. To this end they focus critical analytical engagement 'on the diverse mechanisms through which the actions and judgments of persons and organizations have been linked to political objectives' (ibid:36).

Although these realms stand in alignment, their inter-relation is not one of direct causality but, rather sustained according to 'indirect mechanisms', that are capable of coordinating 'economic, social and personal conduct with socio-political objectives' (ibid:26). Miller and Rose (2008) make purposeful connections here with Latour's (1987) concept of 'action at a distance' and its emphasis on examining the inter-dependence of phenomena separated by physical space. Miller and Rose (2008), apply this problematic to the analysis of modern forms of governmentality. Governance is a pre-eminent mode of action imposed upon the actions of free agents. Indeed, an imperative condition of governance in advanced liberal democracies is a reliance on the 'self-regulating capacities of subjects' (ibid:27). In order to reshape economic life, to make it compatible with broader economic visions, governance is increasingly reliant upon the productive properties of human agency. Indeed, Miller and Rose (2008) argue that the 'self-regulating capacities of subjects' has become a vital instrument, which legitimates the intrusion of the state into 'governing economic life'.

Governmentality, is therefore, essentially concerned with the development and articulation of technologies and procedures that mobilizes the possible field of action of others. To this end, Miller and Rose's (2008) methodological focus seeks to 'highlight the diversity of powers and knowledges entailed in rendering fields practicable and amenable to intervention' (ibid:28). The central objective of this chapter, is to theoretically formulate advertising as a 'heterogeneous assemblage' in, which objects and subjects of governance are rendered amenable to calculation and regulation. To this end it needs to be recognized that in the cultural politics of economic life:

> To keep constant watch over one's representations, or to verify their marks the way one authenticates a currency, is not to inquire…concerning the deep origin of the idea that presents itself; it is not to try and decipher a meaning hidden beneath the visible representation; it is to assess the relationship between oneself and that which is represented, so as to accept in the relation to the self only that which can depend on the subject's free and rational choice. (Foucault 1990:64)

Advertising as Governmental Rationality

The exercise of power, in advanced liberal democracies, has increasingly come to embrace the 'governing [of] economic life' (Miller and Rose 2008:26). In the writings of Michel Foucault we are guided towards an appreciation of the past and present meaning of the word 'government'. Ubiquitous to the Middle Ages and classical antiquity were political treatises providing advice to the sovereign concerning the exercise of power, obedience and the application of 'divine law' (Foucault 1991b:87). According to Foucault, the concurrence of two major social transformations, namely the disintegration of feudalism and Reformation and Counter Reformation unsettled political orthodoxy. From the intersection of this double moment, which established the centralized modern state on the one hand, and religious dissidence on the other, arose 'the problematic of government in general' (ibid:88). By the mid-sixteenth century political treatises began to emerge that were neither 'advice to the prince' nor political science, but rather notations on the 'art of governance'. Foucault states that these political treatises ascribed 'government' with a broader meaning that extended beyond a focus on the sovereign's political structures of state. Works on the 'art of government' began to pay particular attention to the way in, which the conduct of individuals and groups could be indirectly governed. Advice in the art of government did not only refer to the legitimately constituted formal institutions of the state, but also modes of action exacted by those social authorities that sort to superintend the multifarious existence of provinces, communities and families. Thus in the mid-sixteenth century the dominant concern of key treatises of government focused consistently on 'the problem...of the government of souls and lives...[the] government of children and the great problematic of pedagogy...only as the last of these questions to be taken up, there is the government of the state...' (ibid:87). Curiously, all these modes of governance are at one and the same time internal to state and society and 'thus we find at once a plurality of forms of government and their immanence to the state' (ibid:91). A central theme connecting the particular applications and technologies of governing in various dispersed institutions and social spaces is the emergence of 'bio-power' as a coherent political technology. In 'bio-power' the fostering of life and the regulation of individual conduct throughout the social body as whole, is brought into the political realm as a primary form of political rationality. As Foucault expresses it:

> ...one would have to speak of bio-power to designate what brought life and its mechanisms into the realm of explicit calculations and made knowledge-power an agent of transformation of human life. (1998:143)

Biopower coalesced around a preeminent trajectory which operated to implicate knowledge of human regeneration, health and well-being as objects of political attention. In short bio-power coincides with the birth of the human sciences and the inculcation of the study of human life as a new technical and political rationality. Endeavors to analyze and document the state's environment, citizens and demography were closely tied to the new exigencies of mobilizing power, for in the art of government, 'power is tolerable only on condition that it mask a substantial part of itself. Its success is proportional to its ability to hide its own mechanisms' (ibid:86). Foucault documents how the analysis of the human species came to be connected with the technologies of bio-power enabling 'regulative controls of the vitality of life' (Dreyfus and Rabinow 1982:134). Parallel to this eventuality was the emergence of a new problematic in the art of government namely 'how to introduce economy' that is the meticulous management of individual financial well-being, 'into the management of the state' (Foucault 1991b:92). Indeed, the problem of transposing the micro-financial relations of the family economy into political practice was a principal issue in the establishment of the art of government:

> To govern a state will therefore mean to apply economy, to set up economy at the level of the entire state, which means exercising towards its inhabitants, and the wealth and behaviour of each and all, a form of surveillance and control as attentive as that of the head of the family over his household and his goods. (Foucault 1991b:92)

This mode of investigating the framework of government, draws attention to the discursive and practical realms of government; 'law is not what is important' (ibid:95). The boundaries and 'the finality of government' exists 'in the things it manages and in the pursuit of the perfection and intensification of the processes which it directs' (ibid:95). Foucault makes the point that a frequent theme throughout the seventeenth century is that 'the instruments of government, instead of being laws, now come to be a range of multiform tactics' (ibid). The aim of this form of government is to cultivate distinct types of technologies and governmental apparatuses essential in the acquisition of 'knowledge of the state, in all its different elements, dimensions and factors of power…' (ibid:96). This combination of knowledges and technologies, was, according to Foucault termed 'statistics', which literally meant 'the science of the state' (ibid).

One of the great turning points in the art of government occurs in the eighteenth century as part of the demographic expansion connected with the rise of industrial capitalism, and decline of agricultural production. For it is at this conjunction that the political science of the state embraces the problem of population. Whereas statistics had previously revealed the economy of the family, it now makes transparent that population has its own systematic 'aggregate effects' and episodes that are 'irreducible to the dimension of the family' (ibid:99). This knowledge is productive, in that it promotes the existence of a connection between the economic regulations of individual conduct, with the conduct of others dispersed throughout the social body. Foucault suggests that this precipitates the growing importance of economics to the state and that by the eighteenth century the word economy designates 'a level of reality, a field of intervention…' (ibid:93). This is because the field of population becomes above all else the ultimate end of governance:

> I believe, absolutely…and it is from the middle of the eighteenth century that the family appears in this dimension of instrumentality relative to the population, with the institution of campaigns to reduce mortality, and to promote marriages, vaccinations, etc…population comes to appear above all else as the ultimate end of government. In contrast to sovereignty, government has as its purpose not the act of government itself, but the welfare of the population, the improvement of its condition, the increase of its wealth longevity, health, etc.; and the means that the government uses to attain these ends are themselves all in some sense immanent to the population; it is the population itself on which government will act either directly through large-scale campaigns, or indirectly through techniques that will make possible, without the full awareness of the people, the stimulation of birth rates, the directing of the flow of population into certain regions or activities etc. (ibid:100)

Arising from the recentring of the art of government from the family to the population is the sense of continuous and multiple networks linking population, territory and wealth. And this is accompanied by a new political rationality geared towards fostering the connections between the regulation of individual conduct and the well being of the social body. Suffice to say, that:

> the transition which takes place in the eighteenth century from an art of government to a political science, from a regime dominated by structures of sovereignty to one ruled by techniques of government, turns on the theme of population and hence also on the birth of political economy. (Foucault 1991b:101)

Foucault's analyses of government, in sixteenth century political theory, provide the basis from, which to comprehend the exercise of power in modern society. Foucault argued that 'governmentality' is the foundation of modern political thought and practice. The notion of governmentality refers to an 'ensemble formed by the institutions, procedures, analyses and reflections, the calculations and tactics that allow the exercise of this very specific albeit complex form of power' (ibid:102). In order to regulate individual conduct in accordance with the programme of broad economic vision, governmentality has as its strategic target population. And this constitutes 'its principal form of knowledge political economy and its essential technical means of apparatuses of security' (ibid). For it is through, 'the shifting ambitions and concerns of all those social authorities that have sought to administer the lives of individuals and associations' that advanced liberal democracies govern (Miller and Rose 2008:28).

Governmentality in this sense is essentially concerned with the issue of population and the articulation of a kind of rationality that 'indirectly' mobilizes the possible field of action of others (ibid). The concept of 'indirect' mechanisms of governance is an important advance to Foucault's original conception of governmentality. Miller and Rose (2008) argue that the contemporary analysis of governance necessitates an appreciation of the multifarious modes through which subjective meanings, identities and actions are aligned with the political agenda of government. Axiomatic to this assertion is the persuasion that modern political power is exercised through an assemblage of officials, organizations and techniques many of which are only tangentially connected to the formal institutions of the state (ibid:26). For Miller and Rose (2008), this observation engenders a more prescient mode of governmental analysis, one that focuses on the evasive ambitions and relevancies of the multitude of social authorities that have sought to manage the everyday life of subjects and institutions. To this end they focus critical analytical engagement 'on the diverse mechanisms through which the actions and judgments of persons and organizations have been linked to political objectives' (ibid:36).

Although these realms stand in alignment, their inter-relation is not one of direct causality but, rather sustained according to 'indirect mechanisms', that are capable of coordinating 'economic, social and personal conduct with socio-political objectives' (ibid:26). Miller and Rose (2008) make purposeful connections here with Latour's (1987) concept of 'action at a distance' and its emphasis on examining the inter-dependence of phenomena separated by physical space. Miller and Rose (2008), apply this problematic to the analysis of modern forms of governmentality. Governance is a pre-eminent mode of action imposed upon the actions of free agents. Indeed, an imperative condition of governance in advanced liberal democracies is a reliance on the 'self-regulating capacities of subjects' (ibid:27). In order to reshape economic life, to make it compatible with broader economic visions, governance is increasingly reliant upon the productive properties of human agency. Indeed, Miller and Rose (2008:27) argue that the 'self-regulating capacities of subjects' has become a vital instrument, which legitimates the intrusion of the state into the 'governing [of] economic life'.

According to Miller and Rose (2008), economic life has become a site for the intervention of insidious modes of governmental technologies. Invoked within these intrusions is the 'notion of autonomy and self-fulfillment' (ibid:27). For example, advocates of the Direct to Consumer Advertising (DTCA) of pharmaceuticals consistently advance the educational benefits of promotional campaigns. In so doing, these advocates invoke the figure of the autonomous consumer, as a legitimation for advertising incursions at the level of everyday practice. Indeed, advertising discourse is a powerful and persuasive regulatory instrument. Nevertheless it is to misconceive the raison d'être of government, to implicate advertising in the direct coercion of subjects. Rather, it is my contention that Direct to Consumer (DTC) pharmaceutical promotional campaigns constitute indirect mechanisms for the accumulation of information on, and knowledge of populations. This is because, governmental technologies 'have come to rely in crucial respects upon "expertise"' (ibid:26) as disciplinary instruments. The concept of 'expertise' refers to 'the social authority ascribed to particular agents and forms of judgment on the basis of their claims to possess specialized truths and rare powers' (ibid). The theme of expertise, illustrates the idea of a mode of technology that is originally incidental to the state, but is eventually coincidental with the socio-political objectives of governmentality. Miller and Rose argue that:

> …the self-regulating capacities of subjects, shaped and normalized in large part through the powers of expertise, have become key resources for modern forms of government and have established some crucial conditions for governing in a liberal democratic way. (ibid)

In other words, the very process of rendering subjects calculable and devoting attention to their individual well-being simultaneously imbricates subjects within normalizing structures that are both individualizing and totalizing. This is to appreciate the inherently discursive character of governmentality. Miller and Rose (2008) recognize epochal shifts in the function of language in governing economic life, many of which are long term and characterize advance liberal democracies. The governmental field is an authoritative source of knowledge-economy, with vocabularies and rationalities produced, circulated and applied to the structuring of relations between the state and its citizens (Fairclough 2001). As Miller and Rose express it:

> 'Knowing' an object in such a way that it can be governed is more than a purely speculative activity: it requires the invention of procedures of notation, way

> of collecting and presenting statistics, the transportation of these to centres where calculations and judgments can be made, and so forth. It is through such procedures of inscription that the diverse domains of 'governmentality' are made up, that 'objects' such as the economy, the enterprise, the social field and the family are rendered in a particular conceptual form and made amenable to intervention and regulation. (ibid:30)

The concept of 'inscription' points to a number of important developments that can help conceptualize, the intersection of advertising expertise with the political economy of health and healthcare provision in liberal democratic societies. The intervention of advertising into the circulation of performance statistics, 'market' analogues and promotional imagery is evidence of the propensity of advertising to articulate a kind of rationality that is relevant to the process of 'knowing' subjects. Although advertising imagery is partially an immaterial form of inscription, advertising knowledges operate through the categorization of objects and their ordering in what Foucault (1991a:143) describes as 'an analytical space'. This space of analysis is, here, neither a physical territory, nor a material place, but rather 'the rank: the place one occupies in a classification, the point at which a line and a column intersect, the interval in a series of intervals that one may traverse one after the other' (ibid:145-146). Foucault urges us to recognize 'the instruments of government...to be a range of multiform tactics' (Foucault 1991b:95). He is adamant that in modern societies the management of population does not merely involve an aggregate of the collective mass, rather 'it also implies the management of population in its depths and its details' (ibid:102). Advertising considered as a mode of inscription serves this function by establishing the conditions and parameters for social interaction in public and private spaces. It does so both at the level of advertising knowledge and practice, through methods that Miller and Rose (2008) observe of expertise more generally, which involve:

> ...rendering aspects of existence thinkable and calculable, and amenable to deliberated and planful initiatives: a complex intellectual labour involving not only the invention of new forms of thought, but also the invention of novel procedures of documentation, computation and evaluation. (ibid:28)

Governmentality, is therefore, essentially concerned with the development and articulation of technologies and procedures that mobilizes the possible field of action of others. To this end, Miller and Rose's (2008) methodological focus seeks to 'highlight the diversity of powers and knowledges entailed in rendering fields practicable and amenable to intervention' (ibid:28). It is my contention that one such 'heterogeneous assemblage' is advertising, for it exemplifies a condition that makes it possible for the objects and subjects of governance to be rendered amenable to calculation and regulation. A significant appreciation of these processes is provided in the following genealogy of governmental rationality, healthcare and advertising practice.

Advertising and the Psychic Realm of Fordist Corporate Liberalism

The 1970s signaled the meteoric ascendancy of a transnational neoliberal revolution. The conditions precipitating this transnational revolution were the outcome of discontinuous and yet related historical trajectories. In economic terms, the revolution materialized against a background of international crises in capitalist accumulation. Of initial significance was the immediate aftermath of World War II, which had marked the golden era of 'corporate liberalism' (Overbeek and Pijl 2001:11). During this era, economic policy was rooted in a synthesis and complementarity linking private economy, public planning and state regulated markets. In contrast with classical liberalism's specters of unbridled capitalism, corporate liberalism entailed the dismantling of a rigid opposition between capital and labour. In its preference for the 'visible' as opposed to the 'invisible' hand, corporate liberalist policies intervened into markets and public planning to assuage the extremities of capitalist dynamics. These revisionist policies highlighted the indebtedness of corporate liberalism to Keynesian ideals, and the belief that growth and stability could be achieved through government spending and state regulation of the proclivities of productive capital (ibid:10). Against the context of the cataclysmic Wall Street Crash and banking crisis of the early 1930s, state interventionist corporate liberalism successfully stabilized growth; balancing economic activity with levels of aggregate demand.

In Western industrial nations, Fordism pioneered the corporate liberalist state's concern to directly control 'the conditions of capitalist production and reproduction' (Hall 1988:24). In this era, firms increased productivity in the production of consumer durables by applying 'scientific management' (Taylor 1947) to the detailed timing of manufacturing operations. Fordist capitalism's rationalized mass production, in vertically integrated firms, instituted highly bureaucratic modes of labour process control alongside a tacit 'capital labour' accord which directly involved labour in political discourse. This corresponded with a regime of accumulation geared towards, both accelerating the rate of commodity manufacturing and 'in producing the means of production for it' (Overbeek and Pijl 2001:11). Scientific management had accentuated the distinct technical expertise of management, but Fordism's amplified economies of scale necessitated the integration of the labourer's consumption into the productive circuits of capital (ibid:12). In order to balance mass production with aggregate demand and avoid the depreciating profitability of surplus production, capitalists needed to transform workers into consumers. In this context, 'every push of the workers at the level of wages is translated into a push of capital towards the production of commodities necessary for the workers' (Maurino 1974, quoted in Overbeek 2001:12). Scientific management was therefore advancing the degeneration of the self-reliant producer/consumer as a metaphor of economic prosperity. With a vastly expanding productive capacity, capitalists needed to transcend this orthodoxy and abandon the elite market based, traditional supply and demand models of industrial goods consumption. As Stuart Ewen (2001:25) observes, in his seminal genealogy of advertising history *Captains of Consciousness*, 'the manufacturer was required to create an ideological bridge across traditional social gaps – region, taste, need and class – which would narrow prejudices in his favor'.

The consolidation of the productive system required by mass production necessitated a re-definition of labourers into consumers. This entailed a movement away from defining workers merely in their productive capacity. 'Progressive' managerialists were increasingly motivated to transcend, the question of organizing the factory and move towards an understanding of the arenas in which workers might be self-disciplined to commit themselves to the industrial process (Ewen 1977:15). The new 'corporate economy', with its hoards of cheap mass-produced goods needed to produce 'a continually responsive consumer market' (ibid:32). Mass production needed more dynamic market growth both horizontally (from provinciality to national demand), vertically (away from an upper class customer base) and ideologically (ibid:25). The modern mass producer needed to adopt a nationwide plan which extended beyond the traditional dependence on local markets. Manufacturers had little option other than to create national marketing strategies, especially if they were to compete successfully with other manufacturers of the same goods (ibid). The construction of 'national markets' became a definable response, by business communities, to the exigencies of the productive system.

As avarice replaced thrift in the ideology of industrialism, so 'it became imperative to invest labour with a financial power and a psychic desire to consume' (ibid:25). But this required overcoming a culture of parsimony which had tended to define consumption in the literal sense in which it meant 'to pillage', 'to subdue' and 'to exhaust' (Rifkin 1996:19). And businesses could no longer afford to exclusively provide for existing markets; rather foresighted companies began to adopt social scientific expertise in their quest to produce a market place of malleable, reliable consumers. It is within this context that the advertising industry emerged as a tool of Fordist corporate liberalism, with the purpose of 'solidifying the productive process whilst at the same time parrying anticorporate feeling' (Ewen 1977:19).

Advertising in this corporate liberalist era materialized as a specialized vehicle for incorporating workers into the circuit of productive capital. Advertising knowledge had advanced spectacularly in the early 1920s, especially in the flourishing area of psychology (cf., Dill Scott 1909). In its elevation from practice to academic discipline, advertising was a vital component in the new corporate expectation to become 'captains of consciousness' (Ewen 1977, 2001). Industrialists realized that in order extend both commodity markets and control over the worker they must broaden industrial discipline to encompass the social world occupied by the labourer. Indeed, the reproduction of the worker as consumer came to be perceived as much a nodal point to capitalist accumulation as labour power. Ewen (2001:26) observes that knowledge of 'human conduct' became immensely valuable to manufacturing output. As he expresses it 'within an ideal of a "scientifically" managed industry, raw materials and consumers were both viewed as malleable. They both would have to be shaped by the demands of…the newly emergent managerial tools of capital' (ibid). One such increasingly prominent tool was advertising, especially in its endeavour to 'know' the psychic realm of consumer behaviour. Advertising psychologists were developing models of human nature, so as to formulate character traits and map these against the behaviourial predispositions of certain types of consumers. Some evidence of this imperative is provided by advancements in advertising psychology made during the 1950s.

Psychologists at that time were raising intellectual questions which mirrored advertising's concern to gain scientific knowledge of decision-making in order to predict buyer behaviour. The psychological disposition of the consumer became an integral feature of commercial discourse. And advertising was keen to adopt psychology's accrescent constructions of human behaviour. With the advent of Freudian analysis, the intellectual field of psychology increasingly began to articulate challenges to the rational psychic operator (a *homo economicus*). The assumption that there are unconscious mental processes which motivate people to act toward certain goals achieved a significant level of orthodoxy in advertising circles. Indeed by the 1960s advertising professionals generally acknowledged the belief that it was insufficient to merely know the market facts or technical information about a product. Advertising experts also had to 'learn to understand the deeper meaning of the products and services' (Ditcher 1964:v).

Freudian analysis directly informed the theoretical contributions of the Institute of Motivational Research established in 1946. Its director Ernest Ditcher declared the purpose of the institute to be that of 'finding answers to the "why" of human actions in order to develop appropriate strategy to bring about desired results and goals' (1964:vii). At the same time advertising's normative interventions into what traditionally had been perceived as the private realm of psycho-social life extended capitals control over labour. For it is evident that advertising psychology's development of new ways of viewing human nature provided the opportunity for industrialists to socialize and mobilize the private realm of the consumer's life world. As Gramsci (1991:303) observed in his seminal work *Americanism and Fordism*, capital's normative interventions into the private realm of labour 'have the purpose of preserving, outside of work, a certain psycho-physical equilibrium which prevents the physiological collapse of the workers, exhausted by the new method of production'. This element of Fordist accumulation clearly attempted to deflect attention away from the alienating propensity of standardized mass production and focus the resolve of the worker/consumer inward towards their very identity. As Gramsci expresses, normalizing initiatives 'can only be something purely external and mechanical, but it can become internalized if it is proposed by the worker himself, and not imposed from the outside' (ibid). Thus advertising's role as a normative intervention into the ebb and flow of labour's psycho-physical existence, effectively locked workers into Fordist corporate liberalism's circuits of production and reproduction. The result, Ewen argues, was the belief amongst industrialists that advertising could produce a 'homogenous national character' comparable to the civilizing influence of epochal-making democratizing developments in Western history (2001:41).

It is evident that as advertising became central to the production of a homogenous national character, the nature of proletarianization began to dramatically transform. Since the advent of the industrial revolution, capital has persisted in its efforts to coerce labour into adopting the imperatives of mechanical time. Unsurprisingly, Fordism's application of Taylor's time and motion analysis, into the rationalization and intensification of the labour process, placed the issue of time at the centre of tensions between capital and labour. While rationalized production had routinized the labour process at the expense of craft and creativity, members of business communities propagated the 'economic freedom' and 'industrial democracy' affect of mass production (Ewen 2001:27). Part of the optimism stemmed from the propensity for business communities to effectively re-define traditional social divisions (e.g., class) into the concept of 'mass', so as 'to create an "individual" who could locate his needs and frustrations in terms of the consumption of goods rather than the quality and content of his life (work)' (ibid:43). To this end advertising's identification of common human traits and corresponding mass individual markets, provided an ideological bond linking across traditional class based tensions. Thus advertising encouraged labour to substitute for traditional political agitations and protest, the aspiration of cultivating self-identity 'among the uncontestable fruits of the new industrial cornucopia' (ibid:27). In this incantation of democracy and the civilizing self 'the essential political impulse' became one 'of entrepreneurial domination, a structure in which political choice was limited to the prescriptions formulated by business and politicized in its advertising' (ibid:91).

The endowment of advertising with industrial democratic dimensions, also addressed the burgeoning problem of surplus production. Fordism's advances in productive technologies had precipitated a movement towards what Karl Marx had earlier defined as 'relative surplus value' (Marx *Capital Vol. 1* 2003), that is, a shortening of the amount of labour time required to produce 'surplus-value'. Such transformations offered capitalists the opportunity to transform increased leisure into commercial profit. Capitalists, once again linking advertising to industry's commercial imperatives, set about habituating leisure time into 'the exigencies of mass production' (Ewen 2001:29). By transforming leisure into a time for consumption, capital could curtail revolutionary threats by ameliorating their very inception, and translating their very pretext into unpatriotic, 'resistance to the "universal" appeals of modern advertising' (ibid:43). It is evident that this profound effect of acquiescence was enhanced by the Keynesian 'capital labour compromise' which assigned increased control over the state's centralized social organization to managers largely drawn from the public sector, while at the same time integrating labour into political discourses, planning and the implementation of legislation. To this end, Fordist corporate liberalism extolled Keynesian fiscal policies of demand management, along with its emphasis on state intervention to curtail the excessive avarice of private investors and regulation of money capital circulation. This era of state orchestrated centralized planning produced historically unparalleled levels of social welfare, employment and abundant economic growth (Bonanno 1998). Formative adjustments to ruling class hegemony, were significantly facilitated by advances in productive technology, which alongside the growth in the new middle classes, broadened the social gains acquired from commodity culture and purchasing power. In a world where ownership and management of capital were becoming disassociated, capitalist accumulation was adumbrated by promotional culture's capacity to substitute for social and political protest the ultimately insatiable, quest for self-fulfillment through the compulsive consumption of commodities.

In the 1950s and 1960s, Fordism in Western capitalist economies was operating at near optimal levels, achieving an unprecedented economic growth, low inflation and abundance. But this 'Golden Age', of Fordist corporate liberalism, was abruptly disrupted as Britain's latent structural and economic contradictions began to overwhelm the Keynesian regime of capital accumulation. By the second half of the 1960s and through the 1970s, Keynesian was faltering badly, as a series of economic crises catapulted the economy into shorter and shorter 'oscillations between recession and recovery, with a steady underlying deterioration' (Hall 1983:24). In the West, the economic nationalist agenda of the post-war era, gave way amidst vociferous attacks against protectionism, obligatory corporatism and fiscal policies aimed at achieving short-term stabilization of output. In the United States of America (US), this translated as political resistance to the state enforced price controls and social democratic welfare interventions that characterized Roosevelt's 'New Deal'. And in the UK the economic recession that beset the second half of the 1960s 'effectively destroyed the last remnants of the "radical programme" on the basis of which Wilson won power in 1964. And to which he tried to harness a new social bloc' (ibid). The paradigmatic scale of resistance irrevocably displaced corporate liberalism's centralized state regulation. In its place was advanced entrepreneurial cultures and the right of the private sector to flourish in an extended market place.

By the 1970s it became increasingly apparent that deepening economic chaos festered within the spiraling crisis of the international monetary system. Key western nations had, by the end of the 1960s, already collapsed into full-blown recession. In the midst of economic instability, it became increasingly difficult to sustain the Keynesian compromise that had embedded national unions into bargaining between state, capital and labour. The Labour government's crisis management drew desperately from the repertoire of income policy and wage restraint. This latter strategy 'had profound effects in disorganizing and fragmenting working class responses to the crisis itself' (Hall 1983:24). And this progressively translated into confrontations within organized labour, and strikes by powerful unions against business owners. By the mid-1970s, the immediate terrain of political struggle was also dramatically shifting, as global economic crisis dictated 'synchronization between capitalist recession on a global scale, and the crisis of capital accumulation specific to Britain' (Hall 1983:24). The capital-labour accord had greatly strengthened the bargaining power of organized labour. In the context of economic instability, these staple features of Keynesian economics became its central weakness. Thus, as wages soared, inflation began to rise rapidly and the relatively orderly Keynesian system was unraveling with increasing alacrity. More ominous was the dismantling and eventual collapse of the Bretton Woods Agreement's regulatory reins on international finance. Established in 1944, at Bretton Woods New Hampshire, the primary function of the Bretton Woods Agreement was to regulate and stabilize international finance. The Bretton Woods system inaugurated two international finance institutions, the International Monetary Fund (IMF) and the International Bank for Reconstruction and Development (eventually renamed the World Bank). The primary objective of the Bretton Woods agreement was to stabilize international finance on the basis of fixed exchange rates between currencies based on the primary role of US dollar.

Up until the early 1970s, the relatively stable architecture of Bretton Woods successfully regulated financial transactions between international nation states. However, a series of developments irrevocably undermined Bretton Wood's control, which meant that countries could expand without incurring penalties in their balance of payments. Commodity prices increased exponentially with the unraveling of the Bretton Woods system, partly as a result of increased competition between wage markets in different economies. Historic events also compounded the splintering of the Bretton Wood fixed exchange rate system. In 1973 the price of crude oil had risen dramatically mainly as a consequence of an agreement between the Organization of Petroleum Exporting Countries (OPEC), to control the distribution of crude oil in order to amplify its price. OPEC's trade restrictions, sent shock waves through international finance markets as 'oil prices rose by 66 per cent in October 1973 before doubling again in January 1974' (Backhouse 2002:295). The resulting acute shortage of oil affected the productive capacities of Western industries. These events combined with high inflation and spiraling rates of unemployment irreparably confounded the inability of Keynesianism to address the crisis in capitalist accumulation. Indeed, it has been frequently observed 'that the very success of the 'Golden Age' seemed to have undermined its basis' (Glyn 2007:2). It was under these circumstances that a transnational revolution took place leading to a restructuring of the economic, social, cultural and political conditions of capital accumulation. Neoliberalism, it will be argued, emerged from this transformative revolution and precipitated a new political sign economy 'required to disarticulate old formations, and to rework their elements into new ones' (Hall 1983:23).

Advertising and the Political Economy of Neoliberalism

The pinnacle moment in the establishment of the neoliberal hegemony, was marked by the victory of 'Thatcherism' over Keynesianism in the 1979 UK general election. In the United States 'Reaganism' epitomized the rightward march of the new political era, and the inauguration of Ronald Reagan as president in 1981, pinnacled the transatlantic ascendancy of neoliberal economic policy. Indeed, both electoral victories signify the first phase of global neoliberalism, which is a politics, based on an antipathy to notions of centralized collective economic action and the committed promotion of deregulated market capitalism.

In the United Kingdom this monetarist shift was most prominently evident in the Margaret Thatcher's Conservative government (1979-1990), control of inflation; partly through the transfer of nationalized assets into private ownership (i.e., privatization) and 'cut backs' in public sector spending. The substratum underpinning these policy objectives drew disproportionately on: the global economic crisis of the 1970s and the financial incongruence posed by an expansive public sector; Keynesianism's failure to accommodate unregulated global economy; spiraling inflation and the menacing interstice between fiscal expenditure and revenues. This rhetoric of imminent disaster and fiscal crisis was powerful in its auditory.

By the mid-1980s monetarist conjecture came to preeminence in macro-economics and with this privatization became a principal condition of the Thatcher government's second term in office (1983-1987). The centre piece of this reform was the privatization of state-owned utilities such as gas, water and electricity. In this context privatization refers to an attempt to limit the direction of state regulation, through the transfer of ownership of public assets and service provision into the private sector.

Underpinning the Thatcher government's brand of neoliberalism were ideas derived from Milton Friedman and his seminal neoliberalist text *Capitalism and Freedom* and a specific notion of 'freedom' (Friedman 2002:6). For 25 years succeeding World War II (1945-70) Keynesian interventionist macro-economic policy had dominated the political landscape. According to Friedman (ibid:11), Keynesianism's impulse to stabilize capitalism's demand-generation process through collectivist monetary and fiscal economic planning, detrimentally intrudes on individual freedom. Published initially in 1962, Freidman's ground breaking book *Capitalism and Freedom* initially garnered limited recognition (Bonanno 2000). However, the book experienced a spectacular reversal of fortunes in the late 1970s and throughout the 1980s. This is largely because, escalating economic crisis in the mid-1970s was decisive in promoting the breakdown of Keynesianism, and creating a favourable intellectual climate for a substantive restructuring of the post-war socio-economic and political order (ibid:315). Freidman markedly critiqued the Keynesian ideal and his contemplations of economic restructuring signified the potential of a new era.

Contrary to the implications of the standard Keynesian model, the regulation of markets had according to Friedman (2002), largely failed to eradicate class based inequalities. Poverty and marginalization, Friedman asserts, are 'natural' phenomena in a given society. Attempts to address natural patterns in the aggregate inherited differences in individual skills, leads to the decline 'of faith in self-help' (ibid:201). According to Friedman, evidence of this decent 'is of itself sufficient to account for the growth of legislation tending towards socialism' (ibid). In light of this evidence and the economic crisis in capitalism, the burden of proof seemed for Friedman to suggest that centralized control of economic affairs by the state is ultimately a condition of economic unfreedom. Conversely, the market development of competitive capitalism ensures equitable income distribution, as both labour and capital are paid in accordance with what they are worth. Given that market dynamics also presume the existence of supply and demand, rates of employment are comparable with market performance. Within this schema, fiscal policy interventions designed to coordinate the demand-generation process with levels of employment, produce the adverse affect of ever-accelerating inflation and spiraling unemployment; for they disrupt the inherent equilibrium of market processes.

It is a widely accepted historical fact, that matters of social and economic disadvantage were spectacularly exacerbated, in the mid-1970s as spiraling unemployment and rocketing high inflation sent the British economy into crisis. The incorporation of unions into wage bargaining between capital and labour was rapidly disintegrating as; demands for rising fiscal spending began to detrimentally exceed the political capacity to levy taxes. It was Friedman's contention that much of the problem resided with Keynesianism's imperative to unite economic and political power. For 'concentrated power is not rendered harmless by the good intentions of those who create it' (ibid:201).

Evidently Friedman believed that market relations precede, at least in relevance, all other human activity. Indeed, he observed that the basic problem of advanced societies is one of coordinating opportunities. Friedman argued that one of the most effective mechanisms of achieving this was through a model of society organized on the principle of bi-laterally informed, financial transactions within the context of a 'free private enterprise exchange economy' (ibid:13). In its neoliberal political application, Friedman's conception of 'effective freedom of exchange' translated into the rhetoric of 'laissez-faire market society', 'individualism' and 'freedom of choice'. Central to these aspects of economic freedom is the conviction that the market organization of economic activity will protect individual freedom. And thus the market is superior to the state in this regard, because 'the market does this impersonally and without centralized authority' (ibid:15).

Significantly, Friedman's advocacy for a free market does not entirely eliminate the need for government. In its limited capacity as an 'umpire', the state defines the rules of market competition. Furthermore, the economic freedom of markets effectively constrains 'the range of issues that must be decided through political means' (ibid). In so doing markets 'minimize the extent to which government need participate directly in the game' (ibid). Consequently, economic freedom equates with political freedom. For the core threat to individual freedom is the 'power to coerce' (ibid). Markets reduce the control of political authority over the 'organization of economic activity' and thus deliver political freedom from a potential 'source of coercive power' (ibid). In contrast with Keynesian's state regulation of economic life, neoliberalist market based society equates with freedom from the excesses of political authority. Friedman, therefore contends that the primary function of government should be 'to preserve law and order, to enforce private contracts, to foster competitive markets' (ibid:2). Furthermore, the preservation of freedom is reinforced by capitalism's reliance on 'voluntary co-operation and private enterprise', as these socio-economic activities 'insure that the private sector is a check on the powers of the governmental sector' (ibid:3). Set in the context of spirally inflation and economic stagnation, Friedman's suggestion that financial savings could be gained from dismantling the regulatory architecture of Fordist corporate liberalism garnered widespread interest.

In the late 1970s the political environment increasingly mirrored the flourishing intellectual climate for the diffusion of neoliberal ideas. Economic crisis had irrevocably undermined the credibility of Keynesianism's corporatist state intervention. Nationalized industries and public sector service provision had enjoyed statutory protection in their position as icons of Keynesian collectivism. Although symbolizing freedom from class based inequalities, they were subject to government evoked regulatory controls. Over and above the immediate regulation of investment criteria, pricing and distribution, government control sought to establish operational codes of collectivist political practice and ethos; to varying degrees of success. It has been observed, that in the utilities sector nationalized firms could direct the structure of the economy and exploit their monopoly position, partly by controlling the balance and composition of public spending (Glyn 2007:37). But, this functionality was to be radically challenged by the structural transformation of the post-war capitalist system which produced seismic supply-side shocks, crippling Fordist production and precipitating a reconfiguration of capitalist accumulation (Pietrykowski 1999:181). David Harvey argues that it was mainly through 'spatial and temporal displacement' that Fordism survived its major overaccumulation crisis in the period immediately after World War II (2005:185). Temporal displacement defines the switching of resources from immediate to 'future uses' or 'an acceleration in turnover time' (ibid:182). Conversely, spatial displacement involves 'the absorption of excess capital and labour in geographical expansion' (ibid:183). Harvey argues that by the 1970s accelerated production was triggering off high inflation and undermining the value of fixed capital assets (ibid:185). And intensified competition between geographically distinct markets had the unintended consequence of increasing the level of international competition (within the mass produced sector) over a wider geographic area (Pietrykowski 1999:181). The outcome of which left domestic markets struggling to compete with the lower labour costs of their international competitors. These market developments effectively set the stage for 'systemic perturbation in the sequential' ordering of time and space in Fordist production systems (Castells 2000:464). Deficient levels of aggregate demand and uncertainty over transaction costs left Fordist production systems unable to sustain long production runs and undertake the continued investment in fixed-cost specialist machinery dedicated to the production of a single product (Pietrykowski 1999:181). These historical developments set the scene for the rise of neoliberalism's economic regime of 'reflexive accumulation' (Lash and Urry 1999).

Reflexive Accumulation and Neoliberalism

In post-Fordist production 'culture has penetrated the economy itself' (Lash and Urry 1999:61). Signs no longer represent the material world of manufacturing; rather signs permeate the production process. Developments in computer aided design and manufacturing (CAD/CAM) has not only precipitated flexible production, but also penetrates manufacturing with the ephemeral aesthetics of visual culture. Thus post-Fordist production has been defined as an 'economy of signs' (ibid). Accelerated rates of production enable commodities to be rapidly encoded with visual imagery that augments their exchange-value (Wexler 1990:166). It is this translation of exchange-value into sign-value which invigorates the circulation of capital. As Hall expresses it:

> Through marketing, layout and style, the image provides the mode of representation and fictional narrativisation of the body on which so much modern consumption depends. Modern culture is relentlessly material in its practices and modes of production. (1990:128)

Lash and Urry's (1999) concept of 'reflexive accumulation' effectively discerns the progressive significance of signs to capitalist accumulation in advanced neoliberal societies. This is because 'reflexive accumulation' focuses on the ascendency of socio-economies reliant on non-material service products, and the corresponding decline of material production as a basis of economic prosperity. Neoliberal market reforms are axiomatic with this form of capitalist accumulation. And this is most evidently, in the reliance of neoliberal market reforms, on the integration of knowledge and information into the productive process. Knowledge here is not just accentuating the intensity of the aggregation of facts so as to respond to the uncertainties of complex economic environments. Rather knowledge refers also to the reliance, in contemporary productive processes, on the subjective capacities of subjects and their reflexive engagement with the world. In this sense, 'Knowledge on the basis of reflexivity operates via not just a single but a double hermeneutic, in which the very norms, rules and resources of the production process are constantly put into question' (Lash and Urry 1999:61). It is my contention that, informationalism and reflexive knowledge is axiomatic with neoliberal market reforms. Indeed the market reforms introduced into the United Kingdom's (UK) Nation Health Service (NHS) during the Thatcher era (1979-1990) and subsequent neoliberal regimes are emblematic of the extent to which 'production has become increasingly grounded in discursive knowledge' (ibid:60). Even the most cursory perusal of New Labour's *NHS Choices* programme's systems, processes and promotional campaigns provides consistent evidence of what Lash and Urry (ibid) have elsewhere described as a 'democratization of knowledge-intensive production' as part of 'culturally based production'. Indeed, substantial aspects of the New Right, New Labour and current Conservative party's NHS 'choice agenda' correspond with reflexive accumulation. And it is my contention that this has important implications for the analysis of advertising signs and cultural politics in global times.

Semioticization of Neoliberal Market Reforms

According to Lash and Urry (1999:60) the tendency for advanced capitalism to ground production in 'discursive knowledge' is closely related to the growth of 'information-intensive research and development processes' (ibid). Knowledge of the labour process has from, the 1920s time-and-motion studies of Frederick Taylor, become a long established addendum of capitalist production. However, Lash and Urry (ibid) are referring to a process in which 'knowledge-intensive production' has 'succeeded a material labour process' such that information, signs and ephemera now displace the material 'reality' of an economy based on material production. Consequently, Lash and Urry (ibid) propose that advanced capitalism needs to be analysed in terms of the opposition between 'materially based versus culturally based production'. Again this suggestion illuminates dilemmas and processes apparent within the NHS in the UK and also healthcare reform in the United States (US). For instance, in the UK successive governments have introduced performance evaluation measures so as to assess the economic efficiency of the NHS and standards of healthcare delivery. The production and circulation of these measurements (signs) have encouraged the penetration, into the productive economy, of socio-cultural processes. Consequently images of league tables, performance indicators, consumer satisfaction panels, comparative market analogues and other quantifiable measures saturate and overwhelm the political landscape. Thus the concept of reflexive accumulation best describes how in neoliberal market reform 'culture has penetrated the economy itself' (ibid:61). And this refers to 'the extent to which symbolic processes, including an important aesthetic component, have permeated both consumer *and* production' (ibid). Axiomatic with this revelation is the recognition that culture is no longer a realm of representation 'hovering immaterially at a distance from the brute facts of "real" life' (Connor 1992:224). In the new era, culture partially instantiates the real. Consequently, reflexive accumulation 'is partially aesthetic and hence contemporary economies not only involve information-processing capacities but also symbol-processing activities' (Lash and Urry 1999:61). Significantly, these signs relate to symbols that include 'both information and aesthetic signifiers and other non-informational symbols' (ibid). And this has provided a platform for the direct introduction of advertising into neoliberal market reform. For example, in the UK in 2008, New Labour introduced a series of policy reforms dedicated to sanctioning healthcare service advertising and providing a *Code of Practice* (DoH 2008) for the regulation of healthcare promotion.

The integration of production with symbol-processing activities has transvalued the integrity of advertising and its location within the productive process. As signs engulf the exteriority of value so advertising has been promoted 'from a derivative to primary condition of societal maintenance' (Wexler 1990:166). Again clear parallels exist between the ascendency of the advertising sign and the global context of healthcare service delivery in advanced Western liberal democracies. Of particular relevance here has been the meteoric ascendency of Direct to Consumer Advertising (DTCA) as a central appendage of the global pharmaceutical industry. Proponents of Direct to Consumer (DTC) pharmaceutical advertising argue that it serves to educate the public about medical conditions and their treatments. In the UK and more so in the US, the arena of internal markets has effectively transformed patients into consumers empowered with the autonomy bequeathed by a retrenching welfare state. Accordingly, consumers have become more involved and apparently keen to play an informed active role in their healthcare. From the perspective of the government and pharmaceutical industry this translates as a potential beneficial effect of DTCA. For DTCA educates consumers about pharmaceuticals and also raises their awareness about new medicines and treatments. In this sense, DTCA primes the doctor-patient dialogue.

Cultivating the Self and Marketing the 'Soul'

According to Lash and Urry (1999:61), reflexive accumulation is bound-up not only with 'production but also reflexive consumption'. The concept of 'reflexive consumption' is crucial to understanding the extent to which advertising has become an integral dimension of neoliberalist policy and practice. Of particular relevance here is Anthony Giddens' (1993) *Modernity and Self Identity*. He argues that partly as a consequence of globalization, our current era is a de-traditionalized social order i.e., one in which traditional forms of social solidarity (e.g., community networks) have declined. A similar theme is apparent in Lash and Urry's (1999:61) account of the fragmentation and decline of communities and collective solidarities as they express it:

> What is more important is the process of Enttraditionalisierung, of the decline of tradition which opens up a process of individualization in which structures, such as family, corporate groups and even social class location, no longer determine consumption decisions for individuals.

Suffice to say that our current era is 'post-traditional' and 'one in which tradition changes its status. Traditions have to explain themselves, to become open to interrogation or discourse' (Giddens 1998:5). This disembedding of everyday life from traditional processes and calculable expert systems propels individual decision making 'away from the hold of pre-established precepts or practices' (Giddens 1993:20). In this context, individuals become ever reliant upon themselves to define a sense of identity. These conditions are accentuated by the transformation of social relations across time and space. Innovations in communication technologies provide new conditions for the articulation of social relations and personal identities both nationally and internationally. The interiority of the local and global into day-to-day life is transforming of self-identity. For self-identity is reflexively produced as a project 'constituted by the reflexive ordering of self-narratives' (ibid:244). But the claims to reason, tradition and 'truth' which traditionally defined these self-narratives are in decline. Consequently reflexivity, in this post-traditional order, leads to the ceaseless interrogation of the self and this 'is existentially troubling for ordinary individuals' (ibid:21).

In this condition of flux and instability the signifying practices of consumer culture become ever more appealing. This is because, consumer culture provides an important site in which subjects can fashion a sense of identity. Indeed, consumer culture is axiomatic to Giddens' concept of 'reflexive modernity'. Firstly, consumer culture is linked to globalization and the aesthetization of goods into spectacular imaginary. Secondly, recent transformations in advertising language, from utility to sign-value, excite the reflexivity of contemporary culture. For the signifying practices of postmodern advertising directly challenge cultural reproduction and the hegemony of *habitus* as a determinant of choice. And finally consumer culture is axiomatic to Giddens' notion of 'life politics' (1998). Which refers to 'disputes and struggles about how...we should live in a world where what used to be fixed either by nature or tradition is now subject to human decisions' (ibid:15). The implication here is that the reflexive subject of late modernity fashions a sense of identity through the signifying practices of consumption choices. But life politics is not merely a politics of self interest and maximizing individual gain. Rather 'in the domain of life politics individuals or groups take lifestyle decisions that limit or actively go against maximising economic returns' (ibid:102). Consequently the consumer as citizen is a morally privileged subject cognizant of its rights and responsibilities and in this sense in correspondence with neoliberal market reforms.

Reflections and Conclusion

The primary intention of this chapter was to interrogate the integration of advertising into corporate liberal and neoliberal political discourse. In the milieu from which universal rights are disappearing, advertising imposes a moral obligation on subjects to make healthcare provision for themselves and their families well into the future. While some attention has been drawn to the mobilization of collective resistance to neoliberalism (c.f. Harvey 2007), insufficient attention has been paid to the medium of visual culture as both a source of resistance and vehicle for the extension of neoliberalist discursive practice. The logical implication here is that, in advertising cultures, autonomous consumers come to adopt a certain entrepreneurial form of practical relationship to their selves. Enterprise is represented here as playing a vital translating role, promising to align 'political thought and a range of specific programmes for administering the national economy' with the goals of industry and the self-regulating activities of individuals (Miller and Rose 2008:49). More specifically, the languages and techniques of enterprise:

> provide both the necessary distance between political authorities and organizational life, and the translatability to establish an alliance between national economic health, increased organizational effectiveness and progressive and humanistic values. (Miller and Rose 2008:50)

Within this politico-ethical environment, consumers are constituted as both objects of enterprise and instruments of enterprise as they make 'entrepreneurs of themselves, seeking to maximize their "quality of life" through the artful assembly of a "life-style" put together through the world of goods' (ibid:49).

Chapter 2
Governmentality and the Political Economy of the Sign

The primary intention of this chapter is to critically analyse the integration of advertising into neoliberal market reforms of healthcare services in the UK and US. In the milieu from which universal rights are disappearing, advertising imposes a moral obligation on subjects to make healthcare provision for themselves and their families well into the future. While some attention has been drawn to the mobilization of collective resistance to neoliberalism (c.f. Harvey 2007), insufficient attention has been paid to the medium of visual culture as both a source of resistance and vehicle for the extension of neoliberalist discursive practice. The logical implication here is that, in advertising cultures, autonomous consumers come to adopt a certain entrepreneurial form of practical relationship to their selves. Enterprise is represented here as playing a vital translating role, promising to align 'political thought and a range of specific programmes for administering the national economy' with the goals of industry and the self-regulating activities of individuals (Miller and Rose 2008:49). More specifically, the languages and techniques of enterprise:

> provide both the necessary distance between political authorities and organizational life, and the translatability to establish an alliance between national economic health, increased organizational effectiveness and progressive and humanistic values. (Miller and Rose ibid:50)

Within this politico-ethical environment, consumers are constituted as both objects of enterprise and instruments of enterprise as they make 'entrepreneurs of themselves, seeking to maximize their "quality of life" through the artful assembly of a "life-style" put together through the world of goods' (ibid:49). This chapter is divided into four sections. Section one, entitled 'Signs of the Times: Neoliberalism and Aesthetic Accumulation'; examines the rise of advertising as an addendum to neoliberal market capitalist reform. The central theme here is that axiomatic to market reform is the creation of 'market analogues', which take the form of advertising practice, and are directed at enabling market relations of competition and 'choice'. By way of an introduction to this process of translation, consider the following extracts of policy documents and press releases, announcing and debating market reform of healthcare in both the UK and the US:

> Our reform plan is based on the methods of the post-bureaucratic age – decentralisation, accountability and transparency. Applying these ideas to the NHS will help us improve it for everyone and allow us to meet people's rising expectations. Instead of bureaucratic accountability there will be democratic accountability. We will decentralise power, so that patients have a real choice. And by publishing information about the kind of results that healthcare providers are achieving, we will make sure there is no hiding place for failure. If patients don't like what they are offered, they will be able to find something better. This will drive up standards by allowing people to choose the best providers and by encouraging hospitals to compete for patients. (Conservative Party David Cameron 2010)

> So we know that reforming our health insurance system will be a critical step in rebuilding our economy so that our entrepreneurs can pursue the American Dream again, and our small businesses can grow and expand and create new jobs again. That is precisely what the reform legislation before Congress right now will do. Under these proposals, small businesses will be able to purchase health insurance through an insurance exchange, a marketplace where they can compare the price, quality and services of a wide variety of plans, many of which will provide better coverage at lower costs than the plans they have now. (White House President Barack Obama 2009)

> This Code of Practice therefore sets out rules that providers of NHS-funded services must follow when promoting their services…This is an important step towards making choices a reality in the NHS, giving patients the material they need to choose services that suit their needs, and encouraging providers to make their services more responsive to patients. (Labour Party, Department of Health 2008:i-ii)

Section two entitled; 'Neoliberalism, Advertising and the Aestheticisation of Healthcare', demonstrates advertising as an addendum to the market reform of healthcare. Section three, entitled; 'DTCA and the Aestheticisation of Healthcare Services in Global Context', critically case studies the rise of Direct to Consumer Advertising (DTCA) in the UK and US healthcare service. This section uses document analysis to detail cultural politics directed at resisting the spread of advertising cultures in healthcare provision. Section four, entitled; 'Advertising Technologies and the Medicalization of Social Life', examines academic debates intent on criticizing the role of DTCA in the medicalization of social life. While detailed in their critique of DTCA, it is my contention that these studies fail to appreciate advertising's role in what Foucault (1990) describes as the 'cultivation of the self'. For, it is through the cultivation of the self, that 'the self-regulating capacities of subjects shaped and normalized in large part through' advertising cultures 'have become key resources for modern forms of government' (Miller and Rose 2008:26).

Signs of the Times: Neoliberalism and Aesthetic Accumulation

In the UK, the pinnacle moment in the establishment of the neoliberal hegemony, was marked by the victory of 'Thatcherism' over Keynesianism in the 1979 election. In the US Reaganism epitomized the rightward march of the new political era, and the inauguration of Ronald Reagan as president in 1981, pinnacled the transatlantic ascendancy of neoliberal economic policy. Indeed, both electoral victories signify the first phase of global neoliberalism, which is a politics, based on an antipathy to notions of centralized collective economic action and the committed promotion of deregulated market capitalism. Within industrialized countries the neoliberalist revolution translated into: (1) deregulated labour markets; (2) limited state intervention into the operations of market capitalism; (3) emphasis on contracting fiscal investment in public sector service provision; (4) extension of market relations and the private economy into the public sector; (5) the deregulation of financial markets; (6) privatization; (7) weakening of trade unions through legislation designed to obstruct the effective mobilization of strikes; (8) disassembly of the Keynesian capital-labour accord through the establishment of increased management control over the labour process; and (9) dismantling trade barriers and other controls over capital movements; thus opening up the conditions for the transnational circulation of capital. In macro-economic policy these features accorded with 'monetarism', which in simple terms is a doctrine that attributes the primary factor explaining inflation, to rapid destabilizing escalations in 'the quantity of money', i.e., 'the stock of currency in circulation plus the stock of bank deposits' (Backhouse 2002:196). To this end monetarist economic policies counter the Keynesian emphasis on short term increases in the flow of money supply, with market lead regulations engineered to achieve a constant rate of money growth and circulation. When viewed against the repercussions of a Keynesian era in, which rapid monetary expansions lead to destabilizing economic recession, a strategy geared towards controlling the growth of money supply was particularly persuasive (ibid).

In the UK this monetarist shift was most prominently evident in the Conservative Thatcher Government's (1979-1990) control of inflation; partly through the transfer of nationalized assets into private ownership (i.e., privatization) and 'cut backs' in public sector spending. The substratum underpinning these policy objectives drew disproportionately on: the global economic crisis of the 1970s and the financial incongruences posed by an expansive public sector; Keynesianism's failure to accommodate unregulated global economy; spiraling inflation and the Damoclean gap between fiscal expenditure and revenues. This rhetoric of imminent disaster and fiscal crisis was powerful in its auditory as evident in the following extract of Margaret Thatcher's *The Downing Street Years*:

> Privatization, no less than the tax structure, was fundamental to improving Britain's economic performance. But for me it was also far more than that: it was one of the central means of reversing the corrosive and corrupting effects of

> socialism. Ownership by the state is just that – ownership by an impersonal legal entity: it amounts to control by politicians and civil servants; and it is a misnomer to describe nationalization, as the Labour Party did, as 'public ownership'. But through privatization – particularly the kind of privatization which leads to the widest possible share ownership by members of the public – the state's power is reduced and the power of the people enhanced...so privatization is at the centre of any programme of reclaiming territory for freedom. (1993:676)

By the mid-1980s monetarist conjecture came to preeminence in macro-economics and with this privatization became a principal condition of the Thatcher government's second term in office (1983-1987). The centre piece of this reform was the privatization of state-owned utilities such as gas, water and electricity. In this context privatization refers to an attempt to limit the direction of state regulation, through the transfer of ownership of public assets and service provision into the private sector. However, privatization assumed three distinct forms during the Thatcher era: (1) the sale or denationalization of all or part, of publicly owned assets; (2) subcontracting to the private sector, of government financed services and provision; and (3) deregulation of a given state monopoly. Despite these variations central themes connect these practices. For each is premised on the abiding contention 'that markets alone are both all that is required to understand economic behaviour and the only sure means to achieve efficiency' (Crouch 2007:261). It was presumed that privatization would generate rapid financial rewards. Most notably, the belief that cost benefits derived from extricating government control of capital intensive loss-making assets, might, 'reduce government debt and raise revenues, which could be used for further politically popular cuts in the direct rate of income tax' (Evans 2005:35). Additional justifications emphasized the economies of scale and efficiencies that are generated once a firm is introduced to 'competitive private sector disciplines' (Glyn 2007:38). Clear trajectories connect these ideas to the neoclassical economics of Milton Friedman and most notably, the pragmatic rightwing politics of New Right orthodoxy. Both ideologues mounted a systematic challenge to the institutional structures of collectivism, in the belief that demolishing the 'burdensome' relics of collectivist Keynesian would liberate individuals to construct economically successful markets. In this context, opening up sectors that had been formerly restricted by state monopoly protection was axiomatic with, pursuing the natural competitive tendency of economic relations.

Indeed the evident market failures and related suboptimal inefficiency levels of government sanctioned monopolies provided empirical evidence of the potential that 'free' markets might deliver. And this rightward visionary idealism largely informed the Conservative government's relentless, neoliberal regime of utilities privatization during the 1980s. Once this first phase of 'rolling back the state' was firmly established, a second phase of neoliberalism precipitated a 'rolling out' into the public sector of market based policies. This prolonged strategy of market reform is seen by David Harvey (2007:2) as an inevitability of neoliberalism this is because:

> Neoliberalism is in the first instance a theory of political economic practices that proposes that human well-being can best be advanced by liberating individual entrepreneurial freedoms and skills within an institutional framework characterized by strong private property rights, free markets, and free trade.

Neoliberals regarded Keynesian institutions of social protection and expansive governance, to be an iniquitous problem that might be resolved by market relations, coupled with the commercial integration of goods and services located outside the market. State financed monopolies obstruct the competitive role of markets in determining, that factors of production are remunerated according to their worth, thus encouraging an over emphasis on state protection. Moreover, neoliberals propose that, in the absence of market competition, Keynesian forms of public sector governance; stifle entrepreneurial efficiency, impede performance related wealth distribution and lead to a myopic emphasis on bureaucratic interests and professional needs (Dwyer 2000:63). Neoliberalism is said, therefore, to have emanated as an ideological reaction to the crisis in Keynesian social protection and public sector institutions. Given that the crisis in Keynesianism manifested itself in cumbersome Fordist bureaucracies, the neoliberal policy revolution assumed equally spectacular visual images keen to juxtapose cumbersome process against lean market efficiency. The Thatcher government's commitment to market processes effortlessly conveyed a vast reduction in the discretionary power of the state, and the transition towards market-based reforms.

Certainly market practices ally with neoliberal privatization. Marketization is, however, more frequently evident in the absence of private ownership. This is because, marketization has provided an effective adumbrate to the retrenchment, by successive governments, from state subsidies and the deregulation of both private and public sector services. In this context, marketization is based on the permeability of the interfaces between the public and private sectors and the ability of previously ridged dichotomies to cascade into themselves.

Broadly speaking marketization policies instigated the development of 'quasi-markets' in state financed and or state provided services. These 'quasi-markets' entail claiming territory previously separated from markets and subjecting these areas to the dynamics of the market. Thus, 'enabling policy inputs and outputs to be measured in terms of a single cost metric' (Crouch 2007:266). The metaphor of permeability signifies several aspects of quasi-market operations within, and between, Government departments and services. Crouch (2003:4) has observed that following Conservative reforms of the 1980s public sector institutions and Government departments were required to operate market-based relations. This invariably involved trading 'services with other units as though they were in a market relationship, abandoning the professional colleague model that had previously governed their interactions' (ibid). Because the market economy reduces the role of government, quasi-markets within the public sector have established a client–provider model based on the separation of purchaser from provider (Levacic 1995).

It is important to appreciate that, based on the absence of a cash nexus, quasi-markets fundamentally distinguish from their free-market counterpart, 'though few contemporary markets in any field are actually free from government regulation and many of them involve some element of overt or covert subsidy' (Whitty and Power 2000:94). Even more significantly, the integration into the market of goods and services, previously external to commercial market relations 'involves an elaborate procedure of creating barriers of access so that we cannot get them without payment' (Crouch 2003:9).

Public sector products/services traditionally operate in the absence of a price mechanism. Indeed, in 1942 William Beveridge certified the concept of the welfare state as conditional with the universal rights and obligations of citizenship. All citizens had the right, to at least a minimum level of free welfare provision, within specified conditions. A significant focus of the neoliberal ideological onslaught on Keynesian modes of social protection has been the suggestion that Beveridge viewed welfare to be a conditional right that had to be earned through active participation in economic activity (i.e., National Insurance payments). And thus the push for marketization represents a renewed economic ethos equating welfare and financial relations. However, without a price mechanism the scope of public sector marketization is limited. For price achieves two fundamental roles in markets: firstly provides a 'unitary indicator' enabling the comparison of commodities based on their quality and value for money and secondly it acts 'as a rationing device for distribution' (ibid:27). Governments have demonstrated ingenuity in resolving the anomaly of the cash-less nexus. Invariably this requires that the very ideography of the product/service has to be translated, so as to reconfigure previously non-market relations into the market's signifying language.

Throughout the hegemony of neoliberal capitalism this process of translation has involved the creation of 'indicators that can serve as analogues of prices' (ibid:9). Where markets are implied and products/services only virtually traded, as with NHS marketization reforms, there is consistent evidence of recourse to artificial indicators (promotional signs) so as to affect the market-like dynamics of trading. Indeed, the unrelenting determination expressed by successive governments, to subject the welfare sector to the market relations has been axiomatic with the extension of advertising into public sector provision. This phenomenon is acutely evident in National Health Services (NHS) market reforms, most significantly in the aestheticisation of healthcare through the recasting of health into 'internal markets'.

Neoliberalism, Advertising and the Aestheticisation of Healthcare

The NHS has experienced many changes since its establishment in 1948. Nevertheless, an enduring feature of the services provided by the NHS has been the commitment to ensuring that it is free at the point of delivery. Indeed, even amid the recession of the early 1980s, the then Conservative government pledged that 'The National Health Service will continue to be available to all, regardless of income, and to be financed mainly out of general taxation' (DoH 1989:ii). Nevertheless the difficulties encountered in sustaining universal access to free healthcare, amidst a burgeoning financial crisis within the NHS, provided pragmatic justification for the introduction of 'internal markets'.

Markets have always been implicit to the conditionality of welfare as a universal right of citizenship (Marshall 1992). Claims of a history of market absence within the NHS, can also be challenged, for instance Klein (1995:195) insists that 'competition between consultants for funds, beds and merit awards had characterized the NHS throughout its entire history' (quoted in Powell 2000:98). Moreover, the 1980s had already witnessed the introduction of Compulsory Competitive Tendering (CCT) amongst private and non-profit services, for the provision of auxiliary services within the NHS. While it was the case that some precedence existed for the competitive practice, what was distinctive about the reforms introduced since 1989 was, the increased application of market principles and the accentuated competitive pressures precipitated by the introduction of 'internal markets'. The idea of 'internal markets' can be traced to Professor Alain Enthoven; a Stanford University academic who worked for the US President Johnson's administration during the 1960s. Known as the 'father of managed competition' Enthoven was invited to the Nuffield Hospital Trust in 1984 to advise on NHS reform (Porter 1999:255). His cost-benefit analysis recommended a financially integrated healthcare delivery system that would debilitate the monopoly of power operated by NHS suppliers, by compelling them to engage in market-based competition, while also preserving the principle of universal state funded welfare (ibid). According to Enthoven (1988), internal markets, would promote cost-effective, consumer-lead quality services. Enthoven's (1988) ideas provided some of the intellectual raison d'etre behind the Thatcher government's introduction of internal markets into the NHS during the 1980s. Indeed, in many ways the evolution of internal markets within the NHS was instigated in 1989 with the publication of the White Paper 'Working for Patients' (DoH, 1989) which introduced: 'Fund-Holding' General Practitioners, promotion of medical audit; capitation basis for the buying of services for a designated population and capital charges to determine the actual cost of building/services and additional capital assets. These proposals detailed in the White Paper, were the foundation of the subsequent legislative reform – The *NHS and Community Care Act 1990*, which was instituted in 1991.

The underlying principle guiding the Conservative government's NHS reform was the belief that the creation of an internal market, within the NHS, would revolutionize existing processes so as to achieve greater efficiency and improve management. This objective was bullishily actualized with the introduction of the radical 'purchaser/provider split' i.e., the separation of public health functions previously conflated in the role of District Health Authorities. From 1991 the principle role of District Health Authorities (DHA) became that of identifying the healthcare needs of the resident population, situated in the geographical area covered by the DHA, and purchasing resources accordingly. Additional healthcare institutions that were ascribed the role of 'purchaser' included Family Health Service Authorities (FHSA) and 'Fund-Holding' General Practitioners (FHGP). Traditionally, General Practitioners (GPs) are independent contractors to the NHS. Under the system of NHS reform established in 1991, large GP practices could apply for the 'practice fund', to purchase a defined range of services directly from hospitals so as to treat their patients. According to 'Working for Patients', FHGPs are 'in the interests of a better service to the patient' (DOH 1989:5). This is partly because 'GPs will be encouraged to compete for patients by offering better services. And it will be easier for patients to choose (and change) their own GP as they wish' (ibid). Thus, in summary it has been observed that 'the purchasing authority is the citizen's agent in a quasi-market' (Harrison and Wistow 1992:124).

In contrast the 'provider' function designates that healthcare units act as providers of healthcare services to patients, which are purchased by the DHA. As part of this reform, hospitals, community health services, and other units of healthcare provision, previously possessed by the DHA, became providers of healthcare. The 1990 act also encouraged some of these units to be 'self-governing' NHS Trusts 'to own and manage hospitals or other facilities previously managed by health authorities, or to develop new facilities' (DoH 1989/1990:ii). In effect, while remaining within the NHS, Trusts have independence from the NHS in the management of their affairs. A key motivation behind the establishment of NHS Trusts was to harness efficiency by ensuring that these institutions 'will earn revenue from the services they provide' (DoH 1989:4). It was perceived that money would follow patients as NHS Trusts 'have an incentive to attract patients, so they will make sure that the service they offer is what their patients want' (ibid). Alongside NHS Trusts were service providers of which DHAs retained nominal control (i.e., directly-managed units: DMUs). It is noteworthy that all NHS hospitals, whether managed by the DHA or self-governing where ascribed the authority to extend their services to other health authority and to the private sector. Indeed, the government actively encouraged public and private sector partnerships in health provision as is evident from the following extract 'The NHS and the independent health sector should be able to learn from each other, to support each other and to provide services for each other' (ibid:8). Suffice to say, a central outcome of the purchase-provider split was to inject competition into the system as healthcare providers were propelled into direct competition in the pursuit of contracts. As is the logic of market capitalism, those providers and purchasers not catering to client demand would incur diminished revenue, loss of market share and risk foreclosure. Consequently both providers and purchasers were transformed into market players and their interrelations were created through 'contracts' that defined the volume, cost, quality and timing of services (Harrison and Wistow 1992:124).

Market Analogues and the Politics of Healthcare Reform

The ethos of corrivalry situated at the heart of the Conservative government's 1990 NHS reform package, worked in symbiosis with the generation of comparative performance data and a plethora of other indicators that can serve as analogues for decision making in a contract driven market place. The first NHS performance indicator deliberately aimed, to communicate with the public, was the Patient's Charter introduced in 1991 as part of the then Conservative government's launch of *The Citizen's Charter: Raising the Standard.* The Patient's Charter outlined basic rights to amongst other things, 'a wider choice for patients, improved responsiveness to their needs and specific standards for patient services' (DoH 1991:10).

With regards to the operation of internal markets and the 1990 NHS reforms, the creation of market analogues became a categorical national priority with the establishment of the Purchaser Efficiency Index (PEI). The PEI was 'a measure of the year on year change in a purchaser's efficiency' (SCoHR 1998:1). It was presumed that PEI would provide accessible data about the efficiency of healthcare purchasers. Despite their perceived benefits, it soon became evident that the production and large-scale circulation of quantitative market analogues invariably produce market distortions. This is because formulaic analogues have a reductive affect, in that they conflate the qualitative complexity of social activities into easily measurable signs. Once qualitative dimensions of social acts are transformed into commercially viable simulacra, there is a tendency to excessively focus on the marketing of activities that are included as measures of effective performance (Crouch 2003).

With the 1997 electoral victory, New Labour euphorically promised to deliver a 'Third Way' which differs both from the expansionist Keynesian approach of the post-war era and the competitive individualism of the Conservative government's market-based NHS model. In a White Paper entitled 'The New NHS Modern Dependable', New Labour pledged to place the needs of patients at the centre of healthcare. The abolition of the internal market was then seen as axiomatic with 'making the NHS better every year' (DoH 1997:4). New Labour promised to abolish the internal market. Providers and patients would no longer be subject to the fragmenting and divisive ravages of internal market competition:

> Under the internal market, the Purchaser Efficiency Index was the only real measure of performance. But it distorted priorities and – to the universal frustration of NHS staff – institutionalized perverse incentives which got in the way of providing efficient, effective, high quality services. In addition, budgets for emergency care, waiting list surgery and drug treatments were artificially divided, reducing flexibility. (DoH 1997:15)

According to New Labour the Conservative government's 'obsession' with the PEI was at the expense of investing in improvements in other areas of healthcare. For 'the Tories so-called Efficiency Index' counts the number of patient episodes, not the quality or success of treatment (SCoHR 1998:1). Conversely, New Labour promised that the NHS would be run on the principle of 'integrated care' (DoH 1997:1). Dismantling the alienating internal market and replacing its more discordant elements with cooperative partnerships became an unyielding imperative. For instance, New Labour phased out GP fund holding and replaced this system with a more cooperative reduced number of purchasers. Primary Care Groups (PCG), comprising of all GPs and community nurses within a designated Health Authority area, were given the 'responsibility for commissioning services for the local community' (ibid:25). PCGs were allocated responsibility for budgets and 'deploy their resources within the framework of the Health Improvement Programme' (ibid). It was established that over time the PCGs would mature into 'freestanding Primary Care Trusts' (ibid). New Labour retained the separation of purchaser and provider roles with the promise to embed this bifurcation into cooperative relations. Thus explaining the insistence that NHS Trusts, 'will agree long term service agreements with Primary Care Groups…linked to the new National Service Framework' (ibid). It is important to note that a theme running through New Labour's early and present NHS reform is the accumulation and distribution of quality indexes. It is also interesting to observe continuities and accentuation in the disciplinary role of this enduring feature of market-based NHS restructuring.

In New Labour's reformed NHS the 'perverse incentives of Efficiency Index' along with its 'distorting priorities', are bygone relics of 'competitive advantage' (ibid:13). New Labour pledged that NHS performance measures would be based on 'quality of outcome, itself an incentive for effectiveness' (SCoHR 1998:1). The centrepiece of New Labour's reform of public reporting on NHS quality and efficiency was launched in July 1998 in the consultation document *A First Class Service: Quality in the New NHS:*

> The Government's third way involves setting clear national standards but with responsibility for delivery being taken locally and being backed by consistent monitoring arrangements. National yardsticks, drawn up through joint working between the Department of Health and the professions, will guide local decisions by managers and clinicians, not tie their hands. Devolution of responsibility will be matched with accountability for performance – as it has to be in a national public service as important as the NHS. (DoH 1998:4)

A First Class Service introduced a new broader-based schema for evaluating the NHS's performance. The PEI system of performance indicators was replaced with a triumvirate schema of standards monitoring. Firstly, the setting of standards and the promotion of clinical cost effectiveness would be the responsibility of the National Institute for Clinical Excellence (NICE). Alongside NICE's advisory role in the provision of best practice, was instituted National Service Frameworks (NSF) for assessing performance. NSFs assign national standards and 'establish performance measures against which progress within an agreed timescale will be measured' (DoH 1999:4). Advances in the delivering of standards were ascribed to 'Clinical Governance', founded upon 'professional self regulation and lifelong learning' (ibid). The third feature of the triumvirate evaluation schema focused on the monitoring of standards. *A First Class Service* accentuated the need for a performance framework that would report the delivery of clinical outcomes and cost effective consumer focused provision. In April 1999 'The NHS Performance Assessment Framework' (PAF) was instituted. Underpinning PAF was the 'balanced scorecard approach' (DoH 2007). This generic scorecard approach enables organizations to acquire a more holistic perspective of performance by isolating, different key elements of performance and comprehending how alterations in them have implications for others. PAF was initially directed at measuring the performance of Health Authorities. Alongside PAF, *A First Class Service* established the Commission for Health Improvement (CHI), which was ascribed the duty to carry out local evaluations to ensure that monitoring systems geared towards advancing clinical quality were in place. A National Survey of Patient and User Experience of the NHS, was also established to review the quality of NHS care. The survey was designed to be carried out nationally and data derived from 'the results could be used to initiate action to secure improved services' (DoH 1999:4).

The Performance Assessment Framework was intended to overcome the obsession with depthless quantitative signs and instead concentrate on 'measuring what really counts for patients, ensuring that the pursuit of quality and efficiency go together' (SConHR., 1998:1). Thus:

> the Performance Framework will judge how well each part of the NHS is doing to deliver quality services. The Framework will hold local services to account against objective criteria which measure performance from the patients' point of view. It will, for example, publish information about whether patients have fair access to similar services in all parts of the country. (DoH 1998:7)

Despite this commitment to setting quality standards that align with 'integrated care', PAF failed to assuage the concerns of practitioners, largely because of New Labour's unremitting insistence on the accumulation and circulation of quantitative market analogues. As is evident here, amongst other places, '...tackle inefficiency through demanding targets on unit costs and productivity [and NHS Trusts] publish their costs on a consistent basis to help drive out unacceptable variations through benchmarking' (SConHR 1998:1).

There is extensive literature investigating the impact of this early era of New Labour's NHS performance quality measurements. Of pertinence here are the observations of Annandale (1998:219) particularly the suggestion that the market-based commercial ethos transforms patients into organizational currency. As she expresses it 'Patients, who are constructed as discrete disease episodes that are "contracted for", literally become products in a market, caught up in a system which is mystifying and within which they can have little real say about what happens to them' (ibid). Similar challenges are presented by Davies and Lampel (1998). They highlight the growing resistance across the public sector to the development of performance monitoring systems 'which promise information to reform service organization and performance, but which are in fact political in origin, ritualistic in execution, and self sustaining in effect' (ibid:160). Elsewhere, Smith (1995:277), argues that 'the performance indicator philosophy is based on inadequate models of production and control'. Focusing on the behavioural unintended consequences of performance indicators, they identify 'gaming' and 'ossification'. 'Gaming' refers to the deliberate underestimation of performance so as to control the rate of production and gain strategic advantage. 'Ossification' operates to undermine entrepreneurial initiative. It arises from the organizational paralysis generated by the implementation of 'an excessively rigid system of performance evaluation' (ibid:299).

It is clear that the perfusion of performance indices during the first term of New Labour's NHS reform fuelled escalating resistance. And yet New Labour's accumulation and circulation of market based analogues of NHS performance relentlessly continues. In July 2000 New Labour published *The NHS Plan* (DoH 2000). The document makes reference to the Performance Assessment Framework (PAF), and the benchmarks of performance used to monitor health authorities. Its states that 'each year tables are published showing how each health authority has performed against the measures of each category' (ibid:61). Within *The NHS Plan* the system of PAF was extended beyond the initial focus on health authorities to encompass NHS bodies from both sides of the purchaser (e.g., primary care trusts) provider (e.g., NHS hospitals) divide. As part of the rationale supporting this extension of PAF it was stated that 'This will enable both Ministers and the public to understand how efficient and effective the providers and deliverers of health service are' (ibid).

New Labour has also increasingly made use of performance related monetary measures designed to individualize the accountability for the delivery of NHS provision. The most aggressive tool forcing this accountability was introduced in 2004 as part of New Labour's *The NHS Improvement Plan* (DoH 2004). The reforms established a national system of 'payment by results', intended to 'support the exercise of choice by patients, improve waiting times for patients and provide strong incentives for efficient use of resources' (ibid:11). Under this new arrangement NHS care providers will be paid a pre-determined price for each patient treated. A national 'tariff' of prices was created and provided the basis of the majority of hospital and community healthcare. It was intended that financial incentives will invigorate turnover rates for the number of treatments provided. The new 'payment by results' scheme was deliberately created as a mechanism for enhancing efficiency 'as providers take action to bring their costs into line with the tariff, for example by reducing lengths of stay in hospital' (ibid:70). The sustained division between planning and delivery meant that the new system had particular consequences for Primary Care Trusts (PCTS). Of significance are the consequences that stem from the introduction of a national tariff. For this effectively ablated, from the process of commissioning, the need for price negotiation. Thus shifting the 'focus discussion on the quality of care' (ibid:70). It was clearly the intention that 'payment by results' would play a significant role in instilling an entrepreneurial sprit into the delivery of NHS services. And the accent on enterprise was furthered by the initiative to provide 'a lot more choice for patients about how, when and where they are treated and much better information to support that' (ibid:8). To this end the Labour government extended the role of the private sector within the NHS. Thus from 2008 patients were ascribed the right 'to choose from any provider, as long as they meet clear NHS standards' (ibid:9). The centrality of the private sector to this mix of choice is evident here and elsewhere. For The NHS Improvement Plan stated that 'NHS patients will also be able to choose from a growing range of independent providers, with their diagnosis and treatment paid for by the NHS' (ibid:10). Indeed it was forecast that the independent sector would 'provide up to 15% of procedures on behalf of the NHS' (ibid).

The quality assessment and ranking of health service providers, according to recent reports it set to intensify and this will have direct disciplinary consequences for NHS funding. In 2008 health minister Lord Darzi published a ten year plan outlining measures to enable patients to rate the quality of NHS care they have experienced. Based on a twelve month review involving consultations with 60,000 patients and healthcare staff, the report aimed to introduce 'clarity to quality' and to make coherent the 'morass' of existing performance measures (Lord Darzi quoted in BBC 2008). Of particular significance in the report was the announcement of the launch in 2009 of performance measure that enable patients to rate the quality of their NHS care. According to Lord Darzi this initiative 'is about giving more clout to patients' (ibid). He argues that 'by measuring quality across the service and publishing that information for the first time, both staff and patients can work together to make better informed choices about their care' (ibid). In August 2009 the NHS launched a comparison service originally hosted on its NHS Choices website. Patients viewing the website will be able to enter their postcode, rate and compare hospitals online according to performance indices evaluating issues such as mortality, infection rates and patient care. This hospital 'scorecard' system operates in a similar fashion to the internet price comparison sites available in the commercial insurance market. The scheme received some support from prominent NHS practitioners and patient care groups. For example Michael Summers the then chairman of the Patients Association praised the scheme as 'an important web tool' (quoted in Carlowe 2009:420). Similarly, Nigel Edwards, the then director of policy for the NHS Confederation, supported the increased opportunities for patient feedback but warned that for the system to work it requires large volumes of patients to participate into process of inputting their experiences into the computer system. Thus the administrators of the scheme need to make 'sure that the information is reliable and paints a full picture…To work at their best, large numbers of patients need to rate and comment' (quoted in Carlowe 2009:420). Although widely defended by the then health secretary Andy

Burnham and marketed as assuring in a new era of accountability, the new scheme has engendered a recurrent theme of resistance regarding the simplification of complex healthcare processes. Thus for example, Mark Porter, the then deputy chairman of the British Medical Association's Central Consultants and Specialist Committee said:

> I am in favour of open information and of more of this being published, but I am against summarizing vast amounts of information and using a single measure to represent a hospital's overall performance...You are summing up the activities of hospitals that have more than 5,000 employees, 40 clinical departments, and thousands of patients [and] putting them into a single number. It is of no help to patients – the results may be falsely reassuring, accurate, or falsely depressing. The patient has no way of knowing. (quoted in Carlow 2009:420)

Here and elsewhere, it is evident that advertising knowledges have the affect of aestheticising and simplifying the complexities of healthcare, and in so doing translating information into resources relevant to the accomplishment of the governmental objectives of neoliberal market reforms. These processes are particularly evident when we examine the pharmaceutical market and the lucrative effect that government (de)regulation of healthcare promotion has had on the scope and capacity of the global pharmaceutical market.

DTCA and the Aestheticisation of Healthcare Services in Global Context

> In all public services, we are making a radical shift from top-down, target-driven performance management to a more bottom-up, self-improving system built around the individual needs of service users and influenced by effective engagement with the public. Increasingly, improvement will be driven by the choices made by service users and healthy competition between different service providers. The NHS is no exception...Through promotional activity, providers will develop a better understanding of the needs and wants of patients and GPs. This will enable them to respond and reshape services accordingly and deliver services that better meet those needs. (DoH 2007:5)

In the operation and maintenance of choice, advertising has achieved a dramatic incursion into public sector healthcare provision. New Labour's resuscitation of the internal market, sedimented, the concept of advertising, deep into the operational infra-structure of the NHS. From 1 April 2008 patients were gifted the right to select, to receive, routine elective services from any healthcare provider in England, as long as they accord with NHS quality standards and costs. It was recognized that the reality of choice needed to be supported by information and thus NHS patients were provided with access to clinical quality data as well as government sponsored online advice portals such as the NHS Choices website.

As advertising expenditure within the NHS soared, New Labour was increasingly intent to publicly defend the explosion of information detailing NHS service provision. An often stated palliation was that 'the publication of information on the quality of services will increase transparency, and will provide an incentive for service improvement' (DoH 2008:i). It was also emphasized that the infra-structure of choice would motivate healthcare providers to make information about their specific services available directly to patients and referring clinicians. In order to safeguard patients from abuses of advertising the DoH, in November 2006, published a consultation on a *Code of Practice for Promotion of NHS Services* (DoH 2006). In the foreword by the Rt Hon Patricia Hewitt, the then Secretary of State for Health, it was stated that the Code of Practice outlines a 'self-regulatory approach to promotional activity' (ibid:6). Sign-up to the Code was enforced as part of the contacts between PCTs and providers of NHS services and regulated by Strategic Health Authorities (SHAs). The Code of Practice itself was to be self-regulated by the advertising industry and thus would relate to prevailing Advertising Codes administered by the Advertising Standards Authority (ASA). In January 2007, the Promotion Code was criticized by the NHS Association of Healthcare Communicators (AHC) who denounced the regulatory code of practice for promotion as 'too prescriptive and bureaucratic' (quoted in HSJ 2007). The then chair of the AHC is reported to have said 'there are so many mechanisms that hold the NHS to account already. Creating a new one is counter to the current direction of travel of policy' (ibid). Nevertheless, the self-regulatory emphasis of the Code endured.

In 2008 the *Code of Practice for Promotion of NHS Services* completed its period of consultation, culminating in the publication of the *Code of Practice for the Promotion of NHS-Funded Services* on 19 March 2008. This document, refers to the *Code of Practice* as the Promotion Code. This abbreviation is clearly appropriate for the Promotion Code covered a comprehensive range of promotional activity 'including advertising, direct marketing to patients and information directed at referring clinicians' (ibid:5). Thus, NHS providers were granted permission to promote their healthcare services through a wide spectrum of promotional activity, provided they aligned with the ASA's advertising code and operated within the remit of the NHS brand policy. With regards to the latter the Promotion Code states that:

> No promotional activity should be undertaken that undermined the reputation of the NHS, NHS logos or trade marks (or services supplied under those logos or trade marks) or otherwise brings the same into disrepute. Promotional activity should not undermine public confidence in the NHS. The logo is trademarked and may not be used by providers to promote non-NHS services or products. (DoH 2008:32)

Initially intended to self-regulate the promotional activities of 'providers of acute healthcare services' (DoH 2006:7), the Promotion Code was extended to 'apply equally to all providers of NHS-commissioned services, whether they are from the independent sector, NHS providers or charities' (DoH 2008:iv). This significant development follows the prescription of New Labour's choice agenda i.e., 'Choice is fundamental to the delivery of a truly patient-centred NHS' (DoH 2008:i). Choice is constituted in New Labour's rhetoric as facilitated by information processing. In order to facilitate rational decision-making 'high-quality information' needs to be made available and rules need to be put in place 'governing the types of promotional material that providers of NHS services produce' (ibid:ii). New Labour's consultations and publications supporting the introduction of advertising and marketing into the NHS are replete with references to the benefits of informationalism. And these sentiments were echoed by some NHS bodies, for instance the then chief executive of the NHS Confederation (Dr Gill Morgan) is reported to have enthusiastically agreed with the production and publication of Clinical Outcome Indicator Reports (detailing e.g., operation results) as a source of information for the public. When pressed further about consultations concerning the Code of Practice Dr Morgan is reported to have said 'We are trying to change the NHS from being a service where you get what you're given…to a service where patients are much more able to chose what they want… Hospitals needs to understand what patients want, and secondly they need to make GPs – and patients in some cases – aware of what is actually available' (quoted in Berry 2006). Nevertheless even the most cursory perusal of New Labour's documents justifying the Promotion Code provides consistent indication that this venture also marked the further extension of market capitalism into the NHS. For instance, in March 2008, the then Secretary State for Health Alan Johnson, in this forward to the *Code of Practice for the Promotion of NHS-funded Services*, made specific reference to market-based reform and competition. In so doing, provided revealing links between performance evaluation, advertising, NHS reform and market capitalism. As is evident in this extract:

> Choice is only one of the ways in which we are driving quality. The new Care Quality Commission, which is to be established in April 2009, will assess both public and private providers of services to ensure that wherever patients are treated, services meet the high standards that that the NHS expects. Money will follow patients, meaning that providers will compete on the quality of services they offer (rather than on the price of those services) to best meet the needs of patients…For patients to exercise their choice effectively, and to ensure that they receive the treatment that best fits their needs, they need to have accurate information about services available to them…This Code of Practice therefore sets out rules that providers of NHS-funded services must follow when promoting their services…This is an important step towards making choices a reality in the NHS, giving patients the material they need to choose services that suit their needs, and encouraging providers to make their services more responsive to patients. (DoH 2008:i-ii)

In the brave new world of 'payment by results', where money follows patients, healthcare providers are compelled to compete with each other. But this is only part of the story. From 2008, and for the first time in NHS history, service providers have the freedom to advertise direct to patients. The *Code of Practice for the Promotion of NHS Services* (DoH 2006) consultation document included detailed reference to promotional activity directed at the public and referring clinicians. The more advanced, *Code of Practice for the Promotion of NHS-Funded Services* published in 2008, confirmed the DoH's support and acceptance of direct marketing to the public as is evident in the following extract 'Direct marketing to the public, their carers or advocates or to referring clinicians is only permissible where marketers comply with all relevant data protection legislation, the NHS Confidentiality Code of Practice and Mailing Preferences Services requirements' (DoH 2008:36).

Despite consistent reference to 'choice' and patient lead reforms, the Labour government's positioning of advertising as a vehicle for market-based competition received substantial hostile resistance. According to a survey conducted by the market research firm YouGov for the NHS Together alliance of health unions and the TUC, members of the general public sampled were overwhelmingly opposed to the introduction of promotional activity within the NHS (HSJ 2006). Conducted between 25-30 October 2006, the internet survey sample consisted of 2,022 adults and the resulting data was weighted so as to be representative of all GB adults aged over eighteen (TUC 2006:3). Overall the survey findings revealed that the Labour government was significantly failing to gain public support for the NHS reforms introduced since 1997. For example, while 46 per cent of the sample, rated the NHS healthcare they had recently received or indirectly experienced, as 'good', 26 per cent indicated that over the last ten years the NHS has got 'a little worse' and 26 per cent denoted that it was 'much worse' (ibid). When questioned about a central aspect of the Labour government's NHS reforms i.e., the introduction of market based competition, 39 per cent strongly disagreed and 34 per cent disagreed with the statement 'I want to see more competition in the NHS with doctors and hospitals competing for my custom, such as spending money on advertising' (quoted in TUC 2006).

NHS practitioners protested their indignation with similar adamancy. Commenting on the then consultation plan document *The Code of Practice*, Dr Jonathan Fielden, chairman of the British Medical Association (BMA) stated that:

> The Government has created a market-based system to deliver health care which means the NHS is forced to compete against new private providers in delivering NHS services…NHS hospitals will have no option but to invest in marketing tactics, such as advertising, if they are to survive against private firms who will already have large marketing budgets and considerable expertise in selling themselves. This is all the more galling when the independent sector receives advantageous rates for less complex work on guaranteed contracts when compared to the NHS…It is a sad indictment of government policy to

> consider spending public money on advertising NHS services when hospitals are having to make cutbacks in patient care and compulsory redundancies in order to save money. (BMA 2006)

Similar sentiments were expressed by prominent union officials. Of significance were the reservations expressed by the major public service union UNISON. In 2007, this union's healthcare service affiliation represented approximately 450,000 employees. Unsurprisingly UNISON was invited to participate in the Code of Practice's 2007 consultation exercise. In February 2007 Unison published *UNISON Response to DH Consultation Document: 'Code of Practice on Promotion of NHS Services'*. UNISON raised substantial questions concerning what was viewed as a direct threat to the fundamental principles of the NHS as is evident in the following extract:

> The ethos of the NHS is under threat if making money becomes more important than caring for patients. Under the new Code, trusts would be allowed to say that they offer better care than others, which undermines the spirit of collaboration and cooperation that the NHS is built on. (UNISON 2007:2)

Elsewhere in the document there were several clarion calls for interested parties to 'guard against the NHS becoming little more than a brand added to services carried out by a variety of (increasingly private sector) providers' (ibid). UNISON also expressed concerns regarding the tendency for advertising to exacerbate rather than ameliorate competition and this statement of concern is evident in the following extract:

> There are wider concerns to be addressed, given that the need for the Code stems from the ongoing marketisation of the NHS, as represented by the patient choice agenda and driven by the Payment by Results system. UNISON continues to champion reform where this is designed in the best interests of patients and where it allows NHS staff to deliver the highest standards of care. The Code of Practice does, however, provide another telling example of how far down the road towards a fully competitive market the current reform agenda has taken the English NHS. Coming from a leading architect of the health reform programme, a recent article from Professor Chris Ham on the state of the health service was particularly significant as it highlighted the incompatibility between the patient choice agenda and the laudable twin desires of moving care closer to home and ensuring greater integration of care. Essentially this is due to the failure of the market system to encourage collaboration between healthcare organizations, something which the Code sets in stone. (UNISON 2007:4)

Both UNSION and the Trade Union Congress (TUC) challenged the prospect of channeling expenditure on the expansion of marketing and advertising and the self-evident movement towards 'initiatives by hospitals that are now effectively competing for patients under the Government's patient choice agenda' (ibid:2). According to the TUC's then general secretary Brendan Barber 'Voters would rather money was spent on patient care than ads. But advertising is a logical conclusion of the government's mistaken view that the key to NHS reform is to treat hospitals like competing businesses' (quoted in Unison 2006). Elsewhere, the Royal College of Nurses (RCN) expressed grave concern regarding the Promotion Code and the introduction of a celebrity culture of medical advice (HSJ 2007). A reservation also shared by UNISON as they express it:

> There are alternatives to the unseemly prospect of hospitals producing advertising campaigns featuring celebrity endorsements and the denigration of competing providers. The NHS should continue to strive for more effective systems for patients and the public to exercise their voice, rather than treating patients merely as customers or consumers of healthcare. (UNISON 2007:5)

The Promotion Code states that 'Public figures who are likely to be perceived by the general public as medical experts are not permitted to be involved in general promotional campaigns or to provide testimonials' (DoH 2008). Nevertheless, the Promotion Code did state that 'Public figures and medical experts will not be banned from involvement in promotional activity' (ibid:28). It is very difficult to assume this proviso to be anything less than a gateway for the introduction into the NHS of celebrity culture. And if this is to be acceptance, the Promotion Code's reluctance to limit the amounts providers can spend on promotional activity fits efficaciously with the development of an advertising industry within the NHS. Indeed the Promotion Code practically invited this eventuality through the publication of clumsy, non-committal statements such as the following:

> Providers will be expected to recognize the potential effect on the reputation of the NHS of disproportionate expenditure on promotional activity. The cost of TV or cinema promotion is very unlikely to be justifiable. Responsibility for appropriate promotional expenditure lies with provider organization's boards... (DoH 2008:33)

The millions of dollars expended on Direct-to-Consumer Advertising (DTCA), in the US, bears testament to the eventuality of an advertising industry to emerge, once regulatory restrictions are moderated. In 2008, the value of the US market for pharmaceuticals was estimated at $291 billion dollars, with an estimated annual growth rate at 1-to-2 per cent range. It is widely recognized that a substantial part of this colossal revenue is attributable the investment by pharmaceutical manufacturers, in advertising expertise and practice.

In the early 1980s the US's Food and Drug Administration (FDA) became concerned about the appearance of advertisements for prescription drugs aimed direct-to-consumers. Under the exigency of Congress, the pharmaceutical industry and the American Medical Association, in 1983 the FDA initiated a moratorium on DTCA until it considered the regulatory options (Jaramillo 2006:269). Despite concluding that 'direct to the public prescription advertising was not in the public interest' (FDA quoted in Woloshin 2001:1141), the FDA issued in 1985 a briefing notice in the Federation Register stating that acknowledging concerns about freedom of speech and in light of favourable evidence the existing regulations were sufficient to safeguard the consumer from mis-leading advertising material (Wilkes, et al 2000:113). The FDA's 1985, briefing lead to a lifting on the moratorium and sent a clear message to the pharmaceutical industry that they could advertise direct-to-consumers (DTC) provided that they abided by FDA regulations and specified criteria. In 1997, following public hearings and debates around media and DTCA, the FDA revisited its regulation so as to accommodate 'consumer demand for information' (FDA quoted in Jaramillo 2006:270).

The most substantial alterations contained in the FDA's 1997, revision was to relax restrictions on DTC advertising for prescription medicine on broadcast media. In so doing the FDA, opened the floodgates for a meteoric increase in the expenditure on DTCA using commercial communication channels. In 1990, the US pharmaceutical industry spent an estimated $47 million on DTCA (Kaphingst et al 2004:143). While this amount initially appears substantial, it commands less remarkability when one considers that from 1997-2005 the amount pharmaceutical companies spent on DTCA grew on average by approximately 20 per cent annually 'twice as fast as spending on drug promotion to doctors, reaching US$ 4.2 billion in 2005' (*Lancet Editorial* 2007:1). Following regulation revision to broadcast media DTCA, television has galvanized a vase proportion of DTC promotional spending. In 2001 this amounted to an estimated 64 per cent of DTCA was for television commercials a substantial increase from the 13 per cent recorded level of 1994 (Kaphingst et al 2004:143). Justifications for this increasing expenditure on DTCA, parallel the rhetoric extolled in New Labour's *Code of Practice for the Promotion of NHS-Funded Services* published in 2008, consequently developments in the US's maturer DTCA market provides a useful point of comparison.

Proponents of DTC pharmaceutical advertising argue that it serves to educate the public about medical conditions and their treatments. In the UK and more so in the US, the arena of internal markets has effectively transformed patients into consumers empowered with the autonomy bequeathed by a retrenching welfare state. Accordingly, consumers have become more involved and apparently keen to play an informed active role in their healthcare. From the perspective of the government and pharmaceutical industry this translates as a potential beneficial effect of DTCA. For DTCA educates consumers about pharmaceuticals and also raises their awareness about new medicines and treatments. In this sense, DTCA primes the doctor-patient dialogue. Research evidence suggests that exposure to DCTA assists patients in the articulation of their illness. Indeed, studies report that DTCA makes patients more sophisticated and informed in their interaction with physicians (Flynn 1999, Weissman et al 2004). According to Calfee (2002) increased patient knowledge leads to more equitable and informed interactions with healthcare providers. Such conviviality, it is argued, encourages the disclosure of undiagnosed conditions thus enabling physicians to make better informed diagnoses. As patients become partners in their healthcare, their active engagements directly impact on market competition with companies competing to both attract the attention of consumers and secure their product's referral to physicians. Indeed, it has been observed Mintzes et al (2002) that in DTC prescription drug advertising, the patient creates a 'pull' effect dragging the promoted medicines to the attention of physicians. Ultimately the claim that DTCA promotes healthy well-being by educating the public about medical conditions and the availability of therapeutic options hinges on the presumption that advertisers seek to achieve at least one of the following outcomes: (1) encourage the audience member to seek further information; (2) engage in a dialogue with their doctor featuring the promoted medicine/treatment; (3) communicate with a pharmacist about the medication/treatment and (4) speak with members of their immediate and extended network about the promoted medicine/treatment (Huh and Becker 2002:3). Opponents of DTCA criticize the educational role of the pharmaceutical industry. In riposte to the industry's alleged altruism opponents of DTCA pose the insurgent question 'public education or brazen marketeering' (Wilkes et al 2000:116).

DTCA is incredibly cost effective for the US pharmaceutical industry. It is estimated that 'a dollar spent on television adverts returns $1.69 in sales; a dollar on magazine adverts returns $2.51' (quoted in the *Lancet* 2002:1709). It has also been observed that in excess of 50 per cent of DTC advertising is spent on the promotion of just 20 branded medicines (quoted in the *Lancet* 2007:1). Proponents of DTCA argue that it can educate consumers and increase public awareness of healthcare issues. Conversely DTCA's opponents raise questions about this educational function and in so doing interrogate the actual momentum driving the increasing volume of advertising directed at consumers. Critics contend that consumers' actual comprehension of DTCA content falls short of the educational claims made by DTCA's advocates. Based on telephone survey of 329 adults drawn from Sacramento County Bell et al (1999) argue that 'prescription drug advertisement have unquestionably penetrated the consciousness of the American consumer' (ibid:656). But in contradiction with proponents of DTCA, it was found that '…education was not strongly related to awareness' (ibid). Similarly Kimberly et al (2004) identify a tendency for DTC advertising to oversimplify complex medical issues, by decontextualizing information and providing insufficient information about risks.

Rather than educating consumers, oversimplifying complex issues merely compounds the fact that consumers lack specialized medical knowledge. Nevertheless, evidence also suggests that DTCA successfully achieves information transfer and this process of circulation translates into substantial revenues. Some empirical support for this claim is provided by market research analyses. In September 2008 a team of Harvard researchers published an article in the *British Medical Journal* (see Law et al 2008). The article generated controversy because it dare to suggest that 'exposure to US direct to consumer advertising transiently influenced both Canadian and US prescribing rates for Tegaserod, a drug later withdrawn owing to safety concerns' (ibid). The article went on to conclude that 'The impact of direct to consumer advertising on drug use seems to be highly variable and probably depends on the characteristics of the advertised drug, the level of exposure to direct to consumer advertising, and the cultural context' (ibid).

The marketing research and branding consultation company Millward and Brown (2008), amongst other agents with a vested commercial interest in DTCA responded quickly to refute this potentially damming indictment. In their empirical analysis, Millward Brown found that 'DTC campaigns raise awareness for new pharma brands' (ibid). They go on to report that 'In fact, the correlation between advertising and brand awareness is tighter and more direct in pharma than in any other category' (ibid). They substantiate this claim by stating that 'On average, three months after a launch, brands with little or no prior awareness achieve brand awareness levels of almost 50 percent among relevant targets' (ibid). It is not my object here to engage in refutations of DTCA's ability to influence behaviour. Rather, it is my aim to intervene into the consequences of these counter claims. For it is evident that the DTCA in the US sustains a multi-billion dollar industry, that thrives irrespective of its efficacy. Part of this momentum stems from the ability of advertising to generate the needs for advertising. Thus for example, Millward Brown is emblematic of the paradoxical insistence among marketing/advertising/brand consultants that more advertising is the solution to advertising shortcomings:

> An overview of results from sales modeling suggests that only around 10 percent of ads pay back in the short term. Therefore marketers who know that the true value of brand communication is revealed over time must constantly remind and educate those in charge of business of the importance of building brand equity over the long term…The process of brand-building and the role of advertising within that process are the same for prescription drugs as they are for other types of products. The basic requirement is to build awareness. Because pharma marketers don't have access to traditional point-of-purchase tactics such as shelf facing, end caps, price promotion and packaging, they must rely on DTC advertising to reach consumers. (Millward Brown 2008)

The ability of advertising to spawn its propagation provides a novel alternative perspective, to the educational role of DTCA promoted by its advocates. Nevertheless a more substantial criticism of DTCA's educational efficacy is presented by those social scientists that identify DTCA's role in the 'medicalization' of everyday social life.

Advertising Technologies and the Medicalization of Social Life

Medicalization occurs when previously normal vicissitudes become designated and treated as medical problems typically in terms of illnesses or disorders (Conrad and Leiter 2004). It has increasingly been argued that the creation of healthcare markets, in the US and UK, in conjunction with the DTC interventions of pharmaceutical companies, is spectacularly expanding the boundaries of untreatable illness (Conrad 1992, Conrad and Leiter 2004). One of the most straightforward descriptions of this process suggests that, the role of the pharmaceutical industry in relation to new diseases is a commercially driven dialectic. Even the spectacular healthcare reforms introduced to the US electorate by President Obama in 2009 could not avoid the all pervasive stranglehold of pharmaceutical markets. Moynihan et al (2002:324) have previously described the relentless grip of the pharmaceutical industry as follows:

> Within many disease categories informal alliances have emerged, comprising drug company staff, doctors, and consumer groups. Ostensibly engaged in raising public awareness about undiagnosed and undertreated problems, these alliances tend to promote a view of their particular condition as widespread, serious and treatable...A key strategy of the alliances is to target the news media with stories designed to create fears about the condition or disease and draw attention to the latest treatment. Company sponsored advisory boards supply the 'independent experts' for these stories, consumer groups provide the 'victims' and public relations companies provide media outlets with the positive spin about the latest 'breakthrough' medications.

Revelations of these processes have lead to social commentators questioning, disparaging and challenging the advertising motivations of pharmaceutical manufacturers as is evident in the following allegation provided by Wolinsky (2005:612) 'not every new disease for which the pharmaceutical business provides a drug is necessarily a major public health problem, but rather a venue for drug companies to increase revenues'. Pharmaceutical companies are actively involved in both the manufacture and promotion of their products. As part of the creation of markets, pharmaceutical companies are increasingly in league with, medical agencies and practitioners ordinarily dedicated to the identification and treatment of disease. Given the changing medical scene in the US and UK the interventions of pharmaceutical companies here have tended towards 'sponsoring the definition of disease and promoting them to both prescribers and consumers' (Moynihan et al 2002:886). Thus it has been observed that 'the social construction of illness is being replaced by the corporate construction of disease' (ibid).

Studies report adverse correlations between Western capitalist healthcare markets, DTCA and the creation of markets for prescribing prescription medication. Of significance has been research studies focusing on the post 1997 FDA de-regulation of broadcasting media as a channel of DTCA. In an analysis of medicine advertising on television, Jaramillo (2006) draws attention to signifying practices integral to the promotion of the attributes and values of pharmaceuticals products. He argues that 'branding as a subset of marketing' emphasizes the development of symbolic meanings tangential to the actual product, thus 'the actual pill is peripheral to the lifestyle that is being built and promised to consumers, *not* patients' (ibid:271). To this end, the criteria for branding pharmaceutical products positions them in strategically managed cross-platform marketing so as to capitalize on the attributes of other lucrative brands. In recent years the meteoric rise of global pharmaceutical brands evidences the expeditious use of cross-platform marketing. Conrad and Leiter (2004) describes how the pharmaceutical company Pfizer capitalized on the established brand kudos of the US Senator Bob Dole as well as internationally recognized athletes. In March 1998 the FDA advocated Viagra as a medicine for the treatment of erectile dysfunction. Conrad observes that Pfizer tapped into cultural values and social attitudes associated with erectile dysfunction so as to re-configure the market 'by promoting sexual difficulties as a medical problem and Viagra as the solution' (ibid:162).

Pfizer aggressively marketed directly to physicians and consumers. Brand transference formed part of this strategy as the wonders of Viagra sought to convince the public that even high ranking politicians and supreme athletes might require assistance with erectile dysfunction and in so doing 'advertising expended the market to include virtually any man who might consider himself as having some type of erectile or sexual problem' (ibid). Conrad and Leiter (2004) make direct links between the cross-platform spotlighting of global brands in DTCA and increased volumes of prescriptions for Viagra. Apparently, 'physicians wrote 2.9 million prescriptions in the first three months of its availability; in the first year alone, over three million men were treated with Viagra, translating into $1.5 billion in sales' (ibid). Conrad and Leiter (2004) also suggest that 'perhaps 200,000 prescriptions for Viagra are written weekly…with untold more Viagra sold through the Internet…' (ibid). Conrad and Leiter's point about the Internet highlights, the seemingly limitless market-space for global pharmaceutical brands. But, while the meteoric sales of Viagra are a spectacular case-study, what is of significant here is that even the educational propensities of DTCA entails what Foucault observes elsewhere as 'an intensification of the values of private life or the importance accorded to the relations to self is associated with an exaltation of individual singularity' (1990:42). Suffice to say that DTC advertising of pharmaceuticals is dominated by the clarion call that one must 'take care of oneself' and this principle establishes its necessity, presides over its regime of accumulation and codifies its practices.

Timely Reflections

Increasingly, the pharmaceutical industry has found itself under fire, from critics that question the recurrent practice of synchronizing 'public awareness' healthcare initiatives, with advertising campaigns (ibid) It is suggested that the key intention of such alliances is to 'disease monger', i.e., to foster exaggerated anxiety about illness and direct attention to the latest medical intervention (ibid). While these accusations are plausible their underlying theory of social control over simplifies advertising practice and misrecognizes DTCA as a coercive powerful interventionist force. An important framework, frequently overlooked by these studies, is Michel Foucault's (1990) conception of 'the cultivation of the self', for this concept relates directly to political economy, signs and governance.

In *The Care of the Self; History of Sexuality Volume 3*, Foucault (1990) examines texts that inscribe the ethical and moral contemplations of philosophers and physicians throughout the development of the first two centuries. Deliberating only those historical texts that concentrate on, the question of the ethics of 'pleasure', Foucault identifies statements that appear to mark the ascendancy of new interdictions concerning the regulation of the body. In these texts there is an insistence on '...the attention that should be brought to bear on oneself' (ibid:41). But what marks these texts as particularly distinctive is:

> ...the modality, scope, constancy, and exactitude of the required vigilance; it is the anxiety concerning all the disturbances of the body and the mind, which must be prevented by means of an austere regimen; it is the importance attributed to self-respect, not just insofar as one's status is concerned, but as concerns one's rational nature... (ibid)

Among other things, Foucault relates the emergence of these historical pronouncements on the 'cultivation of the self', to the accrescence in the Hellenistic and Roman world 'of an "individualism" that is said to have accorded more and more importance to the "private" aspects of existence...and to the interest that people focused on themselves' (ibid). To this end he argues, that it wasn't an increase in coercive political power that inculcated this form of self cultivation, but rather a moderation of the political and social context governing the everyday lives of subjects. Foucault observes how the weakening of political obligations tying subjects to cities and increased isolation from collective forms of social solidarity lead to an increased reliance, in the first two centuries, upon philosophical rules of conduct. Of particular popularity were those philosophical rules that guided the conduct of the personal patrimonial interests and an excitation into discourse of doctrines focusing on 'the intensity of the relations to self' (ibid:42). The latter refers to a discursive constellation directed at 'the forms in which one is called upon to take oneself as an object of knowledge and a field of action, so as to transform, correct, and purify oneself, and find salvation' (ibid). Suffice to say, the care of the self is in fact an 'art of existence', in which the ever penitent human is dedicated to the cultivation and redemption of the soul.

Prominent to Foucault's analysis of the ethical pronouncements of ancient philosophical texts is an observation of, the way in ancient Greek culture; the cultivation of the self intersects with medical thought and practice. In his analysis of ancient Greek texts Foucault observes notions and schemas intended to encourage subjects to apply clinical practice to the body as a route to correcting the infirmities of the soul. Foucault describes the existence in this era of 'a whole series of medical metaphors…regularly employed to designate the operations necessary for the care of the soul…'(ibid:55). Thus he observes an increased popularization of medical discourse, 'expressed through a particular and intense form of attention to the body' (ibid:56). But this attention is very different from the valorization of the body evident in the stringent fitness regimes of an athlete. For medical involvement in the cultivation of the body is less about treating physical infirmities as true ills. Rather, it is about perceiving the body as the gateway of the soul, and training the body to achieve the deliverance of the soul. As Foucault expresses it:

> …in fact the focus of attention in these practices of the self is the point where the ills of the body and those of the soul can communicate with one another and exchange their distresses: where the bad habits of the soul can entail physical miseries, while the excesses of the body manifest and maintain the failings of the soul. (ibid:56)

The key to the cultivation of the self, in these ancient times, was therefore the intersection points and the cognition that '…one had best correct the soul if one does not want the body to get the better of it, and rectify the body if one wants it to remain completely in control of itself' (ibid). One effect of the apprehension of the body as a vehicle for the cultivation of the soul, '…is the inducement to acknowledge oneself as being ill or threatened by illness' (ibid:57). The implication here being that the soul, in human beings, exists in a state of imperfection and this intersects with the body so that the individual is 'one who suffers from certain ills and who needs to have them treated' (ibid). Part of this therapeutics requires that the individual seek medical correction administered 'by oneself or by someone who has the necessary competence' (ibid). Thus the cultivation of the soul ritualizes the individualized subject into the regime of clinical medical thought and practice. A situation that Foucault describes as one in which 'everyone must discover that he is in a state of need, that he needs to receive medication and assistance' (ibid).

Civic and political activity has obviously profoundly changed its form, in the intervening centuries, but nevertheless significant parallels link these processes of self cultivation with advertising's interventions into the medicalization of everyday social life. Indeed, it is evident that several processes correlate these epochs. Firstly, advertising knowledge is resonant with Foucault's observations of the ancient world, individualism and the medicalization of social life. It is clearly evident that advertising knowledge operates according to a methodological logic, based on the construction of 'need' as a predisposition of the individual consumer.

In recent decades, this reductionism has been accentuated by the 'consumer choice' manifesto of successive healthcare market reforms. As we have seen, the rhetoric that has accompanied NHS market reform has been consistently based on the existence of a free enterprising consumer, exercising agency in the medical marketplace. DTC pharmaceutical advertising trades upon these liberal vistas and in so doing perpetuate a process described by Foucault as 'an exaltation of individual singularity' (ibid:42). This is to argue that the reduction of 'need' as an attribute of the consumer, in DTCA campaigns, ascribes 'absolute value…to the individual in his singularity' (ibid). It is important to understand that this singularity of the self in DTCA also has the effect of surrendering the body to clinical practice. For DTCA offers the individualized subject advice on the medical interventions needed to remedy the body. But this ailing body is partly constituted through the visual cultures, allegory and discursive metaphors of DTCA and thus dominated by the principle that insists one must 'take care of oneself'. As Fuqua (2002:664) also observes:

> …prescription drug advertising reinforces the already existing idea that the patient/consumer is in a state of need and that this need can be met through medical advice and, most importantly, consumption of a particular prescription drug.

One of the most pernicious dimensions of this cultivation of the body is the inculcation of the subject into daily routines devoted to the care of the self. For 'contemplating a life reduced to its essentials' takes time (Foucault 1990:51). And 'this time is not empty; it is filled with exercises, practical tasks, various activities. Taking care of oneself is not a rest cure. There is the care of the body to consider, health regimens, physical exercises without overexertion, the carefully measured satisfaction of needs' (ibid). Thus the cultivation of the self assumes the form of a daily routine, a project that intensifies the relation to the self and transforms this phenomenon into 'an object of knowledge and a field of action' (ibid:42). And this affect is amplified by DTCA's acclaimed educational role in the US and UK's medical marketplace. This is because DTCA's role in the promotion of healthcare and the inculcation of healthcare into the cultivation of the self are interconnected activities. DTCA exists within a socio-economic context in which healthcare has become an explosive political battlefield. In advanced Western societies life expectancy has substantially increased and this coupled with a declining birthrate means that tax receipts necessary to support state healthcare programmes are in freefall. Invariably this adds up to an acute revenue crisis in health service. It is necessary to recognize these factors as primary to a cultural, economic and political context '…in which patients/consumers are being asked to increase the surveillance of themselves and each other, are being encouraged to look at their bodies and the bodies of others from a kind of clinical perspective' (Fuqua 2002:664). And these processes are linked with the regulation of individual conduct in accordance with the programme and broad economic vision axiomatic with modern forms of governmentality.

PART II
Postmodern-Political Caesura

Che Guevara as postmodern cultural politics

Source: AIZAR RALDES/AFP/Getty Images. Image created 01/05/2004. Reproduced by permission of Getty Images.

Chapter 3
Inversions in the Political Economy of Global Signs

Advertising is indexed to the political economy of globalized capitalist accumulation. First and foremost, advertising operates to aestheticize the objects and subjects of political economy. For instance, in Figure 3.1., the iconic image of Che Guevara has been transferred to another object (i.e., the product Mon Bijou), in order to give this commodity a symbolic value resonant with Che Guevara's image. In conjunction with the advertisement's overt appearance, exists a 'latent' meaning, which operates to complete the overt aesthetics. This is because the transference of symbolic value can only be achieved through the identification of the advertisement's audience members. Consequently 'latent' meaning operates to make desirable the aesthetics of the commodity such that its appeal appears accessible through the act of consumption.

In this sense, the signifying systems of modern advertising translate into a form of currency. This economy of signs trades upon established 'referent systems' in society and culture, and expropriates their meaning as part of the transformation of objects from useful things to 'exchange values' (Williamson 2000). And the circuits of symbolic production are mediated by the logic of exchange-value (ibid). It is in this sense that the signifying systems of advertising have an insidious ideological effect. For the process of meaning transfer in advertising denotes a 'labour in which man alienates himself' (Cohen 1978:120). Individuals partake in paid work because they assume that the products of their labour have value, to which they relate, and which regulates their lives as producers. Through advertising, the social reality of oppression becomes invisible as workers, in quite a specific sense, become alienated from their own power, which has passed into things (ibid:120).

This chapter begins by detailing Karl Marx's analysis of 'commodity fetishism'. Writing in the nineteenth century, Marx observed how advances in industrial capitalism had precipitated a transition in the mode of production away from an emphasis on surplus-value 'arising from a simple prolongation of the working-day' (Marx *Capital Vol. 1* 2003:298). Marx defined this mode of surplus-value expropriation as 'absolute surplus-value'. Developments in the technical conditions of late nineteenth century industrialism had revolutionized the productiveness of labour, enabling a reduction in the proportion of the working day during which the labourer must work for his own subsistence 'and by that very shortening, to lengthen the other part of the day, during which he is at liberty to work gratis for the capitalist' (ibid:304). Marx defined the expropriation of value arising 'from the curtailment of the necessary labour-time' as relative surplus-value (ibid:299). It is significant to recognize, that Marx anticipated the extension of relative surplus-value to be dependent on the extension of consumer markets. For instance, Marx states that 'the increase in the productiveness of labour must seize upon those branches of industry, whose products determine the value of labour-power' (ibid). Such processes were evident in the context of accelerated levels of capitalist production in the nineteenth century and continue to have relevance to contemporary regimes of capitalist accumulation. Thus to fully appreciate how contemporary economic relations are expressed and realized it is crucial that one first analyses the social basis of capitalism. Indeed, what particularly interested Marx was that in Capitalist modes of production, social relations between people become transformed into a relation between the fetishistic properties of objects. Part of this process involves the ascription, to objects, of anthropomorphic qualities which obfuscate the inequalities inherent in their production. This Marx refers to as 'commodity fetishism'.

Commodities are the outcome of labour power, but this disappears into them as they transform into an alien force, which rules our lives. Marx saw the reality of Capitalist society as one dominated by commodities, which take the place of the free flow of relations between people. This observation has informed a vibrant tradition of Marxist analysis into advertising and the making of political subjectivity in modern times. Thus the first part of this chapter, introduces Marxist

Figure 3.1 Mon Bijou as Che Guevara

Source: Reproduced with kind permission of Duailibi Petit Zaragoza Propaganda, São Paulo, Brazil.

theories that detail advertising's part in the obfuscation of labour-time's role in the production of value. Judith Williamson's book *Decoding Advertisements*, is extensively reviewed as it remains a foremost Marxian critique. Writing during the 1970s Judith Williamson anticipated a theoretical renaissance in cultural studies' analysis of commodity culture and self-identity. Few writers had observed that 'an attempt to differentiate amongst both people and products is part of the desire to classify order and understand the world, including one's own identity' (2000:13). As a material artefact of modern commodity culture, advertising imagery is resourceful in defining the 'equation of people with things' (ibid). This is because advertisements have to translate 'the inherent qualities and attributes of the products they are trying to sell', into statements that reflect human values and echo human relationships (2003:12). Williamson interiorizes the permeation of exchange-values throughout our cultural life. Figure 3.1., is particularly effective as an illustration of Williamson's argument that advertising signification is homologous with the system of exchange-values; signs have no autonomy outside of the logic of equivalence. Conversely, use-value is grounded in an unsurpassable integrity; for it elides human beings with the harmonious satisfaction of 'real needs'. And the theology of use-value features in 'the ideal relation of equivalence' uniting human beings with nature, labour and its objects, human beings and the visceral body, self and its relation with others (Baudrillard 1981:139). Ideologically this 'true' state of human being is hermeneutically sealed off from the veracious deployment of the commodity-sign. By formulating a metaphysics of utility, Williamson opens up a space in which to embed an idealized vision of the potential of humanity removed from the tenacity and manipulation of symbolic exchange-value. Such impassioned sentimentality is evident in her emphatic concern 'that the need for relationship and human meaning appropriated by advertising…[if] not diverted, could radically change the society we live in' (2000:14).

Certainly advertising is a highly powerful cultural form, and this chapter provides a detailed illustration of Judith Williamson's ingenuity in decoding the ideological meaning of advertisements. But what this exercise reveals is that Williamson's text is inconclusive with respect to its primary objective i.e., to combine Marx's analysis of political economy with a critique of symbolic exchange-value. Of particular concern, is Williamson's narrow interpretation of Marx's (2003:76) observation that 'the mystical character of commodities does not originate, therefore, in their use-value'. To this end, this chapter interrogates Williamson's *Decoding Advertisements* as illustrative of a particular misconception of Marxism, advertising and the constitution of the very subject of cultural politics.

Dialectics of Time and Political Subjectivity

> Economy of time, to this all economy ultimately reduces itself. Society likewise has to distribute its time in a purposeful way, in order to achieve a production adequate to its overall needs; just as the individual has to distribute his time

> correctly in order to achieve knowledge in proper proportions or in order to satisfy the various demands on his activity. Thus, economy of time, along with the planned distribution of labour time among the various branches of production, remains the first economic law on the basis of communal production. (Marx *Grundrisse* 1844/1973:173)

Marxist analysis of capitalist accumulation and commodity culture reveals time as directly implicated in the formation of political subjectivity. Karl Marx (1818-1883) chronicled historical transformations in the tempo of economic life. In *Capital Vol. 1*, Marx identifies how in capitalist regimes of accumulation the labour-process operates as a generalized system of commodity production, based on wage-labour and the conversion of surplus-value into profit. As he expresses it 'The rate of surplus-value is…an exact expression for the degree of exploitation of labour-power by capital, or of the labourer by the capitalist' (*Capital Vol. 1* 2003:209). According to Marx the consciousness of human being achieves fulfilment through labour. This is to recognize that human beings are, first and foremost, material beings existing in relation to the natural world. Our consanguinity with nature is active as opposed to passive, for it is based on production. And this productive activity guides human beings into relations with each other. Consequently, human beings in association with each other actively produce 'the means of the reproduction of their material life' (Harris 1983:180).

Marx elaborates upon this materialist conception of humanity to include an account of self and subjectivity. For, it is through labour that human beings control the 're-actions' between the self and nature (*Capital Vol. 1* 2003:173). By applying labour to the external world, and transforming it, human beings at the same time change their own nature (2003:173). To this end Marx contends that 'At the end of every labour-process [the labourer] not only effects a change of form in the material on which he works, but he also realizes a purpose of his own that gives the law to his modus operandi, and to which he must subordinate his will' (2003:174). Such dedication is 'no mere momentary act' (2003:174). For, it demands 'that during the whole operation the workman will be steadily in consonance with his purpose' (2003:174). In these circumstances 'labour has incorporated itself with its subject: the former is materialised, the latter transformed' (2003:176). Whenever labour is engaged in the whole process of production this has the effect of creating an embodied, meaningful relation to the labour process. However, the propensity of human beings to achieve the fullness of their humanity, in work, is contingent on the conditions under which labour is performed. Throughout history human action has constantly advanced its capacities in the 'appropriation of natural substances to human requirements' (2003:179). Hence the relation of humankind to production is a dynamic process of historical materialism.

Following Hegel, Marx asserts the existence of an inherent dialectic in the development and displacement of modes of production. This dialectic produces contradictions and incongruences between structural elements of the labour-process (i.e., between owners and non-owners of the means of production). According to

Marx, the labour-process in Capitalist production is distinct in its capacities to imbue both economic production and human reproduction with the logic of commodity production. That is to say, the *differentia specifica* of Capitalist production is the procurement and vendition of labour power. In the capitalist system producers are not solely engaged in the selling of goods on the market, but the labour-power itself becomes a commodity. Thus in capitalist regimes of production, the labour-process is transformed 'into the process by which the capitalist consumes labour-power' (2003:180). Labour-power becomes a commodity and 'the labour-process is a process between things that the capitalist has purchased' (2003:180). Marx contends that it is labour which produces value, and surplus labour is converted into monetary profit by the capitalist during the circulation of products on the market. Pivotal to Marx's concept of value is an important distinction between 'useful' and 'abstract' labour (Meek 1979). Use-value can be defined objectively as the utility of the product or subjectively as the usefulness of the labour required to produce it. When use-value is considered subjectively the concept of 'useful' labour emerges (1979:165). Marx defined 'useful' labour as 'productive activity of a definite kind and exercised with a definite aim' (*Capital Vol. 1* 2003:49). Labour in this form creates use-value, but the labour which finds expression in profit according to Marx 'does not possess the same characteristics that belong to it as a creator of use-values' (2003:49). Commodity production's primary aim is not the creation of use-value as such, but the manufacture of goods for sale. In this sense, use-values are of relevance to the commodity producer in so far as consumer expectations need to be taken into account. This is because objects that circulate in a capitalist market system must not only have use-value; they are also required to be attractively useful to others and so have an 'exchange-value'.

As Gamble observes 'production occurs not directly for use but for the exchange of commodities' (1976:115). Thus, of primary significance to commodity production is the 'exchange-value' of objects and this refers to the value attributed to a product when proffered in exchange for other products. Exchange-value exists in reciprocal relation to economic transactions and is indissoluble from commodity markets. One might assume that Marx defines the *moment of exchange* to be therefore, the market place. Indeed, Marx observes that all new capital appears on the market with a monetary value 'that by a definite process has to be transformed into capital' (*Capital Vol. 1* 2003:145). In its simplest form of circulation, new capital is commodities (C) and these are transformed into money (M) as part of the attribution of a definite exchange value. In due course money is exchanged for commodities thus instigating an incessant process of C-M-C. Marx was particularly intrigued by an advanced form of capital circulation; more typical of industrial capitalism, in which money (M) is transformed into commodities (C), which are exchanged for money (M). Marx observed that money which circulates according to the system M-C-M 'is thereby transformed into, becomes capital, and is already potentially capital' (ibid:146). In the simple circulation process involving C-M-C the *moment of exchange* is quite evidently the market place, for it is here that the commodity is detached from its use-value and exchanged for money. Conversely in the more complex system of circulation defined as M-C-M, money is used in order to sell at a profit. And thus money (M) 'multiplies itself within its circuits' (ibid:153). From this analysis it is apparent that what actually ascribes the commodity with value is not a *moment of exchange* in the market place, but rather the existence of an exploitable resource embedded within the commodity itself.

Marx contends that any object, irrespective of whether it is a commodity or not, can only embody value as an outcome of the expenditure of human labour in its production. Consequently 'both exchange-value and use-value must be directly related to the amount of labour embodied in the production of a commodity' (Giddens 1988:46). Nevertheless, Marx also contends that 'exchange-value cannot be derived from use-value' (ibid). Although exchange value necessarily manifest in a purely relative form (i.e., subject to market forces) the value-relationship which commodities bear to one another has expression in an absolute form. This requires that some common quality either inherent in or attached to commodities must be identified as constituting the substance of value. This common quality must also take upon the 'substance that manifests itself in the exchange-value of commodities' (*Capital Vol. 1* 2003:46). These forms, Marx argues are 'abstracted from' in the exchange. In effect commodities regardless of their specific use-values have the capacity to pass as equivalents in market based relations (Meek 1979). We need only consider the popular two-for-one offers at supermarkets to gain a sense of products passing as equivalents. Marx argued that the substance which constitutes a common element across commodities was quite apart from a natural property such as weight, volume etc., 'such properties claim our attention only in so far as they affect the utility of these commodities' (Sayer 1989:51). Once the option of constituting 'that common something' as a natural property is excluded, commodities have only one quantifiable common property left that fulfils the requirements that Marx identifies with value. That inherent quality is based upon 'some quantifiable characteristic of labour' (Giddens 1988:47). To the extent that exchange-value abstracts from the specific characteristics of social relations, so it is that the 'common something' which enables products to pass as equivalents is 'abstract general labour, which can be measured in terms of the amount of time expended by the worker in the production of a commodity' (ibid).

Marx distinguishes 'abstract' labour from 'useful' labour. The former's distinguishing characteristics are axiomatic to production within modern capitalist societies. As Marx expresses it the concept of 'abstract labour' is 'truly realised only as a category of the modern society' where 'individuals pass with ease from one kind of work to another, which makes it immaterial to them what particular kind of work may fall to their share' (quoted in Meek 1979:165). The distinction between useful and abstract labour is axiomatic to Marx's account of the expropriation of profit through surplus value. If a use-value derives value 'only because human labour in the abstract has been embodied or materialised in it' the magnitude of this value is therefore measured by 'the quantity of the value-creating substance, the labour, contained in the article' (Sayer 1989:52). The quantitative measure of labour is derived by the expenditure of time and 'labour-time in its turn finds its standard in weeks, days and hours' (1989:52). Thus:

> Labour has been equalized by the subordination of man to the machine or by the extreme division of labour...the pendulum of the clock has become as accurate a measure of the relative activity of two workers as it is of the speed of two locomotives...Time is everything, man is nothing; he is at most, time's carcass. Quantity alone decides everything; hour for hour, day for day. (Marx 1967:151)

If human labour creates value, the clock is its measurement. The mechanistic metaphors of time used by Marx are commensurate with the objectification of labour in capitalist production. For, the logic of the capitalist mode of production 'is and remains the mass of direct labour time, the quality of labour employed, as the determinant factor in the production of wealth' (Marx 1973:704). Labour power is defined by Marx as 'the aggregate of those mental and physical capabilities existing in a human being, which he [sic] exercises whenever he produces a use-value of any description' (*Capital Vol. 1* 2003:164). In capitalist production, what Marx calls 'the dull compulsion of economics', coerces individuals to sell their labour power as there is little other means of survival other than to enter into a subordinate relationship with capital. Conversely the owners of the means of production retain control over capital and in so doing possess – for the working day – the bodies tied to labour power. The worker for a proportion of the working day is paid back, in the form of wages, the value which is generated from their labour. The capitalist, however, only pays the worker the value of the reproduction of labour power (the sum cost of maintaining the worker at a socially determined level of subsistence). But labour has the curious ability to generate more value than it needs to survive and reproduce itself. The difference between the value of the commodity, created by labour power and the salary supplied to the labourer is surplus value. Thus in capitalist production the exchange of equivalences has been turned around to produce a generalized system of commodity production, based on wage-labour and the conversion of surplus value into profit.

Marx's analysis of capitalist production equates capitalist accumulation with the expropriation of surplus labour time. Marx argued that the value of a commodity is determined by 'the quantity of the value-creating substance, the labour, contained in the article' (*Capital Vol. 1* 2003:46). Marx further argued that 'the quantity of labour...is measured by its duration and labour-time in its turn finds its standard in weeks, days and hours' (2003:46). Thus the primary determinant of a commodity's value is the magnitude of labour time invested in its production, as Marx expresses it 'Every commodity (product or instrument of production) is = the objectification of a given amount of labour time' (*Grundrisse* 1973:140).

Commodity Fetishism and the Dialectics of Political Subjectivity

> The process, then, is simply this: The product becomes a commodity, *i.e., a mere moment of exchange*. The commodity is transformed into exchange value. In order to equate it with itself as an exchange value, it is exchanged for a symbol which represents it as exchange value as such. As such a symbolized exchange value, it can then in turn be exchanged in definite relations for every other commodity. Because the product becomes a commodity, and the commodity becomes an exchange value, it obtains, at first only in the head, a double existence. This doubling in the idea proceeds (and must proceed) to the point where the commodity appears double in real exchange: as a natural product on one side, as exchange value on the other. I.e. the commodity's exchange value obtains a material existence separate from the commodity. (*Grundrisse* 1973:145)

The fundamental insight of Marx's labour theory is that throughout history it is labour and its expropriation that actively creates wealth. Comprehending any actual economy requires an appreciation of labour-time, because it is how labour-time is structured and exchanged that 'provides the material basis of its life' (Gamble 1976:114). Thus to fully appreciate how contemporary economic relations are expressed and realized it is crucial that one first analyses the social basis of capitalism. Indeed, what particularly interested Marx was that in Capitalist modes of production, social relations between people become transformed into a relation between things. This Marx refers to as 'commodity fetishism'. Commodities are the outcome of labour power, but this disappears into them as they transform into an alien force, which rules our lives. Marx saw the reality of Capitalist society as one dominated by commodities, which take the place of the free flow of relations between people. As Marx expresses it:

> The mystical character of commodities does not originate, therefore, in their use-value. Just as little does it proceed from the nature of the determining factors of value. For, in the first place, however varied the useful kinds of labour, or productive activities, may be, it is a physiological fact, that they are functions of the human organism...Secondly, with regard to that which forms the ground-work for the quantitative determination of value, namely, the duration of that expenditure, or the quantity of labour, it is quite clear that there is a palpable difference between its quantity and quality. In all states of society, the labour-time that it costs to produce the means of subsistence, must necessarily be an object of interest to mankind...And lastly, from the moment that men in any way work for one another, their labour assumes a social form. (*Capital Vol. 1* 2003:76)

It is clear from this quotation that the fetishism of commodities refers precisely to the relations between labour-time, use-value and exchange-value. In *Capital*

Marx is conclusive about the materiality of use-value as he expresses it 'so far as it (the commodity) is a value in use, there is nothing mysterious about it' (2003:76). Orthodox readings of *Capital* often assume that Marx, in this quotation and elsewhere, is attributing the production of use-value, with an inherent materiality noticeably separate from the 'mystical character of commodities' (ibid). To this end, labour-time is conceived as producing use-values which have a clearly discernable materiality. In so far as meaning is inherent in their physical constitution, there is little evidence that the production of use-values involves the transformation of objects into 'something transcendent' (ibid). Marx appears explicit in this contention; he writes that 'The mystical character of commodities does not originate, therefore in their use-value' (ibid). According to this reading of Marx, commodities become mysterious purely as a consequence of their entering into a system of exchange-value. At which point a perversion of the article of utility occurs; the object's properties are no longer purely defined as 'capable of satisfying human wants, or from the point that those properties are the product of human labour' (ibid). As soon as the object assumes the form of a commodity it is endowed with an enigmatic character whereby:

> The social character of men's labour appears to them as an objective character stamped upon the product of that labour: because the relation of the producers to the sum total of their own labour is presented to them as a social relation, existing not between themselves, but between the products of their labour. (*Capital Vol. 1* 2003:77)

To make a fetish involves investing something with properties it does not have in itself. In this sense fetishism does not equate with illusion, but rather the misrecognition of properties as belonging to a commodity directly. For example, if we think that the value of a house is an inherent quality, we misrecognize that its value is only a result of a market system created by humans. In essence fetishism involves failing to recognize that the properties of things are not an inherent part of their physical existence, but in fact 'created by their integration into a system of meaning' (Jhally 1987:29). The mystery arises because the social character of production is manifested only in exchange. For example, the many individual labour hours invested in the building of a house are carried out by individuals or groups of individuals labouring independently of each other. Fetishism thus operates to erase 'the mutual relations of the producers, within which the social character of their labour affirms itself' (*Capital Vol. 1* 2003:77). The social character of production is revealed in the process of sale, within which the individual labour hours are aggregated and appropriated as profit. In this sense the market operates as a distributing force transforming the total labour invested, into a socially unifying element, which can be expropriated as profit. Commodity fetishism consists in disguising the fact that in essence humans produce value. In so far as labour produces capital, the sale of a commodity in a market place is just the fetishized offspring of 'congealed labour-time' (ibid:47). The fetishism of commodities performs an erasure of this historical genesis every time social relations between workers 'assumes in their eyes the fantastic form of a relation between things' (ibid:77).

Commodity Fetishism and Visual Culture

It would seem then that commodity fetishism is as much a product of market relations as it is a product of labour producing itself as object and subject of capital (Wayne 2003:191). It also appears that Marx believed, that the mysterious subtleties of the object had little connection to its physical properties and was merely a function of exchange-value (Jhally 1990:28). Indeed, the most typical rendition of commodity fetishism proclaims that Marx assumed that use-values where inherently intelligible and independent of the fantastic forms of exchange value. It is evident that this reading of Marx forms the centrepiece of orthodox Marxian advertising theory. For example, Judith Williamson in her seminal text *Decoding Advertisements* states that:

> Advertisements must take into account not only the inherent qualities and attributes of the products they are trying to sell, but also the way in which they can make those properties *mean something to us*. (2000:12)

It is discernable here and elsewhere, that Williamson takes as given the existence of use-values. Inherent in the product is a 'use' that resides outside of the dynamics of sign-systems and has an unambiguous materiality. The tenacity of advertising resides in its capacity to endow objects with a false materiality that 'violates natural human needs' (ibid:110). Williamson's conception of 'violation' is not grandiose or portentous. At the centre of her approach is the belief that advertisements create systems of meaning, which not only function economically to sell products, but also operate to provide human beings with a sense of ontological security. In order to clarify this assertion it is necessary to situate advertising within the material and historical context of Williamson's text. Writing during the 1970s Judith Williamson anticipated a theoretical renaissance in cultural studies' analysis of commodity culture and self-identity. Few writers had observed that 'an attempt to differentiate amongst both people and products is part of the desire to classify, order and understand the world, including one's own identity' (ibid:13). As a material artefact of modern commodity culture advertising imagery is resourceful in defining the 'equation of people with things' (ibid). This is because advertisements have to translate 'the inherent qualities and attributes of the products they are trying to sell', into statements that reflect human values and echo human relationships (ibid:12).

Williamson's premise is that advertising involves the creation of exchange-values that communicate a concrete use-value embedded within the product. Exchange-value is the mystery that Williamson's deconstruction is directed at decoding. For it is at the level of exchange-value that advertising reproduces a capitalist system in, which production is preoccupied with the exchange of commodities and the expropriation of labour-time is the basis of wealth creation. Williamson is unambiguous about labour-time. Embedded, in the commodity is a use-value created through the expenditure of abstract labour-time which is in turn expropriated as part of capital accumulation. Labour-time is an objective standard and basis of the capitalist market system. What preoccupies Williamson is the complicity of advertising signifying practices in the creation of a world in, which sovereign producers freely sell their labour in exchange for other commodities. It is only in capitalist systems of production that exchange relationships mediate social relations, as part their establishment as the universal form of economic relation. Williamson positions advertising signification as a primary vehicle through which social relations between producers take the fantastic form of value relations between commodities. In capitalist commodity culture much of this activity resides with the 'structures of meaning' created by advertising (ibid:12). Williamson's reference to 'structures' is an intriguing conceptual device intended to re-define mainstream analyses of advertising communication. In contrast with dominant orthodoxy, Williamson rejects a conception of advertising as a singular signifying practice. Rather 'the components of advertisements are variable' and irreducible to a simple semiological model (ibid). This is because advertising signs operate as signifying structures, which decontextualize meaning systems and transform them into symbolic exchange-values.

Integral to the process of meaning transfer is the subjectivity of the audience member. This is partly because 'the advertisement seems to have a life of its own: it exists in and out of other media, and speaks to us in a language we can never identify' (ibid:14). Disembodied and omnipresent, the narrational properties of the advertisement assume metaphysical properties that call the audience member to embody the space 'left where the speaker should be...so that we become both listener and speaker, subject and object' (ibid). While the poetic metaphor of metaphysical spaces is inspiring, Williamson's account of active reception is more convincingly developed in Chapter 2 of her book entitled 'Signs address somebody', as is evident in the following quotation:

> What the advertisement clearly does is thus signify, to represent to us, the *object* of desire. Since that object is the self, this means that, while ensnaring/creating the subject through his or her exchange of signs, the advertisement is actually feeding off that subject's own desire for coherence and meaning in him or her self. (ibid:60)

What is clearly evident here is that the, signifying practices of advertisements operate at two interrelated levels. The outward manifestation of the advertisement is the immediate denotative dimension of the advertisement. In dynamic interplay with this level of signifying practice are the codes and conventions, which orchestrate and instantiate the meanings of imagery, in the process of deciphering the advertisement (Dyer 1993:116). Consequently, the symbolic meaning of the advertisement is partly the outcome of the dynamic interplay of semiotic and aesthetic processes. As Dyer expresses it 'the meaning of one thing is transferred to or made interchangeable with another quality, whose value attaches itself to the product' (1993:117). Advertisements are incessantly engaged in the process of transferring meanings between objects, places, peoples and events.

Certainly advertising is a highly powerful cultural form, and this chapter provides a detailed illustration of Judith Williamson's ingenuity in decoding the ideological meaning of advertisements. But what this exercise reveals is that Williamson's text is inconclusive with respect to its primary objective i.e., to combine Marx's analysis of political economy with a critique of symbolic exchange-value. Of particular concern, is Williamson's narrow interpretation of Marx's (2003:76) observation that 'the mystical character of commodities does not originate, therefore, in their use-value'. In Williamson's interpretation of this conceptual statement, advertising itself is a negation of freedom because it corrodes our natural being and delays the eventual dissipation of the commodity-based world of capitalism. Advertising is an object of critique because it manipulates our genuine 'needs' and creates artificial desires. The concept of 'needs' is at once symbolically effective (because it rediscovers a teleology that captures the essence of the subject), and at the same time fundamental reductionism (because it presupposes a private and autonomous dimension of the self). As Baudrillard observes, 'it establishes the object in its truth, as an essence called use value, transparent to itself and to the subject' (1981:133).

Baudrillard demonstrates that use-value is an effect of exchange-value. Although his early work was not entirely dismissive of Marx's analysis of use-value, all ambivalence is dissipated when Baudrillard later examines the metaphysics of 'needs'. Baudrillard illustrates how over time the category of 'needs' has become erected 'more and more into an abstract system, regulated by a principal of equivalence and general combinative' (1981:135). At this anterior stage of political economy it can clearly be seen that fetishism is at play in the system of needs. For use value and needs are not merely homologous to the system of exchange-value 'it expresses the later in all its depth and perfection' (ibid). The immediate implications of Baudrillard's argument directly foreclose Williamson's naïve assumption that advertising mitigates the expression of a mode of being outside of economic relations. It seems that Williamson's steadfast commitment to the existence of 'genuine use-value' forces her analysis of advertising and the political subject into a limited model of economic determinism, that is unable to comprehend the extent to which the political economy of the sign extends into everyday life; 'down to the very act in which man believes he has rediscovered himself' (Baudrillard 1981:139).

Chapter 4 provides a case study of the spectacular commodification, of the revolutionary Cuban photographer Alberto Díaz Gutiérrez's, 5 March 1960 portrait of Che Guevara. The purpose of the case study is to follow through Baudrillard's critique so as to situate advertising, commodity fetishism and the labour theory of value within the context of global capitalist accumulation. More specifically, the case study examines advertising visual cultures and illustrates their role in spectacularly obfuscating the exploitative relations of power evident in global capitalist accumulation. Axiomatic to this phenomenon, is the propensity for global advertising to transmogrify both the politics of representation and the representation of cultural political resistance to global capitalist accumulation.

Chapter 4
Aesthetic Disruptions in the Cultural Politics of Representation

Alberto Díaz Gutiérrez's (self-renamed Alberto Korda) was the photographer responsible for taking the legendary picture of the Cuban revolutionary Che Guevara. The photograph captures an instant, on 5 March 1960, in which Che Guevara appears at the front of an improvised platform established as part of a memorial service, in Havana, for the victims of the *La Coubre* explosion. In later years Alberto Korda recalls that, it was initially an unremarkable damp cold day, and for the most part his 90mm Leica camera lens apathetically surveyed the figures on the dais. Yet by virtue of an instant, Alberto Korda, suddenly lurched backwards and captured the revolutionary sentimentality that inspired a generation to fight against overwhelming odds. Che Guevara had been standing behind Fidel Castro on a platform and suddenly he stepped forward into the camera's viewfinder, his brown eyes ablaze with remonstration, his single-star emblazoned beret drawn over an unruly mane of flowing locks, as he stared beyond the lens with resolute intensity and steely defiance. As Alberto Díaz Gutiérrez poetically describes it:

> At the foot of the podium draped in black crepe, my eye pressed to my old Leica, I was focusing on Fidel and the people around him. Suddenly, through the 90mm lens, Che loomed above me, I was surprised by his look...By reflex, I snapped twice – one horizontal shot and one vertical. I didn't have enough time to take a third photo, as he stepped back discreetly into the second row. (Alberto Díaz Gutiérrez, quoted in Loviny, C. 2006:78)

Like so many epic portraits, idolatry of the image pursues the instant proclaiming the birth of the icon. Alberto Korda's classic portrait is widely proclaimed to have captured the moment when Che Guevara became a symbol for revolutionaries everywhere. But, the mistake of many commentators is to presume that Che Guevara's political ideals are immediately invoked by this mesmerising portrait (see Figure 4.1).

Born in Rosario, Argentina in 1928, Che Guevara had initially dedicated his life to medicine and dreamed of being an esteemed medical researcher and 'achieving something which might ultimately be of use to humanity' (Guevara quoted in Sinclair 2006:9). Such idealism bore little correspondence with the harsh realities of poverty hunger and disease, Che Guevara witnessed during his motorcycle odyssey across Latin America. He had voraciously digested the complete works of Marx and an entire pantheon of Marxist literatures. But it was

Che Guevara's first hand experience (as recounted in his *Motorcycle Diaries*), of the intolerable degree of exploitation and enslavement licensed by Western imperialism that allied him with Fidel Castro's crusade to emancipate Cuba from the military dictatorship of Fulgencio Batista. The Cuban Revolution was an extremely hazardous military undertaking; its victory in January 1959 is widely attributed to the strategically ingenious guerrilla warfare of Che Guevara. With Fidel Castro at the helm and Che Guevara steering the progressivist fervour the Cuban revolutionary process enthralled the whole world. It was on 5 March 1960 that the now legendry portrait of Che Guevara was captured by Alberto Korda. Che Guevara was attending a funeral service for the victims of a munition cargo ship called *La Coubre*, that had exploded while unloading its cargo in Havana harbour, killing 81 port workers and wounding hundreds more. Alberto Korda was commissioned by the newspaper *Revolución*, to take photographs of Fidel Castro and others attending the funeral. It is a curious fact, that Alberto Korda's famous photograph of Che Guevara, taken during this memorial event, initially had an inauspicious rise to fame. It was originally, merely, relegated to the inside pages of the Cuban newspaper *Revolución*. Indeed, for a significant period of time, the portrait garnered little occasion and remained on the wall of Alberto

Figure 4.1 Che Guevara as philosophy football

Source: Image taken from the Che Cuba flag t-shirt available from www.philosophyfootball.com. Reproduced with kind permission of Philosophyfootball.com.

Korda's studio, until in the early autumn of 1967, when he gifted (without securing copyright) two 10" x 8" prints to the supposedly anti-capitalist Italian publisher Giangiacomo Feltrinelli (Chanan 2001:2).

In October 1967 Che Guevara was captured and killed by the Bolivian army, while trying to instigate a new guerrilla front in Bolivia. His dedication to resisting imperialism had inspired him to 'develop a true proletarian internationalism; with international proletarian armies' (Guevara quoted in Sinclair 2006:45). The appetence for revolution had achieved sparse satiation even with the victorious socialist revolution in Cuba. Guevara's revolutionary imagination idolized the 'daily heroism' of freedom fighters in 'Guatemala, Columbia, Venezuela and Bolivia' (ibid). He envisaged a Latin American liberation propelled by the 'cause of redeeming humanity' and 'establishing a government of socialist tendencies' (ibid). Che Guevara's death at the hands of an oppressive and tyrannical Bolivian army, instantaneously established him as a martyr to the revolution. On Tuesday 10 October 1967 a photograph of Che Guevara's body was published by the Bolivian army and transmitted world wide, in an attempt to expiate his myth and conclude the legend. The futility of this endeavour quickly became evident as Che Guevara's living image exceeded the detail of his death. For it was Alberto Korda's 1960 portrait of Che Guevara that formed the backdrop, as Fidel Castro addressed Che's memorial rally in Havana's Plaza de la Revolución. And soon after Che's death Giangiacomo Feltrinelli used the prints gifted him by Alberto Korda as the front cover of Che Guevara's diaries. Alberto Korda's photograph quickly became a visual emblem of the 1968 student revolution and Jim Fitzpatrick's artistic impression entitled the 'Che Guevara poster of May 1968' visually defined the anti-Vietnam war protests worldwide (see Figure 4.2). Many decades hence Alberto Korda's image of Che Guevara has become ubiquitous; emblazoned on a jamboree of; commodities, disparate artefacts of popular culture and political times.

One might verdantly hypothesize that the iconic status of Alberto Korda's 1960 Che Guevara portrait, is a measure of Che's visionary belief that revolution is imperishable and self-creating. It is evident that the symbolic appeal of Alberto Korda's 1960s portrait has persisted in collective memory. And yet the apotheosis of this image in contemporary consumer culture is diametrically inconsistent with, Che Guevara's aversion to material incentives as a vehicle for economic development. It was Che Guevara's belief that 'for man fully to realise himself, the concept of man as commodity must cease to exist, and society must give him his share in exchange for the accomplishment of a social duty' (ibid:40). But the apotheosis of Alberto Korda's iconic image into commodity culture transcends the life of Guevara 'and the idea or fact of revolution' (Berger 2006:58). For this image has become ubiquitous, a brand spectacle, more symbolic of the absurdities and contradictions of capitalism than the moral imperative of repatriating humanity. Che Guevara fought and died resisting capitalist material excess and yet his image is emblazoned on T-shirts, transformed into pop art and irreverently integrated into the global capitalist market. But how did Alberto Korda's 1960 portrait of

Che Guevara become an artefact, artificially preserved as an object of commodity culture? This chapter argues that, Alberto Korda's 1960 portrait of Che Guevara has become the perfect advertising conduit to a postmodern political caesura. At the basis of this observation is both a direct challenge to and extension of Marxist advertising theory.

Advertising Visual Cultures and the Rise of Global Revolutionary Signifiers

An orthodox Marxist analysis of Alberto Korda's 1960 portrait of Che Guevara and its commodification, would equate advertising practice with commodity fetishism. Advertising would be defined as operating to extend the commodity-form and the logic of exchange-value into the realm of popular culture. And this would be seen as part of capitalism's insatiable drive to accumulate capital through the expropriation of surplus-value. Evidence of this Marxian premise, applied in similar case-studies, is provided in Judith Williamson's (2000) seminal text, *Decoding Advertisements*. Williamson's premise is that advertising involves the creation of exchange-values that communicate a concrete use-value embedded within the product. Exchange-value is the mysterious thing that Williamson's deconstruction is directed at decoding. And this process of decoding involves distinguishing between, the 'overt' and 'latent' manifestations of the advertisement.

Advertising imagery positions its subjects within a cultural economy of time (Odih 2007). Williamson observes this phenomenon as involving the 'synchronic', 'a-temporal location' of the subject or the 'a misplacement of the subject' with regards to their own past 'and the shared past of "History"' (2000:152). Advertising imagery can depict not only an event but also provides cues to recollect memories and future aspirations, as part of its embodiment of narrative time. Such practices are clearly evident in the apotheosis of Che Guevara's image into advertising culture. In April 2007 the *Financial Times* inaugurated an ultra-modern and impressionistic advertising campaign as part of a propitious rebrand of the broadsheet. The campaign revolved around the strapline 'We live in Financial Times'; highlighting the focal role that global business plays in our everyday lives (Pearson 2007). Created by the advertising agency DDB London, the campaign features iconic images that accentuate the *Financial Times*' reinvigorated brand focus on globalization, mergers and acquisitions and entrepreneurship. The visual imagery includes an inventive global cityscape configured by the world's most iconic buildings depicting the spatial concentration of global business in urban cities. Visitors to the site are able to scroll over the cityscape animations and retrieve 'World Business in One Place'; thus signifying the *Financial Times* as a pre-eminent source of global business news. The spectacular 3D affective global cityscape was launched alongside a provocative advertising campaign featuring the image of Richard Branson in a caricature, purposely evocative of Alberto Korda's 1960 portrait of Che Guevara.

According to the *Financial Times*, the campaign was the culmination of an 'extensive programme of global customer research', which confirmed the global pre-eminence of the broadsheet but suggested that it was 'somewhat inaccessible and old fashioned' (ibid:1). It would appear therefore that the application of Alberto Korda's 1960 portrait of Che Guevara is intended to affect a change in the newspaper's brand image. Indeed the, then Global Marketing Director of the *Financial Times*, Frances Brindle, described the paper's new brand advertising as 'a move away from the *Financial Times*' traditional approach' (ibid). She further stated that the company intended to 'create a campaign that would not only promote the excellence of [its] global business coverage, but also capture the excitement and energy of modern business' (ibid). Decoding the advertisement confirms an intentioned application of visual imagery designed to embed Alberto Korda's 1960 portrait of Che Guevara within a discernable inter-textual sign system. Drawing heavily upon the entrepreneurial animation of the Branson brand, the affect of his image morphed into Che Guevara is to formulate a visual inter-textuality, designed to evoke past memory and future expectation. It achieves this by constructing a narrative that conjoins recollected memories with revolutionary expressions of imaginative freedom. While it is evident that advertising trades off memory and future expectation it is important to appreciate 'that in a very real way, everything in the ad is already past' (Williamson 2000:152).

One may for a moment be stimulated by the advertisement's evocation of imagination, but the use of such referencing is designed to focus on sign-value. To this end the image has an established currency. Consequently, Williamson contends that narrative advertising imagery is always finished, 'and the future events are never open, but specifically directed' (ibid). We may experience the visual morphing of Richard Branson into Che Guevara as a cue to recollect memories, but the campaign's prior intentionality transposes onto the spectator 'a closure, a narrative sequence which is inevitably pre-determined' (ibid). This simulacrum is in contrast with the reconstructive nature of time and memory. For the past is an integral part of one's self-concept. Our recollection of experiences inter-weave with one's changing self-knowledge to produce a future of unpredictable eventualities. Conversely, the future horizon of narrative advertisements trails the memories and emotions circumscribed in advertising fictions. It is in this sense, according to Williamson, that 'the closed future belongs to a deterministic and unalterable present' (ibid). But we are so accustomed to being addressed in relation to a predetermined future that we fail to recognize its underlying ideological function i.e., the misplacement of the subject in terms of his own past and the shared past of 'History' (ibid). For, the act of securing closure requires that the events that preceded it are hermeneutically sealed out of the flow of time and locked in an eternal moment. At this point it might assist to reflect once again on the *Financial Times*' campaign featuring Richard Branson as Che Guevara. The pose, expression and configuration of the image explicitly caricatures Alberto Korda's 1960 iconic portrait of Che Guevara. Indeed each fragment of the image is incorporated into a sequence of events in time (e.g., the unruly hair, dishevelled attire and wilful facial hair) and linked to a pre-determined future expectation in, which Che Guevara's revolutionary mythology equates with the commercial aspirations of the *Financial Times*.

Williamson observes that the process of linking past and future is part of the formation of a myth 'and so is synchronic' (ibid:153). She further argues that narrative advertisements reproduce an 'ideology of the synchronic', which in turn refers to 'a category that is used to misrepresent history, since it can represent history as a story…which has an end, and thus might just as well have happened all at once, from the vantage view-point of the present' (ibid:154). It is clear that Richard Branson's portraiture and advertising imagery speaks to the mythology of Che Guevara rather than the actual history of his revolutionary endeavour. Thus for the purposes of visual affect, history is transmuted; condensed into a synchronicity that endlessly reproduces its legacy and projected into an imaginary inflation vaguely equivalent with the original referent. Such observations are not intended to undermine the propriety of the *Financial Times*. Rather it is my intention to highlight the paradoxical dynamics of narrative advertising imagery. When we observe Richard Branson's imagery in the *Financial Times*' advertisement, in the content of Williamson's revelations, it becomes evident that 'There is no real present in advertising' (ibid). This is because advertising is never actually 'a celebration of a pleasure-in-itself', but 'always about the future' (Berger 1972:132). Thus it is apparent that the advertisement interpolates with the past and surges forward in its commercial aspiration to signify a revolutionary regeneration of the brand.

Memory and anticipation are the dimensions of time made possible in an advertisement's visual spectacle. The resulting affect displaces the present moment into the metaphysical future of the advertisement. To this end the advertisement is intended to reconstruct the attributes of an event and fix this imaginative exercise within the confines of a delineated moment. The spectator is therefore visualizing the perpetual details of an eternal instance and thus 'the subject is captured in time' (Williamson 2000:155). Narrative time also works through the meaning constructions of the subject. This is because advertising's creation of meaning structures is only successfully accomplished when audience members make the semiotic connections implicit in the advertising imagery. Thus advertisements invite (or appellate) audience members to accomplish the work of the text by investing in the production of meaning.

The audience member does not passively encounter the advertising imagery, for they are actively involved in the process of meaning production. As Williamson observes, this is because 'advertisements are selling us something else besides consumer goods…they are selling us ourselves' (2000:13). Axiomatic with Williamson's (2000) rendition of audience engagement is the existence of a communicable cultural world inhabited by communities of semiotically adept individuals. Advertisers draw upon reservoirs of shared cultural knowledge as part of their activities in attributing commodities with symbolic value. Williamson defines these systems of meaning as 'referent systems' and she is adamant that they have an aprior existence i.e., they precede advertising practice. For example,

Williamson describes how advertisements borrow from working class cultural history and its political significance is transferred into sign-values that are propitiously attached to commodities. One need only reflect upon the revolutionary warfare and militaristic attire predominant in the above stated advertisement, to gain a sense of the appropriation of working class political culture. What is significant here is that such practices obscure the fact that 'the real distinction between people are created by their role in the process of production, as workers, it is the products of their own work that are used in the false categories invoked by advertising' (ibid:13). Thus, in its efforts 'to make those properties mean something to us' advertising erases the material expressions of exploitative labour-time expended in the production of the commodity. It is in this sense, that advertising has an ideological affect.

Advertising signifying practice 'is the meaning made necessary by the conditions of society while helping to perpetuate those conditions' (ibid:13). And advertising is able to accomplish this role because it operates in a circular formation trading off 'genuine' use-values eagerly received by audience members 'needing social meaning' (ibid:14). Williamson effectively summaries this supposition with the statement 'material things that we need are made to represent other, non-material things we need: the point of exchange between the two is where "meaning" is created' (ibid:14). It is evident here and elsewhere, that Williamson assumes that the fantastic form of the commodity resides with exchange-value. Alongside this mode of analysis is the equally questionable supposition that the *moment of exchange* is instantiated in the market place. By demonstrating a homology between exchange-value and market economy, use-value by implication is located outside the political economy of the sign. Use-value, in this circumscribed mode of analysing advertising, materializes neither as a social relation or cynosure of fetishization. Utility is indifferent to the contradictions and tensions that have beset the historical determination of social class. In effect it has its own finality and thus can be imbued with:

> the promise of a resurgence beyond the market economy, money and exchange value, in the glorious autonomy of man's simple relation to his work and his products. (Baudrillard 1981:130)

Williamson's Marxian rhetoric is equally idealistic; it prognosticates the intrinsic purpose of use-value for the determinacy of subjectivity and reclaiming the political subject. As she expresses it '...the need for relationship and human meaning appropriated by advertising is one that, if only it was not diverted, could radically change the society we live in' (Williamson 2000:14). De-coding advertisements is therefore tantamount to reclaiming political subjectivity in modern times. But this political praxis is undermined by the affect of constituting advertising signification as itself an instance of alienation. The sense of estrangement which workers experience in the production process is, Williamson argues, reproduced by advertising's location within a sign-system of exchange-value. This is because advertising operates to obfuscate the true character of embodied production, which will only be revealed when commodity-based capitalism is dismantled. In other words, our natural being involves a form of production in which 'labour has incorporated itself with its subject: the former is materialised, the latter transformed' (*Capital Vol. 1* 2003:176). So it appears that the symbolic relations, object relations and motivations for the subject's labour have their equivalent in utility and the system of needs (Baudrillard 1981:135). Thus utility is presumed to precede generalizable exchange, indeed utility is 'idealized by opposition to exchange value' (ibid:139).

While exchange-value effaces power inequality and ascribes the commodity with autonomous value, use-value traces the needs and satisfactions which define the human being as an individual. Baudrillard observes a recurrent theme in Marxian praxis predicated on 'its ability to reinterrogate radically the repressive, reductive, rationalising metaphysic of utility' (ibid:139). The consequence has been a convergence of idealized vision on use-value and a celebration of its dissimilitude from exchange-value. At its simplest mode of expression, it is assumed that while the logic of equivalence produces inequity with respect to the purchase of commodities, the inherent functionality of use-value suggests that individuals would be equal with respect to goods recognized as use-value. The principle contours of Williamson's critique of advertising echo this proposition along with its tendency to hermeneutically seal off use-value, from the system of exchange-value. Of particular concern, here is Williamson's narrow interpretation of Marx's observation that: 'production not only produces goods; it produces people to consume them, and the corresponding needs' (quoted in Baudrillard 1981:136). In Williamson's analysis advertising itself is a negation of freedom because it corrodes our natural being and delays the eventual dissipation of the commodity-based world of capitalism. Advertising is an object of critique because it manoeuvres needs and creates artificial desires. Fundamental to this assertion is a failure to recognize:

> that what produces the commodity system in its general form is the concept of need itself, as constitutive of the very structure of the individual – that is, the historical concept of a social being who in the rupture of symbolic exchange, autonomizes himself and rationalizes his desire, his relation to others and to objects, in terms of needs, utility, satisfaction and use-value. (Baudrillard 1981:136)

Axiomatic with this political intervention is a reversal of Marx's position in which the useful properties of the object precede the political economy of the sign. In Baudrillard's observations 'the field of political economy generalizes and saturates itself through the system of use value' (ibid:137). Baudrillard demonstrates that use-value is an effect of exchange-value. And the immediate implications of this directly foreclose Williamson's naïve assumption that advertising mitigates the expression of a mode of being outside of economic relations. It seems that

Williamson's steadfast commitment to the existence of 'genuine use-value' forces her analysis of advertising and the political subject into a limited model of economic determinism that is unable to comprehend the extent to which the political economy of the sign extends into everyday life; 'down to the very act in which man believes he has rediscovered himself' (ibid:139). As shall become evident, Baudrillard largely avoids the economic reductionism that plagues Williamson's analysis and thus advances our understanding of cultural politics and advertising in postmodern times.

Critique of the Political Economy of the Sign

Baudrillard's (1981) *Critique of the Political Economy of the Sign*, collapses Marx's parallel order of exchange-value and use-value into a general political economy. According to Marx's analysis use-value is material and does not incorporate equivalents. This is because the unchanging underlying structure of use-value assumes that a given commodity would constantly be seen to be purposeful for a stipulated task even if it was 'never truly inscribed in the field of the market economy' (ibid:130). Conversely exchange-value is immaterial and analyzed in terms of abstract social domination. Baudrillard challenges this mode of analysis. Far from being a law of static equilibrium, 'use value – indeed, utility itself – is a fetishised social relation, just like the abstract equivalence of commodities' (ibid:131). Baudrillard demonstrates a homology between use-value and sign production and this leads him to argue that 'use value is an abstraction' and in actuality conceived in terms of exchange-value and the commodity (ibid). Just as in Marx's interpretation exchange-value abstracts labour time, so 'the system of needs' is rooted at the heart of the purported contradictions between use-value and the logic of equivalence. If only on a preliminary logical level use-value is nonsensical without exchange-value the two dimensions dynamically reinforce one another; 'for there to be a system at all, use value and exchange value must be regulated by an identical abstract logic of equivalence, an identical code' (ibid). For Baudrillard it is the coalescence of these fetishizations that forms the basis of commodity fetishism. Use-value and exchange-value converge in a two-sided matrix infused with the code of equivalences. In so doing, Baudrillard directly challenges Marx's distinction between the use-value and exchange-value. For the use-value is revealed as a 'construct of the system of exchange value which produces a rationalized system of needs and objects that integrate individuals into the capitalist order' (Best and Kellner 1991:114).

This transformation in the system of needs is located within a particular genealogy of 'simulation'. According to Baudrillard there is a direct correspondence between the birth of the private individual, in the bourgeois era, and the constitution of objects with individually discernable use-values. This homology is a consequence of 'an objective rationalization, the surpassing of old rituals and symbolic constraints' (Baudrillard 1981:132). In pre-modern society objects did not have the social structures of objective relations inscribed into them. In due course 'secularized, functionalized and rationalized in purpose, objects become the promise of an ideal (and idealist) political economy, with its watchword "to each according to his needs"' (ibid:132). In conjunction with this transformation the individual freed from the archaic obligatory ties of ancestry is 'at last private and autonomous' and is formed by a dialectic of reflexive constitution 'through an "objective" activity of transforming nature – labour – and through the destruction of utility for his benefit: needs, satisfactions, use value' (ibid:133). To this extent the rediscovery of the political subject actualized through the satisfaction of needs is an incongruity. For the existence of this subject traces a particular historical trajectory which witnessed the birth of the individual reflexively defined in terms a universal world of objects. It is my contention that an analysis of advertising and cultural politics needs to appreciate that the, history and present of sign-value and the mode in which sign-value mediates the whole social psychic system of needs such that the fetishism of use-value ideologically substantiates the fetishism of exchange-value.

Changing Times, Changing Politics

In pre-modern societies where identities were primarily ascribed at birth through kinship and blood lineage or acquired through affinal ties of marriage, the modern precarious and unending process of achieving and sustaining one's identity through social activity was unknown. However, in modern society, identity becomes ever more absorbing as it is precarious and it begins to be the measure of life – a fluid reflexive process instantiated through the time-space events, which it also serves to constitute (Giddens 1993; Lefebvre 1991). Contrived to forge its own identity the modern subject is presented with the ironic proposition of having 'no choice but to choose' (Giddens 1994:75). Thus in modern times identity becomes a 'personalized problem, the solution of which lay in the future' (Clarke 2000:220). Marketing in the modern era reproduced this conception of subjectivity, in its belief that a relatively fixed system of human needs could be discovered by tracing the development of consumers through time-space events (Odih 2007). And advertising embraced a modernist aesthetic, which ascribes human beings with 'a unique personality and individuality' (Jameson 1985:114).

In this modernist sensibility the object of advertising 'can be expected to generate its own unique vision of the world and to forge its own unique, unmistakable style' (ibid:114). Advertising lives symbiotically on the audiences' reservoir of social and cultural meaning (Proctor et al 2002). Advertisers rummage through everyday culture in the relentless search for symbolic meanings to augment the utility value of commodities. The informal symbolic productions of social relations, in time and space, are a particularly attractive source of raw material for the creation of commodity values. Advertising congruity allies commodities with culturally constituted representations of everyday life. Advertising achieves this by separating 'the intrinsic qualities of being human from actual living humans' and this 'reification imparts a time-lessness to the manufactured product' (Goldman 1995:32). The ebb and flow of everyday interaction is an integral feature of capitalist commodity circuits, as advertisers endeavour to transform the symbolic meaning of informal productions into currency. But the transfer of meaning is only achieved by the creative ingenuity of consumers 'whose interpretations reflect their own experience, social situations and concerns' (Proctor et al 2002:35). Consumption is an active and productive cultural practice, which requires the accomplishment of 'symbolic work' (Willis 2000:69). Symbolic work involves 'symbolic understanding' deployed in the interpretation of sign-values (2000:69). It can be seen as 'sensuous cultural practices' in which socio-symbolic meanings are produced and adapted dialectically to the situated and personal context of consumption (2000:70). Advertising trades upon these contextual meanings turning them into fetishized human qualities which 'become time-bound, contingent on possessing the product's properties' (Goldman 1995:32). Thus modernist advertising requires a 'remembering subject' (Williamson 2000:158) as a source of meaning production. It also depends on the consumer's interpretative skills and their ability to invest symbolic work in making coherent 'the fragments and flows of commodity culture' (Willis 2000:69).

Conversely, the postmodern world of simulation and 'hyper-reality' is a world without 'fixed' references of meaning. Figure 4.2., presents yet another morphosis of Che Guevara and in so doing demonstrates how, in postmodern culture his legend has 'become invisible and ubiquitous' (Berger 2006:53). How has this come about? The extraordinary time/space compression of the postmodern era disrupts the modernist segmentation of culture and the segmentation of life into separate value spheres. And this has direct consequences for the philosophical demarcations of modernist politics. It has been a long-established tradition, in political philosophy, to align culture with 'Romantic political vision' and present irreconcilable differences between this and the liberal ancestry of rights (Cowan et al 2001:3). Acknowledging rights necessitated a disaffirmation of culture, because the presupposition of universal individual rights requires a disengagement from relativism and the specificity of one's values. The figuring of culture and rights in binary opposition is a principle element of modernist political thinking. Indeed, the competing claim of universalism versus cultural relativism has shown a remarkable pertinacity in its power to compel a singular positioning for or against. And this is why the extension of advertising into politics presents a radical challenge to the notion of the subject presupposed in modernist discourse. For, postmodern advertising aesthetics imagine a transition away from fixed identities towards a form of social being that is 'eminently contingent and continually reproduced in specific discursive contexts' (Tribe 1993:4). Drawing upon Baudrillard (1981, 1983, 1985, 1990, 1994, 2005), the following sections argue that the fleeting presence of subjects, objects sounds and sensations in postmodern advertising imagery are evidence of new times in cultural politics.

The Political Economy of the Sign in Postmodern Advertising

Baudrillard observes that with the transition from pre-capitalist to capitalist society, objects begin to function like signs. In line with Saussurean semiotics, this understanding of representation exceeds the reductive notion of the sign as indexed to a real and independently distinguishable material reality. 'The object-become-sign no longer gathers its meaning in the concrete relationship between two people' (Baudrillard 1981:66). Rather the relation between sign and referent are completely arbitrary. The sign obtains its meaning through its 'differential relation to other signs' (ibid:66). Baudrillard traces this transition in signification onto three orders of simulacra: 'Counterfeit...Production...Simulation' (Baudrillard 1983:83). The first-order of simulacra *counterfeit* denoted the predominant scheme of the classical period up until the Industrial Revolution and is underpinned by 'the natural law of value' (ibid). Conversely the second-order, *production* was axiomatic with the industrial era and is based on 'the commercial law of value' (ibid). The third-order simulacra, *simulation* denote the hegemony of the current era and are based on 'the structural law of value' (ibid). According to Baudrillard, these epochs historically accompany two phases in a genealogy of the political economy of the sign; a period of abject alienation in which the masses were brutally oppressed and endeavored to find transcendence through orchestrated revolution and visionary idealism (Gane 2007:128). And a second period in which the masses are psychologized by consumerism and media saturated political democracy (ibid). This era paves the way for the emergence of a third-order simulacrum in which politics enters into a colossal simulation and political desires cannot be determined outside of representational systems (ibid). With regards to the former era, Baudrillard invests pre-capitalist societies with a mode of symbolic exchange non-commensurate with a regime of monetary equivalence or a semiological logic of value. In his book *Simulations*, Baudrillard (1983) describes the historical mutations which precipitated the corruption of the assured and referential symbols of mass political protest.

Real Representation

Counterfeit transpires in the Renaissance and is born out of the dissolution of the feudal order by the bourgeois system 'and the emergence of open competition on the level of the distinctive signs' (Baudrillard 1983:84). Signifying practices, in feudalism were governed by modes of resemblances binding each sign unequivocally to a system of ascribed status. Signs were restricted in number and each one functioned to exclude or forbid an act so as to affirm social order through interdiction. As Baudrillard observed each sign connotes 'a reciprocal obligation between castes, clans or person' (ibid). Any confusion of signs or infraction of the 'symbolic order' directly challenges the integral reality and sodality of the caste system. Thus, the relation between signifier and signified is far from arbitrary. It is with the emergence of the Renaissance that the limited symbolic order of the 'obliged sign', which ferociously prohibits 'free production', encounters 'the proliferation of signs according to demand' (ibid:85). At this moment the morphology of the sign no longer resembles the endogamy axiomatic with the limited order of the obliged sign. For the sign multiplied is, its copy. Baudrillard ascribes to this sign the label counterfeit, not because it is an adulteration of the original sign. Rather, the sign multiplied is a counterfeit because signifiers refer back to the 'disenchanted universe of the signified...the real world toward which no one has any obligation' (ibid).

The emergence in the Renaissance of signs, liberated from their archaic referential obligations, marks the hegemonic moment at which the pre-capitalist principles of symbolic exchange begin to disintegrate. The sign multiplied and freed from pre-modern archaic systems of obligation operate as counterfeits of an extra-systemic referent. To this extent, Baudrillard argues that in the first-order of simulacra, a representation of the real (e.g., a map) is a counterfeit of an exterior reality. Baudrillard (1983) describes how the map is not an identical copy of reality. Nevertheless it suffices as a cultural representation of an independent reality. Returning to our previous discussion of Alberto Korda's portrait of Che Guevara, in so far as the image adheres to the dialectical capacity of representation it functions as a 'visible and intelligible mediation of the Real' (1983:10). Rather than presuppose a material reconstruction, all faith and revolutionary idealism attributed to this image, engages in a wager on representation; 'that a sign could refer to the depth of meaning' (ibid). But what if a simulacrum of the real was so profound in its affect that it impacted on the real? Baudrillard poses a more profound version of this challenge as he dares to enquire 'what if God himself can be simulated, that is to say, reduced to the signs which attest his existence?' (ibid). In this sense the condition of ideality does not gain validity from its equivalence to the real, because reality is inseparable from the circulation of signs.

Production

Capitalism throughout its history has been axiomatic with the annihilation of the referents of referential systems in order to establish a monetary law of equivalence. In industrial capitalism we observe an accentuation of this process with the advent of the second-order of simulacra. This new era of signs is even further removed from the binding restrictions of caste. Signs 'no longer have to be counterfeited, since they are going to be produced all at once on a gigantic scale' (Baudrillard 1983:96). The singularities which arise from concerns about the integral reality of the sign are less relevant. In the era of industrial sign production the only origin the sign 'posses is in the dimension of the industrial simulacrum' (ibid). This is because in a series of equivalent identical objects, each 'become undefined simulacra one of the other' (ibid:97). Central to the equivalence of indifference is the annihilation of the original referent. Once the prototype of the original process can no longer be seen a generalized law of equivalence can be set in motion transforming all 'original being' into a 'series of identical beings' (ibid). It is this generalized law of equivalence, which affectively blurs the distinction between reality and representation. Baudrillard (1983) illustrates this feature of the second-order of simulacra by recounting Borges' fable of the cartographers who constructed a map of Empire, which was so exact that it virtually covered the entire territory. The enchantment and poetry of the map comes alive in the charm of Baudrillard's storytelling:

> If we were able to take as the finest allegory of simulation the Borges tale where the cartographers of the Empire draw up a map so detailed that it ends up exactly covering the territory (but where the decline of the Empire sees this map become frayed and finally ruined, a few shreds still discernible in the deserts – the metaphysical beauty of this ruined abstraction, bearing witness to an Imperial pride and rotting like a carcass, returning to the substance of the soil, rather as an aging double ends up being confused with the real thing) – then this fable has come full circle for us, and now has nothing but the discrete charm of second-order simulacra. (1983:1)

At the hegemonic moment, when the coextensivity of the map and its territory disintegrates, simulacrum is true. Representation presupposes a one to one correspondence between signs and things. Conversely, simulation commences from the displacement of correspondence, at no point do signs exchange for a concrete referent. Rather linguistic representation is based on a system of differences and reality is embedded within a circulation of signs. According to Baudrillard the imperialist ideals that preoccupied the cartographers of Borges' fable, also motivates contemporary politicians that 'try to make real, all the real, coincide with their simulation models' (ibid:2). But this suggests that as an allegory of Empire, a vital component of Borges' fable has disappeared. The fastidious ingenuity of the cartographers implied that they were dedicated to the existence of a sovereign difference between the territory and its representation and this formed the basis of 'the abstraction's charm' (ibid). Modern day politicians are less concerned with reconciling maps with territory. For the metaphysics that instantiates the sovereign difference between real and representation has disintegrated.

Part of the dissolution of the real was precipitated by the Industrial Revolution's technological innovations that made possible the automated replication of advertising. Machine production, enabled the serialization of signs, but the resulting simulacra was resolutely indebted to utilitarian operational models of advertising (Odih 2007). These monopolistic production processes where radically challenged by artistic movements intent on disrupting modernist representations of reality. For example, in the surrealist aesthetics of the 1930s, advertising affected an entreaty to make manifest the mechanisms that produce conceptual meanings and exhibit the disguised workings of truth production. To these observations, Baudrillard adds the extraordinary power of the media, and its ability to challenge the very idea of integral reality. Signs are 'no longer specular and discursive…No more mirror of being and appearances, of the real and its concept' (1983:3). Rather in media technology, 'the real is produced from miniaturized units from matrices, memory banks and command models – and with these it can be reproduced an indefinite number of times' (ibid). If we are to accept that the power of the media now means that the real has dissipated into operational codes, then we are lead to believe that the dynamics of moral teleology and political agency constitutive of Western democratic society are in disarray.

The political has become an integral feature of the age of simulacra and axiomatic to the incessant circulation of self-referential signifiers. The production of political agency has given way to a process of reciprocal corruption in, which the compliance of the masses is assured by the compulsive recourse of political elites to the spectacular amplification of a reality that is already a product of reproduction. The totalizing logic which arises from the discontinuous indeterminism of amplified spectacle produces models of reality that are determining of reality. And it is this feature of simulacra that provides contemporary politics with a means of transforming representation into a vehicle of endless performativity. This observation leads Baudrillard to examine modern political history in terms of the incantation of imaginary effects (e.g., political scandals) for the purposes of 'concealing that reality no more exists outside than inside the bounds of the artificial perimeter' (1983:26).

Baudrillard presents Watergate as a simulacrum of a scandal induced by the total performativity of the media and its ability to obfuscate the defining principle of the real. Watergate was a presidential campaign scandal, precipitated on 17 June 1972 when a group of agents, commissioned by the re-election assembly of President Richard Nixon, were apprehended breaking into the Democratic Party's offices located in the Watergate complex, Washington DC.

Over the next two years repeated attempts to conceal Nixon's imbroglio, lead to the realization that corruption in the White House was rife and that the ill-fated attempt to bug the opposition party's Watergate office formed part of a catalogue of criminal offences. Thanks to the investigative skills of *Washington Post* reporters Bob Woodward and Carl Bernstein and the clandestine disclosures of agent 'Deep Throat', the media latched onto the decaying carcass of a government going off the rails and relentlessly publicized the Nixon administration's absurd attempts to cover-up a multitude of political misdemeanors. Under intense opprobrium the regime began to buckle and its eventual demise was guaranteed, when in 1973 it was revealed at the Senate's special Watergate Committee that the Oval Office superintended audio recordings of conversations that clearly implicated Nixon in the Watergate scandal. Nixon resolutely objected to releasing the tapes. The legal investigation that followed, assailed the heights of the American judicial system culminating in a subpoena being issued. Nixon continued to contumaciously refuse the release of the audio recordings. Instead he audaciously insisted on the sacking of the prosecutor responsible for the subpoena and prompted the attorney-general's resignation. Amidst the ensuing carnage many of Nixon's closest political advisers and a host of senior government officials were charged, convicted and imprisoned.

After two years of irrefutable allegation, the United States Supreme Court intervened and insisted that Nixon release the Oval office tapes. Nixon finally relinquishes the audio recordings. One of the tapes, later to be described as the 'smoking gun', discloses that Nixon sanctioned a cover-up. In July 1974 the House of Representatives voted to commence the impeachment of Nixon. In August 1974 Nixon proclaims, in a live television broadcast, that he intends, for the good of the nation, to resign. Finally true to his word, Nixon resigned in 1974, so as to escape the humiliation of impeachment. The denunciation and disposition of key felons in this political debacle performed a restorative function cleansing American democracy and restoring popular belief in the existence of legal justice. Thus, power staged 'its own murder to rediscover a glimmer of existence and legitimacy' (ibid:37). It is Baudrillard's contention that, everything in the Watergate scandal 'metamorphosed into its inverse in order to be perpetuated in its purged form' (ibid). Journalists became bastions of moral order thus denying their role in the manufacture of news. And the political integrity of the good guys was once again immediately discernable.

According to Baudrillard, the dramaturgy of the Watergate scandal efficaciously coincided with a crisis in the hegemony of the political establishment and the imperative to simulate an 'artificial menace to conceal that they were nothing other than mannequins of power' (1983:37). To this extent, Watergate's pursuit of truth and denunciation of scandal produced a model of the real that became determining of the real. For the denunciation of scandal played homage to the, ultimately improvable, existence of an entirely reputable political order. The scandal also succeeded in widely disseminating the idea that Watergate was the locus of scandal, thus exonerating artifice external to this arbitrary perimeter. As Baudrillard expresses it 'capital, which is immoral and unscrupulous, can only function behind a moral superstructure, and whoever regenerates this public morality (by indignation, denunciation etc.) spontaneously furthers the order of capital, as did the *Washington Post* journalists' (ibid:27). Thus simulacra achieved the intention of purging and reviving the political order by drawing the populace into an engagement in a moral critique that itself was the origin of the simulacrum; 'a simulation of scandal to regenerative ends' (ibid:30). It is equally important to appreciate that the power of simulation is of the same order of the impossibility of controlling semantic effects. This is because:

> simulation is infinitely more dangerous…since it always suggests, over and above its object, that law and order themselves might really be nothing more than a simulation. (Baudrillard 1983:38)

It is evident that a degree of linear continuity links this logic of simulation with the consequences of any act or event calculated to regenerate political credibility. This is because in simulation 'facts no longer have any trajectory of their own' (ibid:32) and the resulting conflation of the fact with its model conveys the indeterminacy of a self-coordinating identity. Baudrillard need not, therefore, have been so despondent over the politics of capitalist culture. For his book *Simulations* provides some recognition that the precision of simulacra can generate indeterminacies of unequivocal magnitude. For simulation not only multiplies signs it accelerates the 'semantic plasticity' of signs (Ryan 1988:568). Every simulation is a mere short-circuit of reality, this is because the absolute reduplication of reality always escapes the model. Thus the simulacrum is admirably ambivalent in its ability to transform the real. It has the potential to create a 'polysemous' excess of meaning (ibid). And this implosion of simulacra can magnificently distort the analytical mode that distinguishes reality from the play of effects. Ryan argues that to envision the polysemony of simulation 'one must see seemingly univalent social phenomena as being capable of giving rise to multiple semantic effects' (ibid). It is my contention that the inherent polysemony of the second-order of simulacra best explains the specter of simulacrum that apotheosized Che Guevara's image in the student revolution of 1968.

1968 Student Revolution: Signification Ablaze

The 1960s witnessed tremendous insurrection, and Che Guevara's death in 1967 coincided with a world revolutionary alignment involving not just the working class, but intelligentsia, students and factions of the traditional middleclass. Conceived as the inspiration of a new revolutionary avant-garde, the student revolution of 1968 stands out as a monumental flash-point, in the tidal wave of protests that swept over capitalist production; and threatened to overwhelm its foremost political doctrines. In the United States students sought to chart a new course for the civil rights movement and raged against the malapropism of the Vietnam War. Enthralled by the concept of rural revolt, the student movement in Latin America flowed out of the countryside to purge the cities of their corrupt elites. In France, President Charles de Gaulle's New Year's Eve 1967 speech praising France's robust capitalist system and confidently greeting 'the year 68 with serenity', proved to be preposterously optimistic (quoted in Taaffee 2008:4). Six months later the French economy was effectively incapacitated by student riots and the levers of power had to realize a force beyond the economic rationality of the market. Revolutionary struggles in England were also in direct confrontation with the establishment. Students entered into political protest by outflanking traditional authority structures and staging mass insurrection. Universities were 'strategic and vulnerable elements of late bourgeois society', and the moderates advocated a democratic mass challenge to the bourgeois order of the university establishment (Barnett 1969:45). By 1968 the insurrection had become visible across English universities as students acquired spaces 'where the cultural and material pre-conditions of revolution' could be assembled (ibid). Within these spaces intellectual persuasion, rather than a rein of political terror, would anchor the student assault on the absurd contradictions of Western capitalism. Elsewhere, in Eastern Europe the student movement mirrored the intellectual commitment of anti-capitalist revolutionaries in the West. Indeed, the spectra of the 1968 student revolution compelled nation states to observe the insidious inequalities that festered within their borders. Not only were the student movements successful in forcing political leaders to look uncomfortably at their polities, the students adopted a mode of protest that changed decisively both the politics of representation and the representation of politics.

1968 signified a spectacular renaissance of political culture. The insidious victimizing adversary of the revolutionary brigade was an object of no physical dimensions, and yet its crushing impact reverberated throughout political culture. To this end the attack on capitalism had to be directed at culture. And thus the 1968 student revolution was ablaze with signs; brandished as protest banners, furiously burned national flags, desiccated army recruitment cards and a colophony of anarchic sights and sounds all directed at signifying a break with the rigid rationaliztic confines of capitalist accumulation. Within this heightened context of

Figure 4.2 Che Guevara poster of May 1968

Source: Reproduced with kind permission of the artist Jim Fitzpatrick.

revolution by spectacle, advertising realized a new power of the sign. Of particular significance was the mesmeric impact of Alberto Korda's 1960 portrait of Che Guevara and its re-interpretation by the artist Jim Fitzpatrick (see Figure 4.2). In Jim Fitzpatrick's artistic impression entitled the 'Che Guevara poster of May 1968', a fascinating dialectical paradox is produced largely because the image is an impression of a photograph and thus unable to colonize the discursive spectra and self-coordinating identity of the original image. And yet it became a prolific emblem of the 1968 student revolution and defined the anti-capitalist student protest worldwide. One of the risks run by historical analysis is that of ascribing to history a linear flow of causality. In so far as Jim Fitzpatrick artistic impression contained the image of Che Guevara it is pure symbolic representation. But if this was the image's sole achievement how might one explain its purpose? For it appears merely to be a copy of an original? It is my contention that the success of this image is a product of the ontological properties realized at the level of sign production, circulation and display. For the image is a curious manifestation of and direct challenge to, what Guy Debord describes as *The Society of the Spectacle.*

Writing in 1967 Debord recognized the tectonic permutation from a society based on commodities to one consumed by the circulation of signs. Modern conditions of production, had transformed life in Western societies, such that social reality now 'presents itself as an immense accumulation of spectacles' (2006:12). The code of signification governing the spectacle is a logic of signs detached from everyday life and embodied social relations. Mediated by the blaze of the spectacle, social relations are apprehended 'in a partial way' as 'a pseudo-world apart' (ibid). Thus with irrefutable dispassion Debord observes 'the deployment of the power of the spectacle' as a defining feature of modern governance (ibid:8). For the spectacle manifests Western capitalism's monopolization of the sphere of appearances and the integration of material life into an amorphous 'universe of speculation' (ibid:17). This eclipse of the real is absolutely fulfilled by the fetishistic properties of the commodity. This is because the hegemony of the spectacle corresponds with a historical moment in which consumption has become an organizing principle of the modern world. As Debord states 'It is not just that the relationship to commodities is now plain to see – commodities are now all that there is to see; the world we see is the world of the commodity' (ibid:29). The commodity thus designates the spectacle's colonization of social life and transformation of 'being' into the outcome of a combination of self-referential signs.

It is only in light of this commentary that we can fully appreciate the degree to which Debord's work interpolated with the ideological fervor of the 1968 student movement. Revolutionary culture demanded intellectual rigor including the necessity to anchor heightened consciousness 'in real encroachments on bourgeois power' (Barnett 1969:44). In this sense the construction of revolution begins with concrete critical reflection in which 'the oppressive force of bourgeois ideology' and its fetishism of commodities 'must be understood and rejected in practice' (ibid:45). Indeed, it is a commonly recognized fact that the revolutionary student movement in Britain directly challenged two co-coordinated dimensions of capitalist society 'its legality and its ideology' (ibid:44). A prominent mode of student insurrection involved negating these dimensions and replacing them with a radical form of 'counter-legality and revolutionary culture' (ibid). Commodities symbolized the monopolizing fervency of capitalism and anti-consumerism became the preferred instrument of revolutionary change. It was in this context that Fitzpatrick's artistic impression of Che Guevara came to embrace the anti-capitalist crusade of the 1968 student movement. Anti-capitalism raged against the spectacle of the commodity, for it represented 'capital accumulated to the point where it becomes image' (Debord 2006:24). One of the central objects of the revolutionary critique targeted the predilection of the spectacle towards the 'specialization of images-of-the-world' and the manufacture of what Debord describes as 'the autonomous image' (ibid:12). In Debord's analysis the autonomous image operates to reproduce the form of capitalist ideology thus producing a situation in which 'deceit deceives itself' (ibid). And this symbolic relation finds its highest mode of expression in the prevailing system of production, whose product is alienation from embodied labour and the transformation of this principal of work 'into a realm of non-work, of inactivity' (ibid:21). For leisure is inextricably tied to productive activity and is itself an artifact of capitalist production. In advanced capitalism the manufacture of use-values has been replaced by the reproduction of signs. The rise of sign-value has transformed the productive work of labour into a realm of non-productive work concerned with the reproduction of signs. 'There can be no freedom apart from activity' declared Debord, but the accumulative reproduction of signs designates a loss because 'within the spectacle all activity is banned' (ibid:21). A corollary of this process is that non-productive work 'has been forcibly channeled into the global construction of the spectacle' (ibid:22). Thus a pre-condition of anti-consumerist resistance required liberation from the tyranny of non-productive leisure. It is evident that this ideological challenge was ontologically embedded in the use-value of Jim Fitzpatrick's 1968 artistic impression of Che Guevara.

In an interview conducted with a fellow artist (called Mir Aleksandra), in 2005, Jim Fitzpatrick describes the technical approach employed in the production of his artistic impression of Che Guevara (Aleksandra 2005). The account commences with a descriptive narrative linking the start of Fitzpatrick's Che Guevara artistic works, in 1967, as part of a commission for the Irish magazine 'Scene'. Fitzpatrick displays significant reverence for Che Guevara and spends much of the interview expressing a desire to commemorate his hero. As the interview progresses it becomes increasingly evident that Fitzpatrick was not merely intent on producing a visual memoriam. Rather, Fitzpatrick's use of non-commodified social-networks to circulate, globally, his artistic impression of Che Guevara, directly confronted the depoliticising, alienating spectacle of the commodity-form. Indeed, it is clearly evident that his artistic practice induced from audience members, forms of productive activity, which had the effect of ontologically impregnating the very existence of the image with a revolutionary ideal.

If we assume that the triumph of the spectacle is founded on the organizing principle of inactive labour, then we must accept that Fitzpatrick's dynamic negation of consumption definitively broke with capitalism's political economy of the sign. It is the omnipresent celebration of exchange-value that transforms social relations between people into the unilateral appropriation of signs. Thus it was imperative that revolution interrogated the normalizing legality of the commodity world. Especially the extent to which 'the humanity of the commodity' infiltrates the 'worker's leisure and humanity', transforming the 'totality of human existence' into 'the regime of the perfect denial of man' (Debord 2006:30). Debord situates the political technology of art within this context, arguing that at the moment that art emerged as an independent form in the modern sense, it became subject to 'the movement governing the history of the whole of culture as a separated realm' (ibid:133). Art's declaration of independence from the realm of embodied symbolic relations marked the 'beginning of the end of art' (ibid). The negation of consumption presupposed in Fitzpatrick's annihilation of the reproductive logic of the code permits a real dialogue commensurate with the language of the spectacle, and yet directly challenges the production of 'the autonomous movement of non-life' (ibid:12).

Dislocated from the logic of the spectacle, Jim Fitzpatrick's artistic impression is not concerned with imaginary coextensivity, since it is not designed to be measured against the original. Rather its purpose is merely operational, i.e., to produce a model that is determining of reality. Indeed, the image transcends the real and speaks instead to the constant demand for a self-realization of revolution. The events that arise from Jim Fitzpatrick's artistic impression of Che Guevara suggest the dynamic of a subject-less transcendence that has disoriented any relationship with the symbolic order of the social. For the artistic impression uses Alberto Korda's original photograph and merely superimposes this image onto a red background. Nevertheless Jim Fitzpatrick's artistic impression was transformed in the melodrama of difference, into an iconic simulacrum that successfully regenerated a moribund principle of student revolution. In an enigmatic reversal the political becomes a new game of reciprocal seduction in, which the ontology of the object (the revolutionary image of Che Guevara) is achieved by the dispossession of the subject as commodity spectacle.

Simulation

In postmodern imagery, meaning is perpetually deferred, constantly slipping beyond our reach. Baudrillard argues that the third-order of simulacra coincides with a loss of a private sphere in which 'the dramatic interiority of the subject, engaged with its objects as with its image, is played out' (1985:128). Whereby the incessant saturation of communication networks in the private sphere effaces its erstwhile distinction from the public arena 'in a sort of obscenity where the most intimate processes of our life become the virtual feeding ground of the media' (1985:130). Axiomatic to the modernist separation of economy and culture, public from private is a subject 'situated within the world and able to make sense of that world through application of its powers of self-awareness' (Rodaway 1996:249). This modernist narrative assumes that the subject 'acts upon an object' and thus is an active agent in relation to the world (1995:249). Moreover, the self has an interior a private universe 'invested as a protective enclosure, an imaginary protector, a defense system' (Baudrillard 1985:130). Conversely in the media saturated world of postmodernity, the 'self is nowhere and everywhere at the same time, totally abstracted, rapidly flitting before us in myriad versions unanchored to concrete experience' (Holstein and Gubrium 2000:66). The self is constantly on display as both a trophy and signifier of commodity culture.

Seduction and the cavalcade of the self, is raised to new levels of intensification and spectacle in postmodern advertising imagery. For instance, consider for a while the imagery contained in Figure 4.3. In 1999 the Churches Advertising Network (CAN) published this image with the intention of problematizing taken for granted models of religious iconography and reversing the, polarity of the religious icon (object) and practicing religious subject. But the affect of visualizing Che Guevara as a veneration of Jesus transcends the image's moral teleology and political agency. According to CAN's own website the advertising campaign generated hostility in the British Parliament with members denouncing it as 'sacrilegious' (CAN 1999). It also incensed the broadsheet media and provoked contentious debates about religiosity and advertising. In response CAN, published an ardent defence of the campaign stating that:

> Jesus was not crucified for being meek and mild. He challenged authority. He was given a crown of thorns in a cruel parody of his claims about proclaiming the Kingdom of God. Our poster has the most arresting picture our advertisers could find to convey all this – the image deliberately imitates the style of the well-known poster of Che Guevara. (CAN 1999)

According to CAN the campaign was 'on the whole highly successful' and this is evident by the extraordinary media spectacle generated by the campaign as 'it was reported in newspapers across all five continents' (ibid). Needless to say the campaign achieved some notoriety, but it is difficult to ascertain whether the message of 'Meek Mild As If' could ever have been homologous with the discovery of the 'real Jesus'. This is because simulation as a vehicle of political agency becomes absorbed into the political economy of the sign.

The modernist episteme positions the Cartesian subject at the fulcrum of existence, for the 'knowing agent [is] contextualised and a locus of power' (Rodaway 1996:251). The metaphysics of presence which explicates this notion of knowledge orientates the subject within the context of experiential time and space (Holstein and Gubrium 2000). The self is able to evaluate experience by linking the social meaning of time-space events into signifying chains. Although this knowledge is never flawless, the subject sought reassurance in the belief that it possessed access to an object with which to compare representation (King 1998:51). Signs assumed a narrational meaning and form which determined their independent relation with the referential world of objects. Conversely in post-industrial society social life is mediated and radically alienated by a new game of seduction far removed from referential meaning and the satisfaction of needs. Thus Baudrillard observes that objects are no longer things nor categories, they have become signs whose value is determined by an insidious featureless disciplinary code. For instance, there is no material reverent with which to compare the imagery in Figure 4.3. Rather the image is a simulacrum 'for the pure and intelligible Idea of God' (Baudrillard 1983:8).

Elsewhere writers have earnestly reflected on the religiosity of the various portraits of Che Guevara and especially the image of his corpse transmitted on Tuesday 10 October 1967. Guevara had been captured leading an insurrection against the Bolivian army. In his contribution to *Viva Che!* John Berger (2006) compares the photograph of Che Guevara's corpse with Mantegna's painting of the dead Christ. Gripped by incoherent emotions, Berger's first reaction is to declare 'Guevara was no Christ' (ibid:56). Nevertheless we are entitled to deduce from the measure of spectacle that accompanied his death, that Guevara had also achieved that rare occurrence in which 'the tragedy of a man's death completes and exemplifies the meaning of his whole life' (ibid). Berger also provides an extract of speech by Guevara in which he is said to have envisaged his own death 'Wherever death may surprise us, let it be welcome, provided that this, our battle-cry, may have reached some receptive ear and another hand may be extended to wield our weapons and other men be ready to intone the funeral dirge with the staccato chant of the machine-gun and new battle-cries of war and victory' (quoted in Berger 2006:57). These moving parallels between the religiosity of sacrifice for 'the intolerable conditions of the world' (ibid:58) and Che Guevara's death affect a degree of reflection from the reader. But little of this sentiment, reflection and contemplation is born out from the iconography impressed in Figure 4.3. Fitted out with a non-diacritical, anti-semiological transcendence of productive referential meaning, the assemblages of signs attach themselves together so as to impress the singularity of a symbolic event. And thus we are apprehended by the reversal of the Cartesian polarity between subject and object.

Baudrillard's concept of 'seduction' engages objects and subjects in an intense metaphysical attraction, with the capacity to 'turn appearances in on themselves, to play on the body's appearances, rather than with the depths of desire' (1990:8). In the enchanted simulation (*trompre-l'oeil*), objects seduce subjects by the 'pure play of appearance' (1990:8). Seduction pronounces a relation between subject and object diametrically distinct from the immense capacity of the modernist subject. In modernist representation the subject has superiority over the unknown object, which it has the power to represent. In the third-order of simulacra objects efface the subject seducing the latter to abandon its claims to sovereignty over the object world (Best and Kellner 1991:129).

Axiomatic to the modernists concept of politics is 'a rational and creative agent individually orientated and critically willing to challenge accepted conventions through the application of reason and science' (Rodaway 1996:248). But this relation of subject and object is radically transformed in the third-order of simulacra. In the postmodern stages of capitalism, cultural representations are no longer linked to an independent reality. Baudrillard describes how cybernetics, media and computerization have produced a 'quotidian reality in its entirety – political, social, historical and economic' (1983:147). One that 'from now on incorporates the simulatory dimension of hyperrealism' (1983:147). Representation no longer blurs the distinction between real and copy; rather there is a detachment from both of these as multi-media simulations become realer-than-real, 'a hallucinatory resemblance' of its own existence (Baudrillard 1983:142). In the third-order of simulacra, technologies gain their own momentum providing a self-referential simulacra of actual events effacing any access to a 'real', which itself is an effect of the code system (Sarup 1996:111). As Baudrillard expresses it:

> abstraction today is no longer that of the map, the double, the mirror or the concept. Simulation is no longer that of territory, a referential being or a substance. It is the generation of models of a real without origin or reality; a hyper-real. The territory no longer precedes the map nor survives it. Henceforth, it is the map that precedes the territory – PRECESSION OF SIMULACRA – it is the map that engenders. (Original emphasis Baudrillard 1983:2)

The extreme eclecticism of postmodern advertising collage, is similarly detached from the concept of representation, mimesis and any relation to an original, which 'is lost in a continuous play of signs' (Rodaway 1996:248). Firat and Venkatesh describe how in Nike advertisements 'the need for a context seems to be increasingly transcended' (1993:234). Similar aesthetics are in evidence in Figure 4.3. Without the dramaturgy of a formalized system of political idealism, Che Guevara's image is reduced to an obeisance of commodity culture. The commodity-sign dominates the advertisement's organizing principle guiding its appropriation and manipulation of signs. Everything in the advertising imagery is no longer a combinatorial practice of political nostalgia and experience, but of a code of exchange-value. Indeed, Baudrillard argues that in postmodernity the relation between sign and referent are completely arbitrary 'determined by its [their] position in a self-referential system of [floating] signifiers' (Featherstone 1991:85). In this sense, signification means simply difference and nothing else. For Baudrillard (1968), the only meaning that signs retain is their difference from other sign. Signs are entirely self-referential, making no attempt at signification or classification, their only point being to make a temporary impact on our consciousness. The advertisement in Figure 4.3 is exemplary in its aesthetic as 'it is no longer a question of imitation, nor of reduplication, nor even of parody. It is rather a question of substituting signs of the real for the real itself' (Baudrillard 1983:4). Devoid of specific referentiality the signifiers in Figure 4.3 assume a materiality of unparalleled intensity as they explode into our consciousness. Jameson describes how, in the absence of a 'meaning effect' or even the illusion of mirage 'the signifier in isolation becomes ever more material – or better still, literal – ever more vivid in sensory ways' (1985:120).

Figure 4.3 Churches Advertising Network as Che Guevara

Source: Reproduced with kind permission of the Churches Advertising Network. Registered charity No. 1096868.

The isolated disconnected signifiers resist any attempt to weave meaning into a coherent narrative sequence or signifying chain. And this directly impacts on our experience of time. According to Ermarth time in postmodernity is a 'local definition, a dimension of an event, a unique and unrepeatable period' (1995:94). Postmodern advertising aesthetics have a similar affect on time. Disengaged from any discernable referent, floating, postmodern signifiers construct time as a function of each isolated position, a dimension of each self-referential event. It is fractured, multiple and discontinuous. Since 'our feeling of identity depends on our sense of the persistence of the "I" over the "me" over time', the subject of postmodern advertising looses the ability to thread 'certain paths' through the image (Jameson 1985:119). The search for an authentic narrative is disrupted by the 'pure' sign, which resides within a self-referential context and almost coincidentally, collides with 'products' (which are themselves mere signs). In postmodern consumer culture goods no longer provide a basis for the construction of fixed identities, but rather 'make people seem different through a collage of fragmentary images' (Proctor et al 2002:34).

Undoubtedly the cavalcades of signs and sounds that saturate our daily lives are splendid; indeed spectacular. In the shopping arcades of the Western metropolis the aesthetic of spectacle gathers momentum as fractal objects, and fractal forms bombard our senses with a single discernable oration 'I am therefore I shop'. But this seduction of the real is achieved through an abreaction. Postmodern advertising visual culture is a 'simplified operational mode…in which all particular contents are annulled at the very moment when they can be transcribed into each other' (Baudrillard 1994:87). It involves the negation of the core dichotomies of modernist thinking. The subversion of differences between real/imaginary, public/private. The dissolution of the classical modernist juxtaposition between subject and object. In modernity such binary modalities garnered 'weighty enunciations' as they protected 'articulated forms of meaning' from the superficialities of culture, and ensured 'that they cannot be translated into each other' (ibid). In postmodern advertising culture the modernist postulation of representation is displaced by the sheer contiguity, irony and hyper-reality of the postmodern sign. The effect of such a breakdown in the signifying chain is to subvert modernism's presumption that the 'meaning of truth preceded and determined the representations that communicated it' (Ryan 1988:559). In this sense, postmodern advertising culture proffers simultaneously the possibilities for the renascence of cultural politics and for its dissipation through indeterminacy.

'Absolute Advertising' as Neutrosemy?

The progressivist aspirations of modernism promised to shape the political sphere into a coliseum for the aporetic enunciation of rational critique, moral teleology and political agency. Haunted by the finite self-consciousness of historical time, political thinking preceded signifying culture and its representation of ethical life. Postmodernism, in its capability to create real simulacrum, exposes the mythic power of aporetic engagement and implodes its distance from the tyranny of commerce. In the new political era, culture instantiates the real. And in so doing, it implodes modernity's differentiation between public and private. In *Simulacra and Simulation*, Baudrillard argues that this phenomenon pre-stages a situation in which the social becomes overwhelmed by its solicitation and 'turns itself into advertising' (1994:88). This morphosis circumscribes a society in which sales pitches for products are indistinguishable from the broadcasts of different political parties selling their policies and public declarations. Sleek political campaigns with appurtenant slogans convey the same rhetorical inertia as advertising's staging of the commodity. As Baudrillard observes:

> It is not by chance that advertising, after having, for a long time, carried an implicit ultimatum of an economic kind, fundamentally saying and repeating

> incessantly, 'I buy, I consume, I take pleasure', today repeats in other forms 'I vote, I participate, I am present, I am concerned' – mirror of a paradoxical mockery, mirror of the indifference of all public signification. (1994:91)

The superficial transparency of 'absolute advertising' can be discerned in Baudrillard's account of the *Political Economy of the Sign* but achieves its denouement in *Simulacra and Simulation*. For it is here that Baudrillard decodes the ascendant triumph and eventual disaffected capitulation of the postmodern advertising sign.

In its golden days the mass production of signs, issuing from the advertising industry marvelled at the utilitarian form of the commodity. Just as the realist archetype of mass produced advertising was bound up with the socio-economic development of market capitalism, so the eclipse of the utilitarian commodity-form was coincident with the rise of modernist advertising. Signs celebrated aesthetics and revelled in the extravaganza and impetuosity of staging the commodity as, itself a mere sign-value. Advertising cavorted with new social and economic relations. Thus it could be observed that while advertising was irrepressively indexed to specific regimes of accumulation and the profiteering management of capital, its signifying practices remained paradoxical and adept in their circumvention of capital's subjugating tenure. Baudrillard is uncharacteristically nostalgic for a semiotically based sign system of advertising in which;

> Whatever the subjugation of publicity to the management of capital…it always had more than a subjugated function, it was a mirror held out to the universe of political economy and of the commodity, it was for a moment their glorious imaginary, that of a torn-up world, but an expanding one. (1994:93)

In this golden era advertising, with its focus on allegory, ambiguity and irrepressibility, exposed the multitude of meanings that audience members can derive in any one signifying system. Advertisements performed the dual function of denoting and connoting the ambiguities of capitalist culture, and their narrative appeal enabled images to be decoded differently depending on their interpretative conventions and cultural environment. Polysemous signs ascribed audience members with a relative autonomy and social theorists propagated their ability to exceed the intentions of textual producers and by pass 'the preferred reading' (Hall 1973, Puntoni, et al 2006). Even as advertising began to ride the cusp of the postmodern cultural wave, polysemy awarded audiences a greater ability to encode signs with new referents or alter the encoding of established ones and in so doing evade hegemonic meaning. According to this conjecture 'polysemy is a political concept and reception in itself may be conceived of as a political act' (Jensen 1990:58). Baudrillard at times recognizes the polysemous dimensions of signs (c.f. the second-order of simulacra and Watergate). Nevertheless the greater emphasis of his debate disregards the polysemic properties of signs and instead forecloses the indeterminate nature of mass-mediated signs in post-industrial society. As he expresses it:

> ...the universe of the commodity is no longer this one: it is a world both saturated and in involution. In one blow it lost both its triumphal imaginary, and, from the mirror state, it passed in some sense to the stage of mourning. (1994:93)

Integral Reality

According to Baudrillard, the erosion of sign-value in advertising imagery is precipitated by the dissolution of the commodity into 'an immense field of the mockery of signs' (1994:92). In the third-order of simulacra objects have lost their deeper symbolic meaning and advertising is no longer preoccupied with the staging of the commodity. Instead advertising is the prefiguration of the commodity's empty form. This is because the paucity of verifiable signifieds erodes meaningful production 'as an independent entity in the dialogical process of reading' (Sandvoss 2005:829). As this aesthetics of disappearance gathers pace, fractal signs and neutral rhetoric affects an 'asyntatic neubla' which encircles us and in so doing squeezes aside the perplexities of 'belief' and 'efficacy' (Baudrillard 1994:88). And this is reflective of a transition from polysemic to neutrosemic signifying practices. Neutrosemy arises here, because the political economy of the postmodern sign does not offer meaningful signifieds, it offers a 'rhetorical continuum of sounds, signs, signals slogans' (ibid:89). At this hegemonic instance in capitalist production and alienation, 'referential value is nullified, giving the advantage to the structural play of value' (1984:60). In more recent times Baudrillard (2005) identifies communication technology, commodity culture and advertising to have produced an 'integral reality' marking the death of 'reality'. What Baudrillard means here is not that the physicality of reality has ceased to exist. Physical reality abides, but the metaphysics and very principle of reality has deceased. Simulation has undermined the singularity of objective reality and in its wake has arisen 'integral reality', which Baudrillard describes as 'a reality without limits in which everything is realized and technically materialized without reference to any principle or final purpose...whatever' (ibid:18).

Baudrillard claims that this is evident in the transvaluation of advertising from a derivative of the political to a transversal contamination, which dissolves any distinction between the economic and the political. As he expresses it:

> As a medium become its own message (which makes it so that now there is a demand for advertising in and of itself, and that thus the question of 'believing' in it or not is no longer even posed), advertising is completely in unison with the social, whose historical necessity has found itself absorbed by the pure and simple demand for the social: a demand that the social function like a business, a group of services, a mode of living or of survival...whereas formerly it was a sort of revolution in its very project. (1994:90)

Promiscuity and seduction reigns in contemporary politics, such that the field of political economy generates and saturates itself through the auspices of political endeavour. And this leads Baudrillard to pessimistically declare 'Quite simply, there is no longer any social signified to give force to a political signifier' (1983a:19).

Baudrillard's disquietude with a postmodern world of simulation, in actuality concerns a recurring theme in his writings; the dissolution of a symbolic order of embodied relations and its devastation in the West by a simulacrum of self-referential signs. The absorption of the social into an amorphous universe of the spectacle has advanced the eruption and dissolution of the symbolic. In *Simulacra and Simulation* Baudrillard convincingly argues that the generation of simulatory models of the world has become an organizing principle of modern politics. In this context advertising has become an active mode of idealistic practice, largely indistinguishable from its incessant manipulation of commodity-signs. In Baudrillard's analysis of *Absolute Advertising*, the postmodern system of advertising signification is resolutely ironic and marks the absorption of political expression into the reproductive logic of the code. If we assume the code to herald the triumph of depthless superficial forms reproduced by the amplification of spectacle, then the code governing political life, has erased the historical time of ethical progress and replaced this teleology with a depthless entropy; an 'instantaneous form without a past, without a future, without the possibility of metamorphosis' (1994:87). Although the triumph of this superficial form is the outcome of intensities produced by the systemic over production of advertising, it is not really advertising itself that perplexed Baudrillard. But rather, a particular model of promotional culture involving, 'a simplified operational mode, vaguely seductive, vaguely consensual' (ibid). The crucial reversal in this advertising aesthetic is the negation of 'weighty enunciations' expressing value, towards the compression of meaning, as progressive ends become 'transcribed into each other', replacing their content with performative codes. In this form of advertising, all distinction between the real and imaginary dissipates into 'a vestige of sociality hallucinated' everywhere and nowhere in particular (ibid:88).

Absolute Advertising emphasizes the triumph of signifying culture and the systematic reduction of political expression into an illusion of operational signs. For Baudrillard, the irascible power of simulation to implode the social, affects an 'aesthetic of disappearance' (ibid:91) and this intensity of destruction is what perpetuates alienation in capitalist society. As he expresses it:

> Like the signs in advertising, one is geared down, one becomes transparent or uncountable, one becomes diaphanous or rhizomatic to escape the point of inertia – one is placed in orbit, one is plugged in, one is satellized, one is archived – paths cross: there is the sound track, the image track, just as in life there is the work track, the leisure track, the transport track, etc., all enveloped in the advertising track. Everywhere there are three or four paths, and you are at the crossroads. Superficial saturation and fascination. (ibid:91)

It is only in the light of this background, that the problematics of Baudrillard's advocacy for an extra-simulationary grounding of transgressive action becomes apparent. What Baudrillard excludes is the discursive contemporaneity between the formation of a postmodern aesthetics of self and the interrogation of the limits of simulacra. The idea of aesthetics of self recognizes ethics as rooted in the stylization of the self as a dedicated creative project (McNay 2005).

Timely Reflections

Modernity apotheosized the separation of the private sphere from the public realm. The civic body of citizens was enshrined by a common commitment to private property, free market and freedom from the unnecessary interventions of government. Natural rights to life, liberty and property ensconced the strict delineation of the public from the private realm. In the private realm the rational subject has the right to procure and exchange their property without interference from the public realm. The modernist vision of civil society, therefore, distinguishes the social organization of life from its representation in signs and language. To this extent cultural politics presupposes a critical distance from the irreverent signs and linguistic metaphors, which saturate promotional culture and its constituent practices. Modernist cultural politics refers to an external set of practices predicated on a dichotomy separating the consumer and citizen. It is based on a commitment to the material effectivity of representation, which grounds political institutions in truth and shields their ideas from the tyranny of commerce. In the new political era, advertising is instrumental in instantiating the real. Advertising simulacra implodes modernity's differentiation between public and private. Chapter 4 will demonstrate that this has direct implications for an understanding of the degree to which the political economy of the sign penetrates contemporary cultural politics.

In the twentieth century, advances in advertising aesthetics witnessed the emergence of the commodity-sign and this precipitated a revolution in advertising promotions. Many of Baudrillard's observation concerning the second-order of simulacra coincide with the controlled logic of the commodity-sign and its location in the new consumer society of modernist self-identity. In this context, sign-values do not circulate freely and indiscriminately, rather the commodity-sign is defined by the logic of the commodity-form. Goldman (1994) identifies the commodity-form in capitalist societies to effect an universalization of social relations. This process manifests according to a specific logic which imposes 'formalized standards and rules of the market…upon social relations to effect a quantitative, standardized process of exchange' (1994:20). In postmodernity, advertising has exceeded its previous vitality. Contemporary advertising cultures make manifest the absorption of dominant cultural forms into 'instantaneous and instantaneously forgotten' signification (Baudrillard 1994:87). This is because postmodern advertising assumes a daringly peculiar form. Undoubtedly the cavalcades of signs and sounds that saturate our daily lives are splendid; indeed spectacular. In the shopping arcades of the Western metropolis the aesthetic of spectacle gathers momentum as fractal objects, and fractal forms bombard our senses with a single discernable oration 'I am therefore I shop'. But this seduction of the real is achieved through an abreaction. Postmodern advertising is a 'simplified operational mode...in which all particular contents are annulled at the very moment when they can be transcribed into each other' (ibid). It involves the negation of the core dichotomies of modernist thinking. The subversion of differences between real/imaginary, public/private. The dissolution of the classical modernist juxtaposition between subject and object. In modernity such binary modalities garnered 'weighty enunciations' as they protected 'articulated forms of meaning' from the superficialities of culture, and ensured 'that they cannot be translated into each other' (ibid). In postmodern advertising the modernist postulation of representation is displaced by the sheer contiguity, irony and hyper-reality of the postmodern sign.

For Baudrillard, the omnipresence of absolute advertising also precipitates its eventual demise. This is because the ephemerality of postmodern advertising has escaped any claim to advertising as informative communication. In so doing, advertising has forsaken the social dramaturgy, crucial to its establishment as efficacious professional practice. It no longer offers signifieds in which symbolic meaning can be invested. In the postmodern era, an internal revolution has displaced the communicative mode of advertising. Exchange-values overwhelm the system of use-values and now the 'medium becomes its own message', thus generating 'a demand for advertising in and of itself' (ibid:90). As Baudrillard expresses, this is why it is futile to deliberate advertising as communicative language:

> ...because something else is happening...a doubling of language (and also of images), to which neither linguistics nor Semiology correspond, because they function on the veritable operation of meaning, without the slightest suspicion of this caricatural exorbitance of all the functions of language... (ibid:92)

According to Baudrillard, these conditions signify the death knell for advertising, not necessarily as a result of our apathy or even a disinclination to heed the clarion call of consumer culture. Baudrillard observes that today advertising is losing its power to another form of language even more adept at simplifying the social. The language, which mesmerizes Baudrillard, is the digitality of computer science. He observes the micro-processing language of cybernetic systems as exceeding advertising's ability to reduce sociality into abstract self-referential signs. The digital language of micro-processing has overtaken advertising's ability to instantiate a 'rhetorical continuum' of sounds and signs; a three dimensional 'total environment' of simulacra (ibid:89). Baudrillard observes that 'the "thrill" of advertising has been displaced onto computers and onto the miniaturization of everyday life by computer science' (ibid). While Baudrillard's observations, appear consistent with contemporary media developments, his account of the intransigence of the code of signification governing advertising visual cultures insufficiently appreciates transgression as a medium of global advertising cultures. Much of this disregard stems from an insufficiently developed account of a postmodern aesthetics of self.

Chapter 5
Semiology of Time in Postmodern Cultural Politics

In 1998 the children of the St. Valentin Institute were the shining stars of Benetton's global advertising campaign, entitled *The Sunflowers*. The campaign featured photo-realist images taken at the St. Valentin Institute for the disabled, located in Ruhpolding in the southwestern part of Bavaria. The St. Valentin Institute specializes in the education of young children with learning disabilities. With state support the institute provides educational facilities for infants and young adults. The institute's programme is designed to develop capabilities for the integration of residents into mainstream employment, or equivalent structures suitable for adults with disabilities. Consequently, tremendous effort is made to sustain a 'natural, uncontaminated environment' for the young people to live (Benetton 1998). In 1998 these youngsters featured in Benetton's Fall/Winter catalogue. They were also the principle subjects of Benetton's advertising campaign press releases. Indeed, in the advertising campaign's main press release Benetton describe the stars of its *Sunflowers* campaign as follows:

> Little Hildegard wearing a polo neck that proclaims love, a group of children ice skating, young cooks preparing and tasting what they've made with their own hands, Manuela posing with her mother and brothers, little Hansi smiling in the country sunshine with his grandparents, parents and a gentle speckled calf, a team of skiers ready to launch themselves on the snow and fourteen year old Stefan imitating Elvis with his guitar. (Benetton 1998)

Ever since the appointment, in 1984, of Oliviero Toscani as art director, Benetton has endeavored to confirm its image as the new radical face of representational politics.

This chapter's empirical focus is keen to highlight advertising practice. The chapter provides some support for writers who adopt a postmodern approach to representational politics. In this alternative discourse advertising is envisioned to give rise to multiple semantic affects. The multiphrenic intensity of postmodern advertising is capable of becoming a social and material force, foregrounding new meanings of cultural politics and its representation. This chapter is designed to illustrate the political valence of postmodern advertising. I will, primarily be concerned with the materiality of language in Benetton's 1998 *Sunflowers* campaign. My method of research investigation involves narrative analysis and specifically Benetton's use of 'autoethnography' in the promotional literature, which accompanies the *Sunflowers* campaign. It is my intention to make transparent the exhilarating political potential of *The Sunflowers* campaign. I am particularly keen to highlight its innovative aesthetic strategies of language, form and figuration.

Sunflowers – Advertising and Postmodern Representational Politics

Cultural theorists often highlight the controversial images of dying AIDS patients, renegade soldiers brandishing human bones and environmental catastrophe, so as to exemplify the heightened dramaturgy of the *United Colors* brand. An often neglected contribution to the *United Colors* political proselytizing is *The Sunflowers* advertising campaign launched in 1998.

The Sunflowers campaign featured photo-realist images taken at the St. Valentin Institute for the disabled, located in Ruhpolding in the southwestern part of Bavaria. The St. Valentin Institute specializes in the education of young children with learning disabilities. According to the campaign's press release the St Valentin Institute is a 'peaceful community where the usual measure of normality is superseded by a deeper feeling of solidarity between human beings' (Benetton 1998). It would appear that Benetton's *Sunflowers* campaign signifies, an important moment in the St Valentin Institute's promotion of social justice with regards to disability. Indeed, Benetton incorporates, into its press release, the endorsement of Sister Michaela (one of the teachers) who states 'we're all delighted that Benetton decided to do its catalogue in our centre…there was a wonderful atmosphere here; it was really an enjoyable encounter and a sign of friendship' (ibid). Benetton's 'ecumenical' mission (Shapiro 1994) is carried through in the iconoclastic rhetoric of, Oliviero Toscani. He justifies his selection of the St Valentin Institute by quoting a famous Dadaist motto: 'Stupid people see beauty only in beautiful things' (Benetton 1998). The overall idea, expressed here, signifies a direct assault on aesthetic ideals reified in mainstream advertising. Thus Oliviero Toscani's claims that 'it is necessary to look for something deeper than superficial beauty…I've chosen these children, these young people, these families, because they are beautiful in the purest sense of the word' (ibid). Elsewhere in the text, of *The Sunflower* campaign press release, Benetton exemplifies crucial links between 'the politics of representation' and 'the representation of politics' (Giroux 1994:7).

The Sunflower's advertising imagery is replete with aesthetic strategies of form and figuration, intent on disrupting the traditional orders of meaning that sustain the cultural discrimination of disability. The advertising campaign's visual imagery strikingly reveals the use of photojournalistic images to appeal to an aesthetic realm, which too often reproduces crude and unthinking distortions of disability. The visual substance, of the photography, is treated with deliberation so as to avoid composing the figures as objects, distanced from the audience. And this methodology has defined the advertisement's photorealist mode of imagery. Obviously, the scenes of motherhood and youth portrayed in *The Sunflowers* advertising imagery are not a purely immanent reality. Nevertheless the inclusion, of the disabled infant adds a level of realism and credibility to the denotation of the imagery. Thus the advertising figures appear as an analogical photograph. For, it is an analogon to the existence of persons with disability. But the image is also deliberately operating as a challenge to simplistic and one-dimensional representations of disability. And it is this dual functionality, which induces one of several, tensions between the contrived aesthetics of the scene and the image of the infant as a perfect analogon.

Photographic Realism – The Medium is the Message

Roland Barthes (1977:17) describes how the analogical perfection, which defines common-sense readings of photographic imagery, depicts it as 'a message without a code; from which proposition an important corollary must immediately be drawn'. To this extent, the photographic image is distinguished from the imitative arts, which are constituted by a denotative message (the analogical perfection) and a connotative message (cultural meaning systems and values). Commonsense, semiosis attributes this dual system of messages to all reproduction with exception of photographic ones. This is because the validity of the photograph professes a 'mechanical analogue of reality' (ibid:18).

Mechanical reproduction carries with it an acclaimed replicability and objectivity. Thus, photography stands apart from other modes of representation. The mechanistic production of the photography image abdicates responsibility from a subjective artist to the scientific precision of a calculative machine. To this extent photography assumes the mantle of being entirely occupied by the denotative message. In this commonsensical semiotics the simulacrum of the photographic image is so convincing that any reference to a second-order semiological system struggles to communicate something alternative to what is depicted. In his book *Image Music Text*, Barthes (1977) reveals that the assumed, entirely denotative, status of the photographical is a mythical ruse. As he expresses it 'there is a strong probability...that the photographic message too – at least in the press – is connoted' (ibid:19). When considering *The Sunflowers* advertising imagery, Barthes' statement is not particularly revelatory. Surely all advertising imagery, contrives to conceal the relations of production through which commodities are produced and in so doing create need? A powerful process Karl Marx in *Capital Vol. 1* (1887/2003) describes as commodity fetishism. However, *The Sunflowers* campaign assumes a status far beyond the commodity fetishism which clearly governs commercial advertising. Evidently Benetton's concern isn't to promote disability citizenship as a means of extending commerce into yet another sphere of social life. But rather to raise awareness of the disabling affect of social exclusion and stigma. And this is particularly evident in the following extract derived from the press release, which accompanies *The Sunflowers* advertising imagery:

> Because of this, the Benetton catalogue, for the first time, will also become a world-wide communication campaign, presenting some of these pictures in the press and on billboards, in order to help break down the wall that surrounds disability as an extreme form of 'difference' and therefore marginalized because it is incomprehensible, frightening and, even more serious in our image-orientated society, unpresentable. (Benetton 1998)

Connotative Procedures

The Sunflowers advertising imagery has a vested interest in achieving a perfect analogon in its depiction of disability. To this extent the analogon assumes an ethical intention 'as though the analogical were a factor of resistance' (Barthes 1977:20) to the treatment of disability in mainstream media. It is political endeavour, which encourages the imbrication of the analogue with second-order messages, designed to portray a semantic structure replete with metaphorical challenges to conventional representations of disability. To this extent, the viewer is afforded an alternative aesthetic realm in which simplistic one dimensional representations of disability are repudiated. For example, each of the figures in *The Sunflowers* campaigns are proudly positioned, so as to encourage the viewer to decipher the signifiers and signified in terms of complex nuanced aesthetic appeals. The viewer is aided in this veritable decipherment by a stock of recognizable guises in the form of posture (vertical and four-square), gaze (forth-right and unremitting) and style (creative and bold). It is worth making mention to the image's use of photogenia i.e., 'the image itself embellished (which is to say in general sublimated) by techniques of lighting, exposure and printing' (Barthes 1977:23). The exhibition of the subjects through lighting and exposure is clearly designed to affect a degree of naturalistic activity. And this mise-en-scene is obviously depicting the quotidian of leisure as neither pronounced nor disabled by bodily impairment. Indeed the entire *Sunflowers* campaign can be semiotically read in this manner; as each of its photographs come together to form a sequence of similar narratives, what Barthes defines as a 'concatenation' (ibid:24). Indeed all the advertising visual images that constitute *The Sunflowers* campaign, identify a sequence of images, which signify repetition and variation along a similar theme, i.e., a forthright challenge to advertising aesthetics intent on inducing conformity and making invisible the disabled body.

Beyond the Normalization of Political Correctness

Very often, in their intention to demonstrate positive representations of disability, creatives pursue the parallel path of caricaturing disabled people in equally distorted 'positive imagery'. Conversely, *The Sunflowers* creatives avoid some of the excesses of political correctness. They achieve this by obscuring the elements of cliché through the decontextualization of the image. We are provided with little sense of context. How did the individuals in the advertising imagery arrive at this moment in time? Do they know each other? Are they related? Our lack of knowledge militates against us jumping to conclusions, on the basis of acculturated narrative plots and characterizations. For, the image provokes neither a literal reading nor mere verisimilitude. Instead, we are confounded 'by the immediacy of the logic of the spectacle' (Giroux 1994:21). Detached from established political, social and juridical codes, the image invites new meaning and new forms of expressions. But, this suppression of history, also restrains the amplitude of meanings that might be used as a reservoir of interpretation. This is because we experience the a-historical spectacle of the image as individualized subjects. To this extent Giroux is consistent in his claim that Benetton's advertising imagery produces an 'aestheticization of politics' which 'foregrounds our fascination with the hyperreal and positions the viewer within a visual moment that simply registers' the image (ibid:22). And Giroux is convincing in his claim that underlying this visual symbolism is a sense that Benetton offers 'unity' amid a society that denigrates and alienates its 'Others' (ibid:6). Stripped of its historical context the aesthetics of photo-realism astounds our senses as images 'appear to mean something by themselves' (Barthes 2000:143). But what is suppressed in Giroux's discourse is an appreciation of the connotative procedures of text and image.

Roland Barthes in his book *Image Music Text*, argues that 'the press photograph is a message' (1977:15). It is 'an object endowed with a structural autonomy' (ibid). Congenitally it is important to recognize that the configuration of the photograph is not a hermitical structure. For, the photograph is in dialogue with the text, which accompanies it. The communication of information is thus conveyed by the photographic imagery and the linguistic content of the text. Barthes observes that 'these two structures are co-operative but, since their units are heterogeneous, necessarily remain separate from each other' (ibid:16). This is because the image is comprised of shades and shapes, whilst the text is constituted by words. Moreover, the two occupy there own distinctive space. In the context of Benetton's *Sunflowers* campaign the advertising imagery is separated off from the press release; each has a separate identity. Barthes proposed that a semiological analysis should proceed by focusing on each separate structure of the text/photograph dyad. For, it is only when the analysis of each distinct structure is exhausted can the manner in which they complement each other be discerned. And it is at this point that the forms our society uses to ensure normative order are revealed. To this extent Barthes was keen to bestow a technique which enabled observes to grasp the magnitude, detours and implicit functions of signs. With similar intention, my analysis of *The Sunflowers* advertising imagery, in conjunction with its press release, aims to make apparent Benetton's radical intervention into normative representations of disability.

Aesthetic Strategies of Language

Common to each of the *United Colors* campaigns is the circulation of a press release, which foregrounds the advertising imagery. The political valence of this textual artifact is more evident when we consider Barthes' (1977) poignant remarks concerning the semiological dimensions of the text which accompanies press photographs. Firstly, the text has the affect of accelerating the connotation of the image 'with one or more second-order signifieds' (ibid:25). This is in some respects a classic preformulation of how we encounter the press release. By denying specificity Benetton's advertising imagery heightens the 'immediacy of translation' (Barthes 1979:72) and this exacerbates the desire for meaning. In this situation 'it is not the image which comes to elucidate or "realize" the text, but the latter which comes to sublimate, patheticize or rationalize the image' (1977:25). Consequently, while it is certainly evident that Benetton's decontextualized advertising imagery foregrounds an aestheticization of politics as mere spectacle. These conditions accentuate the desire for an informational resource. And this has enabled the text to load 'the image, burdening it with a culture, a moral, an imagination' (ibid:26). It is precisely at this pinnacle frontier, that *The Sunflowers* press release agitates discordance.

To this effect, Benetton's press release, launching *The Sunflowers* campaign, is replete with narrational devices intent on belying commercial intent. Instead of polarizing or erasing the injustices of disability, *The Sunflowers* text features charming figurations of cherubic children. The literary warmth and sincerity invokes a sense of trust, which invites the penetration of advertising aesthetics into the immediacy of our consciousness. But the deliberate authorial style of the press release does more than simply amplify an assemblage of connotations already present in the advertising imagery. The central intention of this chapter is to illustrate how Benetton's use of 'autoethnography' provokes an ethics of self, through which we come to care and are receptive to Benetton's representational pedagogy. To this extent, *The Sunflowers* campaign forms part of the vast assemblage of visual technologies, which subjects, in contemporary societies, have 'to constitute their sense of self as – among other things – citizens of ever expanding communities' (Meijer 1998:247).

Postmodern Advertising and Autoethnography

The visual imagery of *The Sunflowers* campaign is accompanied by an edifying press release. Of real significance is the moral work and ethical practice inscribed into the text of the press release. For the text represents a vehement, and pronounced riposte to attitudes, which fail to recognize disability as the affect of a hostile social environment. To this end, *The Sunflowers* campaign is determined to address, what it perceives as a vital component of the problem, i.e., the omission of experiences of disability from cultural depictions of everyday life. Cultural images of the disabled body, determine far greater than biological fact, the extent to which disabled people fit the profile of citizenship. It is self-evident that the lack of naturalistic cultural representations of experiences of disability 'contributes to the "Otherness" of people with disabilities' (Wendell 1996:43). The absence of disability from, cultural depictions of everyday life perpetuates the misconception that 'their lives are inconceivable to non-disabled people' (ibid). Mainstream media confirms existential fears of the disabled body, by omitting authentic depictions of the prosaic and quotidian experiences of disabled people. A marked absence of these quotidian events provides little challenge to the belief that disabled bodies live disabled lives. The ramifications of this emphasis on functional 'incapacity' are particularly acute when they form the basis for a broader calibration of the individual as 'invalid' (Barnes, et al 1999). Benetton's *Sunflowers* campaign is clearly designed to challenge this medicalization of disability.

The creative intervention, that informs Benetton's *Sunflowers* campaign, is clearly cognizant of the power of culture to construct society's conception of bodily difference. Such concerns are evident in the form and figuration of the press release which accompanies the advertisement's visual imagery. The challenging format and content of the press release displays multiple layers of consciousness connecting the Otherness of disability to the cultural. The ability of the text, to achieve this crucial association is primarily an outcome of its 'autoethnographic' style. Autoethnography is a genre of writing that connects the autobiographical to the cultural. More specifically autoethnography 'is an autobiographical genre of writing and research that displays multiple layers of consciousness, connecting the personal to the cultural' (Ellis and Bochner 2000:739). Autoethnography aims at achieving nuanced expressions of personal experience and thus it works with narratives derived from the interviewee's life world, and also that of the author. Personal experience and meaning interpretation correspond in autoethnography to exactness in quantitative measurement. We as subjects attribute meanings to the world we inhabit and thus the social world is subjectively meaningful. Autoethnographic research seeks to elucidate the Gestalt (patterned meaning) that defines a culture. Integral to these frameworks of understanding are the author's schemes of interpretation. This is to recognize that our 'objects' of observation are 'subjects' which, have the capacity to orientate their actions to the actions of others and adapt competently to the field of observation. Moreover, autoethnography recognizes that social phenomenon display multiple layers of sensibility, connecting the personal to the cultural. Consequently, the meaning of social phenomena is dialectically revealed through the use of one's own 'self' to apprehend the meaning of other peoples' lives.

Similar sensibilities are evident in Norman Denzin's account of 'creative interviewing', He describes this as a 'process in, which two or more persons creatively and openly share experiences with one another in a mutual search for greater self-understanding' (1989:43). Autoethnography is also concerned with sharing biography as 'authors use their own experiences in the culture reflexively to bend back on self and look more deeply at self-other interactions' (Ellis and Bochner 2000:740). This involves a process in which;

> back and forth autoethnographers gaze, first through an ethnographic wide-angle lens, focusing outward on social and cultural aspects of their personal experience; then they look inward exposing a vulnerable self that is moved by and may move through, refract and resist cultural interpretation. (Ellis and Bochner 2000:739)

Suffice to say, autoethnography is inherently reflexive and weaves between affective first person narratives and reflections on culture. Ellis and Bochner (2000:740), observe that autoethnographers vary their reliance, on the research process (*graphy*), on the medium of culture (*ethnos*), and on the self (*auto*). An emphasis on the self (*auto*) locates the researcher at the centre of the process. And an emphasis on culture explores the interplay between a personally engaged self and cultural process. It is in the combined effect of self reflection and cultural reflexivity that autoethnography provides a challenge to the representation of disability in mainstream media. Indeed, theorists have elsewhere identified the power of autobiography 'to expose how dramatically social representations determine the nature of the disabled body and the forms of self-knowing attached to it' (Sieber 2001:737).

It is my view that the press release, which accompanies Benetton's *Sunflowers* campaign, uses autoethnography as an effective tool to expose how dramatically social representations affect social attitudes to disability. The text achieves this by detailing personal observations derived from subjects using their own senses, their own bodies and movements. These subjective observations are articulated by an ambient authorial voice, which eloquently links personal narratives with an outward focus on social and cultural processes. This form of autoethnographic intervention is evident in the following extract derived from *The Sunflowers* press release:

> The catalogue pages show children and youngsters with disabilities, happy and sad like all young people…The photos give an impression of unstrained genuineness, innocence and hope. They are pictures that, as Tamaro emphasizes, 'speak of a world with no defences, no limits, no preconceptions. A world that presents itself by offering the immediacy of its love'. (Benetton 1998)

Evident, in this extract, is the seamless interweaving of concrete action ('the catalogue pages show…') with the narrator's subjective impression ('genuineness, innocence and hope') in conjunction with the introspections of a personally engaged self ('Tamaro emphasizes "speak of a world…"'). The interplay of these layers of personal experience is intended 'as much on examining a self autobiographically as on interpreting a culture for a nonnative audience' (Ellis and Bochner 2000:740). This enables the text to assume a cultural reflexivity in, which it bends back on itself and examines more incisively the self-other interaction, which defines our perception of disability.

Autoethnographic narratives are presented throughout the press release, which accompanies the inauguration of *The Sunflowers* campaign. And these assume distinctive forms. Of real significance is the style adopted in the second paragraph of the press release, for it evokes a personal writing akin to the genre of literary memoir. The paragraph to which I refer reads as follows:

> The new catalogue is called *The Sunflowers* because, in her introduction, the writer Susanna Tamaro tells of how these flowers can be seen from a window of her home and of how she associates 'their stubborn joy and...the docility with which they follow the sun' with the smiles of the children of the Ruhpolding institute. The catalogue pages show children and youngsters with disabilities, happy and sad like all young people, their families, teachers and specialist Institute staff: all together in a sort of extended family, in a peaceful community where the usual measure of 'normality' is superseded by a deeper feeling of solidarity between human beings. 'We're all delighted that Benetton decided to do its catalogue in our centre', said sister Michaela, one of the teachers 'there was a wonderful atmosphere here: it was really an enjoyable encounter, and a sign of friendship'. (Benetton 1998)

In this extract the press release turns towards intimate self-conscious writing. We are informed that the writer Susanna Tamaro created the title *The Sunflowers* based on her observations, from a window of her home, of young disabled children playing. Tamaro describes these 'flowers' as radiating 'their stubborn joy' and admires 'the docility with which they follow the sun' (Benetton 1998). Her experience provides the reader with a platform from which to think of disability as a self–other interaction. By writing Tamaro into the text, as a major character, the text challenges the accepted view that moral work and ethical practice involve objective knowledge. In this sense, Tamaro's memories are personal disclosure and thus the antithesis of political-ethical principles which sanitize disability issues. Thus Tamaro's memories function as moments of self-discovery for the narrator and the reader. For we are encouraged to realize that caring and empathy can be a basis for moral work and ethical practice. And even where the text moves beyond the merely personal, it continues to interweave the intimate with the cultural to suggest that, established metaphors and meanings are narrativized into the exclusion of disability issues from our everyday lives. This form of dialogue involves the interweaving of relational and institutional stories, which 'zoom backward and forward, in ward and outward' (Ellis and Bochner 2000:739). An example of this evocative form of self-conscious writing is evident in the following extract derived from *The Sunflowers* press release:

> The photos give an impression of unstrained genuineness, innocence and hope. They are pictures that, as Tamaro emphasises, 'speak of a world with no defences, no limits, no preconceptions. A world that presents itself by offering the immediacy of its love'. Because of this, the Benetton catalogue, for the first time, will also become a world-wide communication campaign, presenting some of these pictures in the press and on billboards, in order to help to break down the wall that surrounds disability as an extreme form of 'difference' and therefore marginalized because it is incomprehensible, frightening and, even more serious in our image-orientated society, unpresentable. (Benetton 1998)

In this extract the text's autoethnographic gaze moves back and forth, first zooming its ethnographic lens inwards, to embrace Tamaro's memories of disabled children playing and then expanding its focus outward, so as to challenge cultural interpretations. In so doing, 'distinctions between the personal and cultural become blurred, sometimes beyond distinct recognition' (Ellis and Bochner 2000:739). Employing autoethnography, therefore has the effect of connecting a personally engaged self with cultural interpretations of disability. And this highlights the need for embodiment, as a foundation for change and in so doing creates a space for dialogue. As is characteristic of autoethnography the writing recognizes 'the power of emotion as an incitement to action' (Moloney 2007:121). Thus what might initially appear to be gratuitous self-disclosure is in fact altruistic engaged embodiment. Moreover, Tamaro's prose is inconsistent with media messages, which encode impairment with the signs and symbols of disability. Instead we are drawn into an experiential discourse, intent on showcasing the affirming experience of impairment. To this end Tamaro visualizes disability as speaking 'of a world with no defenses, no limits, no preconceptions. A world that presents itself by offering the immediacy of its love' (Benetton 1998).

Timely Reflections

Benetton's revolutionary conjunction of advertising and commerce has clearly agitated the modernist separation of politics from business. The modernist vision of civil society proposed that moral principles can only be considered valid if they are judged to be objective. Above all judicious political intervention should observe a critical distance from commercial intercourse. Conversely, the *United Colors* campaign invites the penetration of commerce into 'the politics of representation and the representation of politics' (Giroux 1994:7). Thus Giroux observes that 'Within Benetton's worldview, the relationships among identity formation, commerce, pedagogy and politics are being re-worked' (ibid:7-8). Giroux is highly critical of Benetton's 'pedagogy of representation' (ibid:8). He argues that Benetton's configuration of cultural politics highlights how moral instruction 'can be conscripted into the service of relations of identity and difference that promote an apolitical egalitarianism veiled in an appeal to international harmony' (ibid:8).

Giroux situates the *United Colors* campaign within a vortex of post-Fordist production and the postmodern condition. He dispels the suggestion that postmodernity merely amplifies existing cultural processes. For, it is clearly evident that the ability of advertisers to galvanize the logic of postmodernism exemplifies a significant disjuncture between modern and postmodern advertising. As Giroux expresses it '...mass advertisers have seized upon the postmodern condition with its celebration of images, its proliferation of differences, and its fragmented notion of the subject...'(1994:60). Giroux describes this insatiable expropriation of postmodern culture as 'often pernicious efforts to rearticulate the relationship among differences, human agency and community' (ibid). To this extent the *United Colors* '...succeeds in its promotional mission: to disguise the political nature of everyday life and appropriate the vulnerable new terrain of insurgent differences in the interests of a crass consumerism' (ibid).

Arguably, Benetton's style of representational politics is unyielding in its tenacious alliance of social conscience and business enterprise. Nevertheless, Benetton's integration of signification with cultural politics is resonant with the postmodern aesthetics of some contemporary forms of politics. Postmodern cultural citizenship proclaims the demise of modernist, stable categories of self-identity. It is precisely this freeing of subjects, from traditional categories of being, that is celebrated in postmodern cultural politics. For it is argued that the demise of modernist structures frees subjects to become 'active agents in themselves, creating and evoking new substances, new social forms, new ways of acting and thinking, new attitudes, reshuffling the cards of "fate" and "nature" and "social reality"' (Ryan 1988:560-561). It is on this periphery that a liberated culture can be dissimulated from the constraints of traditional political institutions. And 'it is on this margin that culture, seemingly entirely autonomous and detached turns around and becomes a social and material force' (ibid). Within this view, we are urged to adopt a more reflexive appreciation of the performative autarchy of consumer culture. Consequently, we are prompted to extend beyond the well practiced claim that Benetton's advertising is merely extending capitalism's relentless commodification of the social in the postmodern age. In the discourse of postmodern cultural politics Benetton's advertising, might alternatively be discerned, as providing new technologies of self from which subjects can reflexively explore the rights and responsibilities of citizenship in postmodern consumer culture. This framework rests on the principle that advertising is 'a means to create positive notions of contemporary citizenship' (Meijer 1998:236).

The chapter examined advertising and the signifying practices of postmodern cultural political. *The Sunflowers* innovative appropriation of auto-ethnography and exemplary visual dramaturgy, invokes a new reinvigorated cultural politics liberated from the rigidities of the modern self. In this discourse cultural signs are 'detached from the ontological, natural and moral foundations that give political, social and juridical institutions their meaning as representations of a prior referent or truth...' (Ryan 1988:561). Cultural signs, alternatively, 'are revealed to be the instruments of the creation of new grounds, new meanings and new institutions' (ibid). Such ideas directly challenge the critical theorists, which argue that the fetishistic properties of advertising imagery corrupt autonomous creative thinking (e.g., Giroux 1994). These texts too often lose sight of the analogous proposition, that consumers discern the content of advertisements as part of the ethics of self actualization. Consequently this chapter has sympathetically explored the extent to which, advertising plays a central role 'as a form of public communication and a setting for the actualization of notions of contemporary citizenship' (Meijer 1998:235).

PART III
Geo-Political Caesura

Fashion chain protest

Source: Photographed by Peter Macdiarmid (23 June 2008). Reproduced with kind permission of Getty Images.

Chapter 6
Political Economy of Citizen Branding

Fair Trade is a revolutionary geopolitical challenge to the exploitative relations of global capitalist accumulation. The Fair Trade movement supports sustainable and ethical relations of exchange and production, in countenance to the socially and economically destructive relations characteristic of global capitalist accumulation. Fair Trade emerged in the 1940s and 1950s as a form of fairer international system of goods exchange coincident with the development regime of the Bretton Woods era (Fridell 2006:9). Established in 1944, the Bretton Woods system inaugurated two international finance institutions, the International Monetary Fund (IMF) and the International Bank for Reconstruction and Development (eventually renamed the World Bank). Alongside these institutions was formulated a development regime orientated towards international market regulation as a primary means for the improvement of the economic plight of Southern producers. Consequently economic development in this era focused on the imposition of international controls on capital flows and international market regulations of commodity production. For its part, the Fair Trade movement in its formative era (i.e., 1940s-1970s) fostered the re-embedding of international trade into a system of equitable economic trade-relations that benefited Southern producers (ibid:10). It was optimistically anticipated that Fair Trade networks would lay the foundations for a new trading system constituted by 'alternative trade organizations that would form part of a new international economic order based on strong state intervention at the national and international levels' (ibid). Although the Fair Trade movement remains committed to the alleviation of poverty and propagation of sustainable development, its strategic approach changed markedly in the 1980s in reaction to the spread of global neoliberalism (ibid). In the neo-liberalized markets and declining capital controls of international trade, it was no longer apposite to promote sustainable development in terms of the state regulation of international markets. In response Fair Trade introduced a new conception of Fair Trade built on voluntaristic trading partnerships between producers and exporters, based upon reciprocal benefits and geared towards the alleviation of poverty. This chapter outlines the political economy of the Fair Trade citizen branding of textile products.

Brand Politics of Fairtrade

The Fair Trade movement supports sustainable and ethical relations of exchange and production, in countenance to the socially and economically destructive relations characteristic of global capitalist accumulation. Fair Trade emerged in the 1940s and 1950s as a fairer form of international goods exchange, and coincident with the 'Trade not Aid' development regime of the Bretton Woods era (Fridell 2006). Established in 1944, the Bretton Woods system inaugurated two international finance institutions, the International Monetary Fund (IMF) and the International Bank for Reconstruction and Development (IBRD). A significant function of the IMF has been to superintend the international monetary system. Axiomatic with this role is the distribution of loans designed to assist member countries manage balance of payments predicaments. The IBRD, from its inception, has operated as an international source of financial assistance. In this capacity, IBRD provides leveraged loans, to developing countries, for capital programmes geared towards the building of social facilities and healthcare infrastructure. As part of the Bretton Woods system and alongside the IMF and IBRD, was formulated an international development regime geared towards the regulation of commodity markets. Critics of free markets, question the unfair affect of capitalist pricing structures for developing countries, particularly as the rise of transnational manufacturing operations shifted the terms of trade against the exports of developing nations (Leclair 2002:949). In these circumstances, developing countries have little option other than, to export a perilously unsustainable increased volume of goods, in order to conserve their level of imports from Western countries. Debt crisis in the poorest countries of Asia and Africa is an undeniable direct outcome of free market profiteering, rather than a coincident occurrence. In an attempt to address this inequity, economic development in the Bretton Woods era, focused on the imposition of controls on capital flows and the institution of alternative systems of international trade, as a means of encouraging sustainable development for marginalized producers, especially in the Southern hemisphere. For its part, the Fair Trade movement in this formative era (i.e., 1940s-1970s) fostered the re-embedding of international trade into a system of equitable economic trade-relations that benefited producers in the developing world (Fridell 2006:10). As a form of ethical goods exchange, this international solidarity movement created alternative trading channels consisting of face-to-face trading relationships between a network of producer cooperatives and commercial importers. It was optimistically anticipated that Fair Trade networks would lay the foundations for new relations of exchange constituted by 'alternative trade organizations that would form part of a new international economic order based on strong state intervention at the national and international levels' (ibid). Consequently, the earliest incarnation of Fair Trade was resolutely committed to market regulation as a means of addressing the exploitative inequities of international trade.

Although the Fair Trade movement remains committed to the alleviation of poverty and propagation of sustainable development, its strategic approach changed markedly in the 1980s in reaction to the global spread of neoliberalism (ibid). In the de-regulated markets and declining capital controls of the global neo-liberal economy, it was no longer apposite to promote sustainable development in terms of state regulated international markets. In response Fair Trade introduced a new conception of fair trading built on voluntaristic commercial partnerships between producers and exporters, based upon reciprocal benefits and geared towards the alleviation of poverty. Thus the objectives of the Fair Trade movement were dramatically re-orientated in the 1980s, as its networks sought to reform conventional markets by harnessing, the mechanisms of neoliberalism, to the ethics of sustainable development. The resulting voluntaristic ethical trading relationships with commercial corporations have been described elsewhere as 'market-driven ethical consumption' (Clarke et al 2007) and an 'enterprise solution to poverty' (Booth and Whetstone 2007).

There are strongly integrated global branding issues mobilized by Fair Trade's commitment to the creation of alternative trading channels between producers, in developing countries, and the set of industrialized countries that constitute the Global North. This is because the Fair Trade movement in the industrialized world, 'has been conducted primarily through storefront operations that offer products from the developing world at subsidized prices' (Leclair 2002:949). In the late 1980s, European ethical consumption movements, in the Netherlands, began labelling their Fair Trade products so as to mark their entry into conventional markets. The introduction of national Fairtrade certification trademarks and labelling schemes was initiated in 1988, by the Max Havelaar Foundation under the enterprise of the Dutch development agency Solidaridad (Fairtrade 2009a). The Max Havelaar labelling initiative was successfully imitated in other markets across Europe resulting in the introduction of the 'Transfair label' (in Germany, Austria, Luxemburg and Italy) and the 'Fairtrade Mark' (in the United Kingdom and Ireland). In 1997 these national labelling initiatives were affiliated under the patronage of the Fairtrade Labelling Organizations International (FLO), which was established in Bonn, Germany for the purposes of creating a global brand, and 'worldwide standards and certification' (ibid). FLO's attempts to formalize the disparate array of national Fair Trade labelling schemes, thus provided the conditions necessary to certify mainstream trading companies wishing to meet FLO's fair trading criteria.

Cognizant of the role of branding as part of the rich tapestry of a neo-liberal market economy, in 2002 FLO launched a new international Fairtrade Certification Mark. Described in Fairtrade literatures as 'The Symbol of a Cheering Person', the visual imagery is said to 'represent the people at the heart of the Fairtrade system – it could be a farmer holding up their products a shopper reaching to purchase, or a campaigner fighting for greater justice in international trade' (Fairtrade 2009).

Principles and Politics of the Fairtrade Brand

Though the international trade in Fair Trade products has grown substantially in the era of neoliberal globalization, this progress has been driven by the meteoric ascendancy of ethical consumerism and its embodied resistance to the exploitative market conditions of global neo-liberalization. Products that carry the Fairtrade label signify a non-governmental approach to sustainable development. This approach exceeds the preoccupation, by conventional ethical trading movements, with the relations of commodity exchange. In contrast, Fair Trade focuses on both the relations of exchange and relations of production implicated in the global chain of commodity-based exploitation. To this end, Fair Trade's cultural politics embodies a commitment to achieving a 'shaped advantage' for the most disadvantaged producers in the developing world. According to the principle of 'shaped advantage', the cultivation of a nation's institutional capacity, social capital, and economic infrastructure, can assist low-income producers advance their position in the global economy. As Fridell (2006:13) expresses it, Fair Trade is partly:

> an exercise in enhancing the 'social and cultural capital', 'institutional capacity', and marketing skills needed for poor producers to enter the global market under more favourable conditions by taking advantage of a socially conscious 'market niche' in Europe and North America.

In the Fair Trade marketplace, microeconomic adjustment occurs at the local level through skill transfer programmes and the construction of cooperative trading networks. Indeed, The Fair Trade Foundation's advocacy for producers to organize into cooperatives reinforces the widely held view that it is 'a project that assists local organizations in developing the capacities and infrastructure required to help offset the negative impact of globalization' (ibid:9).

While the imperative of market competition and unethical business virulently prevail globalized neoliberalism, Fair Trade advances an alternative trading model. Fair Trade countenances competition with its promotion of cooperative exchange relationships. Fair Trade interrogates market dynamics through its commitment to social justice, economic security and environmental sustainability. It is also a movement that seeks to rehabilitate the very infrastructure of the global economy, at the same moment in history, that economic liberalization reforms (such as the Export Processing Zones discussed earlier), are being championed by the World Bank and the IMF. Right now, in many places around the world, the Fair Trade movement represents a corporate form that although existing within the market, harnesses the mechanism of the market to support alternative and just trading relations in the face of globalization. While this suggests a paradox, in which the market is used to reform global capitalism, Fair Trade's ethical principles directly challenge market capitalism's emphasis on self-interested material benefit. Indeed, and paramount to these ethics, is Fair Trade's commitment to overcome the fetishistic properties of commodities. Commodity culture indulges in the mysteries and dissimilitude of capitalist production, and in so doing, veiling the contradictions and exploitative relations that are axiomatic with capitalist accumulation (see Chapter 4). To its credit Fair Trade directly challenges capitalist relations of both production and exchange. And, in terms of cotton production, persuading the modern consumer of the Fair Trade message has provided a good testing ground for Fair Trade's brand of ethical politics. Let's briefly consider these ethics for they are the platforms that make the Fair Trade ethical brand value transfer, in the global textile production commodity-chain, credible.

Cotton: Tackling Poverty and Empowering Producers Through Trade

It is estimated that in excess of a 100 million small-scale farming units, are engaged in cotton production in 70 countries around the world (Fairtrade 2009f). It is also evident that the world price for cotton is in sustained decline, indeed the current value of cotton is 'only a third of what it was in the early 1980s' (ibid). Pressure to address the dwindling market value of cotton has precipitated aggressive counter measures from Western exporters. Of particular concern has been the United States' agriculture and trade practice of 'dumping', its cotton exports onto international markets at prices so artificially low that they fall below the costs of production. This has the affect of depressing global prices and inequitably reducing the profit margins of cotton farmers in developing nations. The plight of these cotton producers is further exacerbated by the preferentially subsidized cotton industry in the United States, European Union and China. It has been observed that 'cotton producers in the United States receive approximately US$4.2 billion in government subsidies…[and that]…This is equivalent to the value of their entire crop' (ibid). Unjustifiably, US cotton producers can, therefore afford, to 'dump' an estimated three quarters of their yield onto the international market. The inadequacy of current international systems of commodity support works to further impoverish the plight of cotton producers in developing nations, for they seldom receive government subsidies. Against this background, Fair Trade offers cotton farmers in developing nations a root for 'tackling poverty and empowering producers through trade' (ibid).

Fairtrade's ethic of equitable trading is manifest in its register of ethical standards necessary for each stage in the commodity-chain to achieve Fairtrade certification and for cotton products to bear the Fairtrade Mark. In 2004 FLO separated into two non-governmental organizations, entitled FLO International and FLO-CERT. FLO International is a worldwide network of national Fairtrade labelling initiatives ascribed authority to licence the Fairtrade certification trademark on products. In the UK the Fairtrade labelling initiative is administered by the Fairtrade Foundation, which was established in 1992 by a coalition of charities, including Oxfam. In the United States licence for the Fairtrade certification mark, to appear on products, is provided by TransFair. These and other national labelling initiatives are also responsible for promoting Fair Trade in their territory.

For products to be branded as Fairtrade their conditions of production and exchange need to meet Fairtrade standards designated by FLO International. These standards are formulated through consultation with Fairtrade stakeholders (i.e., actors directly or indirectly involved in the Fairtrade commodity chain). Linked to a more nuanced perspective on the capacities of ethical consumption to combat extreme poverty, the Fairtrade standards are not simply a set of benchmarks for the achievement of socially responsible production and exchange. Rather, the Fairtrade standards are purposely designed to 'support the development of disadvantaged and marginalized small-scale farmers and plantation workers' (Fairtrade 2009b). Fairtrade achieves this objective by ensuring that its standards address three key areas of sustainable development; social, economic and environmental. As Fairtrade express it, the key objectives of its standards are:

> [1] ensure a guaranteed Fairtrade minimum price which is agreed with producers, [2] provide an additional Fairtrade premium which can be invested in projects that enhance social, economic and environmental development, [3] enable pre-financing for producers who require it, [4] emphasize the idea of partnership between trade partners, [5] facilitate mutually beneficial long-term trading relationships, [5] set clear minimum and progressive criteria to ensure that the conditions for the production and trade of a product are socially and economically fair and environmentally responsible. (ibid)

In its efforts to make manifest these standards, Fairtrade engages with smallholders working in cooperatives (or other small-scale democratically controlled organizations) and employers that hire paid labourers. For these stakeholders, the gains of entering the Fairtrade network include vastly improved labour process, market access, financing and distribution. Fairtrade explicitly excludes capitalist exploitative working environments i.e., those based on alienation and the expropriation of surplus value. And there are important criteria instituted to guarantee that workers control the labour process.

It has been observed that in modern corporations 'accountability' and 'transparency' enter the organizational repertoire with the dedication and relevance of buzz words. Conversely for the Fair Trade movement accountability and transparency are 'cornerstones of Fair Trade business operations' (DeCarlo 2007:53). 'Collective self-management' directly opposes capitalism's propensity for competitive and exploitative relations of production (Hudson and Hudson 2004:137). Even more significantly, producer cooperatives operate as an intermediary between the market and the producer, thus creating an incentive for small farmers to collaborate their efforts to control the terms of trade. In this respect cotton farmers have very specifically and directly benefited. In 2004, Fairtrade established its first minimum prices for cotton; which is designed to vary depending on the producing region. Fairtrade is prideful of the fact that the minimum prices for cotton 'always cover the costs of sustainable production' (Fairtrade 2009g). So as to provide a crucial safeguard against the reported 'dumping', by the US, of cotton onto the world market, the minimum price that the buyer of Fairtrade cotton is obliged to pay the cooperative, is guaranteed in the producer organization's export contract. Moreover, Fairtrade stipulates that the 'minimum prices for organic cotton are set 20 per cent higher than the Fairtrade conventional minimum prices' (ibid). Negotiations between the producer and purchaser can exceed this amount; nevertheless it is initially set at a level which guarantees that the producer organization achieve a price that covers the cost of sustainable cotton production (ibid). Providers are therefore insulated from adverse changes in market conditions; most especially the catastrophic affect on farmers of markets plummeting below a sustainable level. Moreover, Fairtrade stipulates that certified cooperatives are paid market price for their cotton, when the market price exceeds the Fairtrade minimum price; thus providing a further shield from exploitative trading conditions. And in addition to these safeguards, cotton farmers can if they request, receive 'pre-export lines of credit', which can be 'up to 60% of the purchase price' (ibid).

In addition to securing these terms of trade, the Fairtrade standards stipulate that producers are paid a Fairtrade Premium. The Fairtrade producer network of small family cotton farms (organized into cooperatives) and democratically governed farms specializing in Fairtrade cotton farming, can expect that 'buyers must pay a Fairtrade Premium of US$ 5 cents per kilo of Fairtrade seed cotton' (ibid). Fairtrade producer organizations are required to democratically decide how to invest, this premium, in community development programmes. This often involves selecting amongst, e.g., healthcare infrastructures, education, improved processing facilities and environmental initiatives. The latter development theme is further advanced by the FLO sustainable development standard, prohibiting cotton farmers from the use of agrochemicals.

It is the responsibility of FLO Standards Unit to fix the premium 'in the same way as the minimum price and [the premium] remains the same, even if the producer is paid more than the minimum price for the product' (2009e). And these two mechanisms of instituting fair trading, collectively, are successful in generating long term, reliable relationships between producer and buyer. Thus Fairtrade achieves more than the guarantee of a fair price for producers. It enables the development of a stable and sustainable system of trade and sediments into trading relations based on mutual respect and collective rather than self-interest.

Given that importers pay a premium for commodities, so as to guarantee fair prices and equitable social relations for producers, it is vital that Fairtrade's ethical branding has a way of competing in the ethical products marketplace. The Fairtrade brand relies significantly on its process of producer certification and trade auditing, as a primary mechanism for building integrity into the Fairtrade brand. FLO-CERT is integral to this process, as is evident in the following abbreviated account of Fairtrade's producer certification and trade auditing:

> Producer certification. FLO-CERT…is responsible for the inspection and certification of producer organizations and traders against Fairtrade standards… Trade auditing. As well as producer organizations certified, for a product to carry the Fairtrade Mark, all the traders in the supply chain must be registered and their products certified. All processors and exporters in the producer country must have their products certified by FLO-CERT. The products of importers and companies outside the producer country are certified either by FLO-CERT or by the local Labelling Initiative. The Fairtrade Foundation is responsible for certifying Fairtrade products in the UK…*Producer certification process*. The certification process begins with a written application to FLO-CERT from the producer organization, often with the support of a trading partner such as the exporting company. If the application is accepted, the organization will be

> physically inspected against Fairtrade standards by a regionally-based FLO-CERT inspector. The inspector's report is then considered by the FLO-CERT Certification Committee which takes the final decision on whether or not to certify. Producers are issued with a certificate valid until an agreed date (usually for one year), and this certificate can be renewed following re-inspection. (Fairtrade 2009d)

FLO-CERT's independent inspections of producers and traders are intended to sediment integrity into the ethics of the Fairtrade brand. Inasmuch as each participant along the commodity chain is committed to the creation, and maintenance, of a viable community of associated producers, this constructs a 'socialised market' that underscores the ethics of the Fairtrade brand (Elison 2002). To this end Fairtrade cotton production appears to be an effective answer to the problems posed by the inequitable imbalance of power that pervades the global capitalist production of this commodity. Indeed, the Fairtrade brand is remarkably convincing and few would question its ethical integrity. And this appears to have impacted positively on the sales of Fairtrade cotton products. In the UK, sales of Fairtrade certified cotton products have increased dramatically from a tentative £0.2m in 2005, to a substantial £4.5m in 2006; with further increases in 2007 to £34.8m, and in 2008 to the staggering heights of £77.9m (Fairtrade 2009h).

Textile Production: Tackling Poverty and Empowering Producers through Trade

The manufacturing of garments is one of the most globalized industries in the world. The global expansion of industrial garment production traces a legacy of trade globalization and economic restructuring. It has been observed that from its inception in the 1950s through to the 1980s the industrial production of garments migrated 'out of the West; first to Japan, then to Asian newly industrializing countries, particularly Hong Kong, South Korea, and Singapore and finally to almost every country around the world' (Ho et al 1996:390). This was partly due to developing countries appropriating intensive industrialization programmes after World War II. In conjunction with this, and encouraged by the International Monetary Fund's liberalizing orthodoxy, developing nations adopted export-oriented industrialization strategies linking them to global apparel manufacturing chains. Indeed, the rapid development of industrialization in developing countries, coupled with the liberalizing agenda of the World Trade Organization (WTO) has encouraged many developing countries to become Export Processing Zones (EPZ). This invariably involved abandoning a strategy of state sponsored 'import substitution' (which focused on the substitution of imported goods for their domestic production), for a system of export-led production. Export production involves the liberalization of home markets, adumbrated with such lucrative incentives as tax relief, access to cheap labour markets and the lifting of regulatory restrictions on importing/exporting (Ho et al 1996:390). In recent years these inducements have encouraged the direct foreign investments of trans-national corporations (TNC). Moreover, it can be observed that the simple technology, relatively inexpensive start-up costs, and scale economies have favoured clothing production in EPZ locations where labour expenditure is low. Analysts concur that clothing production within these EPZ is mostly carried out by females, indeed 80 per cent of workers within the industry are female and the vast proportion of this labour-force is unskilled or semi-skilled labour (Dicken 2007:256). The level of skill coupled with insidious gender divisions of labour often mean that 'such workers are easily hired and fired and have no protection over their working conditions' (ibid:258). Even where countries have a legal minimum wage 'in some cases this is lower than a realistic minimum living wage' (Allwood et al 2006:x).

It was through these channels that China and South East Asian countries established subcontracting relations with brand retailers in offshore zones and guaranteed trajectories in international markets. The immense success of textile producers in the developing world encouraged Western countries to instigate the regulation of global trade and in so doing shield their indigenous textile and apparel producers. From 1974 to 2005 China and South East Asia's textile and clothing export was regulated by the Multi-Fibre Arrangement (MFA), which was an international quota agreement 'imposed by developed economies...to attempt to protect their own manufacturing interests' (Allwood et al 2006:8). An unintended consequence of MFA was the geographic dispersion, in the 1970s, 1980s, 1990s of textile and clothing production, to developing countries. This was largely a result of producers in Far East countries quota-hopping, subcontracting or relocating to countries that either had low or unspent quotas (EMCC 2004:3). As a result countries such as Sri Lanka and Indonesia were able to develop a significant textile and clothing export industry. Many feared that with the abolition of MFA these export markets would struggle to compete with 'those countries offering the lowest labour costs, most efficient production and most developed transportation and telecommunications infrastructure' (ibid).

MFA officially ended on 1 January 2005, thus guaranteeing free-market conditions. By 2006 the clothing and textile industry had increased to approximately 7 per cent of world exports (Allwood et al 2006). It is estimated that 3.5 million tonnes of clothing and textiles stream through the UK each year – approximately 55kg per individual (ibid:2). The UK exports 1.15 million tonnes of clothing and textiles per annum and employed around 182,000 workers in 2004 (ibid). UK output stabilized in 2007, despite a decrease in exports (Textile Intelligence 2008). China has one of the fastest growing internal markets and the largest proportion of world trade. Over a quarter of the world's production of textile and clothing is in China, which has expanded exports by over 19 per cent (Textile Intelligence 2008). It is estimated that by 2010 China will galvanize 50 per cent of the world's textile and clothing exports (EMCC 2004:2). This increased market share is largely due to China's access to mobile and low-cost labour force (workers earn about US$120 per month) coupled with technological advances and economies of scale in domestic production (ibid). Impressive growth rates are also evident elsewhere in South East Asia. In 2004 textile and clothing production in Thailand constituted approximately 4 per cent of GDP (Pangsapa 2007:5). In 2005, textile exports from Thailand increased by 6.5 per cent to US$2,011 million (Osaka Senken 2005). Similar increases in textile export volumes are evident in Japan and South Korea (Textile Intelligence 2008).

Time/Space Compression and Technological Innovation Trends in Global Supply-Chain Management

It is generally accepted that much of the rapid increase, in the export volume of textile and garments, is directly related to technological innovation. Evidence of this relation is provided by indicators of productivity formulated by the American Apparel Manufacturers Association (AAMA). Using a physical measure of the ratio of output to labour inputs, the AAMA in 1976 compared the productivity rates of six standard garments between 1960 and 1975 (Bheda and Singla 2003). Direct labour productivity indicators for the category of garments defined as shirts, reveal that with the optimal technology available, a manufacturer in the 1960s could produce 3.76 shirts per hour and 5.50 shirts an hour for the year 1975 (ibid:13). In 2003 shirt manufacturers in Hong Kong reported productivity indicators of 20.87 pieces per hour (ibid). Assuming that these units were formulaic all-year-round styles with a limited range of colours, increased productivity would mostly have been due to the adoption of lean supply-chain networks. It is generally accepted that 'the focus of lean supply management is the elimination of all waste, including time, to enable a level schedule to be established' (Bruce, Daly and Towers 2004:153). Lean supply chain strategies, emphasize lean inventory management facilitated by collaborative planning, forecasting and replenishment. Operating conditions for 'lean retailers require rapid replenishment of products and shipments need to meet strict requirements in terms of the delivery times, order completeness and accuracy' (ibid). Taken together these practices are geared towards sequencing and moderating the manufacturing process in order to limit lead times. And the resulting time/space compression has significant affects for the retail and manufacturing process as Abernathy (1999:9) expresses it:

> Product proliferation and shorter product cycles, reflected in ever-changing styles and product differentiation, contribute to general demand uncertainty for both retailers and manufacturers, thereby making demand forecasting and production planning harder every day. In a world where manufacturers must supply an increasing number of products with fashion elements, speed and flexibility are crucial capabilities for firms wrestling with product proliferation, whether they are retailers trying to offer a wide range of choices to consumers or manufacturers responding to retail demands for shipments. (Abernathy, et al 1999:9)

In recent years it has become evident that the power over retail production has become concentrated with buyers; that is the retailer and the corporate brand merchandiser. It is increasingly evident that retailers own the stores where products are sold and the key to retail profitability depends on flexible cheap responsive production. As Dicken (2003:329-330) expresses it:

> The highly concentrated purchasing power of the large retail chains gives them enormous leverage over textiles and garments manufacturers. When the market was dominated largely by the mass market retailers, demand was for long production runs of standardized garments at low cost. As the market has become more differentiated and more frequent fashion changes have become the rule, manufacturers are forced to respond far more rapidly to retailer demands and specifications. Under such circumstances, the time involved in meeting orders becomes as important as cost.

Advances in electronic communication enable manufacturers to map consumer preferences through Quick Response (QR) management systems. According to Cammett (2006:32), QR systems were first defined in 1985 and are so named because they dramatically accelerate the supply chain 'by speeding up order fulfilment and enabling retailers to respond quickly to shifting consumer tastes through improved information and merchandise flows'. Cammett suggests the emergence of QR, in the 1980s, coincided with an extended period of flagging sales and the imperative for retailers to stimulate consumer engagement in fashion. Formulating multiple fashion 'seasons', was a central marketing strategy, designed to invigorate relatively inelastic demand. It has been observed that 'by the mid-1980s, the standard six-month season was fragmented into at least six fashion cycles and many retailers began to offer about twelve distinct product lines annually' (ibid:31). Innovations in marketing management systems needed to be matched by retailers and their suppliers. It became imperative that retailers maintained perpetual turnover, limited costs, advanced forecasting and delivery reliability so as to curtail inventory risk. In and of themselves these innovations are insufficient without concomitant changes in manufacturing. Retailers needed suppliers that could keep pace with the relentless demands to replenish fast-selling stock. It has become increasingly evident that the manufacturing solution to accelerated apparel production cycles is, outsourcing. But to who's cost?

Feminized Flexibility and Spatially Disaggregated Textile Production

Textile and apparel production has for decades involved offshore outsourcing. Current patterns of outsourcing are driven by constricting 'fast fashion cycles' and the necessary imperative to reduce operating costs and increase flexibility. In the information-age economy flexibility equates with technological innovations and corporate strategies geared towards the global disaggregation of apparel production

(Odih 2007b). To this extent the apparel industry has been characterized as an innovation of the New International Division of Labour (NIDL). According to this argument, flexibility has replaced the sequential operation of Fordist production. And advances in global transportation and communication technology networks have enabled the synchronization of international manufacturing processes. Competitive manufacturers have technologically advanced logistics and transportation functionality. The resulting economies of time/space have accelerated the production cycle reducing 'the cost of working capital by increasing the velocity of its use' (Dicken 2007:259). For example, electronic point-of-sale (EPOS) technologies now enable manufacturers to distribute directly to retail outlets. In so doing, manufacturers reduce the cost of time lag produced by the protracted time delay caused by the need to communicate orders from the manufacture's distribution centre to the retailers distribution centre and then to the retail store. Consequently multinational corporations can out-source segments of the manufacturing process to whichever regions, throughout the world, that can deliver the most cost effective combination of capital and labour. For many analysts these technological developments are 'helping companies to differentiate their product offerings and to operate more efficient supply chains' (Textile Intelligence 2008). But the transnational disaggregation of supply-chains has precipitated exploitative conditions of work and employment.

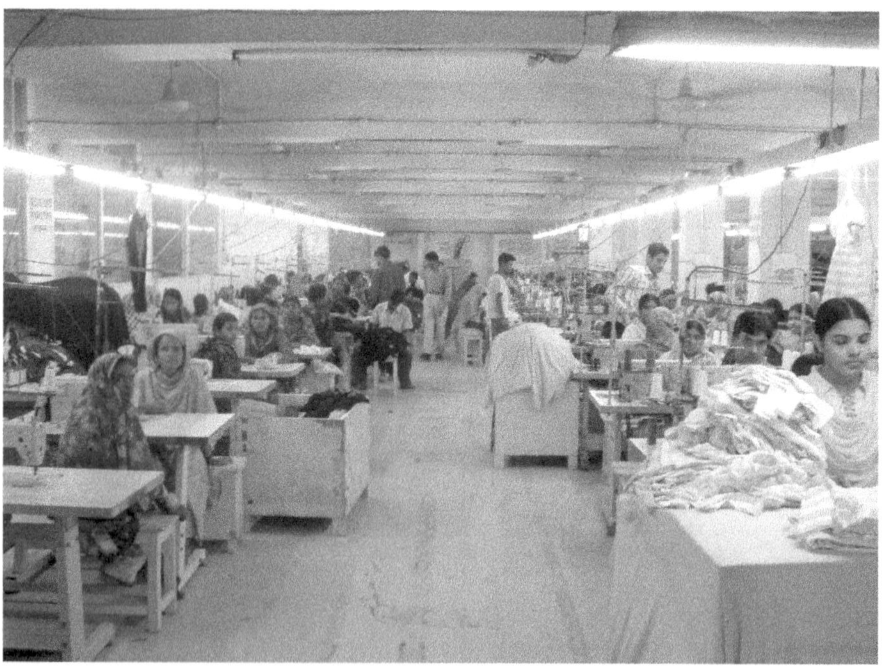

Figure 6.1 Garment workers in a textile factory

Source: Photographed by G.M.B. Akash. Reproduced with kind permission of War on Want.

Official statistics suggest that globally, the workforce involved in textile and clothing production was approximately 26.5 million in 2000 (Allwood et al 2006). A substantial amount of evidence indicates that these statistics under-estimate the scale of informal labour. The rapid development of industrialization in developing countries, coupled with the liberalizing agenda of the World Trade Organization has encouraged many developing countries to become Export Processing Zones (EPZ). Analysts concur that clothing production within these EPZ is mostly carried out by females, indeed 80 per cent of workers within the industry are female and the vast proportion of this labour-force is unskilled or semi-skilled labour (Dicken 2007:256). The level of skill coupled with insidious gender divisions of labour often mean that 'such workers are easily hired and fired and have no protection over their working conditions' (ibid:258). It has been observed that a vast proportion of these workers are 'employed in contravention of government employment regulations' (ibid). Even where countries have a legal minimum wage 'in some case this is lower than a realistic minimum living wage' (Allwood et al 2006:x). Each month new and more sensational accounts of the 'sweatshop' working conditions experienced by women and children in EPZ are beamed into our lives. Global media diligently broadcast the disgraceful working conditions of unregulated sweatshops, where unions are prohibited and unscrupulous factory owners demand excessive working hours, with little regard for unions, health and safety protection or fair wage.

Global fashion labels exacerbate these conditions. This is because their histrionic public renunciation of 'sweatshop' practices contradicts their adoption of lean supply strategies that subject manufacturers and buyers to intractably contracting delivery times. Consequently, while it might be the case that a global brand will stipulate the codes of practice to which its supplier must adhere, the constricting delivery times of global supply chains put pressure on suppliers to subcontract production. It is here that the clothing industry's low levels of capital investment attract small scale manufacturers producing garments in small plants with limited technology and high labour intensity. The labour force in these less regulated provinces of the global supply-chain is often poorly educated, unskilled women and children. And these exploitation conditions of labour have been the focus of resilient cultural politics. Some evidence of this fervent political activity is detailed in the following discussion of the UK clothing retail brand Primark.

Primark and the Fashioning of Cultural Politics

In April 2007 the launch of Primark's flagship retail store in London's Oxford Street, was besieged by hundreds of stampeding bargain-hunters. The furore fulfilled retail expectations as the flagship store sold in excess of a million garments in its first ten days. In September 2007 Primark opened an 85,000 sq ft store in Liverpool, which also attracted frenzied consumers and enthusiastic media coverage. In the financial year 2006/2007 Primark's outlets galvanized 4.8 million sq feet of prime retail selling space (Primark 2008:1). It has 177 stores across Ireland, Spain and the UK and employs in excess of 25,000 people (ibid). Primark's advertising model targets fashion percipient under 35s offering this cohort 'high quality fashion basics at value for money prices' (ibid:3). Half of its sales are in womenswear and a quarter of total sales focus on menswear and childrenswear. It has achieved a myriad of industry awards including 'High Street Retailer of the Year', 'GMTV High Street Fashion Award', and 'Value for Money Award' (Primark 2008a:1). Primark attributes its success to 'super competitive prices', which are the result of 'technology, efficient distribution, supply and volume buying' (ibid). Its brand communicates a commitment to 'value-based' 'high-quality'. In 2006 the UK's prospering budget clothes market was worth an estimated £7.8bn (McVeigh 2007).

In recent years Primark has increased its share of this market. According to the research firm TNS Worldpanel Fashion the largest market share of the budget clothing market is held by Marks and Spencer with 11.4 per cent, followed by Primark, which achieved an astonishing 2 per cent volume share leap in 2008 to 10.1 per cent (quoted in Drapers 2008). Primark's market share is hotly pursued by Tesco with 9.3 per cent and closely trailed by George at Asda with 8.7 per cent (ibid). Other high-street brands have prospered less favourably, Matalan's market share descended from 5.7 per cent to 5.1 per cent. Thus at a time when other retailers are facing merchandising challenges, Primark's 'Look Good Pay Less' philosophy has seen its market share dramatically increase. Market analysts predict that by 2009, Primark will be taking £1 in every £10 spent on clothing in the UK, thus eclipsing its rivals to become Britain's biggest mass-market clothing retailer (McDougall 2008).

Part of Primark's success has been its ability to beguile both the avaricious high-street shopper and the reactionary fashionista. Realizing that contemporary retail profits are driven by speed-to-market dividends, this Irish conglomerate specializes in satiating the Western consumer's un-remitting appetite for cheap up-to-the-minute fashion. Its buying and merchandising teams located in Reading and Dublin 'travel internationally to source and buy up-to-the minute fashion basics that best reflect each season's key fashion trends' (Primark 2008:3). Evidently, significant effort is invested in 'developing a corporate culture that is dynamic, resourceful and customer focused and that accurately reflects the product offering' (ibid:2). However, in June 2008 *The Observer* newspaper exposé and a BBC *Panorama* investigation threatened to unravel Primark's seraphic allure. It was claimed that Primark's trademark affordable fast-fashion masked 'the brutal reality of a supply chain that sees children as young as 11 sewing T shirts which costs shoppers just a few pounds to buy on high streets across Britain' (McDougall 2008:1). It has been further reported that the price war between the three retailers Asda, Primark and Tesco has relentlessly driven down the price of clothing to less than 50 per cent that of other clothing retailers (McVeigh 2007:2). The acute cost margins, demanded by powerful retailer dominated supply-chains, place immense pressure on manufactures.

Violations in working conditions appear to be directly linked to the unremitting speed-to-market demands made by retailers. It has been observed that 'even the Ethical Trading Initiative have agreed that the buying practices of the UK retailer sector are driving wages and having a negative effect on working practices' (quoted in McVeigh 2007:2). Similar assertions were made in the wake of the media expose regarding Primark's manufacturing links with three suppliers in Southern India. It was claimed that 'the investigation found that in the refugee camps of southern India young children had been working long hours in foul conditions to sew designs' (McDougall 2008:2). Media reporters declared this practice as part of 'the race to the bottom' a phrase coined to describe the ebullient practices of 'international retailers employing developing world contractors, who cut corners to keep margins down and profits up for western paymasters' (ibid:4). On 16 June 2008 Primark announced that it had sacked three of its clothing suppliers located in Southern India. It admitted that these suppliers 'had sub-contracted the embroidery and sequin work on a small number of designs to unapproved sub-contractors without Primark's consent or knowledge' (Primark 2008c:1). Furthermore, Primark confirmed that 'the sub-contracting involved home working and in some instances children were also found to be working at home' (ibid). Such practices are in direct contradiction with Primark's voluntary membership of the Ethical Trading Initiative's (ETI) voluntary code of conduct. As part of its membership the company 'has committed to monitoring and progressively improving working conditions in the factories that supply Primark's merchandise' (Primark 2008b:2). To this effect Primark defended its actions by issuing a statement on Ethical Trading stating that:

> The company's system of audits has to date proven very robust and extremely effective at raising supplier standards. Primark uses third party audits, including SGS, a world-renowned audit firm. As a result, Primark takes this lapse in standards in its embroidery supply chain very seriously indeed. In addition to sacking the factories at fault, Primark has taken urgent steps to further tighten control of suppliers. The company has already summoned suppliers to meetings to reinforce the stringent trading standards it expects and to emphasise that it will not tolerate this type of sub-contracting. (Primark 2008c:1)

In addition to the expedient sacking of the three southern Indian suppliers, Primark withdrew from sale the embroidered garments at the centre of the allegations. It claimed that the affected garments represented only 0.4 per cent of the company's world wide sourcing and thus, we are lead to assume that a speedy disposal would quickly stem their circulation. In a further act of contrition it was announced that a 'Primark Better Lives Foundation' would be established and that this will 'provide financial assistance to organizations devoted to improving the lives of young people' (ibid:2). Primark confirmed that 'in addition to the initial funding Primark is endowing the Foundation with any profits made from the affected garments' (ibid:3). It is generally recognized that Primark's expeditious actions ensured that its reputation was restored and brand kudos repaired long before many of its consumers even realized a contravention had occurred. But, even if we accept Primark's resolution to never breach its own code of conduct, can we as consumers be truly confident that high-street stores are ethically satisfying our desire for up-to-date affordable fashion? Such reflections are ever more pertinent when we consider the multitude of high-street brands that are regularly accused of achieving fast-fashion through exploitative sweatshop conditions. For an increasing number of consumers, these concerns are assuaged by the expanding markets of Fair Trade clothing products.

Fair Trade Clothing Commodity Chain

> The Fairtrade Foundation exists to secure better market and trading opportunities for disadvantaged farmers and workers, as well as to raise awareness and promote action amongst UK citizens and consumers. By allowing certification of composite products, the Foundation can maximise huge new opportunities for producers, deepen the positive impact that Fairtrade can have for them, as well as increase the range of products available to consumers, enabling people to integrate Fairtrade purchase into their regular shopping habits. (Fairtrade 2009i)

In its efforts to extend the Fairtrade market place, mainstream textile manufacturers and high street retail brands are being invited to embrace Fairtrade as part of their business ethics and corporate responsibility. A vehicle for achieving this aspect of the Fair Trade neoliberal voluntaristic model (discussed earlier), has required that Fairtrade, amends its labelling policy so as to redefine what is meant by 'composite products'. According to Fairtrade publications, it is presently the case that a vast proportion of its products (e.g., tea, coffee, chocolate etc.) are 100 per cent Fairtrade, however an increasing portion of its commodity range contain a composite of Fairtrade and alternative sourced materials. While welcoming this form of vertical integration, Fairtrade has also been keen to ensure the ethical integrity of these products. Consequently, Fairtrade has developed standards based on FLO policy and specifically relevant to composite products. To this end, the Fairtrade Foundation in 2008 established a composite policy on cotton. Launched on 17 December 2008, this policy stated that 'filled and blended products which are made from less than 100 per cent Fairtrade cotton can now be certified' (Fairtrade 2009f). This agreement has significantly extended the repertoire of textile products that can carry the Fairtrade Mark. Fairtrade cotton products now include 'multiple textiles' (e.g., garments layered using cotton and synthetic fibre) and 'multi-component textile' (e.g., duvet comprised of cotton casing and feather interior). These developments in the classifications of composite products have further contributed to the Fair Trade success story. It is estimated, by the Fairtrade Foundation that the range of certified products made from Fairtrade cotton is in excess of 1,500 (ibid).

The numbers of retailers cooperating with the Fairtrade Foundation in the sale of cotton products saw an increase to 20 in 2008 and at least 10 include the biggest UK high-street names. Given that the Fairtrade Mark is not designed or intended to certify companies, a focus by high street brands, on Fairtrade ethical commodities is a shrewd mechanism for attracting ethically conscientious consumers. It would appear as though the numerous recent high-street conversions to the Fairtrade brand have, at least partially, been motivated by a market change towards a more virtuous arena of commodity production and exchange. But this observation is somewhat overshadowed by the scale and scope of resources that, key high-street brands, are investing into the ethical production and exchange of textiles. For examples, in January 2007, the UK based retail giant Marks and Spencer, launched an ethical business initiative entitled *Plan A*, which set out 100 organizational and business trading commitments to be achieved over five years. *Plan A*, is part of Marks and Spencer's 'Look Behind the Label' campaign, which was launched in 2006 and according to Marks and Spencer 'was the first major campaign by any retailer to focus on the way products are sourced and made' (Marks and Spencer 2009b). Both initiatives tap into the growing appetite amongst UK consumers for Fairtrade products. Evidence of this growing consumer market is reinforced by research commissioned by the Fairtrade Foundation, and carried out by the research company TNS CAPI OmniBus. Based on a sample of 25,000 households, the TNS CAPI OmniBus market research into brand recognition found that 72 per cent of those surveyed had recognition of the Fairtrade Mark (Fairtrade 2009i). And this brand awareness appears to be translating into increased retail sales. The Fairtrade Foundation estimates that, the UK retail sales of Fairtrade products increased from £286.3m in 2006 to approximately £712.6m in 2008; a vast proportion of this retail sales increase was constituted by certified cotton products (Fairtrade 2009h). Awareness of these escalating market trends are reflected in press releases issued during 2006-2009, by Marks and Spencer's then chief executive Sir Stuart Rose. In a press release staged to coincide with the launch of the campaign 'Look Behind the Label' Sir Stuart Rose stated that 'Customers want good value, but they care more than ever how food and clothing products are made' (quoted in BBC 2006). He went on to state that:

> Launching Fairtrade cotton builds on our innovative work in areas such as sustainable fishing, reducing fats, salts and additives in our food and banning harmful chemicals from children's clothing. (Sir Stuart Rose quoted in BBC 2006)

In 2006 as part of the 'Look Behind the Label' campaign, Marks and Spencer became the first prominent high-street retailer to sell an extensive Fairtrade clothing range. By the time Marks and Spencer launched its *Plan A* ethical business programme in January 2007, other leading high-street brands such as Topshop, Gap, Katharine Hamnett and American Apparel were also offering ethical products. It is evident that several of these high-street brands, as with Marks and Spencer, have signed up to the Ethical Trading Initiative (ETI), which is an alliance of commercial companies, trade unions and voluntary organizations dedicated to ensuring that:

> retailers, brands and their suppliers take responsibility for improving the working conditions of the people who make the products they sell. (ETI 2009)

In accordance with this corporate responsibility, Marks and Spencer's £200m ethical programme, *Plan A*, has as one of its 100 ethical commitments the pledge to convert '20 million clothing garments including £5 plain t-shirts, women's strappy vests and oxford shirts to "Fairtrade" cotton – equal to 10% of all M&S cotton use' (Marks and Spencer 2009). Aggrandized by a national press and digital media campaign, the five year ethical trading plan has already proved lucrative for Marks and Spencer. According to its own estimates, in 2008/2009 Marks and Spencer sold in excess of 8 million Fairtrade certified cotton garments and home products (ibid). Marks and Spencer estimate that in '2008/09 Fairtrade certified cotton usage was equivalent to around 2,600 tonnes or 4% of all the cotton [it] used' (ibid). The cotton is sourced from Fairtrade small-scale farming networks, mostly located in India. Thus it goes without saying, that Marks and Spencer's Fairtrade certified cotton products are produced and exchanged in accordance with practices that establish social justice and also promote sustainable development. And this is evidently, also the case for Topshop, Gap, Katharine Hamnett, American Apparel and other leading brands that have signed up to the Ethical Trading Initiative. With regards to leading high-street retailers that have Fairtrade clothing ranges, an important additional initiative is, the retailer Debenhams alliance with Sir Steve Redgrave's UK based charity FiveG. In 2008 Debenhams' existing Maine New England brand teamed up with Sir Steve Redgrave' FiveG men's leisurewear label to launch a new men's wear collection made from Fairtrade certified cotton. The FiveG, Maine New England brand label is exclusively available only from Debenhams. According to Debenhams' promotional material:

> In addition to the economic support that Fairtrade cotton gives to the lives of cotton growers and their families in West Africa and India, FiveG also raise funds for the Steve Redgrave Trust. (Debenhams 2009)

Nevertheless, while it is irrefutably the case that the business ethics of these brands has impeccable integrity, for a growing amount of academics this mode of mainstreaming the Fairtrade brand 'is a way of reforming a broken system, instead of replacing it with a more just alternative' (DeCarlo 2007:61).

Chapter 7 argues that part of the problem resides with the model of the ethical consumer embedded within the advertising practices employed by these and other brands, which have launched Fairtrade clothing ranges. The complexity of this problem is clearly apparent when we examine the main constructs of the ethical consumer, reproduced in Fair Trade advertising knowledges and promotional practices. It is evident that four dominant constructions of the ethical consumer presently, pervade the advertising campaigns of commercial textile retailers of Fairtrade certified cotton. These constructs are as follows: (1) the consuming subject as a postmodern political entity, (2) the information processing consumer sovereign, (3) the self-reflexive consumer citizen, and (4) the ontologically ethically 'relational' consumer. While each of these constructs has interesting genealogies, it is even more significant to examine their (mis)articulation into advertising and brand promotions associated with the selling of textile garments made from Fairtrade certified cotton.

Conclusion

In recent decades there have been unprecedented transformations in capitalist economies of time and space. Capitalism is now global capitalism and its mode of production 'shapes social relationships over the entire planet' (Castells 2000:471). It is evident that the more advanced the capital the 'more extensive the market over which it circulates' (Marx 1973:539). And the more expansive 'the spatial orbit of its circulation' the greater the necessity for capital to strive for the 'annihilation of space by time' (1973:539). The global expansion of capitalism is consistent with the necessity for advanced capital to speed 'towards the universal development of the forces of production' (1973:540). But the universalizing proclivity of capital 'drives it towards dissolution' (1973:540). This is because 'capital is a limited form of production' (1973:540). Nevertheless global capitalism continues to increase the velocity of circulation and multiply its value. This suggests the need to re-examine capital's political economy of time and its relation to the global distribution of labour.

New technologies enable transnational corporations (TNC) to setup decentralized production networks, by outsourcing to different parts of the globe (Peterson and Lewis 1999:403). Such forms of 'vertical disintegration' (Sayer 1989) coincide with a drive towards export-oriented industrialization by Third World nations. Neo-liberal economics is convincing in its claim, that developing nations can only prosper once they have harnessed their economies to the international division of labour. Indeed the integration of Third World labour markets into the global economy has been axiomatic to a revolution in information technology and the emergences of global textile production. And these flexible forms of decentralized production have precipitated spectacular advances in the velocity of circulating capital. In global capitalism, profit is generated, increasingly in decentralized production networks embedded 'in the timeless space' of the 24hr global economy (Castells 2000:472).

In the 24hr global economy decentralized production intensifies the systematic use of subcontracting as a mechanism for 'deskilling, wage depression and labour intensification' (Taplin 1996:192). This is because subcontracting establishes patterns of decentralized production, in which firms can 'export labor intensive and low valued-added tasks' to other firms integrated in a global hierarchical network (Taplin 1996:192). In such circumstances flexibility means the speedy delivery of goods in working conditions in, which skill development is seen as a costly and time consuming luxury. Women are the primary workers in the global economy's 'vertically disintegrated' (Sayer 1989) methods of production. This is because the technology used in decentralized production depends on the existence of labour market differentiation among the skilled and unskilled (Balakrishnan 2002). Firms downsizing and subcontracting to smaller operators create 'labour market segmentation between firms in networks' (Taplin 1996:192). The extent to which this segmentation translates into gender segregation depends on the distribution of skills between the sexes and the resilience of prevailing labour law. Given that the compulsive logic of 'vertical disintegration' is towards the automation of high skilled, high paid jobs the emerging labour processes tends towards a blend of work intensification and low skilled batch production (1996). Consequently work in these markets 'is inevitably seen as part of secondary labor markets, with low pay, few benefits, and little job security' (1996:197). Women are particularly over represented in these labour markets. This is because skill distribution is often differentiated by sex. And on a global scale most subcontracted, labour intensive work is carried out by women, who have historically been marginalized from skill development training. Of particular concern is the experience of women in the global textile industry.

The first part of the chapter examined how technological innovations in clothing production are integral to the proliferating fashion cycles, which have since the 1980s dictated women's fashion. It is evident that the prêt-a-porter glitz and short product cycles of women's' fashion has disconcerting trajectories in the spatial disaggregation of global textile production. The pathology of speed has been the emergence of an 'ungovernable world economy' (Hirst and Thompson 2002:6), in which trans-national corporations (TNCs) face little threat 'from any viable political project' (ibid). Writers invariably forestall the helplessness of workers against the inexorable agility of multinationals. It has been observed that 'in some countries the right of workers in the sector to form associations (unions) to represent their concerns in collective bargaining is suppressed' (Allwood et al 2006:x).

Women and children are typically the exploited victims of the industry's speed-to-market, global supply chains. Indeed, it is argued that the clothing industry epitomizes many of the intractable gender issues precipitated by global trade and production. Fashion retailers' demands for speed and flexibility, in conjunction with low costs; have propelled the global clothing industry to capitalize on 'agile' supply chains (Bruce and Daly 2004). Key to 'agile' manufacturing and supply is rapid response methods fuelled by advances in transportation and communication. These processes increase the agility of multinationals enabling them to disperse, components of the supply chain, to whichever regions of the world that can guarantee profitable combinations of capital and labour. According to this argument labour-intensive processes are disaggregated from capital-intensive activities, 'and dispersed to low-wage areas around the globe, while capital-intensive activities remain in heavily capitalized industrialized nations' (ibid:364). Thus, the global disaggregation of the textile supply-chain has become paramount to the manufacturing drive towards competitive cost effectiveness. But central to this process has been the outsourcing of component-production overseas or the relocation of manufacturing to countries with lower employment costs. For low-income developing countries the outsourced textile-apparel supply chains in the Western hemisphere provide propitious inroads for export diversification. There is significant evidence to sustain the argument that retailers are achieving competitive advantage by exploiting a model of feminized 'flexibility' and 'just-in-time' delivery, so as to transfer the costs and risks of business on to producers 'who in turn pass them on to working women' (Hocking and Wilding 2004:4). Cultural political action has sought to the challenge situation of women within global clothing production circuits. Of particular significance here is the geopolitical revolution of the Fair Trade movement.

Chapter 7
Aesthetics as the Transgressive Politics of the Self

This chapter critically examines constructions of the consumer in advertising for Fairtrade labelled products. It is evident that advertising for Fairtrade labelled products is engaged in an extensive project geared towards dismantling the isolation endemic in commodity capitalism and replacing this with signifying practices that 'differentiate on the basis of production processes rather than (or at least, in addition to) the characteristics of the final product' (Hudson and Hudson 2003:421). This is accomplished through an appeal to the socio-symbolic realm of advertising communication. As part of the sale encounter, the advertising of Fairtrade labelled products 'attempts to increase the visibility of long-term and global economic connections involved in day-to-day economic transactions through the education of the final consumer' (ibid). The evocation of relationality is predicated on imaginatively extended moral geographies, rather than an attempt to build concrete social connections between the consumer and the producer. Thus, given the non-sentient properties of inanimate objects, any attempt to instantiate sentimentality with the object will require that the consumer activates imaginative faculties, 'when understanding themselves to be interacting, not with the product per se, but with the producer of that product' (Watson 2007:271). In contrast to the hedonistic myopic object centred relations that pervade capitalist commodity culture, advertising in the Fair Trade sector is geared towards creating a 'producer-oriented cognitive frame' (ibid).

The advertising of Fairtrade labelled products involves 'meaning making as a situated material practice, where an "economy of semiology" constructs an emotional…bridge between cosmopolitan consumers and "Third World" producers' (Dolan 2008:311). Advertising, here, operates as a technology of reconnection, semiotically invoking a cultural political dialogue based on the symbolic representation of the production process rather than the 'fungible, abstract utilities of conventional global commodity chains' (ibid). The first part of this chapter critically examines the translation of Fair Trade ethical philosophy into the practice of advertising Fairtrade labelled products. Central to this translation has been an advertising focus on the self-reflexively ethical consumer citizen as a primary market driver. Clearly influenced by academic writings within the sociology of modernity, advertising knowledges reproduce the emergence of a mode of subjectivity and self-identity tied to late modernity and the imperative of self-actualization, constituted against a background of dynamic change and unparalleled globalization. Consumers of Fairtrade labelled products are individually, and collectively, engaged in re-moralizing reflexive practices against the backdrop of global transitions and transformations. Indeed it is evident that the consumer is, increasingly being constituted, in this aesthetics of secular ethics, as a self-reflexive political agent in a global movement for redistributive justice.

In its advocacy of a 'beautiful life' (Foucault 1991:349), advertising is promisingly relevant to the promotion of:

> a very strong structure of existence, without any relation with the juridical per se, with an authoritarian system, with a disciplinary structure. (Foucault 1991:348)

This is to envisage the possibilities of advertising beyond its conventional imbrications with the problem of discipline and the 'techne of the self' (ibid). In a way it is to imaginatively conceive of advertising in terms of the 'techne of life, the techne tou biou, how to live' (ibid). This, in turn, leads to an appreciation of advertising as belonging among the cultural inventions and 'treasury of devices, techniques, ideas, procedures, and so on, that cannot exactly be reactivated, but at least constitute, or help to constitute, a certain point of view which can be very useful as a tool for analyzing what's going on now – and to change it' (ibid:349-350). In many respects advertising, therefore, represents a modern secular ethics no longer grounded in externally imposed political, social and economic structures. Rather, advertising's celebration of a 'de-traditionalised' (Giddens 1993) postmodern consumer culture provides a novel source of encouragement for academic scholars, that seek to rid us of the idea 'of an analytical or necessary link between ethics and other social or economic or political structures' (Foucault 1991:350). It partially succeeds in this advocacy, most especially through its promotion of life as a tapestry for the application of art. In the resolve for a more beautiful life, advertising has clear resonances with Foucault's concept of 'the bios as a material for an aesthetic piece of art' (ibid:348). And this idea relates to the fact that the aesthetics of advertising visual cultures tend not to associate ethical problems with externally imposed quasi-juridical structures. Rather, in the advertising of Fairtrade labelled products the consumer is presented with what Foucault describes as the 'problem of personal choice, of aesthetics of existence' (ibid). Indeed Foucault observed that 'From the idea that the self is not given to us, I think that there is only one practical consequence: we have to create ourselves as a work of art' (1991:351). In this articulation, ethics is transformed into a creative activity and ontologically bound up with the making of 'ourselves as a work of art' (ibid:351). Advertising, in this sense forms part of the struggle against the production of ethics that attempt to normalize populations and governmentalize individuality. The kind of relationship that advertising invites us to have with ourselves calls upon an aesthetics of ethics 'which determines how the individual is supposed to constitute himself [sic] as a moral subject of his own actions' (ibid:352). And this implies a unique mode of subjectification, in which individuals are invited to recognize their moral obligations through commodity culture. So political power is exercised by the consumer through an aesthetics of, self-forming, ethical activities in, which the consumer applies deciphering techniques 'in a choice about existence' (ibid:361). As part of 'making one's life into an object...for a *techne* – for an art' (ibid:362), the consumer becomes committed to the application of aesthetic values to 'one's life, one's existences' (ibid).

This chapter asks important critical questions about the possibilities of transgressive aesthetics in the context of ethical marketing and advertising practice. Elsewhere, it has been recognized that organizational practices, such as those deployed by the Fair Trade network Traidcraft, 'serve to make available policies, campaigns and especially repertoires of ethical consumption to consumers in such a way that the resultant opportunities help to govern the consuming self, in a process whereby caring for distant others is achieved through the cultivation of care of the self' (Barnett et al 2005:36). Moreover, Barnett et al (2005:34-36) are concerned with identifying how:

> Organizations such as Traidcraft serve to articulate the contexts of consumer choice, and to mediate consumer conduct by providing opportunities and practice devices through which ethical conducts can be shaped...The resulting repertoires of ethical conduct require continual re-articulation and reinforcement as particular devices suffer from performance fatigue on the part of both consumers and the representative. However, the organizational mediation by Traidcraft and its local representatives provides a constant regulation of ethical consumption in these spheres, and provides many consumers with their principal channel of acting ethically in relation to Fair Trade.

While in agreement with Barnett et al's (2005) Foucauldian account of the cultivation of the self, it is my contention that reference to Traidcraft in terms of providing 'a constant regulation of ethical consumption' (ibid), conceptually hinders an analysis of consumers as agents who dynamically create expressions of ethical disposition. This is because Barnett et al (2005) insufficiently recognize the importance Foucault (1991:362) attributed to 'the principal work of art' in the making of a secular ethics committed to the idea that 'one must apply aesthetic values' to 'one's life, one's existence'. Drawing on Foucault's (1991) concept of the 'aesthetics of existence' this chapter has as its primary focus the possibilities and problematics, of a secular ethics of how to live (*techne tou biou*), presented by the advertising aesthetics employed by commercial retailers that have been licensed to label their produce with the Fairtrade Mark. The chapter will theoretically deconstruct the knowledges that inform advertising practices employed by Fair Trade retailers, so as to evaluate the extent to which their advertising aesthetics enable the making of a self, which is unencumbered by the quasi-juridical, authoritarian dedicates of normalizing technologies.

Mapping the Subject of Fair Trade

The political rationalities of Fair Trade branding, advances a whole new dynamics of advertising communication and this is directly impacting on the order of economic and cultural life. In post-Fordist production the utility-value of the commodity is subordinated to the sign-value. And this is part of a wider shift from a society based on production – and the manufacture of goods with inherent use – value – to a society based on consumption and the circulation of signs. Consumer society is defined by aesthetic practices and it concerns the perfusion of signs throughout everyday life. As Baudrillard (2003) observes, in the consumer society goods are consumed for their sign-value rather than to satisfy a pre-existing physiological need. In consumer societies the consumption of goods resides at the core of existence, as we become ever more reliant on the symbolic meanings of material possessions, to create a sense of self-identity. To this extent, consumerist societies progressively transform consumption from an enjoyment or pleasure to 'the duty of the citizen' (ibid:80). This raises important issues regarding the cultivation of the self in the context of an increasingly sophisticated genealogy of ethics articulated through advertising truths and the self-reflexive cultivation of identity, a process that Knights and Study (1997) describe as the 'marketing of the soul'.

Technologies of Signs and the 'Marketing of the Soul'

In the writings of Michel Foucault we are challenged to interrogate liberal humanist ethical virtues. For more than twenty years of his academic career Foucault was concerned to trace a history of the manifold ways in Western culture 'that humans develop knowledge about themselves...' (1988:18). In a text entitled *Technologies of the Self*, Foucault clarifies very important conceptual tools necessary for decoding liberal humanism and rendering it intelligible as a system of knowledge with, 'specific "truth games" related to specific techniques that human beings use to understand themselves' (ibid). These techniques, assume four major forms of 'technologies' and each mode constitutes a vehicle of practical reason. The first is 'technologies of production', which permit the transformation of natural objects into resources for the mobilization of human interests. Foucault recognizes synergies here with dialectical materialism, 'for instance one sees the relation between manipulating things and domination in Karl Marx's *Capital*, where every technique of production requires modification of individual conduct – not only skills but also attitudes' (ibid). The theme of transformation is evident in, 'technologies of sign systems', the second mode of technology that humans use to organize social life and develop knowledge. Foucault describes this technology as modes of discourse and discursive practice, 'which permit us to use signs, meanings, symbols, signification' (ibid). In his book *Discipline and Punish*, technologies of sign systems enter into a matrix of practical reasoning that functions in a manner, which exceeds a positivistic ontology of the image as representing a mirror of the world that merely needs decoding. Instead, technologies of sign systems are integrated into penal practice and in so doing operate as modes of administration, regulation and discipline. Technologies of sign systems work in conjunction with the third specific technique that human beings have created to know themselves, i.e., 'technologies of power'. Foucault's focus here is premised on elucidating technologies that 'determine the conduct of individuals and submit them to certain ends or domination, an objectivizing of the subject' (ibid). These objectifying technologies form a recurrent theme in *Discipline and Punish.* And in Foucault's (1998, 1992, 1990) later work technologies of power, are detailed in conjunction with the fourth of Foucault's technologies i.e., 'technologies of self'. These permit individuals to voluntarily carry out practices 'on their bodies and souls, thoughts, conduct, and way of being, so as transform themselves in order to attain a certain state of happiness, purity, wisdom, perfection or immortality' (ibid). According to Foucault, these four technologies often operate collaboratively, 'although each one of them is associated with a certain type of domination' (ibid). That is to say that each involves a regime of training and modification in the individual, directed not merely at the acquisition of skills but also in the development of attitudes. It is my intention to apply, Foucault's (1988) concept of sign technologies to render intelligible advertising in terms of an, aesthetics of ethics articulated in the promotion of Fairtrade labelled textile products.

Liberal Humanism and the Reflexive Cultivation of the Self

Foucault's (1982, 1991) interrogation of the production of truth, examines liberal humanist ethics in terms of practices concerned with the regulation of bodies in time/space, the government of conduct and the formulation of the self. Thus, Foucault is sceptical of the 'theme of liberation' in so far as it refers 'back to the idea that there does exist a nature or human foundation which...found itself concealed, alienated or imprisoned in and by some repressive mechanism' implying that 'it would suffice to unloosen these repressive locks so that man can be reconciled with himself' (1988a:2 cited in Simons 1995:47). For, 'the man described for us, whom we are invited to free, is already in himself the effect of a subjection much more profound than himself' (Foucault 1991a:30). In so far as power is embedded in the 'social nexus', subjectivity exists in reciprocal relation to power. Individual self consciousness is configured through the exercise of power within, which apprehensions of personal identity come to be engendered. As Foucault expresses it:

> ...the individual is not a pre-given entity which is seized on by the exercise of power. The individual, with his [sic] identity and characteristics, is the product of a relation of power exercised over bodies, multiplicities, movements, desires and forces. (Foucault 1976, in (ed.) Gordon 1980:73-74)

Accepting that power is multiple and ubiquitous thus involves appreciating that there can be no 'true' essential subjectivity to be liberated from power. To this extent, power is positive in its existence and productive of self-identities along with their regimes of truth; rather than manifest in 'interdiction and operating by repression and deduction' (Dean 1994:156). Within the scope of this micro-physics of the self, Foucault depicts liberation movements, and their quest to emancipate subjects from the abuse of arbitrary power, as in fact bound up with disciplinary technologies directed at both constraining and enabling the power of subjection. For, it is evident that power/knowledge directly imply the preservation of the liberal humanist ethical autonomous self, against constraints that would undermine its sovereignty. Liberalism's propensity is not freedom but unfreedom as it binds us ever more 'tightly to our subjectivities through our efforts to liberate ourselves' (Simons 1995:47). Indeed, the historical emergence of liberalism, also marks the ascendancy of disciplinary technologies that make possible the accumulation of capital and 'a political take-off as the traditional, ritual, costly, violent forms of power were superseded by a subtle, calculated technology of subjection' (Sheridan 1994:157). The two processes were interlinked as technologies of sign systems transformed a knowable population into an electorate, mandated with the power to elect a representative form of government, while the liberal postulation of the autonomous self was an effective disciplinary technique accelerating the circulation and accumulation of capital. More significantly this suggests that as a mode of entrapment, technologies of sign systems are based on an antimony of totalization and individualization.

Initially conceived, as a quest for the freedom of the sovereign individual from arbitrary power, the advancement of liberalism has been accompanied by the evolution of disciplinary technologies and normalization processes (Foucault 1982:213-4). The object of these technologies is the 'soul', to be understood as an entity, unlike in the Christian theological sense as a supernatural quality 'born in sin and subject to punishment' (Foucault 1991a:28). Rather, Foucault's account of the soul, regards it as a substantive category, 'born...out of methods of punishment, supervision and constraint' (ibid). As he expresses it:

> This real, non-corporal soul is not a substance; it is the element in which are articulated the effects of a certain type of power and the reference of a certain type of knowledge, the machinery by which the power relations give rise to a possible corpus of knowledge, and knowledge extends and reinforces the effects of this power. On this reality-reference, various concepts have been constructed and domains of analysis carved out: psyche, subjectivity, personality, consciousness, etc.; on it have been built scientific techniques and discourses, and the moral claims of humanism. (ibid:29-30)

It needs to be emphasized that Foucault is not assuming that the real human subject and, object of intellectual knowledge has been substituted for a non-corporal soul. The micro-physics of power permeates the entire society and operates through the soul on the body (Sheridan 1994). Thus 'a soul inhabits him and brings him to existence, which is itself a factor in the mastery that power exercises over the body. The soul is the effect and instrument of a political anatomy; the soul is the prison of the body' (Foucault 1991a:30). Suffice to say, that the soul is the product, and instrument, of technologies of: production; sign systems; power and the self. The raison d'étre connecting these technologies is the exercise of power upon the body, 'the body and its powers and capacities which are to be transformed in the processes of individualization, and the body and its desires which are transformed in the construction of the self' (Marshall 1996:114). It is my contention that advertising practices and knowledges geared towards the promotion of ethical consumption are resonant with Foucault's observations regarding the cultivation of the soul and the self-reflexive production of an ethical identity. Both processes of self-characterisation raise very important issues regarding subjectification and 'the way a human being turns him- or herself into a subject' (Foucault 1982:208). The following sections outline four mainstream models of the ethical consumer. These constructs are as follows: (1) the consuming subject as a postmodern political entity, (2) the information processing consumer sovereign, (3) the self-reflexive consumer citizen, and (4) the ontologically ethically 'relational' consumer.

Consumer or Citizen? The Consuming Subject as a Postmodern Political Entity

The concept of 'consumer citizen' expresses a systemic disjuncture in the classical philosophical demarcation separating the role of the economic and that of citizenship. In the classical liberalist writings of Thomas Hobbes (1588-1679) and John Locke (1632-1704) the viability of the civic body, is based on the freedom of private individuals to pursue their interests and depends on the cultivation of 'self-government'. Hobbes' (1651:1968) account of man in *Leviathan*, reduces human essence to the pursuit of self-gratification and the proprietorship of one's substantive capacities. Similarly, Locke's *The Second Treatise on Civil Government* sets out an account of individualism that corresponds with a virtue of independence embodied in productive labour. Though the earth is common to all human beings, the fact that 'every man has a "property" in his own "person"', presupposes an inscriptive enclosure of the commons in, which 'labour being the unquestionable property of the labourer' produces objects that 'no man but he can have a right to' (1690:1986:20). In short, the broad classical liberalist hypothesis is that all individuals possess the right to property, the existence of which establishes a dichotomy between the public and private realm. The social contract is based on an agreement; limiting government to the public realm of commercial enterprise while also protecting, the private realm of social life, from excessive government intrusion (Faulks 1998:16). Consequently, citizenship in classical liberalism 'involves the balance between the liberty enjoyed by autonomous individuals, including rights they hold to protect that liberty, and the authority of the state, including duties it can demand from citizens to ensure its survival' (ibid:17). In this rational, autonomous, egoist model of the citizen, 'there is no sense of duty to others other than to respect the fact that all humans will act in a similarly self-interested way and their right to do so should be respected' (ibid).

In citizenship studies it is traditionally the case that the classical liberalist formulation of the 'citizen' is counterpoised with the civic republican critique. The civic republican model of citizenship, as espoused by Jean-Jacques Rousseau (1712-78), begins with the premise that human beings are inextricably tied to community. The prominence of the sovereign individual and its abstraction from communitarian obligations is anathema to the civic republican model. In the *Social Contract*, Rousseau (1762/1968) sets out the polemic of the 'social pact'. Here he argues that man (sic) in the state of nature reaches a level where the obstacles to survival exceed the separate resources of any one individual. Once this inevitability arises the only solution to self preservation, is to unite their separate powers 'and act in concert' (ibid:14). Having forged a collective, it becomes tacitly admitted and recognized that 'no individual associate has any longer any rights to claim; for if rights were left to individuals, in the absence of any higher authority to judge between them and the public, each individual...would soon demand to be his own judge in all; and in this way the state of nature would be kept in being, and the association inevitably become either tyrannical or void' (ibid:15). But, 'since there is no associate over whom he does not gain the same rights as others gain over him, each man recovers the equivalent of everything, he loses, and in the bargain he acquires more power to preserve what he has' (ibid). The resulting political community is positive, for its citizens 'share in the sovereign power' (ibid) and their rights have responsibilities. By extension, the 'public possession' of goods is, according to Rousseau, 'more irrevocable than private possession' (ibid:22). This is because; one can never completely guarantee the right of the initial possessor of private property against the rights of the community. Thus civic republicanism substitutes classical liberalism's idea that individuals possess natural rights to life, liberty and property with a belief that the community accepts into its collective possession the property of an individual. Hence the main role of politics is to transform individuals into citizens by eliminating self-interest and dependence on possessive individualistic acquisition. In this form of political community, citizens:

> begin to unite before they possess anything, and spreading over a territory large enough for them all, proceed to enjoy it in common, or, alternatively, divide it among themselves either equally or in shares determined by the sovereign. In whatever manner this acquisition is made, the right of any individual over his own estate is always subordinate to the right of the community over everything; for without this there would be neither strength in the social bond nor effective force in the exercise of sovereignty. (Rousseau 1762/1968:24)

This aspiration leads to Rousseau's well known bifurcation separating economics and civic status. The propensity for individuals, in modern societies, towards possessive individualism amplifies the degenerative potential in the state of nature for man (sic) to pursue self-interest as opposed to 'uniting their separate powers' (ibid:14). Consequently the salvation for modern society resides with the collective activities of citizens located in, inter-dependent communities, and uninhibited by, the self-interested pursuit of materials possessions.

Clearly, the private acquisition of material possessions is a key subject of contestation separating classical liberal and civic republican theories of citizenship. However, this neat distinction between economics and civic virtues becomes particularly strained when we consider their poignant unification in twentieth century social democratic political practice. For example, William Beveridge, in 1942 inscribed into the architectural design of the UK's welfare state system, monetary structures which guaranteed its contingency on the financial obligations of citizens. All citizens have the right, to at least a minimum level of free welfare provision, but they also have the responsibility of regular financial contributions to national insurance. Alongside this view, emerged a conception of the social rights of citizenship enshrined in the work of T.H. Marshall (1950). The profound belief that the Nation State could deliver social security and prosperity, underpinned Marshall's advocacy for a conception of civic status based on the provision of a minimal level of material and non-material capital to all citizens (Needham 2003:12). Thus Marshall's social dimensions of citizenship ascribe to the citizen rights and responsibilities tied to material capital. And in so doing, Marshall has contributed profoundly to contemporary debates on public life especially with regards to the inclusion of culture as a dynamic of the civic. In recent times advertising has featured prominently in this debate.

Of particular interest here, is the direct relevance of 'advertising's construction of so-called civic capital' (Meijer 1998:236), to advertising campaigns promoting textiles made with Fairtrade certified cotton. Press releases derived from the web-pages of important players in the UK's Fair Trade retail market sector, provide important empirical resources detailing advertising activities in the context of Fair Trade ethical branding. Indeed the press or news release is often wrongly dismissed as a mundane artefact of organizational communication and self-publicity. Conversely it is recognized here, and elsewhere, that 'as communication to external groups, press releases do impact on the formation of corporate image, and do reflect retailers strategic decision-making processes' (Whysall 2004:31). This is because the press release performs a crucial act of translation; converting organizational ideals into the important symbolic capital of brand image. Thus the role of the press release, as a mode of stakeholder engagement, in the advertising of Fairtrade labelled products, offers partial evidence of meaning production in the formation of material practice.

Advertising and the Articulation of the Consuming Subject as a Postmodern Political Entity

> Everyone from super models to high street fashionistas are getting behind eco initiatives.
>
> Get Lily's look this spring with the Limited Collection T-shirt dress £15 and bag just £12 both made from Fairtrade cotton, be stylish and help people in the developing countries.
>
> Lily Cole, face of Limited Collection: 'I see my role working in the fashion industry as a natural opportunity to support various ethical causes. I can use my position as a fashion model to raise awareness of certain issues. I love the idea that eventually, we will all be able to buy anything we like without feeling guilty, and items won't be labelled "ethical" – fashion will just be ethical.'
>
> M&S is the biggest retailer of Fairtrade cotton in the world and offers Fairtrade cotton clothing for all the family as well as for the home. From socks to sheets everyone could bring a little Fairtrade into their lives and help improve the quality of life for others. (Marks and Spencer 2008)

In the postmodern cultural politics, of Fair Trade promotion, advertising might alternatively be discerned, as providing new technologies of self from which subjects can reflexively explore the rights and responsibilities of citizenship in contemporary consumer culture. Some indication of this dynamic is evident in the, above featured, press release from Marks and Spencer (2008). The text is presented as a press release, but is clearly designed to operate as an advertisement. And this process of transmogrification is a recurrent advertising mechanism through which sustainable consumption is imbued with polysemic meanings, relevant to the production of the consumer as an agent in postmodern cultural politics.

This framework rests on the principle that advertising is 'a means to create positive notions of contemporary citizenship' (Meijer 1998:236). The decentring of cultural politics, through the imbrication of advertising, brings with it the possibilities of a reinvigoration of civic society. To this extent, Fair Trade advertising's re-articulation of politics into the aesthetic world of consumption is 'a setting for the actualization of notions of contemporary citizenship' (ibid:235). Let us spend a moment examining empirical examples of this assertion. Firstly, Irene Meijer (1998:228), following Mary Douglas and Baron Isherwood (1979), is keen to positively emphasize that commodities are a vital resource through which humans make meaning of the world, articulate this meaning to others and situate themselves within culture. Given the increased significance of the symbolic realm to social interaction, technologies that are capable of transforming material and immaterial artefacts into social communicators will inevitably become a 'rich source of information about daily life' (ibid). Considered as a mode of meaning making, the expansion of advertising generally, and its extension into the civic realm of politics, is a response to the need for new cultural values and dynamic signs to enable humans to express new meanings in a rapidly changing globalized society. Returning now to the commercial retailers that have used the internet to advertise textile ranges that contain Fairtrade certified cotton. What is common to the advertisements that feature on both the Marks and Spencer website for Plan A and the Debenhams website for FiveG, is the use of narratives that are effectively designed to convey semiotic stories depicting the global relevance of localized consumer action. This is clearly the case in the following extract derived from the Debenhams website for The FiveG Collection:

> Many farmers and workers in developing countries struggle to provide for their families. Poor market access and unFair Trade rules often mean that the price they get for their crops does not cover the cost of production. Fairtrade certification is a rapidly growing international system which aims to improve the terms of trade and increase access to international markets for farmers and workers in the developing world. A product that is Fairtrade certified carries the Fairtrade Mark, an independent consumer label, which is your guarantee that disadvantaged farmers and workers are getting a better deal.
>
> …
>
> By choosing products made with Fairtrade certified cotton you can make a real difference to the lives of small-scale cotton farmers in developing countries. Fairtrade certification ensures the farmers receive a fair and stable price for their cotton, that covers the cost of sustainable production.
>
> …
>
> Choosing Fairtrade cotton products gives disadvantaged small-scale cotton farmers the power to improve their livelihoods.
>
> Look for the Fairtrade Mark on cotton products your independent guarantee they have been made from Fairtrade certified cotton. (Debenhams 2009)

According to Meijer (1998:247) advertising's ability to construct uniquely revelatory stories about the contemporary world, should be greeted with optimism. This is because, stories such as the text derived from the FiveG promotional campaign, 'should be seen as part of the wide array of practices and technologies with which individuals nowadays have to constitute their sense of self as – among other things – citizens of ever expanding communities' (ibid). At the same time the ability of postmodern forms of advertising aesthetics to abstract and disembed images, might engender in the audience, ambivalent feelings of irritation, fascination and even condemnation. Examples of this emotionality are obviously subjective, but one possible illustration is the tendency for Fair Trade commercials to feature rural producer communities in isolation from the more modern urban cityscapes which also exist in developing countries. From Meijer's perspective the emotionality evoked by, the visual trope of the rural producer communities, is an optimistic feature of advertising. For, although this may 'annoy us' or 'offend our fellow citizens', in so doing it may 'inspire new civil attitudes and lifestyles' (ibid). And this generative feature of advertising aesthetics is particularly the case of postmodern advertising techniques that juxtapose unrelated or even oppositional visual metaphors, in such a manner that their collision generates new meaning. Similarly, Meijer makes the convincing argument that the creative propensities of advertising has already extended into the civic realm and conflated modernist dichotomies separating consumption from politics. And this has invigorated cultural politics. Thus, Meijer argues that rather than seeing advertising as 'the designer tools for daily spiritual deprivation' (ibid:238), we should 'consider consumer culture instead as an as yet unmined source of civic capital' (ibid:247).

In the new era of postmodern political culture, advertising ingenuity is a mode of instantiating civic capital. But this fusion of spheres creates, not a culture, of autonomous individuals engaged as citizens in the maximization of self interest in the context of limited state intervention. Indeed, postmodernism is the antithesis of 'a culture that creates a political individual characterised by critical distance, alienation and reflexive rationality' (Wexler 1990:169). Rather the subject is decentred and its self, defined across shifting interests, subject positions and social categories. The relations between subjects are similarly, defined as fetishistic properties of commodities. And this obviates power inequalities as structural differentiations dissipate into the self-referential play of sign values. In a culture devoid of structural differentiation, subjects 'are bereft of spatial coordinates and practically...incapable of distantiation' (Jameson 1991:48-49). Indeed critical theorists express immense concern that 'distance in general (including critical distance in particular) has very precisely been abolished in the new space of postmodernism' (ibid:48). The consequences of this demise have, in some quarters, marked the end of the rhetorical power and material affectivity of representational politics. But let us examine this incisive critical reflection of the postmodern cultural politics with a more direct focus on Fair Trade and the construct of the ethical consumer.

The Shopping Cart Arithmetic of the Neo-Liberal Information Processing Consumer Sovereign

In the 1970s and 1980s with the rise of neo-liberalism, the relationship between the role of the economic realm and that of the civic became even more complexly intertwined. For example, Milton Friedman (1962), in his seminal neoliberalist text *Capitalism and Freedom* introduced a conception of citizenship that was directly linked with commercial freedom. Friedman believed that market relations precede, at least in relevance, all other human activity. Indeed, he observed that the basic problem of advanced societies is one of coordinating opportunities. Friedman argued that one of the most effective mechanisms of achieving this was through a model of society organized on the principle of bi-laterally informed, financial transactions within the context of a 'free private enterprise exchange economy' (2002:13). To this end, citizenship is equated with market autonomy such that 'as far as possible his activities as a citizen should be modelled on his behaviour in the economic market, taken to be a paradigm of rationality' (Miller 2000:50). However, and according to neo-classical economists, the consumer citizen defines a new constellation of socio-economic practice, which can be clearly distinguished from the rational economic practice of 'consumer sovereignty' (Dickinson and Carsky 2005). Often associated with traditional economic models of consumer demand, the concept of 'consumer sovereignty' is a translation of the principle of democratic freedom (and respect for personal autonomy), to the realm of the market (Korthals 2000). Consumer sovereignty is more specifically defined as the individual right of the consumer to decide 'what is good for himself, rather than have someone else play a paternal role' (Lerner 1972:258). In economic discourse, this social construct is related to the concept of efficiency, 'in the use of resources for the greatest possible satisfaction of the needs and desires of people' (ibid:1972). To this end, the economist A.P. Lerner states that the strong emphasis on maximizing the highest utility per unit cost to the consumer, explains why it is that 'the full achievement of consumer sovereignty has been called 'ideal output'' (ibid). The importance of this observation is even more apparent when we recognize that from its conceptual evolution in the 1930s, consumer sovereignty also defined the power of consumer demand to determine the market for the range of commodities offered by producers (Dickinson and Carsky 2005:29).

Significant resonances exist between the construct of consumer sovereignty and, the tendency for Fair Trade advertising campaigns to presuppose the existence of an information processing ethical subject. An illustration of the articulation of consumer sovereignty into Fair Trade advertising is evident in the following extract derived from the Fairtrade Cotton section of Marks and Spencer's Plan A web-pages:

> The Fairtrade Mark is one of the most recognized product certification labels in the UK. But what does it actually mean? Watch the film to find out how M&S Fairtrade cotton makes a difference. (Marks and Spencer 2009)

The instruction for the audience member to digest information ('watch the film') is indicative of the problems of translating Fair Trade principles into conscientious consumption. The overall aim of presenting the consumer with information detailing the social conditions surrounding production is, so that they can knowingly purchase ethically sourced products. It has been similarly observed that Fair Trade promotional campaigns attempt to actuate 'consumers to use their purchases less as a means of signalling their own social status and more as a means of affirming the claims made on behalf of the Third World producers for fair terms of exchange' (Watson 2007:270). Accordingly, it has been stated that Fair Trade campaigners aim to intervene in the commodity fetishism that, arises when conventional advertising frames, consumption decisions as 'calculations that privilege impersonal categories such as demand, supply and price' (ibid:271). Given the high involvement of rationalizing discourse evident in examples of informational communication, it is questionable that an appeal to the symbolic properties of commodities is actually the primary intention of this form of advertising. Indeed, it is evident that rational decision-making theory is integral to understanding informational models of advertising communication. This is because these informational practices invariably insist that 'the role of consumerism in achieving long-term sustainability lies in the fundamental decision-making power of the individual consumer' (Strong 1997:33). Consequently, much effort is dedicated to the fine tuning of communication content so as to enable 'consumers to feel that they have the ability to make a difference' (Wright and Heaton 2006:424). An often cited mode of achieving this is to embed, into the product's packaging, 'producer stories' (ibid). Fair Trade products are often replete with narrative descriptions of the product's producer communities. As is evident in the following extract derived from the Marks and Spencer Plan website:

> Basically, Fairtrade helps small-scale farmers and farm workers in developing countries to invest in their communities, by guaranteeing them a fair and stable price and a Fairtrade Premium for investment in community development projects.
>
> In the Kita region of Mali, Africa, the Fairtrade Premium has been used for digging wells to provide access to clean drinking water and to build a storage facility for grain. Just by having a dry secure warehouse, the community is no longer forced to sell its excess crops, and can store vital fertilisers and seed, too.
>
> In the village of Dougourakoroni, also in the Kita region, the cotton producers co-operative has used the Fairtrade Premium (on top of the Fairtrade price that we pay for their cotton) to build a block of two classrooms, with a further two planned for the following year. This has helped to persuade the government to pay for four more to be built.
>
> …
>
> Another Fairtrade standard is guaranteeing more involvement for women, at every level. Binto Dambile, Board Member of the Union of Cotton Producing Co-operatives in Mali says, 'Before, the women were not invited, not asked, not consulted. We were sad. We are pleased now we are included at the same level as the men. We know that men can't do everything without us. Women are valued now'. (Marks and Spencer 2009)

The inclusion of narratives describing the life and experiences of the producer, offers the consumer the added benefit of using this knowledge to conscientiously participate in the market correction of global capitalism. Thus Fair Trade can be seen as a device, which sophisticated consumers use to 'exercise their sovereignty in the marketplace, supporting ethical business and punishing unethical ones' (Dickenson 2001:98). An important issue here is that of rationality. The obvious counter position is to question the efficacy of human rationality. An interim position of some interest is raised by recent economic analyses of Fair Trade consumption decisions. It has been suggested that while it may appear that consumers are making judgment based decisions based on rational information, there are also rational reasons to suggest that the consumer 'may feel that they are establishing relationships, however tenuous, with the suppliers of their staple products' (Booth 2007:31). In other words, becoming a consumer of Fair Trade commodities is neither predictable in its motivation nor calculable in its outcome.

Products that carry the Fairtrade Mark signify a non-governmental approach to sustainable development. From the rational economic perspective of consumer sovereignty, the primary role of advertising is to promote the physical and economic characteristics of the commodity, and in so doing encourage consumers into multiple purchases of Fairtrade labelled products. Considered from this perspective Fairtrade labelled products are indistinguishable interchangeable units. Advertising's function is to maximize the sale of these units. The money raised can then be channelled back into the sustainable development of the social, economic and environmental context experienced by the producers of Fairtrade labelled products. Taken to its logical extreme, the conscientious rationally economic consumer, could maximize his/her support for Fair Trade by bulk purchasing hundreds of the same units of a Fairtrade labelled product (e.g., bananas). Even the most cursory observation of the buying of Fairtrade produce, in supermarkets, highlights the implausibility of this supposition. Indeed, the erroneous simplicity of the rational consumer sovereignty model deflects attention away from the complex signifying practices at play in the advertising of Fairtrade produce. It is clear, that the success of Fairtrade advertising rests on its ability to encourage consumers to select commodities with a Fairtrade Mark over non-Fairtrade labelled products (Hilowitz 1997:219). This involves persuading consumers to displace their ascribed role, in capitalist commodity culture, as self-interested entities, and instead use their purchases to affirm their political commitment to improving the social and environmental conditions of producers in the developing world. In other words, advertisements for Fairtrade labelled products are coupled, in the public consciousness, with Fair Trade's primary goal to improve the livelihoods of producers by extending the socio-economic relations of ethical trade throughout the commodity chain. Central to this objective is an insistence on extending the moral geographies of economic transactions so as to create within commodity chains, long term inter-dependent relations between buyers and sellers.

The advertising for Fairtrade labelled products is, therefore, engaged in an extensive project geared towards dismantling the possessively individualistic, isolation endemic in commodity capitalism and replacing this with signifying practices that 'differentiate on the basis of production processes rather than (or at least, in addition to) the characteristics of the final product' (Hudson and Hudson 2003:421). This is primarily accomplished through a remarkably sophisticated appeal to the socio-symbolic realm of commodity exchange. Advertising is constantly involved in the transference of meaning onto objects and the transformation of the symbolic properties of commodities. However, in the advertising of Fairtrade labelled products this process of cultivating symbolic meaning takes on an entirely more fascinating dimension of ethical treatment.

The unique semiological dynamics of this genre of advertising strategy is highly distinguishable at the final point of sale. Given that the product is an inanimate object devoid of an ontologically given moral status, 'it can never be the object of mutual sympathy' (Watson 2007:271). This presents advertising creatives with the formidable task of how to transfer the extended moral geography of Fair Trade production onto the non-sentient properties of a product. Part of the problem is addressed through the presence of the Fairtrade Mark. This inscriptive guarantee of ethical trade, enables the advertising of Fairtrade labelled products:

> ...to increase the visibility of long-term and global economic connections involved in day-to-day economic transactions through the education of the final consumer. (Hudson and Hudson 2003:421)

In addition to the Fairtrade Mark's pedagogical function, advertising creatives apply semiotic techniques designed to create a platform for the establishment of social bonds connecting the life of the consumer with that of the producer. The evocation of relationality is insightfully predicated on imaginatively extended moral geographies, rather than an attempt to build concrete social connections between hitherto divided parties. Nonetheless, this does not undermine the importance of the imaginative act of sentimentality that the advertising of Fairtrade labelled products attempts to instantiate. At the point of sale, advertising operates to activate the imaginative faculties of the consumer so that he/she understands 'themselves to be interacting, not with the product per se, but with the *producer* of that product' (Watson 2007:271). In contrast to the hedonistic myopic object centred relations that pervade conventional commodity fetishism, the advertising of Fairtrade labelled products sets out to create an ethically motivated 'producer-oriented cognitive frame' (ibid). In so doing, advertising attempts to replace the myopic object-centred gaze, of conventional capitalist commodity culture, with a cognitive frame that motivates the consumer to:

> ...recognize the legitimate moral status of the producer and accept that the producer is consequently worthy of ethical treatment. (ibid)

This approach exceeds the preoccupation, by conventional ethical trading movements, with the relations of commodity exchange. In contrast, Fair Trade focuses on both the relations of exchange and relations of production implicated in the global chain of commodity-based exploitation. To this end, the advertising of Fairtrade labelled products is geared towards 'a process of meaning making as a situated material practice, where an "economy of semiology" constructs an emotional...bridge between cosmopolitan consumers and "Third World" producers' (Dolan 2008:311). Advertising operates as a technology of reconnection, reuniting the hitherto divided members of the commodity chain. The spatially disaggregated geographies of global textile production (Odih 2007) ensure that consumers and producers will invariably remain geographically distant strangers. The striking and remarkable audacity of advertising, for Fairtrade labelled products, relates to the techniques it uses to bridge the physical distance that separates human beings in the global exchange economy. In general terms, this involves semiotically invoking a cultural political dialogue based on the symbolic representation of the production process, rather than the 'fungible, abstract utilities of conventional global commodity chains' (Dolan 2008:311). It has been observed that advertising attempts to re-personalize, the commodity chain, by making visible, at the point of sale, the stories, histories and experiences of producer groups (Hudson and Hudson 2003:421). While a focus on the advertising practices used to physically embed exchange relations, is of relevance here. It is equally important to recognize that these practices are the end product of advertising knowledges and ideals that are, in themselves fascinating windows, into the construction of consumer subjectivity in our current era of global cultural politics. Of particular fascination is advertising's recent focus on the self-reflexively ethical consumer citizen as a primary market driver. In the sociology of modernity, writers draw attention to the emergence of a mode of subjectivity and self-identity tied to late modernity and the imperative of self-actualization, constituted against a background of dynamic change and unparalleled globalization. Writers here constitute Fair Trade consumers as both, individually and collectively involved in re-moralizing reflexive practices against the backdrop of global transitions and transformations. Similar constructs of the consumer are evident in advertising practices. Indeed it is evident that the consumer is, increasingly being semiotically constituted, in Fair Trade advertising practices, as a self-reflexive political agent in a global movement for redistributive justice. But let us spend a brief moment reflecting on the sociological traditions to which this advertising framework is beholden.

Reflexive Modernity and Self Identity the Self-Reflexive Consumer Citizen

Our current era is characterized by systemic disjunctures propelled by the dynamics of 'time-space distanciation', 'expanding disembedding systems' and 'detraditionalisation' (Giddens 1993). At the centre of these transformations is the intensifying centrifugal force of globalization. So as to signify an acute intensification in the globalizing dynamics of modern society, it is conventional, within the sociology of modernity, to regard these global transformations as precipitates of 'late modernity'. Indeed, it has been argued by Anthony Giddens (1993:1), in his hugely influential text *Modernity and Self Identity*, that:

> one of the distinctive features of modernity...is an increasing inter-connection between the two 'extremes' of extensionality and intentionality: globalising influences on the one hand and personal disposition on the other.

If one accepts Giddens' line of thought, the permanence of change in late modernity is propelled by the immense force of globalizing influences that penetrate into the day-to-day quotidian creation, and re-affirmation, of social institutions. And this imagery of change dovetails with transformations in the parallel dimensions of time and space. In early modernity the Cartesian subject inhabits a world of pre-given boundaries and stands in relationship to modernising change at specific points in time and fixed coordinates in material space. Conversely, the subject of late modernity inhabits a landscape configured by the reticulating dynamics of 'global institutions of communication, polity, economy and sanction' (Spybey 1996:152). In the context of global capitalism's networked society (Castells 2000), instantaneous international commerce and 24hr communication really showcase the global transformation of our local times and spaces. Of particular fascination, here, is the propensity for advanced technologies to 'disembed' social relations by elevating them from their 'local contexts', and 'recombining them across wide time-space distances' (Giddens 1993:2). In the case of high-technology communication systems, the materiality of space and ridged boundaries of clock time, have become increasingly overwhelmed, by the ability of advanced technologies to unfetter social relations from their immediate locales. The result for the individual subject is not merely an increased exposure to globalizing systems, for, it has been observed that large-scale systems are emerging alongside 'the transformation of local, and even personal, contexts of social experience' (ibid:5). As Giddens has expressed it 'local lifestyle habits have become globally consequential. Thus my decision to buy a certain item of clothing has implications not only for the international division of labour but for the earth's ecosystem' (ibid). It is this profound recognition of the dynamic dialectic between the local and global that forms the basis of, theoretical analyses of, reflexive modernization and the transformative nature of self-identity.

Despite notable differences in emphasis, Giddens' (1992, 1993, 1998) analyses of the protean propensities of self-identity allude to an earlier modern time, when matters of self, ethics and morality were established through the orthodoxy of locally embedded expert systems (e.g., philosophers etc.). Indeed, a significant element of the historical break from early modernity has involved an estrangement from, the assemblage of ancestral authorities and erudite knowledges, received from exalted figures imbued with metaphysical power. Modernization has heralded the spread of knowledge-based disembedding mechanisms, arming modern subjects with the tenacity to agitate the foundations of accumulated knowledge. In other words traditional systems are exorcised by the expansive repertoire of modern knowledge and practices. Thus the immense scope of modernization both transforms and extends beyond the key structures and institutions of modern society. For, the very epistemological basis of the principles of modern society itself, have become the target of intense reflection. Ultimately this leads to the interrogation of the whole of social life. This is because, the transmutations of modern society have institutional ramifications that 'interlace in a direct way with individual life and therefore with the self' (Giddens 1993:1).

It is often incorrectly assumed that disillusionment with modernity encourages the emergence of reflexive faculties, which predispose subjects to an increased consciousness and mastery over the uncertainties of everyday life. Rather than engendering control, the tremendous scope and endless proliferation of authority sources, in late modern times, are 'frequently internally contested and divergent in their implications' (ibid:3). Thus, in these global times of flux and vacillation modernity has transformed into a 'post-traditional order' (ibid:2). One might assume that Giddens is referring here to advancements in the capacities of modern rationalities to control risk and guarantee with 'certitude' the probability of future eventualities. But rather than marking a world in which risk has been tamed, the 'post-traditional order' signals the permeation of 'doubt' into the minutiae of everyday life; such that uncertainty 'forms a general existential dimension of the contemporary social world' (ibid:3). This is because; 'systems of accumulated expertise' at one and the same time constitute crucial disembedding influences and locations for the contestation of expertise (ibid). And these transitions, in turn, signify that 'when modernization reaches a certain stage it radicalizes itself' (Beck et al 2003:1).

To this end, it has been observed that 'modernization becomes reflexive modernization to the extent that it disenchants and then dissolves its own taken-for-granted premises' (Beck et al 2003:3). Central to this discourse of modernity, is the concept of 'detraditionalisation' and the parallel process of self-reflexivity. For it is not just a case that traditional orthodoxy has been dispelled. Rather, accumulated expertise, in late modernity, has to dramatically moderate its status. As Giddens expresses it; '[in] a post-traditional order...traditions have to explain themselves, to become open to interrogation or discourse' (1998:5). In this highly reflexive social atmosphere individuals must become self-reliant erotectic purveyors of all sorts of information, relevant to their daily lives, and occasionally act on the basis of their filtering systems.

Globalization has lead to the expansion of diverse information systems that both relativize cultural values and disembed social relations from their traditional locales. The shear magnitude of this expansion, coupled with the associated reorganization of time and space has radicalized and globalized 'pre-established institutional traits of modernity' (Giddens 1993:2). And the coexistent disembedding of everyday life from traditional processes and calculable expert systems propels individual decision making, 'away from the hold of pre-established precepts or practices' (ibid:20). In this context, individuals become ever reliant upon themselves to define a sense of identity. These conditions are accentuated by the transformation of social relations across time-space and the subsequent re-negotiated relations of trust in expert systems and a range of specialists with whom the individual may never have face-to-face contact (ibid:6).

Innovations in communication technologies provide new conditions for the calculation and regulation of social relations both nationally and internationally. In the multi-media world of 24hr broadcasting we can easily apprehend the global relationality of local lifestyles. But, while the interiority of the local and global into day-to-day life 'reduces the overall riskiness of certain areas and modes of life', globalization has so increased the variety of interconnections between distant others, that the everyday is now subject to 'new risk parameters largely or completely unknown to previous eras' (ibid:4). Giddens describes these new parameters as including 'high-consequence risks: risk deriving from the globalized character of the social systems of modernity' (ibid). Of the major high-consequence risks to besiege contemporary social life, none looms more menacingly than the widely pronounced apocalyptic consequences of intemperate globally liberalized trade.

In the post-traditional era of late modernity and against the background of rapacious globalizing forces 'self-identity becomes a reflexively organized endeavour' (ibid:5). Central to this discourse of identity, is the notion that an individual subject is capable of developing an awareness of its own self and can proficiently monitor its activities and conduct. Modern self-identity is reflexively produced through the ongoing dialogue between the components of the self that George Herbert Mead (1967) eloquently described as the 'I' and the 'Me'. In Mead's composition, the self is a symbolic entity, actively constructed through an individual's ongoing social engagement with the 'generalized other' and tenacious reconciliations with the inimitable 'I'. To this end, identity is continuously emerging, re-formed and redirected, as part of the individual's uniquely social interaction with cultural resources and symbolic meanings.

In *Being and Time* Heidegger's account of *Dasein* informs our comprehension of human identity as stretched across time (Thomas 1996:51). *Being* is dispersed through the chronicles of time. The existential time of *Dasein* possesses an intense immediacy, uniquely relevant to the person. And yet *Dasein* as a concept also draws attention to the way subjectivity is always lived in embodied form (Thomas 1996). Subjects live time/space events as well as being constituted by them. Time is, therefore, inextricably bound up with places, spaces and the body. For people 'do not so much think real time but actually live it sensuously, qualitatively' (Urry 1995:6). The identity, which emerges in the process of the self, stretches across time as 'the person one is now has a historical connection with the person whom one was yesterday' (Thomas 1996:45). By reflecting upon previous experience, present contingencies and future desires, the self is consistently bringing itself into existence (ibid:52). Narrativity is thus axiomatic to modern self-identity. Indeed, Giddens (1991:76) describes how the production of an interpretative self-history is central to self-identity in modern social life. The 'reflexive monitoring' of self 'forms a trajectory of development from the past to the anticipated future' (p. 75). Giddens describes the future as resonant with possibilities, 'yet not left open to the full play of contingency' (1991:77). Foucault (1979), in particular, demonstrates the profound historicity of modern subjectivity. Society and culture provide specific 'technologies of the self' through which identities are constituted. The self is a developing site of cultural inscription (Thomas 1996:47). Our existential experiences of time are re-inscriptive of society's social rhythms rather than mere representations. The modern self as a narrative text is always lived in an embodied form so that 'subjects are dialogical, bringing specific personas, discourses and voices to contexts of negotiation and domination' (Thrift 1991:461 quoted in Thomas 1996:47).

Thus the scope and limitations of self-identity are indexed to the material conditions, routines and practical situations, which define day-to-day life (Elliott 2001:43). Suffice to say 'there is a social process out of which selves arise and within which further differentiation, further evolution, further organization take place' (Mead 1967:164). As Giddens observes, self-identity is ordinarily reflexively produced as a project 'constituted by the reflexive ordering of self-narratives' (1993:244). But, as everyday lives become ever more subject to internationally centralized systems of control, and previously unimaginable levels of relatedness intensify interconnections across time and space, traditionally defined self-narratives are in decline. As Giddens expresses it,

> In the post-traditional order...The reflexive project of the self, which consists in the sustaining of coherent, yet continuously revised, biographical narratives, takes place in the context of multiple choice as filtered through abstract systems. (ibid:5)

In the wake of fragmenting traditional collective solidarities and proliferating expert systems, individuals must decipher for themselves the project of the self, and do so against the raucous din of globalizing systems. Consequently reflexivity, in this post-traditional order, leads to increased cognitive work as choices and their possible outcomes are mediated by the interrogation of the self.

The more traditional orthodoxies are interrogated, and the more expertise loses its differential hold, the more significant the self becomes to the conditions of modern existence. Thus in the discourse of reflexive modernity the self is a resilient construct, it does not dissipate into a fragmented array of transient existences bobbing erratically in the interminable flux of postmodernity. Rather the self is axiomatic with the globalizing tendencies of modernity and the inherent dynamic of choice. This is because 'the narrative of self-identity has to be shaped, altered and reflexively sustained in relation to rapidly changing circumstances of social life, on a local and global scale' (ibid:215). The result for the individual is that, the very private experience of self-identity formation is increasingly indexed to the intensifying local dynamics of an individualizing social life firmly embedded in a globalized world. Consequently, in late modernity self-reflexivity directs personal identity towards the discovery of a personal destiny encumbered with global considerations. This is to recognize that the self as a reflexive project is not only premised on the self-monitoring of personal action. Indeed self-reflexivity is axiomatic with an action-oriented model of social change, and this builds into the process of self-formation the transformative potential of social responsibility and culpability (Lee 2006:356).

The Longue Durée *of Consumer Citizenship as Life Politics*

Expectations about the globalizing changes associated with late modernity draw attention to risk in terms of reflexive modernization's dialectic of the local and the global. Here the discussion focuses around the putative impact of institutional legitimacy and trust concerning risk acceptability. The rise of globalizing influences is not just a case of, individuals being affected by distant centralizing systems of regulation. Neither is it only about the development of knowledge-based self-reflexive faculties. Rather, the 'risk culture' of late modernity is fundamental to the way in which publics, individuals, and experts organize their social world (Giddens 1993:3). This is partly because in late modernity 'the future is continually drawn into the present by means of the reflexive organization of knowledge environments' (ibid). The future is transformed into a terrain for the application of knowledge and expertise. It is 'colonized', in the belief that the application of advanced, abstract systems can manage the probability of risk and render the inevitability of uncertainty knowable. Yet, it is increasingly evident that the expansion of disembedding abstract systems produces greater differentiation and diffuses responsibility for guaranteeing that safeguarding systems are adequate. Moreover, the globally networked character of modern institutions coupled with the mutable and frequently controversial nature of risk management organizations, mean that 'most forms of risk assessment, in fact, contain numerous imponderables' (ibid:4). The result for the individual is an unavoidable habituation to the proliferation of decision processes in powerful organizations and the realization that, their choices about risk management, will have implications that exceed the context of their immediate environs.

Thus the global relationality of local dynamics provides the conditions for the negotiated self-reflexive strategies of individual subjects to actively shape their futures (Larsen et al 2005:362). A central presupposition derived from this observation is, 'the emergence of life politics' (Giddens 1993:209). According to Giddens:

> life politics concerns issues which flow from processes of self-actualization in post-traditional contexts, where globalising influences intrude deeply into the reflexive project of the self, and conversely where processes of self-realisation influence global strategies. (1993:214)

Evidently, the concerns of life politics are resonant with, elements of, the emancipatory politics of life chances. Both are political machinations that argue against the inequities of social hierarchies and the reformulations of traditional constraints. And both consider the after effects of a world in which the conditions of hierarchical domination have been interrogated and disassembled. Nevertheless, an implication in Giddens' account of life politics is its unique historical timing. As Giddens expresses it; 'Although life-political issues can be traced further back, life politics only emerges as a fully distinctive set of problems and possibilities with the consolidating of high modernity' (ibid:214). Life politics epitomizes transformations in the location of politics in reflexive modernity. As Binkley (2009:96) observes 'where previously struggles developed around those steering mechanisms by which the direction of modern advance was determined...today political processes take place within the spaces of those second-order consequences and risks once excluded from the realm of politics'. In this 'second modernity', politics involves individualized interventions into the unusually amplified risks and adverse consequences of an earlier modern era's unrestrained subjugation of nature to the appliance of science, its ethics of technological progress, its unbridled intensification of production and arbitrary rationalization of society (Beck 1992, Binkley 2009:96). In a context where the 'planning mechanisms of industrial modernity' are rapidly being eroded by globalized market forces, these amplified risks become our daily reality (Binkley 2009:96). It is in this sense that previously mundane lifestyle choices have become political responses to the unavoidable immediacy of the 'risk society' (Beck 1992, Giddens 1993). Thus, in contrast with the dialectical materialism of the emancipation of life chances, life politics suggests the continuing effort to remodel modernity as an unfinished excavation of 'those moral and existential questions repressed by the core institutions of modernity' (Giddens 1993:223). Giddens builds his argument around his observation, that questions of morality, in postmodern discourse, have become fragmented cultural vocabularies against the background of the beleaguered desolated self. While making analytical use of aspects of the postmodern condition, especially issues that effectively describe reflexive modernization's radical break from modernity's own foundations, Giddens agitates at the limits of postmodernism. Of particular concern is the presumed failure of postmodern cultural theory to consistently explain why moral and ethical concerns increasingly pervade social life. For, life politics emerges in spite of the rapidly transforming circumstances of modern society. And this, according to Giddens, is in contradiction with postmodern concepts of the self. It is often the case that in anti-foundational postmodern paradigms, the embattled, decentred subject is depicted as seeking sanctuary from the phantasmagoria and media spectacle of contemporary politics (c.f. Gergen 1991). In so doing, the postmodern subject constitutes the self 'through a defensive rejection of politics in favour of a tightly confined personal realm' (ibid:209). Conversely, life politics is central to the contemporary reflexive modernization of social institutions; across traditional notions of politics.

Thus the politics of life emerging from late modernity appears to proffer increased individual emancipation. But this formulation of the self differs markedly from the aggrandising politicized subject of left wing Marxist theory. For it is not the consciousness of capitalist exploitation that determines the revolutionary potential of the new ethos of self, but 'rather the ethos of self-growth signals major social transitions in late modernity as a whole' (ibid). This is because, the encumbrance of accentuating institutional reflexivity, in conjunction with transitions towards the greater scope of disembedding abstract knowledge systems and, the increasing interpolation of the local and the global, necessitate a social engagement and reappropriation of the politics of life. With regards to the form and agenda of this politics, it is clear that 'life politics does not primarily concern the conditions which liberate us in order to make choice: it is a politics of choice' (ibid:214). In other words, life politics concerns the essential relevance of choice to self-actualization in a reflexively ordered post-traditional environment, 'where that reflexivity links self and body to systems of global scope' (ibid). The power of the new ethos of choice arises from its index to, the prevalence of forms of knowledge authority, vested in abstract information systems distanced across space and time, as part of the spread of globalized culture. As the certainties of tradition are displaced by the deliverance of knowledge from a wide range of mediated abstract systems, the individual must re-embed this diversity of information 'in such a way as to connect future projects with past experiences in a reasonably coherent fashion' (ibid:215). This necessitates that tradition is replaced by the development of a framework of trust and continuity against the backdrop of contemporary social and cultural transformations. Giddens develops the concept of 'ontological security', to describe the experiential creation of a sense of continuity. 'Ontological security', refers to a unity of *being* and *becoming* against, which evaluations of present changes can be comprehended in terms of the lifespan of past and future. As Giddens (1993:243) expresses it 'ontological security…[is] a sense of continuity and order in events, including those not directly within the perceptual environment of the individual'. According to Giddens, the development of a narrational self, reflexively sustained in the context of the interpenetration of the local and the global, is a vital resource for dealing with a world consumed by the runaway effects of modernization. It is from this perspective that life politics 'concerns debates and contestations deriving from the reflexive project of the self' (ibid).

In this theme of reconstruction in reflexive modernization, life politics emerges at the limits of the 'internally referential systems of modernity' (ibid:224). This is because life politics is decisively confrontational, for it focuses on 'questions of how we should live our lives in emancipated social circumstances' and thus incorporates into the agenda of self-actualization moral and existential concerns. And these forms of concern require a moralizing of social life long since sequestered away from the institutions of modernity. As Giddens expresses it, 'Life-political issues supply the central agenda for the return of the institutionally repressed' (ibid). Here Giddens is referring to the limits modernity has encountered as a consequence of the extension of modernist rationality. These limits relate firstly to 'the invasion of the natural world by abstract systems' (ibid). Suffice to say media documentaries and countless publications have exposed the cataclysmic consequences of excessive human control over nature. Nevertheless, the continued extension into the natural world of abstract rationality has provoked environmental risks, of such magnitude, that it prompts the return of 'repressed existential issues, related not just to nature but to the moral parameters of existence' (ibid). In this context the limits of modernity engenders strategies for overcoming the ontological insecurities of living in a society in, which the actualities of environmental degradation press themselves onto the daily agenda of social existence. Pragmatically life politics involves the utility of individual freedom to profile risks, as part of the asking of moral and existential questions about the relevance of these externalities for self-actualization in a reflexively mobilized social order. And as Giddens observes 'as with other substantive moral questions', these issues of environmental degradation will 'in some way involve lifestyle options' (ibid:225).

The concept of lifestyle can be misleadingly simplistic. In the context of life politics lifestyle assumes increased complexity. For, it refers to 'a time/space "slice" of an individual's overall activities, within which a fairly consistent set of social practices is followed' (ibid:243). To this end, Giddens observes that the moral and existential problems raised by environmental degradation is one of the global crises, that involve the adoption of social practices by self-reflexive individuals in the realization that local actions have global ramifications. And this observation encourages Giddens to identify globalization itself as a major 'focus for the expansion of modernity's internally referential systems' (ibid). For, the global time-space distancing scope of abstract expert systems along with the proliferating array of information they provide inevitably becomes a source of moral and ethical debate. The question of 'how we should live?' becomes ever more prescient as global disembedding abstract systems redraw the epistemological and ontological boundaries erected by modernity. Ontological security therefore, relies upon, the capability of individuals to collectively fabricate morally commendable forms of social life, in a post-traditional order and against the background of globalized local values. Thus life politics is 'a politics of life decisions' (ibid:215). This suggestion interpolates with the detraditionalizing affect of global forces and the alternative value systems of globalized locales. For, life politics concerns contestations and debates deriving from the forging of self-reflexive identities in rapidly changing global times. And, this suggests an extended capacity for reflexivity stretching beyond the immediate time, space and place locales of everyday existence while at one and the same time incorporating these 'locales into novel and complex social dynamics' (Adams and Raisborough 2008:1169).

Misarticulating the Longue Durée *of Love and Value into the Branding of Ethical Textile*

Life politics 'is a politics of life decisions' (Giddens 1993:215). It emerges as a consequence of the individually negotiated strategies that subjects adopt, in order to shape their futures in relation to 'the rapidly changing circumstances of social life, on a local and global scale' (Giddens 1993:215). In late modernity, such political decisions have become internally self-referential as the certainties of tradition dissipate into the post-traditional order. In other words, the 'politics of life decisions', is reflexively achieved within the context of a transforming modern society. Axiomatic with a life politics which utilizes individual freedom to address change, is the reflexive achievement of self-identity. Self-identity in late modernity is reflexively achieved through the meaningful actions of individuals, capable of sequestering themselves from their own practices and even standing back from the process of reflection itself. This entails the configuration of a narrative of self-identity, which is (re)formulated in relation to the global dynamics of modern times. But in this context of rapid change, the self is more insecure and heavily reliant on the affirming properties of trust so as to formulate ontological security. This means that the subject of late modernity must develop and express 'an inner authenticity' (ibid). In response the subject finds a source of expression from the signifying practices of contemporary culture. Like all acts of cultural engagement, this process is one of reflexive appraisal in which 'contestations deriving from the reflexive project of the self' are articulated through signifying practices (ibid). At the same time, and in several intercalating ways, the signifying practices of contemporary consumer culture are becoming evermore appealing. This is because, the spectacular rise of commodity capitalism and the profusion of mesmerising signs of postmodernity, provides for a culture of consumption through, which subjects can cultivate and express a unique sense of self-identity. Thus the creation of a reflexively sustained self-identity in late modernity 'opens up the project of the self' to forms of lifestyle created through the effects of commodity capitalism. Although this is true, the corresponding point of view decrying consumer culture as narcissistic and disparaging the pleasures of consumption as occluding more substantive political interests, fails to apprehend the 'ordinarily ethical dimensions of shopping' (Barnett et al 2005:28). And much the same is true of Giddens', largely dismissive observations regarding the articulation, into advertising practice, of self-identity formation in late modernity. For example, he draws attention to 'the very corruption of the notion of "lifestyles", reflexively drawn into the sphere of advertising' (Giddens 1993:197–198). More specifically Giddens states that:

> Advertisers orient themselves to sociological classifications of consumer categories and at the same time foster specific consumption 'packages'. To a greater or lesser degree, the project of the self becomes translated into one of the possession of desired goods and the pursuit of artificially framed styles of life…The consumption of ever-novel goods becomes in some part a substitute

> for the genuine development of self; appearance replaces essence as the visible signs of successful consumption come actually to outweigh the use-values of the goods and services in question themselves. (1993:198)

Giddens' observations of self-reflexive life-politics in late modern times are incisive, which makes it even more surprising that his critique of advertising fails to interrogate advertising's role in the production of 'cultural economies of time' (Odih 2007). For, an integral feature of advertising is its ability to transform a future aspiration, desire or risk in time, into a commodity that can be consumed in the present.

The symbolic construction of time in the commodity-sign is predicated on the existence of a discursive frame to render the flow of time meaningful and 'achieve the necessary closure around the commodity it promotes' (Lee 1993:155). The latter issue of 'closure' in the context of time and advertising practice is effectively detailed by Williamson (2000). As a starting point, Williamson (2000:152) argues that the time of the advertisements is always already past, 'since the picture is finished and the future events are never open, but specifically directed'. The spectator is situated, by the advertisement, in a position of closure, whereby the narrative sequence and its apparitional future has been determined in advance by the logic of the commodity-form. The narrative instantiates a social meaning of time in which the present is a state of lack and the product signifies a connection to a more satisfied state of being. This narrative of time is in contrast to the flow of time in everyday social relations.

Williamson observes how in time and advertising narrative, the open future of everyday interaction is transformed into 'a deterministic and unalterable present' (2000:152). The closed future of advertising narrative has a demonstrable ideological function. It operates to disengage subjects from the natural follow of time and ascribe their being a 'synchronic status' in which events unfold within a kind of 'eternal moment' (ibid:152). The 'ideology of the synchronic' misrepresents history as a horizon of events which occur simultaneously when observed from 'the vantage view point of the present' (2000:154). It might assist for you to read through the following extract of text originally displayed on Marks and Spencer's Plan A web-page:

> Fairtrade cotton
>
> The Fairtrade Mark is one of the most recognized product certification labels in the UK. But what does it actually mean? Watch the film to find out how M&S Fairtrade cotton makes a difference.
>
> Basically, Fairtrade helps small-scale farmers and farm workers in developing countries to invest in their communities, by guaranteeing them a fair and stable price and a Fairtrade Premium for investment in community development projects.

> In the Kita region of Mali, Africa, the Fairtrade Premium has been used for digging wells to provide access to clean drinking water and to build a storage facility for grain. Just by having a dry secure warehouse, the community is no longer forced to sell its excess crops, and can store vital fertilisers and seed, too.
>
> …
>
> In the village of Dougourakoroni, also in the Kita region, the cotton producers co-operative has used the Fairtrade Premium (on top of the Fairtrade price that we pay for their cotton) to build a block of two classrooms, with a further two planned for the following year. This has helped to persuade the government to pay for four more to be built.
>
> Fairtrade makes a real difference. You'll find Fairtrade cotton products ranging from men's chinos and lingerie vests to kidswear. You'll even find Fairtrade wine at your M&S. Click here to see the range – remember, every Fairtrade product you buy will help farmers and workers in developing countries to invest in their communities.
>
> To find out more about some of the Fairtrade cotton farmers we work with click here. (Marks and Spencer 2009)

The opening statement of the Marks and Spencer text has the effect of constructing time as a continuum in which events are inseparable and merge together in the present. This is achieved by situating the history of the Fairtrade Mark and its meaning as immediately comprehensible by merely watching a video screen. In place of a diachronic flow of time, through which the self-reflexively constituted identity is cultivated, the time of the advertisement has a given beginning and determined end which we can observe from the vantage point of the present. For example the narrative time invoked in the statement 'Fairtrade makes a real difference', begins in the present as a response to a situation of lack and culminates in the present as this lack is defined and satisfied by a guaranteed solution vis-à-vis the statement 'every Fairtrade product you buy will help farmers and workers in developing countries to invest in their communities'. By extension, Williamson (2000) argues that the ideology of the synchronic operates to deny the possibilities of our present as it contrives to map a sense of need onto our experience of the advertisement. As she expresses it 'no present pleasure exits because in the actual present you are looking at the ad anticipating but not enjoying' (2000:155). The advertisement substitutes our lived embodied present with a 'false' present. Within this context we are encouraged to decipher the advertisement's chronological and sequential articulation of time. Thus the material existence of synchronicity 'must be outside of real time, since all time is available to us at once as we stand in real time, in front of the ad' (2000:155). The advertisement in this sense attempts to capture the *Longue Durée* of the Fairtrade brand, both in regards to the re-constructed present and the dislocation of the spectator from the natural flow of time. Several aspects of the individualizing propensity of advertising's construction of, the consumer as a reflexive citizen are addressed by an alternative model of the 'relational' consumer. Indeed, models of the 'relational' consumer provide a valuable re-structuralization of, the conceptual basis of consumption, in relation to the ontological motives and routine negotiation of practical choices about ethical values learned through the disembedding abstract systems of advertising. This approach is consistent with Daniel Miller's (1998) observations concerning ontology and *A Theory of Shopping.*

Love, Value and the Shopping for Self Cultivation

In terms of happiness and fulfilment in life, there is a tendency in the analysis of consumer culture to simplify exchange relations and in so doing reduce their complexity to abstract, market relations motivated by narcissistic self-interest. Consumers are construed as manipulable victims, seduced by transient ephemeral pleasures. In their pursuit of narcissistic delights, consumers apparently, fail to appreciate the extent to which commodity culture undermines their substantive human need for real intellectual autonomy and authentic creative expression. Consumer culture is therefore to be deplored because it perpetuates the alienation of subjects from their substantive needs and, in so doing, sustains modes of depolitization necessary for the reproduction of commodity capitalism. It is unquestionably evident that relations of power are infused into the very cosmology of capitalist commodity culture. And yet it has become increasingly difficult to dismiss contemporary patterns of consumption as inauthentic folly.

Even the most cursory perusal of market trends in ethical consumption suggests that consumers' decisions are not inevitably market-like, rational and utility-maximizing. We have already reviewed statistical evidence of market growth in the purchase of Fairtrade commodities. The spectacular rise in sales of Fairtrade certified products in the UK from £439 million in 2007 to £712.6 million in 2008 suggests in itself that it is difficult to easily dismiss exchange relations as always individualistic and hedonistic. Indeed, what is becoming particularly apparent here is that a vast proportion of shopping is based on an ethics of care. This is to propose that the activity of shopping is intrinsically indexed to 'the activity of constructing a life by negotiating practical choices about personal conduct' (Barnett et al 2005:28). It is from this conceptual basis that Barnett et al, develop their Foucauldian inspired account of ethics so as to present the idea that, 'everyday consumption routines are ordinarily ethical' (ibid). For Barnett et al (2005), clear parallels exist linking the cultivation of the self and the habitual taken for granted dimensions of consumption. This is to presume 'that everyday consumption practices are always already shaped by and help shape certain sorts of ethical dispositions' (ibid:28). From the perspective of social ritual, it is important to appreciate the tacit ethical competences employed even in the act of routine shopping. For, it is by reference to the morality of money, the value of credit and the utility-value of quality, that we accomplish routine consumption practices. And these 'ordinarily ethical' skills and competences, involve procedures and formulas drawn upon as part of the cultivation of the self.

Thus the practice of consumption is not necessarily in contradiction with forms of sociality that involve particular attention to the desires and needs of others. Indeed, it has been empirically observed that 'the purpose of shopping is not so much to buy the things people want, but to strive to be in a relationship with subjects that want things' (Miller 1998:148). A core finding of Daniel Miller's (1998) ethnographic narratives of the social meaning of shopping within families in North London has been, to further confirm the relational sociality of shopping exchanges and highlight the substantively meaningful significance of contemporary shopping. Reading through the richly textured ethnographic narratives presented in Miller's *A Theory of Shopping*, it is convincingly clear that complex dynamics of social inter-relationship, duty and even acts of sacrifice are invoked in the accomplishment of shopping. This is because shopping requires cognizance of the needs and desires of others. However, these altruistic rationalities are often motivated by the hopes, fears and aspirations that the individual shopper ascribes to the subjects and objects of their devotion. It follows that shopping is the 'material culture of love' (ibid:137) instantiated as part of captivating 'family and friends into becoming the ideal subjects that desire what is given to them' (ibid:149). It is 'the siren's song' (ibid), of devotion gilded with the luscious signifying practices of consumer culture and thus even more captivating in its allure.

One implication of this might be to assume that possessions and their signs lure the enchanted shopper into an ephemeral Dionysian reverie that emotionally overwhelms the subject to the point of extinguishing the substantively significant meanings of shopping practice. However, it should be realized that the analogy between love and shopping 'is not the romantic ideal of love' (ibid:150). The concept of love refers, here, to the ideological foundation for complex ascribed and negotiated relationships that exist between kinfolk, friends, marital partners and household members (ibid). In this sense, it is possible to appreciate that love is imbued with dynamic relations of power. And thus 'love as a practice' can be experienced as reciprocal pleasures or in terms of more invidious coercive pressures (ibid). Notwithstanding the ability of love to ideologically structure iniquitous relations, the key issue here is that shopping intrinsically involves a relationality premised on the ethic of care. And this sociality is axiomatic with the cultivation of the self, for 'what the shopper desires above all is for others to want and to appreciate what she [sic] brings' (ibid:149). Thus, instead of the Dionysian pleasure chasing consumer that predominates, studies of recreational shopping, the premise here is that the act of shopping is ontologically relational. That is to say, the act of shopping fundamentally involves the construction of an 'other as the desiring subject' (ibid:148). This point is certainly valid for explaining the act of shopping for others, and it is also relevant to the act of shopping for oneself. This is because both social actions require some reference to an, other, albeit it a generalized other in the case of shopping for oneself. Sayer (2002:353-354) similarly observes this phenomenon and states that 'shoppers may also sometimes seek to buy "treats" for themselves, but even here the egotistical stereotype of shopping needs modification because shopping for treats is defined precisely as the exception to the rule of shopping for others'. It follows that the sociality tied to the act of shopping can embroil the subject into both positive and negative relations, and the later can revolve around 'an often obsessive concern with the micro-trajectories of a few key relationships to which love can be ascribed' (Miller 1998:149). This duality also relates to Miller's very incisive observations concerning the 'dialectic of subjects and objects of devotion' (ibid:148).

An important dimension of the ordinarily ethical basis of shopping is the fundamental affinities that align the act of shopping with the divine religiosity of sacrifice. According to Miller shopping is a dynamic social relation, which has misleadingly simplistic synergies with the act of sacrifice. A cardinal premise of religious sacrifice is the presumed existence of a divine entity (god) that is instantiated through the practice of immolation and thus created 'as a desiring subject' (ibid:148). And much the same is true of consumption, for 'the purpose of shopping is not so much to buy the things people want, but to strive to be in a relationship with subjects that want these things' (ibid). To this end, the act of shopping constructs the subjects of devotion as desiring entities. And thus shopping 'far from being, as it is inevitably portrayed, the essence of ungodliness, becomes as a ritual the vestigial search for a relationship with God' (ibid:150).

Ironically part of this peculiarly secular religiosity, involves the tendency for consumers to align shopping with thrift. According to Miller (1998), saving is an often overlooked and mistakenly foregrounded dimension of shopping. This point is certainly valid when saving is interpreted as a richly symbolic activity and certainly more socially complex than merely the act of spending less money. Indeed, Miller argues 'that is best understood not, as one might suppose, as a means towards some other end, but rather as an end in itself' (ibid:49). The consumer practices of thrift, whilst diverse in their creative permutations and indexed to specific shopping events, all express a paramount concern with 'modesty and an aversion to excess' (ibid:56). Thrift clearly has resonances with quintessential British taciturnity and cautious reserve. But this feature of shopping also has wider relevance to the historical root of Western capitalism. For such self-disciplined probity extend across social classes as Miller (1998:57) states:

> It is possible therefore for thrift to be as powerful a factor for either class, and yet by being manifested through different strategies nevertheless demonstrates the clear symbolic opposition between the classes. Many middle-class shoppers will patronize second-hand and charity clothing shops that working-class shoppers would not dream of using, but the same middle-class shoppers would have considerable difficulty using supermarkets such as Kwiksave and Poundstretcher…

Some indication of the historical significance of thrift is echoed in the edifying expectations of many late nineteenth and early twentieth century social commentators concerned with the relation between consumption and morality. They countenanced capitalist consumption and the insatiable striving for materialism, with a belief in the exemplary life marked by labour and thrift. According to Max Weber (1930), the formal rights and legal procedures of citizenship inter-twined with the moral core of the Protestant Ethic, to provide the psychological impetus for the spread of rationalized entrepreneurial capitalism. Thus the citizen at the heart of Weber's *Protestant Ethic and the Spirit of Capitalism* is prudent, frugal and virtuous. Indulgence and impetuosity equates with mental and bodily indiscipline and threatens the worldly asceticism and self-determined entrepreneurial drive of the citizen.

It is evident that the self-regarding virtues of prudence and frugality conjoined with Christian belief to form the foundation of the Protestant Ethic. Indeed it has been observed that the Protestant Ethic operated as both a categorical influence on the formation of an economic ethic 'and as a final level of causality implicated in the rise of the rational-legal state and of legal citizenship' (Colin 1980:931). Data drawn from the nineteenth century provides fascinating accounts of moralist expositions that drew upon this account of the Protestant Ethic as a basis for chastising against excessive materialism. For example, the Owenite inspired cooperator William Thompson in 1824 once stated 'The consumer (monkey, king, bishop) devours the fruits without return' (quoted in Trentmann 2005:7). Such negative imagery raised profound concerns about the spread of materialism and the effects of profligate living on society's moral values. The very fabric of capitalism relied upon the calculation and predictability of financial markets. Only in a context of ethical beliefs and practices could long-term commercial ventures be established. It would appear that Miller's (1998:56) observations concerning, modern shopping and the 'pride of thrift' link back to this historical trajectory. And thus the 'aversion to excess' and related thrift practices are in tune with the enduring legacy of the Protestant Ethic and the spirit of self-disciplined capitalist work.

From the point of view of expectation, neither the objectified values of thrift nor the eclectic array strategies intended to edify the other, can every be guaranteed in their outcome. And this is implied in Miller's ideology of love and his suggestion that the consequences of propitiatory actions designed to expiate the desiring subject are never certain. Consumers and religious devotees might summon rhetorically the belief that their actions are merely to 'provide for the given wants of their subjects' (ibid:148), but in both cases the action of sacrifice is tinged with the expectation of rejection. Thus beyond the immediacy of the altruism of the gift exchange lies the consequences of failure which introduces risk and jeopardy into both the trajectory of actions carried out by the consumer and the religiosity of the worshipper. It is in this sense, that sacrifice embroils agents into circles of alienation which, Miller (drawing on Hegel) states; presumes 'a form of self alienation which constructs the dynamic of its own subject' (ibid:151). And this introduces into the homology of ritual structure the dimension of time.

A central analogy aligning religious sacrifice and the act of shopping is that both rituals involve the transformation of objects across the temporal dimensions of past, present future. And intrinsic to this is the construction of a reflexively accomplished self-identity. In ritualistic religious sacrifice this transpires as the metamorphosis of ordinarily profane objects into symbols of a higher realm of symbolic value 'where they partake of a relationship which constitutes the divine' (ibid). Similarly in the act of shopping the object transforms its expression from an indistinguishable artefact of commodity culture, into an act of objectification through which the other is uniquely constructed in relation to the shopper. The basic homology of ritual here involves a subjectifying process in which we reflexively 'explore ourselves and develop each other in terms of the potential of the relationship' (ibid). While this observation is in itself interesting, it is particularly valuable to examine the translation of the ordinarily routinely ethical aspects of shopping, into advertising discourse. This is because advertising discursive practices in the context of ethical marketing have resonance with the idea of aesthetics of the self unencumbered by traditional orthodoxy. Such observations are best supported by the theoretical analyses of Foucault (1990, 1991) especially with regards to the transgression and the possibility of the creation of a transgressive aesthetics of the self. But let us briefly examine what Foucault (1990:44) means by the concept of the 'art of existence' and the relevance of this to the creation through advertising of a transgressive ethical consumerism.

Transgressive Aesthetics of the Self

Foucault's oeuvre consistently isolates techniques of power in, which attempts at liberation have the affect of reinforcing oppression. And this observation forms a vital link between three domains of Foucault's genealogy. In the first axis of genealogy, Foucault explores a historical ontology of the self, in terms of an epistemic disruption in *The Order of Things*, which gave rise to the human sciences and the corresponding rendering of 'ourselves as subjects of knowledge' (Foucault 1991:351). In his *Archaeology of Knowledge*, Foucault (1992) traces an epistemic break in the threshold between classicism and modernity. Fundamental to this epistemological disjuncture, is that the representation of the mind and body of the human being ceased to be entirely governed by an objective transcendental mode of order. In the classical era, codes of classification traversed the living embodiment of the subject's consciousness and in so doing, rendered human being as merely an object of nature. Part of modernity's displacement of the notion of human transcendence, involved a double movement in both the ascendancy of knowledge and a modification of what is known about human consciousness of the world. Emanating from the domain of the human sciences, this double movement, constituted a mode of thought 'that takes as its object man as an empirical entity' (Foucault 1997:344). If all knowledge is rooted in the ability of the human being to unveil its experiences as living, labouring and speaking subject, a certain number of enviable consequences become comprehensible. Foucault observed that the imperious unity of knowledge opened up by the human sciences freed the subject in the sense of demystifying subjectivity from the classical order of things. But this freedom is at the cost of the fragmentation of human subjects, through their 'entry into [the] objectivity of something that has long remained trapped within beliefs and philosophies' (ibid:387).

With the advance of modernity, this diffuse agglomeration of objectifying powers becomes annexed to disciplinary technologies, intent on transforming the subject into a malleable object of normative classification and regulation. It is important, here, to recognize that an often misconceived evaluation of the 'carceral society' derives from the assumption that:

> Foucault's conception of the subject as the product of disciplinary techniques imposed on the body left no systematic theoretical space for his own intellectual revolt against what he saw as a ubiquitous process of subjectivization and normalization. (Freundlieb 1995:333)

Such observation fails to apprehend the inextricable co-existence of objectify powers and a ubiquitous process of subjectification, 'in relation to a field of power through which we constitute ourselves as subjects acting on others' (Foucault 1991:351). It is this notion of 'the way a human being turns him- or herself into a subject' (Foucault 1982:208) that forms the basis of the analysis of 'ethics', Foucault's third domain of genealogy. In this axis Foucault counterposed a conception of 'morals' with 'ethics'.

The principle framework of Foucault's analysis of sex and sexuality is to elucidate a history of morals. Methodologically this has involved distinguishing between 'acts' and 'moral codes'. The concept of acts refers to 'the real behaviour of people in relation to the moral code (prescriptions) which is imposed on them' (Foucault 1991:352). Ethics, relates to a side of moral prescriptions, uniquely defined by Foucault (ibid) as 'the kind of relationship you ought to have with yourself, *rapport à soi*'. This infers an element of dynamism concerning self formation, which is unsurprising given that Foucault (ibid:351) extolled the belief 'that the self is not given to us' and thus we are left with 'only one practical consequence: we have to create ourselves as a work of art'. Indeed, Foucault's historical ontology, in relation to ethics, focuses on 'how the individual is supposed to constitute himself as a moral subject of his own actions' (ibid:352).

In short, implicit in the ethical axis of Foucault's genealogy of the self is an examination of ethics in conjunction with power and knowledge, as a way of transgressing limits and redeeming the notion of the subject as a self-determined free agent. And this observation accords with Foucault's analysis of correspondences, between ethics, and the subjectifying propensities invoked by the way in which subjects are invited or impelled to acknowledge their moral obligations. It is at this point that Foucault incisively poses a series of questions highlighting different modes of subjection to moral obligation:

> Is it, for instance, divine law, which has been revealed in a text? Is it natural law, a cosmological order, in each case the same for every living being? Is it a rational rule? Is it the attempt to give your existence the most beautiful form possible? (Foucault 1991:353)

Each mode of subjection relates to a self-reflexive insistence on the attention that should be brought to bear on one's own moral actions. This, in turn, indicates the existence of ethical practices that are bound by externally imposed institutional systems and normative codes. In these circumstances subjectification occurs through the individual's ethico-political choices mediated by moral codes founded on regulatory conventions and governmental rationalities. These quasi-juridical formulations, of moral codes, imbricate individuals in ethical practices for fear of committing an objectively definable, morally indefensible action and punishable offence. Counterpoised to moral codes entrenched in the perspicacity of political, social and economic structures, Foucault explored the possibilities of the formulation of the self by the self, based on a freedom from prescriptive rules of conduct. The possibility of freedom is 'centered on a problem of personal choice, of aesthetics of existence' (Foucault 1991:348).

'Aesthetics of existence' refers to a notion of morality oriented towards a mode of self-referential ethics rather than a set of external norms. The possibility of life as a tapestry for the application of artistic practice fascinated Foucault. Indeed, Foucault lamented the fact that 'art has become something which is related only to objects and not to individuals, or to life' (ibid:350). In modern society aesthetic concerns have been sequestered to the province of creatives and artistic experts, they refer to interior decoration of our homes and are less relevant to 'the *techne* of life, the *techne tou biou*, how to live' (ibid:348). Foucault was passionately committed to resurrecting the art of existence as is evident in the following edict:

> ...we should not have to refer the creative activity of somebody to the kind of relation he has to himself, but should relate the kind of relation one has to oneself to a creative activity. (ibid:351)

From the idea of aesthetics of existence, Foucault developed also the possibility that ethics can be artistic practices, 'a very strong structure of existence' uninvolved in political norms and thus 'without any relation with the juridical per se, with an authoritarian system, with a disciplinary structure' (ibid:348). The mode of subjectification generated through an ethics of self-applied technological or strategic measures is an aesthetic relation to oneself life. In this context technology does not relate to the disciplinary structures of scientific knowledge. Rather, Foucault is keen to draw attention to the fact that:

> Among the cultural inventions of mankind there is a treasury of devices, techniques, ideas, procedures, and so on, that cannot exactly be reactivated, but at least

> constitute, or help to constitute, a certain point of view which can be very useful as a tool for analyzing what's going on now – and to change it. (ibid:349-350)

In these cultural artefacts, drawn from the arts and the sphere of aesthetics, one is unlikely to find normalizing technologies. Rather, the principal resource presented by this bricolage of artefacts is 'only a problem of choice...to live a beautiful life, and to leave to others memories of a beautiful existence' (ibid:341). A point of significant concern to Foucault is that despite our access to these alternative resources for the making of a secular ethics, our ethico-political choices have become constrained by quasi-juridical normalizing judgements and the corresponding belief, that there were analytical relations linking ethics and the fundamental institutional structures of society. In response, Foucault advocates that 'we have to get rid of this idea of an analytical or necessary link between ethics and other social or economic political structures' (ibid:350). In place of a reliance on normative judgements, it should be a case of making 'one's life into an object for a sort of knowledge, for a *techne* – for an art' (ibid:362).

It is in this sense that Foucault dedicates much of the historical ontology of ethics to a study of the conceptual conditions that framed the ancient Greek and Hellenist relations of self to self. In *The Care of the Self; History of Sexuality Volume 3*, Foucault (1990) examines texts that inscribe the ethical and moral contemplations of philosophers and physicians throughout the development of the ancient Greek, Hellenist and Roman world. Deliberating only those historical texts that concentrate on, the question of the ethics of 'pleasure', Foucault identifies statements that appear to mark the ascendancy of new interdictions concerning the possibility of freedom in relation to moral and ethical discovery of the self. While Foucault did not claim to endorse the principles underlying the aesthetics of self mastery advocated in ancient Greek society, he was clearly drawn to the mode of ethical self-formation. Rather than having to conform to the externally imposed moral codes espoused from religious institutions, legal systems and politics dictates, a citizen of the ancient Greek world was more concerned with the problem of personal choice, that is 'which *techne* do I have to use in order to live as well as I ought to live?' (ibid:348). It is this aspect of the mode of ethics in antiquity that clearly inspired Foucault's conception of ethics as he expressed it:

> In antiquity, this work on the self with its attendant austerity is not imposed on the individual by means of civil law or religious obligation, but is a choice about existence made by the individual. People decide for themselves whether or not to care for themselves. (ibid:361)

The mode of ethics in antiquity has significant contemporary relevance for Foucault, mainly as he thought that ethical concerns in today's society had reached a degree of impasse, due to the stifling imposition of large-scale normalizing systems. The incessant regulation of ethico-political judgement is, according to Foucault also affecting the transgressive efforts of recent liberation movements, as he expressed it:

> Recent liberation movements suffer from the fact that they cannot find any principle on which to base the elaboration of a new ethics. They need an ethics, but they cannot find any other ethics than an ethics founded on so-called scientific knowledge of what the self is, what desire is, what the unconscious is, and so on. (ibid:343)

This observation in turn leads Foucault to operationalize the mode of ethics in antiquity, so as to transgress the discursive hegemony of our modern day normalizing ethical regime and enable the exploration of alternative discourse. It is in this respect that I indeed to make analytical parallels between Foucault's analysis of an aesthetics of ethics in antiquity and the secular ethics perpetuated through the art of the advertising of Fairtrade labelled products. For both, focus on 'the idea of the *bios* as a material for an aesthetic piece of art' (ibid:348).

Aesthetics as the Art Fairtrade Advertising

The advertising of Fairtrade labelled products is characterized by a diversified or pluralistic range of subjectifying strategies, where the search for a degree of connectivity between the consumer and producer of highly differentiated products and services is both the condition and consequence of an ethical social identity. Individuals in their capacity as ethical consumers engage with a proliferating multitude of Fairtrade labelled products for the purposes of 'fashion[ing]' (Bauman 1988:808) a distinct and differentiated subjectivity. Ethical identity, in this formulation, does not relate to fixed attributes of personality or self, still less to certain fixed forms of behaviour. Instead, as Giddens states, identity resides 'in the capacity to keep a particular narrative going' (1993:54). It has acquired the status of an ongoing 'project' (1993:54). Identity construction in the late modern era has become a story:

> which a person writes and rewrites about him/herself, never reaching the end until he/she dies and always rewriting the earlier parts, so that the activity of writing becomes itself part of the story. (Gabriel and Lang 1995:86)

Analytical parallels link advertising and 'the will to live a beautiful life, and to leave to others memories of a beautiful existence' (Foucault 1991:341). In the advertising of Fairtrade labelled products, can be elicited a continuity of ethical themes evident in the aesthetics of existence practiced in ancient Greek society. Of particular comparison is the extent to which in both contexts the *techne* of life is primarily concerned with how to live (*techne tou biou*) and 'the problem is to take care of himself [sic]' (ibid). In his analysis of texts derived from antiquity Foucault identifies a recurring insistence on '…the attention that should be brought to bear on oneself' (1990:41). But what marks these texts as particularly distinctive is:

> …the modality, scope, constancy, and exactitude of the required vigilance; it is the anxiety concerning all the disturbances of the body and the mind, which must be prevented by means of an austere regimen; it is the importance attributed to self-respect, not just insofar as one's status is concerned, but as concerns one's rational nature… (ibid)

Among other things, Foucault relates the emergence of these historical pronouncements to the accrescence in the Hellenistic and Roman world 'of an "individualism" that is said to have accorded more and more importance to the "private" aspects of existence…and to the interest that people focused on themselves' (ibid). Foucault is keen to delineate this form of individualism and highlight its subjectifying propensities. He associates the Hellenistic and Roman world with an intensification 'of the relations to self', translated as 'the forms in which one is called upon to take oneself as an object of knowledge and a field of action, so as to transform, correct, and purify oneself, and find salvation' (ibid:42). This self-formation refers to the active development of what Foucault denotes as the 'cultivation of the self', which he defines as a valorisation of the process in which humans self-reflexively turn themselves into ethical subjects, 'wherein the relations of oneself to oneself were intensified' (ibid:43).

The idea of the cultivation of the self, Foucault claims, became a more reflexive practice in the Hellenist and Roman era, this is because it became ruled 'by the principle that says one must "take care of oneself"' (ibid). According to Foucault 'the care of oneself' is tied to an 'art of existence', which is traditionally associated with a philosophical meaning of the 'veritable cultivation of the self' (ibid:44). As Foucault expressed it:

> What interests me in the Hellenistic culture, in the Greco-Roman culture, starting from about the third century B.C. and continuing until the second or third century after Christ, is a percept for which the Greeks had a specific word, *epimeleia heautou*, which means taking care of one's self. It does not mean simply being interested in oneself, nor does it mean having a certain tendency to self-attachment or self-fascination. *Epimeleia heautou* is a very powerful word in Greek which means working on or being concerned with something…It is therefore a very powerful word; it describes a sort of work, an activity; it implies attention, knowledge technique. (Foucault 1991:359–360)

Having worked loose from its original moorings the imperative 'of care of oneself' acquired new dimensions in the Hellenist and Roman era. Foucault observes that the ethic of self-care assumed 'the form of an attitude, a mode of behaviour; it became instilled in ways of living; it evolved into procedures, practices and formulas that people reflected on, developed, perfected and taught' (1990:45). Suffice to say, the cultivation of the self became a social ritual and identity, mediated by practices and designated forms of exchanges and communication. What is significant here is the application of knowledge to the practice of 'taking care of one's self'. It is often assumed that the application of scientific knowledge to the cultivation of the self is a product of modern disciplinary power. Foucault, was keen to highlight a distinction in the form and function of knowledge in the classical care of the self. As he expressed it:

> Knowledge played a different role in the classical care of the self. There are very interesting things to analyze about relations between scientific knowledge and the epimeleia heautou. The one who cared for himself had to chose among all the things that you can know through scientific knowledge only those kinds of things which were relative to him and important to life. (Foucault 1991:360)

Within this chapter I have discussed a similar application of knowledge relevant to the art of Fairtrade labelled products. In their emphasis on narratives, semiotics and trademarks the advertisers transfer highly varied, symbolically charged visual meanings about the: (1) rational decision-making required to voluntaristically support sustainable development through consumption, (2) global consequences of local actions within the context of an increasingly globalized society, and (3) the imperative of love and sacrifice in the ontology of shopping. Consumers actively manipulate these meanings (Campbell 1995) with the deliberate intention of sending signs to others about their integrity as ethically responsible subjects. Consumption is a means of self-construction and 'shopping is not merely the acquisition of things; it is the buying of identity' (Clammer 1992:195). This is because, meaning is constantly cascading from Fairtrade labelled products aided by the ethically minded efforts of advertising creatives. And in so doing, advertising offers the subject personal choice in the production of an aesthetics of existence. Because of the voluntaristic basis of Fairtrade consumption the ethical making of one's life, in this context partakes in an ethics of choice 'for a *techne* – for an art' (Foucault 1991:362). Consequently, 'the same market which offers freedom offers also certainty' (Bauman 1988:61).

Prominent to Foucault's analysis of the ethical pronouncements of ancient philosophical texts is an observation of, the way in ancient Greek culture; the cultivation of the self intersects with medical thought and practice. In his analysis of ancient Greek texts Foucault observes notions and schemas intended to encourage subjects to apply clinical practice to the body as a route to correcting the infirmities of the soul. Foucault describes the existence in this era of 'a whole series of medical metaphors...regularly employed to designate the operations necessary for the care of the soul...'(1990:55). Thus he observes an increased popularization of medical discourse, 'expressed through a particular and intense form of attention to the body' (ibid:56). But this attention is very different from the valorization of the body evident in the stringent fitness regimes of an athlete. For medical involvement in the cultivation of the body is less about treating physical infirmities as true ills. Rather, it is about perceiving the body as the gateway of the soul, and training the body to achieve the deliverance of the soul. As Foucault expresses it:

> ...in fact the focus of attention in these practices of the self is the point where the ills of the body and those of the soul can communicate with one another and exchange their distresses: where the bad habits of the soul can entail physical miseries, while the excesses of the body manifest and maintain the failings of the soul. (ibid:56)

The key to the cultivation of the self, in these ancient times, was therefore the intersection points and the cognition that '...one had best correct the soul if one does not want the body to get the better of it, and rectify the body if one wants it to remain completely in control of itself' (ibid). One effect of the apprehension of the body as a vehicle for the cultivation of the soul, '...is the inducement to acknowledge oneself as being ill or threatened by illness' (ibid:57). The implication here being that the soul, in human beings, exists in a state of imperfection and this intersects with the body so that the individual is 'one who suffers from certain ills and who needs to have them treated' (ibid). Part of this therapeutics requires that the individual seek medical correction administered 'by oneself or by someone who has the necessary competence' (ibid). Thus the cultivation of the soul ritualizes the individualized subject into the regime of clinical medical thought and practice. A situation that Foucault describes as one in which 'everyone must discover that he is in a state of need, that he needs to receive medication and assistance' (ibid).

Analytical parallels exists here linking the concept of the soul in the discourse of ethics evident in antiquity and the self-reflexive cultivation of identity in the advertising of Fairtrade labelled products, a process that Knights and Study (1997) describe as the 'marketing of the soul'. Writing in the late nineteenth century Karl Marx made decisive steps in challenging market society and the reproduction of the relations of capitalist production. While it is evident that Marx recognized the social dimensions of economic phenomena, it has been argued that he insufficiently appreciated 'the human "wants" which commodities satisfy and perhaps the deeper and more complex motivations which they reflect' (Diggins 1978:101). In Marx's dialectical materialism commodities define the alienating propensity of capitalist production. For the progression of capitalism is axiomatic with the enslavement of the worker within a world of fetishized objects and exploitative relations of production. In accordance with this interpretation of Marx's dialectics, alienation is a consequence of the objectification of the labour process, a situation in which 'the "alien medium" of money comes between man and his objects and human relations are now externalized by exchange value, a relation that relates only "thing to thing"' (ibid:101). Marx, it is presumed, disinclined the symbolic value of commodities, and instead focused exclusively on the materiality of objectified relations in capitalist production. To this end writers challenge his dialectics, for insufficiently recognizing that 'the psychological bond between subject and object, between person and thing, is never completely dissolved' (ibid). It is precisely at this theoretical conjecture that Thorstein Veblen (1899/1994) presented his *Theory of the Leisure Class* as a direct challenge to Marx's formulation of reification. This said, a decisive step in Veblen's analysis is that the fetishistic properties of commodities resides in their symbolism and the ability of sign-values to confer 'spiritual well-being' (ibid:63). Veblen's anthropological observations and analyses of the predatory social traits of primitive communities, convinced him in 'the survival of archaic traits of human nature under the modern culture' (ibid:13). Of significance is the role of 'pecuniary emulation' in defining social status and power. In traditional economic theory the acquisition of goods is explained in terms of the accumulation of inter-changeable objects. Conversely, Veblen's anthropological observations demonstrated that objects convey symbolism and sign-values. Commodities radiate distinctive quasi-social attributes. This is precisely because 'commodities are rich with human meaning, but that meaning exists solely in the mind of the interpreter' (Diggins 1978:103).

This anthropomorphic propensity to project onto matter subjective meaning has the affect of transforming inanimate things into animate meanings, which form the basis of 'invidious distinction' (ibid). Indeed, it is evident that 'wherever the institution of private property is found, even in a slightly developed form, the economic process bears the character of a struggle between men for the possession of goods' (Veblen 1994:16). For Veblen this is because, with the exception of self-preservation, emulation is possibly one of the most powerful factors motivating human behaviour. Veblen's observations of commodity culture in the nineteenth century lead him to further argue that 'this propensity for emulation expresses itself in pecuniary emulation; and this, so far as regards the Western civilized communities of the present, is virtually equivalent to saying that it expresses itself in some form of conspicuous waste' (ibid:68). The ritual of conspicuous waste operates in tandem with the industrial efficiency and accelerated output of capitalist production. And this brings us back to the current era and the advertising of Fairtrade labelled products. According to Veblen the apprehension of value, in terms of invidious distinction, is a source of the animism in human beings. This is because, '...the standard of expenditure which commonly guides our efforts is not the average, ordinary expenditure already achieved; it is an ideal of consumption that lies just beyond our reach...' (ibid:64). In its role as an effigy to Fair Trade ethics, advertising in this sector has become a spectacular staging of emulation 'the stimulus of an invidious comparison which prompts us to outdo those with whom we are in the habit of classing ourselves' (ibid). It is precisely this feature of promotional culture that leads Veblen to argue that the alienation of commodities resides, not solely as a feature of their material production. For reification is as significantly in operation when:

> the conspicuously wasteful honorific expenditure that confers spiritual well-being may become more indispensable than much of that expenditure which ministers to the 'lower' wants of physical well-being or sustenance only. (Veblen 1899/1994:63)

And this observation raises serious questions about the advertising of Fairtrade labelled products in terms of a mode of subjectification, in which individuals are invited to recognize their moral obligations through commodity culture. It is evidently clear that political power is exercised by the consumer through an aesthetics of, self-forming, ethical activities in, which the consumer applies deciphering techniques in 'a choice about existence made by the individual' (Foucault 1991:361). But, as part of 'making one's life into an object…for a *techne* – for an art' (ibid:362), the consumer becomes committed to the application of aesthetic values to 'one's life, one's existence' (ibid). This chapter has asked and answered important critical questions about the outcomes of this mode of subjection. Elsewhere, it has also been recognized that the 'ordinarily routine' (Barnett et al 2005:23), practices of consumption constitute the substance for the:

> ways in which everyday practical moral dispositions are re-articulated by policies, campaigns and practices that enlist ordinary people into broader projects of social change (ibid).

While in agreement with this observation, it is has been my contention that such readings of Foucault insufficiently recognize the importance Foucault attributed to 'the principal role of art' in the making of a secular ethics committed to the idea that 'one must apply aesthetic values' to 'one's life, one's existence' (ibid:362). Drawing on Foucault's (1991) concept of the 'aesthetics of existence' this chapter's primary focus has been the possibilities and problematics, presented by advertising's relevance to the making of a secular ethics of how to live (*techne tou biou*), which is unencumbered by the quasi-juridical, authoritarian dedicates of normalizing technologies.

Conclusion

In his analysis of antiquity Foucault (1991), was keen to trace the circumstances that might encourage an intensification of the conditions that lead to such a spectacularly aesthetic, ethical relation with oneself. According to Foucault, it wasn't an increase in coercive political power that inculcated this form of self cultivation, but rather a moderation of the political and social context governing the everyday lives of subjects. Foucault observes how the weakening of political obligations tying subjects to cities and increased isolation from collective forms of social solidarity lead to an increased reliance, in the first two centuries, upon philosophical rules of conduct. Of particular popularity were those philosophical rules that guided the conduct of the personal patrimonial interests and an excitation into discourse of doctrines focusing on 'the intensity of the relations to self' (1990:42). The latter refers to a discursive constellation directed at 'the forms in which one is called upon to take oneself as an object of knowledge and a field of action, so as to transform, correct, and purify oneself, and find salvation' (ibid).

Suffice to say, the care of the self is in fact an 'art of existence', in which the ever penitent human is dedicated to the cultivation and redemption of the soul.

In late modernity the dynamics of individualization, coupled with the highly reflexive self and rise of life politics provide the conditions for 'reflexively organized life-planning' (Giddens 1993:5). In this context, self-actualization refers to the process of confronting uncertainty in terms of risks that transude from a proliferating array of abstract knowledge systems. Such methods of the structuring of self-identity tend to be pragmatically managed in relation to the global implications of local lifestyle choices. And this involves subjects in the pursuit of alternative value systems, which although being indexed to their immediate locale involve a re-moralized tolerance on many levels of global interaction. Even the most affirmative invocation of consumer sovereignty would refrain from linking it with the altruistic endeavour to 'maximize overall consumer welfare' (Dickinson and Carsky 2007:29). This is because the market economics of, consumer sovereignty, transforms social relations into bilateral relations (between a buyer and a seller), which are 'established for the duration of the transaction' (Needham 2003:13). It is this transient aspect of economic exchange, which motivates direct contrasts between the concepts of the consumer sovereign with the practice of 'consumer citizenship'. As Dickinson and Carsky (2007:29) express it:

> That consumer sovereignty would in some sense maximise overall consumer welfare, is of course, an absurdity. Firms have their needs and desires and produce what is in their best interests to produce...Consumers also have their needs and desires, as do governments. The resulting markets are influenced by all kinds of factors including the impact of these three: firms, governments and consumers. (Dickinson and Carsky 2007:29)

Thus the consumer as citizen refers to a category of social responsibility in, which self-regarding subjects make reflexive preferences in the context of rights and responsibilities (Needham 2003:15). The concept of reflexivity is crucial to understanding the phenomena of the consumer citizen, and its articulation into the brand politics of Fair Trade advertising. This is because the advertising of Fairtrade labelled products operates as a conduit of symbolic values through which meanings, moralities and ethics are circulated in the cultural political relationships interconnecting the consumer and producer. Though the international trade in Fair Trade products has grown substantially in the era of neoliberal globalization, this progress has been driven by the meteoric ascendancy of ethical consumerism and its tenacious resistance to the exploitative market conditions of global neo-liberalization. Products that carry the Fairtrade label signify a non-governmental approach to sustainable development. Indeed, as we have seen the signifying practices of Fair Trade advertising intervenes into the hedonistic fetishism that pervades capitalist commodity culture. It achieves this by emphasising the ethically driven relationships between producers and importers. Indeed, strict procedures established by FLO International and certified by FLO-CERT's inspections embed into the Fairtrade brand visible recognition of the integrity of the commodity. This is because Fairtrade ensures that importers are forced beyond a myopic isolated concern for the commodity, towards a more altruistic concern 'with the producers themselves, their social relations of production, and the ecological character of the interactive process of transformation between humans and nature' (Hudson and Hudson 2003:421). To this end the presence of the Fairtrade Mark operates as a point of differentiation, not in terms of the product's attributes, but rather its differentiates on the basis of the ethically mediated production process (ibid).

This approach exceeds the preoccupation, by conventional ethical trading movements, with the relations of commodity exchange. In contrast, Fair Trade focuses on both the relations of exchange and relations of production implicated in the global chain of commodity-based exploitation. To this end, Fair Trade's cultural politics embodies a commitment to achieving a 'shaped advantage' for the most disadvantaged producers in the developing world. Central to this approach has been a focus on the self-reflexively ethical consumer citizen as a primary market driver. In the sociology of modernity, writers draw attention to the emergence of a mode of subjectivity and self-identity tied to late modernity and the imperative of self-actualization against a background of dynamic and unparalleled globalization. Writers here constitute Fair Trade consumers as both, individually and collectively involved in re-moralizing reflexive practices against the backdrop of global transitions and transformations. Although such choices are partially expressed in the rejection of lifestyles that sustain the inequities of traditional social hierarchies, they are also manifest through the signifying practices of consumer culture. It is therefore necessary to examine, the role of advertising as a symbolic resource relevant to the actualization of the self-identity of the ethical consumer.

But, it needs to be recognized that advertising presents simultaneously possibilities for an, aesthetics of ethical existence and for its neutralization as a mode of subjectification in which individuals are self-disciplined into an incessant regime of invidious distinction. Foucault (1991:362) was cognizant of this tendency for the translation of the 'cult of care' to override its transgressive potential, as he expressed it:

> In the Californian cult of the self, one is supposed to discover one's true self, to separate it from that which might obscure or alienate it, to decipher its truth thanks to psychological or psychoanalytic science, which us supposed to be able to tell you what your true self is. There, not only do I not identify this ancient culture of the self with what you might call the Californian cult of the self, I think they are diametrically opposed. (Foucault 1991:362)

This chapter has sought to examine advertising's role in the promotion of a mode of secular ethics predicated on the art of existence. The aesthetization of cultural politics through the advertising of Fairtrade labelled products is evident and formidable in its scope. Firstly, advertising is inextricably linked to the art of existence perpetuated by the Fairtrade brand and its global recognition. Secondly, recent transformations in advertising language, from utility to sign-value, exercise the reflexivity of contemporary culture. And this is enhanced by the fact that, the signifying practices of postmodern advertising have detraditionalizing properties, which directly challenging cultural reproduction and the hegemony of *habitus* as a determinant of choice. As Clarke et al (2007:10) express it 'consumer culture features a populist and quasi-egalitarian impulse, asserting that everyone is entitled to consume and to consume what they want. It disrupts conventions and hierarchies of taste and access'. And finally advertising is axiomatic to Giddens' notion of 'life politics' (1998). Which refers to 'disputes and struggles about how…we should live in a world where what used to be fixed either by nature or tradition is now subject to human decisions' (Giddens 1993:15). The implication here is that the reflexive subject of late modernity fashions a sense of identity through the signifying practices of consumption choices. But life politics is not merely a politics of self interest and maximizing individual gain. Rather 'in the domain of life politics individuals or groups take lifestyle decisions that limit or actively go against maximising economic returns' (ibid:102). Consequently the consumer as citizen is a morally privileged subject cognizant of its rights and responsibilities. But this is also a source of tension, especially because 'relying on individualistic notions of choice and consumer sovereignty rests on the dominant idea that the market is an avenue for democratic expression that is, in many ways, superior to the political arena' (Hudson and Hudson 2003:426).

PART IV
Techno-Political Caesura

Techno-politics in global times

Source: Piccadilly Circus London, May 2009, photographed by Pamela Odih.

Chapter 8
Technoscapes and the Geo-Politics of Global Advertising

In recent decades there have been unprecedented transformations in the rhythms of capital circulation. 'For the first time in history, the capitalist mode of production shapes social relationships over the entire planet' (Castells 2000:471). Marx and Engels had long since anticipated that 'the need of a constantly expanding market' would chase 'the bourgeoisie over the whole surface of the globe' (1985:37). Since the 1970s flexibility has developed as an efficacious adumbrate of capital accumulation. Flexible accumulation has broken down the vertically integrated rigidities of Fordist production. And this has been an integral condition for the transition to a more technologically dynamic circulation of capital. In as much as capitalist accumulation depends on the production of surplus value, the circuits which capital travels 'appears as the time of devaluation' (Marx 1973:538). This is because the speed of circulation directly determines 'the speed with which the production process is repeated' (ibid:538). Since this is the case, the fundamental operation of the capitalist economy is to multiply 'how often capital can be realized in a given period of time' (ibid:538). Indeed businesses, which fail to accelerate turnover time risk surrendering their profits to competitors. Consequently capital must on the one hand strive to eradicate spatial barriers to exchange and on the other hand strive to 'annihilate this space with time, i.e., to reduce to a minimum the time spent in motion from one place to another' (1973:593). The more advanced the capital, the more predicated it is upon the continuous expansion of market relations and the more it strives for 'greater annihilation of space by time' (ibid:539). To this extent capitalist accumulation 'cannot exist without constantly revolutionizing the instruments of production' (Marx and Engels 1985:37). This translates into continuous transformations in the modes of production as all fixed relations are swept away and 'all newly-formed ones become antiquated before they can ossify' (1985:37).

Transformations of this magnitude are currently revolutionising Western capitalism. This is because unparalleled advances in micro-electronic technology have intensified knowledge-based productivity. In the new 'informational' economy, innovation is the essential revenue 'of productivity growth' (Castells 2009:33). Capital accumulation proceeds and profit is generated 'increasingly in the global financial markets enacted by information networks in the timeless space of financial flows' (Castells 1996:472). Axiomatic to the revolution of informationalism is the fragmentation of power which 'is no longer concentrated in institutions (the state), organizations (capitalist firms), or symbolic controllers'

(Castells 1997:359). Rather, power is diffused into global networks of capital, information, real and virtual images 'which circulate and transmute in a system of variable geometry and dematerialised geography' (ibid:359). These ongoing processes of globalization and market liberalization have accentuated the persistent exploitation between capital and labour. In the 'network society', the central anxiety for labour is its marginal capacity as mere executants of instructions orchestrated by the manufacturers of innovation in the informational global economy. As dominant functions and processes in the informational age, become pervaded by networks, the greatest insecurity is to be 'invisible to the programs commanding the global networks of production, distribution and valuation' (Castells 2009:33). Indeed, the accentuation of the social and cultural exclusion, of vast segments of the world's population from the power centres of global networks, has become a formidable obstacle to sustainable development. It is the backlash of the alienated in the form of anti-globalization movements that constitutes the empirical focus of this chapter. On balance the rise of networked global capitalism has paralleled the development of geopolitical strategies organized in the form of global networks. Given that 'the specific structure of communication of a given society largely shapes social movements' (ibid:301), it is unsurprising that organized resistance to globalized market capitalism is increasingly structured around networks. However, what is uniquely interesting about, globally networked social movements is the integration of multimodal digital communication processing technologies, into geopolitical strategies. Part of the motivation fuelling this micro-electronic technological revolution can be explained in terms of global times, and the increasingly acute distinction between the 'space of flows' and the 'space of place'. In traditional social theory, space provides a material context for enacting, simultaneously, shared social practices. To this end, 'space defines the time frame of social relationships' (Castells 2010: xxxi). Space in this sense is contiguous with the physicality of material place. And thus, the 'space of places' is 'the space of contiguity' (ibid). Advances in micro-electronically operated digital communication technologies have transformed the spatiality of social interaction by decoupling the contiguity of space-time, as a boundary to the communicative interaction of social actors. The emerging re-configured spatial context has been called 'the space of flows' (ibid:xxxii). This form of spatiality is defined as 'the material support of simultaneous social practices communicated at a distance' (ibid). It refers to a radical transformation in communication technologies and the new 'possibility of practicing simultaneity without contiguity' (Castells 2009:34). Given that the dominant logic of global capitalism is the relentless annihilation of space by time, alternative projects for the structuration of trade will involve an engagement with the fact that global capitalist accumulation is rapacious in its annihilation of the space of places. In global times, the disaffected are deeply fragmented by the double logic of their exploited inclusion and alienated exclusion from the space of flows. The resulting local demands for solutions to global problems, have directed the concerns of 'alternative trade' initiatives. Organizations such as the Fair Trade movement directly challenge international commercial relations that operate around abstract market principles that devalue and exploit producers and the environment. In their endeavour to create a more socially and ecologically sustainable society, alternative trade initiatives are orientated towards the 'translation' of global political spaces into local political concerns.

In Chapter 7, I examined the semiotic strategies used to re-embed global commodity circuits within local ecological and social relations. These transgressive aesthetics need also to be understood in terms of material structures of actor-networks concerned with the production, articulation and processing of informational flows. In Actor Network Theory (ANT), the construction of alternative trade networks can be appreciated in terms of the articulation, by actor-networks, of interests and their 'translation' into networked structures. Invariably this process of 'translation' involves a process in which, agencies enrol other agencies into the shared belief that the achievement of, alternative trade certification, is a solution to their divergent problems. In ANT, translation is defined as 'the process through which an agency enrols other agencies in order to forge alliances in situations of organizational struggle and conflict' (Ezzamel 1994:218). In more generic terms, the process of translation is said to be constituted by four 'moments'; 'problematization', 'interessement', 'enrolment' and 'mobilization' (ibid).

In so far as, alternative trade networks are market-based political movements, moments of translation require 'the development of localities as nodes of these communication networks, and the connectivity of activities located in these nodes by fast transportation networks operates by informational flows' (Castells 2010: xxxii). In their endeavour to convince agencies to bring their commodity supply chains, into compliance with alternative trade based codes, enrolling agencies are increasingly ceasing upon the versatility and networking capability of advertising technoscapes. In the 'software universe' of modern advertising communication, space can be traversed literally in 'no time' (Bauman 2000:117). Global trends in the digital convergence between traditional mass media and internet-based communication have radically reshaped the infrastructure of advertising. Traditional agency practice involved coordinating planning decisions across vertical communication channels comprising telephony, visual communication and data (Ancarani and Shankar 2003:57). Global electronic communication has precipitated a new digital convergent industry, which has revolutionized the logic of traditional advertising. In this new multimedia industry content production converges horizontally with transmission, packaging and reception (ibid:57). Consequently there has been a transition from information distribution 'dependent on content, specific technology and dedicated hardware' towards an 'independent content system distributed through a shared infrastructure' (ibid:57). Advertisers can now supply a more heterogeneous service in a more synergistic way. In the brand new world of digital convergence, commercials and programme content are delivered synchronously through the mixing of horizontal communication modes of interactive networks (e.g., social networking sites) with vertical networks of multi-media advertising channels; at any place and time of day. Advertising in our brand new global times, is a multimodal internet-based communication network. Where these features have combined with the digitization of content, advertising 'is self-generated in content, self-directed in emission and self-selected in reception' (Castells 2010:xxx).

It is precisely because, contemporary advertising technoscapes are multimodal using both convergent communication networks and mainstream advertising media, that they are able to translate divergent commercial interests, into the autonomous capacity, of alternative trade networks, to shape the process of political change. Focusing on the network structure of the Fairtrade Foundation, this chapter identifies advertising technoscapes as integral mechanisms, for the re-embedding of international commodity-chains into relations of solidarity between globally dispersed actor-networks committed to achieving sustainable development through alternative trade.

Technoscapes and Network Morphology

Manuel Castells (2001:157) deftly weaves the sparse threads of the concept of 'information society' previously developed by social scientists; most notably Daniel Bell's (1976) *The Coming Of Post-Industrial Society*. Castells clearly supports the observation that in post-industrial society information and knowledge are becoming central to wealth, power and work. However, knowledge and information have throughout history been necessary components of social formations. To this extent, Bell's assertions about information and post-industrial society represent a mere anthropological continual evident in all human societies. Notwithstanding the continued relevance of knowledge to the economy, what is distinctive about the role of information in our current era is 'a new technological paradigm ushered in by the information-technology revolution' (Castells 2001:158). In this current information revolution, there is a dynamic coming together of 'the technology of information processing and the impact of this technology on the generation and application of knowledge' (ibid). Evidently it is this feature, of recent transformations, that disinclines Castells to use either the concept of information society or the knowledge economy. Instead, we are encouraged to apprehend the new technological revolution using the concept of 'informationalism', which is defined as:

> a technological paradigm based on the augmentation of the human capacity in information processing around the twin revolutions in microelectronics and genetic engineering. (Castells 2001:159)

The technological capabilities captured by the informationalism concept, relate specifically to three distinctive features of the micro-electronic revolution, which has exploded into the material infrastructure of Western capitalism. Firstly, micro-electronic based technologies (e.g., computers and their networking) are infinitely more advanced in their 'self-expanding processing capacity in terms of volume, complexity and speed' (ibid:160). For example, the micro-electronic based technologies which support web-advertising enable users, in real time, to interactively modify the form and content of a mediated advertisement (Steuer 1992:2). Experientially, interactive websites intensify the audience member's exposure to advertisements. And in terms of revenue generation, economies of scale are achieved by the electronic transformation of messages into micro-fragments, which need not take up an entire circuit and allow for an economical use of transmission capacity. Interestingly, one of the more progressive features of the interactivity of a web-advertisement has been the recent development of push applications inserted into online advertising broadcasting streams. In an effort to remind consumers of the credentials that underline the ethical trading initiative *Plan A*, the UK based retail company Marks and Spencer, in 2009, launched its 'Doing the Right Thing' campaign. Initially designed as a marketing push for its five year, 100 pledges sustainability plan, the campaign was circulated across print formats, broadcast media, in-store and on the internet. Part of Marks and Spencer's sustainability plan involves a long term commitment to the use of Fairtrade certified cotton (see Chapter 6). Suffice to say it aims to convert '20 million clothing garments including £5 plain t-shirts, women's strappy vests and Oxford shirts to Fairtrade cotton – equal to 10% of all M&S cotton use' (Marks and Spencer 2009). This aspect of the *Plan A*, campaign is supported by a website entitled Fairtrade Cotton. The website is interesting mainly because of the innovative array of push applications that it contains. For example, on entry into the website the user is prompted to navigate an interactive banner, which initiates a video of the Fairtrade farmers that are the producers of the cotton for Marks and Spencer's Fairtrade labelled textiles. Additional interactive devices include a 'WWF Footprint Calculator'. Users can input into this device information that enables them to measure their eco footprint. Having activated promotional hyper-text links on the web-page, the user enters an electronic gateway of promotional information and additional offers directly relevant to the Fairtrade product range. Impulse Response (IR) formats are also an especially useful means of gaining information from the audience member. In this mode of application, when various prompts are activated an overlay automatically appears on the screen containing text and graphics designed to illicit information. Advertisers value IR platforms for their ability to create a 'return path' that capacitates 'the advertiser to close the loop: to listen to and answer the viewer' (Johnson 2002:36). Implied in this definition is the ability of interactive advertisements to generate unforeseen combinations of information inputs from the audience. And this is particularly pertinent to a second technologically distinctive feature of the micro-electronic revolution.

Castells argues that the material foundation of this new economic era is pervaded by micro-electronic technologies that are capable of recombining information in innovative ways. As he expresses it:

> Recombination is the source of innovation, particularly if the products of this recombination become themselves supports for further interaction, in a spiral of increasingly meaningful information. (2001:163)

It is worth reiterating here that Castells is disinclined towards the use of the concept of the knowledge society and this is further borne out in relation to the notion of recombination. A self-expanding mass of recombined information will eventually require the application of theory so as to transform this into knowledge. However, 'the ability to experiment with this recombining from a multiplicity of sources considerably extends the realm of knowledge' (ibid). Thus the notion of informationalism substantially exceeds the innovative capacities of the knowledge economy. And this leads to a third distinguishing feature of the new era, namely the concept of flexibility. While it is often considered that technology restructures the relations of capitalist production, the revolution in micro-electronic based technologies, 'in allowing the distribution of processing power in various contexts and application', has precipitated a new social morphology of flexible capitalism (ibid). Castells names this new form of social structure 'the network society' and his analysis of informationalism provides the basis for his overarching conclusion:

> dominant functions and processes in the Information Age are increasingly organized around networks. Networks constitute the new social morphology of our societies, and the diffusion of net-working logic substantially modifies the operation and outcomes in processes of production, experience, power, and culture. (Castells 2000:500)

Bourne from the material fabric of micro-electronic based technologies, the network society has permeated the organizational relations of production, consumption and reproduction in Western capitalist societies. Network morphology is expeditiously provoking the rational linear boundaries of 'organized capital' (Lash and Urry 1999). Industrialization brought linear synchronicity to the assembly lines of Fordist factories. It heralded clock-time as the central organizing principle of modernist production. But this linear, predictable time is being radically challenged in the network society. For, it is striking how:

> networks are self-reconfigurable, complex structures of communication that ensure, at the same time, unity of purpose and flexibility of its execution by the capacity to adapt to the operating environment. (Castells 2004:4)

In a network society, the chronological time of mass production is displaced by a contextual relativity 'to the temporality of other firms, networks, processes or products' (Castells 2000:468). It is a spatially disaggregated, techno-economically networked globalization that now propels flows of capital. And this provides some sense of the new social structures' complex assemblage.

Built around micro-electronic based technologies, 'a network is a set of interconnected nodes' (Castells 2009:19). A node is the position 'at which a curve intersects itself' (ibid). While it is indeed the case that networks have existed throughout history, the microelectronics at the heart of modern networks has dramatically reinvigorated the flexibility of this structural form. This is because the foundations of informationalism provide advanced technological solutions to 'the coordination and steering problems', which have thwarted the operational efficiency of networks throughout human history (Castells 2001:168). Such reflections clearly attest to the competitive advantage gained by open networked structures, against forms of social organization based on vertical-hierarchical organizations. Much of the advantage here stems from the fact that networks are not built around a nucleus. For the structural form defined by networks consists of interconnected circuits, intersected by nodes of inconsistent sizes and relevancies. The concept of relevancy designates a mode of congruity discerned by the ability of a node to contribute to the goals of the network. Thus the vitality of a node does not stem from its specific dimensions, but rather its ability to further 'the values and interests programmed into the networks' (Castells 2009:20). Consequently, organic rhizomatic growth drives the formation of this structure, such that:

> when nodes become unnecessary for the fulfilment of the network's goals, networks tend to reconfigure themselves, deleting some nodes, and adding new ones. Nodes only exist and function as components of networks. The network is the unit, not the node. (ibid)

Given that in all possible social formations 'networks are communicative structures' it has been argued that 'networks process flows' (ibid). In developing the concept of 'flows', Castells defines this phenomenon as 'streams of information between nodes, circulating through the channels of connection between nodes' (ibid). The dynamic rhizomatic growth of networks is axiomatic with communicative structures that circulate information about the intentionality and goals of the network. Defined as the network's 'program', these goals are constituted in the form, 'of codes that include valuation of performance and criteria for success or failure' (ibid).

Programmes, Switches and Networking Power

When perceived as an assemblage of interconnected nodes, the material basis of networks appears to operate in accordance with a binary logic of inclusion/exclusion (ibid). To this extent, nodes can be discerned as 'switches and protocols of communication, following a networking logic rather than a command logic in their performance' (ibid). Consequently, nodes are not the locus of power in network morphology. 'Nodes only exist and function as components of networks. The network is the unit, not the node' (Castells 2004:3). To this end, power is circulated through the mechanisms that interconnect networks. As Castells expresses it, in networking logic, complex flows of actions control power. The net result of this complexity is the pre-eminence of networked relations over individual social actions. When applied to a formal analysis of power it is apparent that, where social relations are built on networks, the ability to exercise influence depends on two principle mechanisms: (a) the dexterity of social actors and institutions to programme/reprogramme the collective intentionality of a given network and (b) the ability to create connection points linking strategically valued networks, 'by sharing common goals and combining resources, while fending off competition from other networks by setting up strategic cooperation' (Castells 2009:45).

Castells (2009) calls the first axiom of power, 'programmers' and the second, 'switches'. In developing this network logic, Castells depicts 'programmers' and 'switches' as social entities that incorporate a complexity of repertoires, which are with difficulty reduced to the actions of individuals. Indeed, these mechanisms operate at the interface between structured groups of social actors. Thus, Castells suggests 'that in many instances the power holders are networks themselves' (ibid:45). This consideration is even more revelatory when we unravel the workings of the two main exercisers of power in the world of networks i.e., 'programmers' and 'switches'. First of all, the programming of a network's intentionality induces a social determination that will pervade and transform all domains of the network's social and economic existence. Thus, despite its reliance on institutions and social actors to inscribe meaningful programmes, once its goals are configured 'information networks, powered by information technology, impose their structural logic on their human components' (Castells 2001:167). For instance, let us here consider the evolution of the Fair Trade global network (detailed in Chapter 6). During its first incarnation, within the context of the Bretton Wood era, Fair Trade networks focused on macro-economic policies for sustainable development. It has been suggested that this era in the evolution of Fair Trade 'was highly process-focused and supply rather than demand driven' (Nicholls and Opal 2005:230). In the 1980s, the adoption of neo-liberal, market-lead promotional strategies, precipitated a dramatic reprogramming of Fair Trade networks. In their efforts to mainstream distribution channels network intermediaries began to engage with conventional retailers.

Consequently the Fair Trade network, in the late 1980s, was reprogrammed, that is to say, it reconfigurated itself in terms of the development of flows and the formulation of new nodes so as to achieve its re-directed goals. It is striking how the ability to transform the goals of the Fair Trade network was predicated on the establishment, from the late 1980s of national and then international labelling and certification initiatives. The consolidations of these labelling initiatives lead to the establishment of the Fairtrade Labelling Organization International (FLO). Set up in 1997, the primary remit of FLO was to communicate a world standard for Fairtrade labelled products. Suffice to say this structure operated in accordance with the networking logic of flows, i.e., as a stream of 'information between nodes, circulating through the channels of connection between nodes' (Castells 2009:20).

It was FLO's role in the circulation of information that tied together the intention, visions and projects of actors within the Fair Trade movement strengthening their connectivities. Thus, when in 2004 the main Fairtrade labelling institutions split into FLO International (which creates Fairtrade standards) and FLO-CERT (which inspects and certifies producer cooperatives and audits the practices of traders) the newly reconfigurated network was, in terms of structure and nodes, more able to achieve its goals. The dynamism of FLO International and FLO-CERT are testament to the fact that power in the network is embedded in processes of communication. Ultimately the goals of the network are received on the basis of the exposure, of its constituent members, to the processes of communication (Castells 2009:46). Thus, 'control of, or influence on, the networks of communication, and the ability to create an effective process of communication and persuasion along the lines that favour the projects of the would-be programmers, are the key assets in the ability to program each network' (ibid). Indeed, the evolution and diffusion of the Fair Trade global network demonstrates that, the ability of a network to reconfigure itself depends on the capacities of would-be programmers to enact processes of communication. And in so doing, programmers constitute one of two prominent 'fields of power in the network society' (ibid).

Alongside programmers, power in networks is configured around the networking capability of 'switches'. Castells (2009:46) defines switches in terms of 'the control of the connecting points between various strategic networks'. It is important not to confuse switches with less significant ordinarily routine connections between groups (e.g., Freemasons). For switches partake of a higher order of social connectivity. This is because, 'these are specific interface systems that are set on a relatively stable basis as a way of articulating the actual operating system of society beyond the formal self-presentation of institutions and organizations' (ibid). It is precisely because switches 'translate' the mode in, which jointed parts are linked that they have important implications for the analysis of alternative trading networks and their embedded advertising technologies.

Network Technology and the Translation Flows of Alternative Trading Switches

Network is a figurative apologue for the flows of 'translations' that human and non-human actors foster in making connections (Mutzel 2009:877). According to Latour (1987:108) translation refers to 'the interpretation given by the fact-builders of their interests and that of the people they enrol'. Thus, translation is the process through, which the explicit interests of an agency, and those of another agency, are associatively enlisted so as to affiliate common definitions. Translations create moments of convergence in the chains of arguments that associate different arenas. To this end, the process of translation involves procedures, employed by agents, to transform both human and non-human resources, into complex networks of power directed at engineering strategic alliances; while retaining the heterogeneity of allied parties. Enacted through multifarious actor-networks, processes of translation in alternative trading networks can be delineated into four interconnected moments: 'problematization', 'interessement', 'enrolment' and 'mobilization' (Ezzamel 1994:219).

Translating the Problematization of Alternative Trading Networks

Problematization refers to the (re)articulation of a complication, by an agency so as to enrol other agencies into the reassurance that an alliance of interested parties is strategically the most efficacious solution to their respective problems. In terms of the translation effect of network switches, problematization provides a moment in which disparate interests held by agents form the basis of powerful networked alliances. The translation of problems, thus initiates relevancies (Latour 1987:127), through which circulate the chains of argument that link different agents and their explicit interests. Such processes of translation are presently networking affinities between alternative trade social labelling initiatives and the corporate responsibility objectives of global brands. Of particular significance is the mobilization of the Fairtrade Mark as a vehicle through which commercial and non-commercial bodies have reformulated their respective problems. An apposite example of how advertising technology fosters a translation of these two arenas can be derived from a brief case study of the environmental sustainability and alternative trading commitments, of the UK based global confectionary company Cadbury. Established in 1824, Cadbury has since expanded its 'business throughout the world by a programme of organic and acquisition led growth' (Cadbury 2009d). It is now a leading global competitor amongst the world's 50 largest confectionary markets.

Central to Cadbury's governing objective is a commitment to sustainability. Specifically, Cadbury has a stated dedication to 'Promoting responsible consumption through thoughtful marketing, product innovation and better nutritional labelling' and 'Ensuring ethical and sustainable sourcing including the Cadbury Cocoa Partnership to support farmers and their communities' (Cadbury 2009). To this end, Cadbury states that 'We see corporate social responsibility and sustainability as key to our future success – helping us create a world in which we can grow and thrive' (Cadbury 2009). In July 2007, Cadbury launched its *Purple Goes Green* environmental responsibility campaign. It pledged to reduce its carbon emissions by 50 per cent and achieve a 10 per cent reduction in excess packaging. In order to implement this initiative Cadbury is committed to working with its supply chain 'to reduce the size of our collective carbon footprint' (Cadbury 2009a). Billed as an absolute commitment to address climate change, *Purple Goes Green* was also expressed by the then Chief Executive Officer (Todd Stitzer) in more commercial terms. For example it was stated that 'Not only will this have a strong social and environmental impact but also a positive economic impact too in the longer term' (ibid). Cadbury's mixing of ethical practice and commercial profit is also evident in the following extract derived from its Sustainability Commitments:

> As well as being the right thing to do, they also create value and competitive advantage, helping to strengthen our business, build our reputation, and motivate our people. (Cadbury 2009)

The articulation of sustainability commitments into 'business opportunities' and revenue growth is even more evident in *The Cadbury Cocoa Partnership*, which was established in January 2008. The partnership initially involved Cadbury entering a networked alliance with rural cocoa farmers in Ghana, local government representatives, the United Nations Development Programme and Non-Governmental Organizations (NGOs). According to Cadbury, *The Cadbury Cocoa Partnership* is committed to securing the livelihood 'and environmental sustainability of around a million cocoa farmers and their communities in Ghana, India, Indonesia and the Caribbean through a £45 million investment over ten years' (Cadbury 2009b). In January 2009 the press media were notified that *The Cadbury Cocoa Partnership* had been activated across 100 Ghanaian communities. This landmark also coincided with the 100th anniversary of cocoa trading between Cadbury and Ghana.

In 2009, Cadbury, in its efforts to extend its partnership commitments to Ghana, sought Fairtrade Certification for Cadbury Diary Milk confectionary bars. This strategic endeavour constituted a moment of translation achieved through the process of problematization. This is because, for products to be awarded with the Fairtrade Mark their conditions of production and exchange need to meet Fairtrade standards designated by FLO International. These standards are formulated through consultation with Fairtrade stakeholders (i.e., actors directly or indirectly involved in the Fairtrade commodity chain). Linked to a more nuanced perspective on the capacities of ethical consumption to combat extreme poverty, the Fairtrade standards are not simply a set of benchmarks for the achievement of socially responsible production and exchange. Rather, the Fairtrade standards are purposely designed to 'support the development of disadvantaged and marginalized small-scale farmers and plantation workers' (Fairtrade 2009b). Fairtrade achieves this objective by ensuring that its standards address three key areas of sustainable development; social, economic and environmental. Ever since the late 1980s this remit has emphasized the enrolling of conventional retailers into the Fair Trade network. In 2009, Cadbury in its efforts to accomplish its £45 million ethical trading investment agreement actively enrolled into FLO International's criteria for the labelling of products as Fairtrade. It is at this moment that we witness translation through problematization i.e., an 'agent's efforts to make other agents subscribe to their own conceptions by demonstrating that they have the right solutions to, or definitions of, the others' problem' (Ezzamel 1994:219). This form of convergence between disparate agendas is articulated in the press statements that the Fairtrade Foundation and Cadbury simultaneously released so as to publicize, on 4 March 2009, their newly formulated partnership. Extracts derived from the press releases are as follows:

1. Cadbury and the Fairtrade Foundation today announced plans to achieve Fairtrade certification for Cadbury Dairy Milk, the nation's top selling chocolate bar, by end of Summer 2009. This groundbreaking move will result in the tripling of sales of cocoa under Fairtrade terms for cocoa farmers in Ghana, both increasing Fairtrade cocoa sales for existing certified farming groups, as well as opening up new opportunities for thousands more farmers to benefit from the Fairtrade system. (Fairtrade 2009k)
2. Todd Stitzer adds, 'By working together, the Fairtrade Foundation and Cadbury believe we can get more people in the UK to buy Fairtrade products and achieve more for this cause than we ever could individually. This Fairtrade initiative is part of our ongoing commitment to cocoa farmers in Ghana where we originally established cocoa farms 100 years ago and last year launched the Cadbury Cocoa Partnership – after all, what's good for the farmers is good for our customers and our business.' (Cadbury 2009e)
3. The Fairtrade Foundation sees this as just a first step in a long partnership to improve livelihoods for cocoa growers. Harriet Lamb continues, 'The Fairtrade Foundation set out an ambitious strategy last year to double its positive impact for producers by 2012, by opening up opportunities for more and more farmers to join the system, and for those already in the system to be able to sell more under Fairtrade conditions. It is precisely this kind of big commitment by a major player such as Cadbury that could make it possible to achieve these goals.' (Fairtrade 2009k)
4. Cadbury will also be sourcing cocoa from Kuapa Kokoo, one of the first groups to be Fairtrade certified, with over 40,000 registered cocoa farmers across Ghana. Although they are currently only selling a small percentage of their cocoa as Fairtrade, they have been able to implement community projects like building primary school classrooms, constructing wells, and investing in corn mills. Now Kuapa Kokoo will have the opportunity to sell cocoa to Cadbury on Fairtrade terms, which will increase their Fairtrade premiums, and therefore the range of farmer support and community development programmes they can implement. (Fairtrade 2009k)

During the process of problematization chains of arguments that connect different problems become entangled. In their efforts to mobilize advocacy for particular entanglements, actors explore the potential of linking-up to solve their respective problems. Problematization then involves the articulation of interests across a diversity of positions; 'channelling people in different directions' (Latour 1987:117). Methodologically, the task of the analyst is thus to trace the diversity of positions and strategies employed to mobilize support for a way of mutually approaching separate agenda. Working analytically with the above press release, we can observe a process in, which agendas are collectively redefined; such that actors enrol each other into a shared way of thinking about the others' problems. As Latour (1987:110) states 'the easiest means to enrol people in the construction of facts is to let oneself be enrolled by them!' The successful confluence of actors and their respective agendas generates a shared space in commensurability to the new approach to which actors have mobilized support. As Latour (2007:219) expresses it:

> Every time a connection has to be established, a new conduit has to be laid down and some new type of entity has to be transported through it.

It is important to recognize that although the boundaries of the 'new conduit' are partially coordinated by human actors, the process of translation can and does enfold both human and non-human actors. In Actor Network Theory (ANT), the analyst is concerned to trace the simultaneous presence of multifarious organic and inorganic agencies, each nested in heterogeneous actor-networks. Social connections are envisaged to be achieved because of, rather than in spite of, the incommensurability of aligning material and social agencies. This is because 'Any course of action will thread a trajectory through completely foreign modes of existence that have been brought together by such heterogeneity' (Latour 2007:75). The result of such renderings of associations over space and time is that it produces 'mediators', which operate as vehicles for different groups to mobilize their respective interests.

According to Latour (2007:38), 'it makes a huge difference whether the means to produce the social are taken as intermediaries or as mediators'. 'Intermediaries' are simple structural processes 'even if it is internally made of many parts' (ibid). An example of an intermediary might be an electronic archive containing press releases. Although its directories will have sub-divisions and complex indexing, ultimately it is merely an archive that regularly receives, indexes and stores press statements. In ANT, the structural processes of intermediary forces are directly contrasted with the more complicated structural processes of 'mediators'.

'Mediators' are multifaceted structures constituted by complex layers interweaving micro-networks of interacting actants (i.e., unformulated potential actors) and actors. Consider for a moment the differing levels of relevancies presented by the content of an archive of press releases. If that archive is located off-line its very nature of connections with humans will be limited by geographies of time and space. However, if this archive is then transformed into a fully net-worked online archive the potentiality and scope of this resource is infinitely multiplied. It is, in this sense that Latour (2007:39) states that mediators, 'cannot be counted as just one; they might count for one, for nothing, for several, or for infinity'. Indeed, the multifaceted structural processes of mediators excite the analysis of actor-networks. Intermediaries, no matter how complex their internal parts, merely operate as transports of 'meaning or force without transformation; defining its inputs is enough to define its outputs' (ibid). When thinking about an off-line archive of press releases, the input of press statements is commensurate with the archive's output i.e., either no alteration of meaning or a negligible transformation might have occurred to the meaning of the archive objects. As Latour expresses it 'no matter how complicated an intermediary is, it may, for all practical purposes, count for just one – or even for nothing at all because it can be easily forgotten' (ibid). Conversely, the multifaceted processes of a mediator amplify its capacities for multiple directions of meaning transformation. To this end, 'No matter how apparently simple a mediator may look, it may become complex; it may lead in multiple directions which will modify all the contradictory accounts attributed to its role' (ibid). For example, consider the relative influence of the above stated press release by Cadbury and Fairtrade on 4 March 2009. As artefacts situated in off-line archives these respective documents are somewhat mundane in their relevance to globally dispersed networks. However, as documents hosted in the archives of websites belonging to global brands, these artefacts are re-invigorated; offering transformational descriptions of themselves. In ANT it is the potential of human and non-human actors to shift from being intermediaries to mediators and visa versa that really excites the analytical imagination. As Latour expresses it:

> it is this constant uncertainty over the intimate nature of entities – are they behaving as intermediaries or as mediators? – that is the source of all the other uncertainties we have decided to follow. (ibid)

As expressions of human and non-human agency, mediations circulate the transformation of meaning from site to site. Once the process of translating divergent problems into shared solutions commences, mediators circulate through the spaces and conduits which constitute the networking process. Consequently, 'What circulates…"inside" the conduit are the very acts of giving something a dimension' (ibid:220). This premise invites application in many directions. One key issue, foregrounded by the analysis of multifaceted interconnections, is that 'if an account employs either a symbolic or a naturalistic type of causality, there is no reason to include it in the ANT corpus' (ibid:10). Rather, the potential for mediations to re-form into intermediaries and visa-versa builds into the analysis a cognizance of serendipity, transgressive agency and disruptions in flows of meaning transfer. Thus the flows of mediations linking-up human and non-human agents can serve to actively transform the connotations that are relevant to the broader structural problems connecting the diverse domains of acting-networks. As Latour (2007:220) expresses it:

> Whenever a locus wishes to act on another locus, it has to go through some medium, transporting something all the way; to go on acting, it has to maintain some sort of more or less durable connection. Conversely, every locus is now the target of many such activities, the crossroads of many such tracks, the provisional repository of many such vehicles.

When analysed from the perspective of ANT, the Fairtrade Mark is recognized as a type of connection 'that makes possible the transportation of agencies over great distance[s]' of space and time (ibid:221). Conceived as a resource for the mobilization of divergent interests, configured together through processes of problematization, the meaning of the Fairtrade Mark takes on new dimensions of counterintuitive possibility. This is to re-emphasize that ANT, conceptualizes non-humans as actors 'and not simply the hapless bearers of symbolic projection' (Latour 2007:10). In this sense, the Fairtrade Mark can be perceived as an enterprising mobile actor that intersects the organizational landscape of conflicting policy agendas. As a symbol nested in local bundles of complex entanglements, the Fairtrade Mark succeeds in connecting corporate alternative trading initiatives (e.g., Cadbury's *Purple to Green* initiative) with broader cultural political mobilizations (i.e., Fair Trade). In so doing, the Fairtrade Mark exemplifies the geometric dimensions of translation. As Latour expresses it 'Translating interests' involves 'offering new interpretations of these interests...[and]...the results of such renderings are a slow movement from one place to another' (1987:117). Such mobile mediations, linking the human world and the object-world of non-human actors are even more evident when we consider advertising's role as a primary connecting site for the Fairtrade Mark.

Chapter 7 extensively examined the advertising of Fairtrade labelled products in terms of subjectification, the care of the self and transgressive aesthetics. When examining the Fairtrade Mark in terms of networks of divergent agents and the mediations that are axiomatic with these convergences, it is evident that the advertising of Fair Trade assumes a more networked morphology. The application of ANT to the marketing and advertising of Fairtrade labelled products is a new and emerging academic field. One of the fundamental characteristics linking prominent contributions to this area is the presupposition that the Fairtrade exchange process is best conceptualized in relation to 'multi-directional network theory, rather than in terms of uni-directional commodity chains' (Nicholls and Opal 2005:163). While both forms of analysis emphasize marketing communications, the application of ANT enables a focus on exchange in terms of information flows and the inscription of commodities with ethical signification. Thus marketing applications of ANT are less interested in the identities of agents within the exchange relationship, but rather the central point of concern is the way actors connect with each other through activities. Some further sense of this marketing application and its focus on acting networks is provided by the following description of 'Fairtrade Towns', derived from the Cadbury Dairy Milk website:

> Let's talk about Fairtrade Towns. There are hundreds of them in the UK, but what does it actually mean to be a Fairtrade Town? And what are they committed to do? Here's the scoop. A Fairtrade Town is a town, city, village or borough that has made a commitment to supporting Fairtrade and using products with the Fairtrade Mark. Garstang in Lancashire...declared itself 'the Worlds first Fairtrade Town' in April 2000. The move captured the imagination of local people and the interest of politicians, inspiring other towns, villages and counties to work towards Fairtrade status in their communities. (Cadbury 2009f)

One gains, from the above extract a sense that a significant shift has occurred in traditional marketing. In traditional commodity chain approaches to consumer behaviour, the dominant node in the network is the producer. Conversely, the above extract exemplifies a transition in marketing practice away from producer/retailer centric model 'to the dominant node being the consumer/retailer (a place focus) best seen in an actor network context' (Nicholls and Opal 2005:177). As with mainstream ANT, marketing academics highlight the simultaneous presence of human and non-human agencies as intermediaries in constructing heterogeneous networks (ibid:175). For example, Nicholls and Opal (2005) in their account of the evolution of Fair Trade marketing strategies, describe a new emerging approach that has social networking practices as its primary focus. In the language and logic of market segmentation, the social networking marketing approach is designed to enrol consumer groups, that are defined as having 'weak ethical concerns, but are still engaged with social and environmental issues' (ibid:172). When social network marketing is conceived in terms of ANT and applied to the marketing of Fairtrade labelled products this involves extending the central concept of 'consumer-producer connectivity' so as to embrace 'fresh market segments by identifying new nodes within the extant, but emergent, network and making strategic use of the information flows across them' (ibid:177). Operationally, this marketing mechanism has involved mobilizing activists, situated locally in towns and cities, to gain accreditation for their local area to be awarded the title of a 'Fair Trade Town'. The Cadbury Dairy Milk website describes this process as thus:

> Here are the five goals of a Fairtrade Town, visit the Fairtrade website for more information on any of these goals and more information about how your town can join the movement:
>
> 1. Local council passes a resolution supporting Fairtrade, and agrees to serve Fairtrade products (for example, in meetings, offices and canteens).
> 2. A range of Fairtrade products are readily available in the area's retail outlets (shops, supermarkets, newsagents and petrol stations) and served in local catering outlets (cafés, restaurants, pubs).
> 3. Local workplaces and community organizations (places of worship, schools, universities, colleges and other community organizations) support Fairtrade and use Fairtrade products whenever possible. A flagship employer is required for populations over 100,000.
> 4. Media coverage and events raise awareness and understanding of Fairtrade across the community.
> 5. A local Fairtrade steering group is convened to ensure the Fairtrade Town campaign continues to develop and gain new support. (Cadbury 2009)

The enrolment of locally situated agents into the campaign involves the use of a 'network intermediary' marketing process (Nicholls and Opal 2005:176). This refers to the grass-root generation of mass-market engagement (activism) stimulated by inter-personal networks and also 'word of mouth' flows. In its efforts to 'epitomize the town as a place of [Fair Trade] consumption', the marketing of place 'is contingent on the network effect itself creating patterns of agency' (ibid:175-176). But these entities are themselves nested within social networks; consequently 'the Fair Trade Town defines itself in its connectedness with Fair Trade values, but also contributes to them as a marketing communications agent' (ibid).

Recent developments in Fair Trade marketing and advertising practice clearly illustrates the relevance of ANT when tracing the embedding of promotional culture into the very ontology of the Fair Trade exchange. In many respects Nicholls and Opal (2005) succeed in highlighting the dynamic marketing of Fair Trade Towns. Moreover, Nicholls and Opal's (2005) employment of ANT demonstrates the 'powerful network effects' of the marketing of place, especially in the Fair Trade Town's 'enactment of the linkages between producer and consumer via both human and non-human nodes, intermediaries and the interactions between them' (ibid). However, Nicholls and Opal's (2005) application of ANT struggles to contend with the realization that translation will, and does, involve the redefinition of meaning and the transformation of actor-networks. As is evident in the following extract:

> Callon and Law's (1992) concept of network intermediaries created by the interactions of network actors and defining and ordering the networks they describe also defines the marketing information flows so crucial to Fair Trade communications concretized in certification, labelling and supplier narrative, as well as civic signage and Fair Trade events. (ibid:176)

In a more meticulous account of ANT, the multifaceted interconnections of actor-networks are understood as occupying a more precarious networked relation. Indeed, the suggestion that marketing communication flows become 'concretized in certification' fails to recognize that both marketing and advertising flows exist as translations between mediators. Looking at it from the ANT framework of Latour (2005), what is traced when analysing the information flows of Fair Trade promotion networks, are not tightly integrated fixed entities. This is because these networks are the localized global responses, to the divergent interests of agents, intent on enrolling each other into a reformulated global solution to distinct local problems. What circulates, inside the shared spaces fostered through translation, are the very acts of negotiating the dimensions and relevancies, for respective actor-networks, of the Fairtrade Mark. Methodologically this suggests the need for an analysis of the process through, which incommensurable symbols and other actors are translated across divergent interests and the mechanisms employed to sustain reciprocity in the agenda of these divergent interests.

Interessement: Translating Negotiated Relevancies

In order to empirically account for the fact that translation 'is entirely dependent on the new unexpected allies that have been made to be relevant' (Latour 1987:127), writers have been keen to develop concepts to explain interventions linking relevancies. Formulations include the concept of 'interessement'. Latour (1987:108) defines 'interessement', in terms of the explicit interests, which intervene between actors and their goals. According to Latour this creates tensions 'that will make actors select only what, in their own eyes, helps them reach these goals amongst many possibilities' (ibid:108-109). Elsewhere it has been observed that 'interessement involves the interference of the enrolling agency between the target agency and another agency' (Ezzamel 1994:219). This, at first involves, the enrolling agency deciding on the identity of the target agency, 'and then developing and cementing links between itself and the target agencies' (ibid). Thus potential allies need to be mobilized so as to provoke support for the entanglement of disparate agenda, and convergence around a collectively redefined solution. Interessement, accounts for the translation role of FLO International, within the bundles of entanglements, agents enter into when they enrol into the assertion, that the Fairtrade Mark provides a solution to their respective problems.

As is the criterion for all Fairtrade labelled products, farmers and exporters located within the producer country are compelled to abide by the trading standards established by FLO International. It is FLO International that directs the target actor-networks (producers and suppliers) through the repertoire of designated Fairtrade standards. But this responsibility is only accomplished through the certification function of FLO-CERT. Indeed, the capacity of 'interessement' is evident in FLO-CERT's inspections and its monitoring of producer organizations and traders; so as to ensure that both these agencies comply with Fairtrade standards. Significantly, the issue of compliance relates to ensuring the certification of both producer organizations/traders in the commodity supply chain and their products. Thus enrolment involves the creation of alliances between human and non-human actors. Indeed the Fairtrade labelled product emerges, to a greater extent, as the embodiment of the explicit political interests aligning actor-networks. Thus an integral feature of the translation, between the explicit interests of the Fair Trade network, and those of commercial agencies, is achieved through 'channelling the target agency through a set of unique and well-defined practices (obligatory passage points) that are under the control of the enrolling agency' (ibid). This translation is stabilized through the creation of reciprocal relations between FLO International, FLO-CERT, Fair Trade partners and micro-networks 'enrolled' into the Fair Trade commodity chain. The concept of 'enrolment' is therefore of much significance for it partially explains the efforts made by Fair Trade partners to integrate global advertising into the process of 'enrolling' micro-networks into the meaning translations of alternative trading networks.

Enrolment: Translating Technoscapes

While in some respects the general concept of interessement highlights the linking-up of actors and their alliances into the creation of mutually beneficial relevancies, the concept of 'enrolment' spotlights the multifarious kinds of actors that constitute actor-networks. This is because 'Enrolment involves the construction by agencies of alliances and coalitions between the memberships to reach agreement on the ends which they desire to pursue' (Ezzamel 1994:219). Enrolment provides a conceptual platform from, which to analytically explain recent innovations in the application of advertising technologies to the supply chain sustainability of alternative trading networks. More specifically, the emphasis of alternative trading networks on sustaining local communities has motivated a focus on advertising as a means of enrolling local communities into the ethics and practices of Fair Trade. An effective example is provided by Cadbury's Dairy Milk Fairtrade multi-media advertising campaign launched in 2009. Created as part of Cadbury's *Glass and a Half Full* production, the campaign exemplifies the integration of advertising into the enrolment processes of alternative trading networks. This is because, the Cadbury's Dairy Milk Fairtrade campaign illustrates how, alternative trading networks are employing the global reach of multi-media advertising, as a mechanism for entangling their macro-objectives with the more local interests of micro-networks.

Cadbury Fairtrade Certified Confectionary and the Enrolment of Ghanaian 'Zingolo'

In March 2009, Cadbury announced that it has achieved Fairtrade Certification for Cadbury Dairy Milk chocolate in Britain and Ireland. In August 2009 Cadbury announced that it was extending these newly formed markets for its mainstreaming of Fairtrade labelled confectionary. Fairtrade labelled Dairy Milk bars are now available in Canada, Australia and New Zealand. Cadbury has calculated that this extension of the market propelled its mainstreaming of Fairtrade 'to a new global level' (2009c). More specifically Cadbury state that:

> ...around one quarter of Cadbury Dairy Milk global sales and 350 million Cadbury Dairy Milk bars will be Fairtrade certified in 2010. Combined with existing Fairtrade market in Britain and Ireland, the five markets will quadruple Fairtrade cocoa sales from Ghana, adding an additional 15,000 tonnes – from 5,000 tonnes in 2008 to 20,000 tonnes in 2010...Cadbury's partnership with the Fairtrade Foundation in Britain and Ireland – which saw Fairtrade Cadbury Dairy Milk bars coming off shelves in July – has already resulted in £500,000 transferred to Ghana, the first instalment of the Fairtrade social premium. This is part of Cadbury's overall investment into cocoa sustainability though the Cadbury Cocoa Partnership. (Cadbury 2009c)

In September 2009, Cadbury launched a multi-platform advertising campaign focusing on Ghanaian music, culture, arts and crafts. The campaign continues from the ethical promises established as part of the ten year *Cadbury Cocoa Partnership*, initiative set up in 2008. A central pledge of the *Cadbury Cocoa Partnership* is the investment of £45 million, by Cadbury, into securing the economic, social and environmental sustainability of its cocoa farmers in Ghana, India, Indonesia and the Caribbean. It was Cadbury's 100 year history of sourcing cocoa from Ghana that formed the central theme of the multimedia advertising campaign that was launched in September 2009. Some indication of the ethical trading ethos that inspired the advertisement is provided in the following press release statement by the then Chief Executive of Cadbury:

> Lots of people think that organizations' commitment to Fairtrade is all about reputation, marketing and the brand – about getting an ethical 'badge'. But for us it's much more fundamental. It's about supply chain sustainability. We realised that we needed to be much more active – right across the economic, social and environmental aspect of cocoa farmers' lives. Profit and principle can go hand in hand. (Todd Stitzer – Cadbury Chief Executive Cadbury 2009i)

Following the award winning success of its previous *Glass and a Half Full* advertising campaigns, Cadbury re-commissioned the technologically innovative advertising agency Fallon. Working closely with Cadbury, Fallon created a multimedia campaign to launch the Fairtrade certification of Cadbury Dairy Milk. The campaign has a vibrant ethnic theme and this is underscored by the fact that, Cadbury filmed the advertisement in cocoa villages in the East Akim and Fanteakwa districts situated in the Eastern region of Ghana during the summer of 2009. In order to further enhance the production's Ghanaian cache, Cadbury commissioned local Ghanaian artists. The large tribal head raining cocoa pods as it travels through a Ghanaian village, which features as a centre piece in the Cadbury's Dairy Milk Fairtrade advertisement, was carved by local sculptures using traditional styles drawing on ancient Ghanaian cultural heritage. In a press release entitled *Ghana Inspires Cadbury Dairy Milk's Innovative Advertising of Fairtrade*, the Ghanaian artist Jasper Teshie is showcased as the artistic talent that produced the hand painted art work that formed the basis for the advertising print campaign (Cadbury 2009f). Jasper Teshie is clearly an accomplished artist. Indeed, the press release informs us that his art work takes inspiration from traditional Ghanaian murals inscribed with West African signwriting. Jasper Teshie is also acclaimed for having painted spectacular murals in Kof Town, Ghana.

These classical references to Ghana's cultural heritage were combined with contemporary Ghanaian pop music. Of particular significance was the production of the first *Glass and a Half Full* music album, which is inspired by the vibrant soundscapes of West Africa. The first single, 'Zingolo' features the Ghanaian music celebrity Tinny. Tinny is acclaimed to have successfully produced a fusion of native Ghanaian 'high-life' music and Western hip-hop rhythms. Tinny fronts the single and accompanying music video for the track 'Zingolo', which we are informed, 'means, "Enjoy it" in Ga, one of the languages of Ghana' (Cadbury 2009f). The four minute music video also features members of Ghana's cocoa farming community, alongside a Ghanaian dance group called the High Sprit Dance Crew. Described as a highly acrobatic street dance collective, the group had previously featured on television programmes accompanying Ghanaian music celebrities and is considered as the country's most acclaimed dance troupes.

The music video was made available to preview on the Cadbury Dairy Milk blog. With regards to broader media platforms, a sixty second taster advertisement featuring the music video was aired during ITV1's popular reality television show *X Factor*. The entire music track of Zingolo was made available for preview, purchase and download from iTunes. Cadbury has pledged, to donate its share of the profits derived from the sale of the single, to the charity CARE International. This charity is a member of *The Cadbury Cocoa Partnership* and is dedicated to insuring that Cadbury's profits, from the sale of the track Zingolo, will be channelled to support the financing of education programmes instituted in cocoa farming communities in Ghana. These charitable commitments succeeded in enrolling further public support from the Fairtrade Foundation as is evident from the following press release statement:

> The essence of Fairtrade is all about local communities being able to improve their own lives. So it's been really important this whole process has worked with Ghanaian people, from the musicians, dancers and artwork to the crafts people, and ordinary villagers and cocoa farmers. And we're delighted that all the profits from the music single will also go back into Ghanaian communities too. We hope this slice of Ghanaian joy will inspire everyone in the power of positive change, making Fairtrade chocolate their everyday choice. (Director of Communications and Policy for the Fairtrade Foundation Cadbury 2009)

As part of its efforts to enrol support, from Ghanaian cocoa farming communities, Cadbury avidly showcased public viewings of the Zingolo music video. On the 9 October 2009 Cadbury held a meeting of the Cadbury Cocoa Partnership Board at its Ghana headquarters. The meeting was attended by senior representatives of Ghana's government ministries, NGOs, prominent farmers' unions, academics employed at the University of Ghana and leading figures within the cocoa farming community. The central objective of the meeting was to review policy initiatives for developing a sustainable supply chain of cocoa farming practices in Ghana. It was decided that the Zingolo music video would be screened during this meeting. The specific reasoning behind this decision was that 'it will of course support education projects in Ghana's cocoa growing areas' (Cadbury 2009h). The audience response was reportedly rapturous as has been remarked by the Managing Director of Cadbury in Ghana:

> People's immediate reaction to the video was of applause and excitement and the general feedback was that the video appealed to everyone. Everyone was clamouring to take home a copy of the video after the event, so I think that shows how popular it was! We are happy to have received such a positive reaction to this video which showcases Ghana's talented performers. (ibid)

On Saturday 17 October 2009, the Zingolo music video was exhibited at key events in the Ghanaian cocoa farming communities of Oslem and Adjeikrom. According to Cadbury 'Everyone was in high spirit as Ghana had won the under 20's football world cup the previous evening and there were cheers and applause as people spotted the familiar faces of their neighbours amongst the dancers in the video, filmed in Ghana' (Cadbury 2009h). Members of Cadbury Ghana returned to the village the following day to gauge reaction to the showcasing of the Zingolo video. Villagers were reported to have expressed pleasure and support for the song. Examples of the community's statements of approval included the following:

> Cocoa is our livelihood. We saw our fathers cultivating it when we were young and we have continued the tradition. We saw the Cadbury film last night. I enjoyed the dancing the most.
>
> We are happy that Cadbury is showcasing us to the world. We hope this friendship will last for a very long time (ibid)

Cadbury's attempts to enrol members of the Ghanaian cocoa community into its Dairy Milk Fairtrade advertising campaign, is particularly fascinating when we consider the attention, Cadbury has invested into also enrolling members of the Ghanaian diaspora located in the UK. Some examples of this activity include the following:

> On Friday 27 November 2009 Rt Hon David Lammy, MP for Tottenham and Minister of State for Higher Education and Intellectual Property and Tinny, visited the Bruce Grove Youth Centre, a £3million state of the art building which attracts local young people in the 13-17 year age group from Bruce Grove and across Tottenham and Haringey. Tinny performed with the young people attending the youth centre, toured the facility and spoke to staff and volunteers about Ghana and Fairtrade. Many of the young people had recently taken part in a series of Fairtrade workshops and were keen to hear Tinny's perspective on the impact of Fairtrade upon Ghana's cocoa farming communities. (Cadbury (2009j)
>
> On Monday 30 November, Tinny spoke to year 5 and 6 pupils at Langley Manor School, with Ali Law from the Cadbury Corporate Responsibility Team and Joanna Brightwell from the Fairtrade Foundation. The students had been learning about Cadbury and Fairtrade and had a range of interesting questions to put to Tinny, Ali and Joanna. That evening Tinny attended the New Horizons

> community centre in Mitcham and took part in an open Q & A with a group of 1st, 2nd and 3rd generation British Ghanaians. The attendees asked Tinny about every aspect of his life, from his musical career, to his opinions of the UK and his involvement with Fairtrade and cocoa farming. He finished the event with a performance of the Zingolo single. (Cadbury 2009j)

According to Cadbury Corporate Affairs Director the advertisement for Cadbury's Fairtrade certified Dairy Milk confectionary bars:

> ...celebrates Ghana's music, dance and artistry, and shares the irrepressible Ghanaian spirit with the UK public in a relevant and intriguing way. From Tinny's irresistibly catchy beat and the originality of the High Spirits dancers to Jasper's distinctive murals, we hope our innovative take on Fairtrade will put smile on faces. (Cadbury 2009f)

Clear tensions are evident in the Corporate Affairs Director's description of the campaign. Part of this tension resides with contradictions around the symbolic dimensions of ethnic identity. Symbolic tropes enlisting high spirited traditional African communities, vibrant music and frenetic gaiety are hazardous racialized stereotypes reminiscent of colonial exploitation. It can be argued that the exotic landscape depicted in the advertisement merely mourns the passing of a space destroyed by racial domination. Rosaldo (1993:68-69) provides important theoretical reflections on colonialism and visual imagery. Drawing upon Michelle Rosaldo's eclectic fusion of ethnopsychology with anthropology (1980), Renato Rosaldo (1993:68-69) interrogates the paradoxical tendency for colonial vistas to portray nostalgic visual imagery idyllically depicting bygone eras, which have since been destroyed by colonial expropriation. As he expresses it 'people destroy their environment, and then they worship nature' (ibid:70). Rosaldo defines this disturbing dialectic as 'imperialist nostalgia' (ibid: 68-70). The insidious propensity of this phenomenon transpires where 'imperialist nostalgia uses a pose of "innocent yearning" both to capture people's imaginations and to conceal its complicity with often brutal domination' (ibid:70). MacCannell (1999) provides an account of touristic display which develops the concept of 'imperialist nostalgia'. According to MacCannell (1999) the commercial exchanges in touristic display implicitly attempt to ameliorate a collective guilt that moderns hold for the systematic destruction of primitive societies (Dicks 2003:60). The concept of 'imperialist nostalgia', in this sense, explicates the performance of indigenous cultures precipitated by the exchange relations that define touristic display. Clear parallels exist here between these observations and the visual imagery that features in the television and print advertisements for Cadbury's Fairtrade certified Dairy Milk confectionary bars. Imperialist nostalgia is evident in the stylized tropes depicting, excitable African people displayed in the advertising imagery. And this stylization appears to, at least in part, to be a response to a mythological ideal intent on sustaining the racialized ideology of the primitive 'Other' in modern times.

Given the facile and stereotypical visual imagery displayed in the Zingolo production and the accompanying print advertisements, it is unsurprising that the Advertising Standards Authority (ASA), in 2009, received complaints accusing the television advertisement of perpetuating demeaning racial stereotypes of African people. According to Michael Todd (Policy and Public Affairs Officer for ASA), the ASA received '33 complaints about the television ad by Cadbury, which launched the company's new Fairtrade chocolate'. These complaints were received 'between the end of September and the end of October 2009'. During our e-mail communication Michael Todd, further stated that 'the complaints felt that the ad was racially offensive by perpetuating the stereotypes of African people'. Cadbury was, cleared of this accusation, indeed Michael Todd stated categorically that 'the ASA decided that there was no case to investigate the ad as we did not believe the ad would be seen by the majority of people as racially offensive'. Although Cadbury was exonerated of allegations of racism, it is noteworthy that prominent members of the West African community were amongst those that voiced complaints about the advertising campaign. It has been reported that the founder of Ligali, an African Human Rights organization based in the UK, complained that:

> The video makes Africans look like buffooning simpletons. The biggest presence on the advert is a giant mask that people fall about in front of. Part of being able to use the Fairtrade brand should also include a responsibility to advertise ethically…The fact that Ghanaian musicians and artists were involved is sad, but it does not excuse it. (Quoted in *The Independent* UK 2009)

The advertisement for Cadbury's Fairtrade certified Dairy Milk also provoked displeasure from the UK branch of the Ghanaian political opposition association the Convention People's Party (CPP). It has been reported that the chairman of CPP sent a letter of protest to the Cadbury board 'on behalf of his party and British Ghanaians' (ibid). The chairman of CPP is alleged to have stated that 'People are disappointed. It's like making an advert about America and only showing images of Harlem…It's a colonial mentality and stuff like this just brings the country down' (ibid). Members of the Ghanaian Migrants Information Services (GMIS) also expressed indignation, stating that the advertisement's theme and visual imagery had outraged members of the Ghanaian diaspora because 'it's racist and it doesn't present an accurate picture of Ghana' (ibid). In response, to these allegations and the formal complaints expressed to the ASA, the marketing director of Cadbury rejected the accusations stating that 'This campaign has been widely welcomed by Ghanaians, including community leaders both in Ghana and in the UK' (ibid).

These complexities, concerning visual tropes and the representation of race, appear to have been heightened rather than ameliorated by the inclusion of hybrid black music cultures into the advertising campaign for Cadbury's Fairtrade certified Dairy Milk confectionary bars. This is because, hybrid black music cultures, combine diverse diaspora, syncretically in struggles to fix their reading of ethnic identity (Gilroy 1987). To this end, black music cultures are a site of political struggle for globally dispersed diaspora. These tensions provide attractive vehicles for advertising creatives keen to underscore their productions with edgy world music and provocative hybrid black music soundscapes. Indeed, Cadbury's commissioning of the Ghanaian music sensation Tinny, is further evidence that black music cultures from, diverse regions of the world, are migrating from outside 'the frame' (Hall 1987) to the centre of advertising cool. But it is necessary to also appreciate that, the hybridity infused into black music soundscapes serve a transgressive function; they signify a 'culture of resistance' (Gilroy 1987). This connection with music and transgressive politics is in contrast with the enduring legacy of the Frankfurt School and especially Adorno's (1947) chastisement of popular music as pseudo-individualistic and formulaic. Adorno (1947) defines the pseudo-individualistic format of popular music to be an integral feature of the industrialization of culture. Standardized formulaic music is integral to the stability of capitalism. And to this extent the products and processes of the music industry enable the enduring hegemony of capitalist relations of power. From this perspective, advertising integrates into consumer culture the political effectivity of black music cultures. However, rather than subduing dissent, the agitated response provoked by the campaign, among members of the Ghanaian community, provoked passionate resistance to what was seen as a facile and stereotypical commodification of Ghanaian music cultures.

Curiously, although the television advertisement for Cadbury's Fairtrade certified Dairy Milk confectionary bars, provoked impassioned objections from prominent members of the Ghanaian community in the UK; it has been favourably received by members of the social networking website YouTube. By 13 October 2009 the campaign had attracted over 140,000 viewings on YouTube (Stitzer 2009). Support from members within other, similar social networking platforms was also impressive. For example, the campaign was exhibited on Facebook, where 15,000 fans congregated in a Facebook group dedicated to Zingolo (ibid). Elsewhere, it appears that not all prominent members, of the Ghanaian community in London, rejected the advertising campaign for Cadbury's Fairtrade certified Dairy Milk confectionary bars. Cadbury has gratifyingly reported that the Ghanaian community group Noviha wholeheartedly supported the campaign:

> At a preview of the advert shown in central London on Thursday 17 September, members of the local Ghanaian community present enthused about the television and print productions. Gabriel Goka, from community group Noviha said 'This is a great partnership for mutual benefit – for the farmers so they can get a better price and for the consumer so we can buy more Fairtrade chocolate. I love the series of advertisements. The whole design is wonderful – very, very imaginative. It says so much about Cadbury, Fairtrade and Ghana – I like best the print ad with the Ghanaian flag in the centre – it says that this initiative wants to be at the middle of Ghana's development. (Cadbury 2009i)

The fact that the *Glass and a Half Full* production, for the Fairtrade certified Cadbury Dairy Milk confectionary bars, provoked a diversity of reactions is perhaps unsurprising. After all advertisements throughout history have been designed to shock! However, what is unusual is that the diversity of approving, and disapproving, responses were mostly articulated as a consequence of agitated competition between networks. Some explanation for this can be discerned from Castells' account of the dynamics of power in network society. According to Castells:

> Networks (and the sets of interests and values they embody) cooperate or compete with each other. (2009:20)

Cooperation is predicated on informationalism and the ability for flows of communication to circulate between networks. These cooperative alliances between networks are axiomatic with 'the existence of codes of translation and inter-operability between the networks (protocols of communication) and on access to connecting points (switches)' (ibid). 'Codes of translation', clearly link the operating system of the Cadbury network with that of the Fairtrade Foundation. Indeed, Cadbury's vision of corporate responsibility appears attuned with Fair Trade's commitment to the sustainable development of farming communities. Codes of translation uniting these ideals include Cadbury's commitment to 'supply chain sustainability' and 'Principled Capitalism'. The latter concept is defined by Cadbury as thus:

> Using wisdom, judgement and perspective we can balance the positive focus of a profit motive and delivery of shareholder value, with values. In Cadbury we call it being 'performance driven and values led'. And we know that it makes for a more successful and sustainable business. (Stitzer 2009a)

Cadbury's concept of 'supply chain sustainability' is encapsulated by the *Cadbury Cocoa Partnership* established in 2008 and the pledge to invest £45 million across the economic, social and environmental conditions of its cocoa farmer's lives. According to Cadbury, this commitment to supply chain sustainability was the primary factor that initiated networking with Fair Trade; 'We came to Fairtrade because of the value it can bring to our supply chain and because of our values' (Stitzer 2009). 'Said another way…quality cocoa for us…and a better quality of life for thousands of farmers, empowered through Fairtrade to reinvest in their own farms and communities' (Stitzer 2009a). These codes of translation have also produced cooperative links with NGOs, charities and governmental agencies concerned to ensure the future sustainability of farming communities in Ghana. Thus Cadbury is keen to promote the fact that in 2009 Todd Stitzer (Cadbury Chief Executive), visited Ghana and had meetings with 'President Atta Mills…village Chiefs and elders…development agencies like the United Nations, Worldvision, Care and VSO…as well as those closest to Ghanaian cocoa growing…such as CocoBod and the Kuapa Kokoo farmers' cooperative' (Stitzer 2009a).

Because of its concern to enrol local support for global supply chain sustainability, the inclusion of Ghanaian artists and farming communities into the advertisement for Cadbury's Fairtrade certified Dairy Milk confectionary, appears to have been a logical extension of its network programming. To this end, the cooperative responses, to the advertising campaign for Cadbury's Fairtrade certified Dairy Milk confectionary, received from cocoa farming communities in Ghana, can be explained in terms of a synergy between the programming of these micro-networks and the Fairtrade Foundation's partnership with Cadbury. As Cadbury express it:

> Together...we will quadruple the amount of Fairtrade cocoa coming out of Ghana from 5,000 to 20,000 tonnes in 2010. This will bring value to both our brand...and the Fairtrade brand. Fairtrade is at a tipping point for consumers – and we want to help. We're providing mainstream consumers with an easy, everyday option. Their favourite chocolate, with the same taste and price, but with added ethics. For the Fairtrade movement it means millions of new consumers...So our new Cadbury Dairy Milk campaign aims to take that kind of connection one step further, and raise awareness of Fairtrade with a totally new audience...Just like the rest of the Glass And a Half Full Campaigns, it aims to make you smile. This time Ghanaian style. Filmed in cocoa villages, it fuses traditional as well as modern Ghanaian pop-culture with a good splash of our trademark quirky glass and a half imagination. To demonstrate the irrepressible Ghanaian spirit – in a relevant and intriguing way. And...it's more than an ad – it's a record – release, with the proceeds raised going to cocoa growing communities...And I tell you, when we previewed it to Ghanaian community representatives on Thursday, it was great to hear of their pride in seeing their country and culture getting this kind of platform and positive attention. The Ghanaian High Commissioner himself said the ad really captured the spirit of Ghana. So from our perspective, the signs are pretty good for a tipping point. This partnership has really touched a nerve within the company. A tipping point in supply...with more farmers benefiting. A tipping point for consumers...with more people choosing Fairtrade. And a tipping point for business...with more principled capitalists joining the movement. From Cadbury's perspective it is truly great to be part of this. (Stitzer 2009a)

It is evident from this press release, that the advertisement's multi-media platform provided the scope and scale to enrol local groups into Cadbury's translation of global supply chain sustainability. Cadbury had in previous years cultivated the social networking patterns of the Facebook generation. In October 2008 it re-launched its confectionary brand Wispa, having achieved 'over 40,000 people talking on Facebook' (Cadbury 2008a). The, then Marketing Directory of Cadbury, highlighted the significance of computer mediated communication to the re-launch of the Wispa brand stating that 'thousands of fans have continued to showcase their love for Wispa across social networking sites' (ibid). Indeed, the advertisement's multi-media platform explains why aspects of this translation were so successful amongst members of the social networking sites YouTube and Facebook. According to the Chief Executive of Cadbury, 'since its launch [in September 2009] the campaign has achieved over 140,000 viewings on YouTube and 15,000 Facebook friends, with many Ghanaians and Africans posting comments expressing their excitement at the positive profits it gives Ghana' (Stitzer 2009). It might alternatively be suggested that the cooperative response, achieved amongst these online communities, was largely a consequence of inter-operability between the protocols of communication that define both multi-media advertising and online social networking sites. For example, the advertisement's transmission on the internet based social networking sites YouTube and Facebook provided audience members with direct access to connecting points (switches) linking both Cadbury and Fairtrade. The advertisement's video format synergized with the protocols of communication that govern the YouTube network. And the 'Facebook friends' infra-structure enabled the demonstration of cooperation between the Fair Trade network, Cadbury and globally dispersed members of the online community Facebook. It might be argued that one witnessed here an instance of 'cognitive mapping' (Jameson 2008:51). That is a model of political culture, which seeks to reconnect and disalienate spatially dispersed individual subjects. In its empirical form, 'cognitive mapping in the broader sense comes to require the co-ordination of existential data (the empirical position of the subject) with unlived, abstract conceptions of the geographic totality' (ibid:52). In terms of the Cadbury Fair Trade partnership, the support apparently gained for its multi-media advertising, among social networking sites exemplifies a process of disalientation in which, spatially dispersed individuals cognitively mapped their 'individual social relationship to local, national and international class realities' (ibid). In so doing, these groups reveal how 'the political form of postmodernism, if there ever is any, will have as its vocation the invention and projection of a global cognitive mapping, on a social as well as a spatial scale' (ibid).

Mobilization of Support

Attaining support for the construction of alliances between networks also requires processes for the stabilization of reciprocal translations between enrolling agencies and those enrolled. In Actor Network Theory (ANT) this process of stabilization is defined as 'mobilization'. As Ezzamel (1994:219) expresses it 'Mobilization refers to how the enrolling agencies control the enroled agencies or ensure that representations of interests remain fixed'. Even the most cursory perusal through press statements, released by Cadbury, announcing its Fair Trade commitments, reveals consistent attempts to stabilize representations of translations. Resistance encountered by Cadbury, from prominent members of the Ghanaian community, suggests that the effectivity of mobilization is contingent on a network's superior operating ability. According to Castells (2009:20), 'Competition depends on the ability to outperform other networks by superior efficiency in performance or in cooperation capacity'.

Cadbury's multi-media platform, advertising campaign for its Fairtrade certified Dairy Milk confectionary, demonstrated spectacular superior efficiency in terms of its inter-operability between social networking sites and consumer markets. However, the agitated resistance and clashes between Cadbury and prominent networks of UK resident Ghanaians suggests that competition can be a source of turbulence in alternative trading networks. As Castells (2009:20) expresses it, 'Competition may also take a destructive form by disrupting the switches of competing networks and/or interfering with their communication protocols'. The challenges presented by the Ghanaian groupings Ligali (an African Human Rights organization based in the UK) and from the UK branch of the Ghanaian political opposition association the Convention People's Party (CPP), both attempted to disrupt the switches of the Cadbury and Fairtrade Foundation alliance. While each of these groups has distinct political legacies it is evident that they shared indignation at Cadbury's articulation of Ghanaian culture. Part of the tension between the networks was the outcome of resistance to Cadbury's attempt to penetrate the networks of prominent Ghanaian groups with its translation codes and valuation of performance. According to Castells (2009:20), 'to alter the outcomes of the network, a new program (a set of goal-oriented, compatible codes) needs to be installed in the network – from outside the network'. This observation is of particular relevance here. Suffice to say that African nations, having unshackled from colonial rule, have for decades struggled to reconcile their independence, with the realization, that total self-reliance is a 'nationalist fiction' (Said 1996:349). The economic map of post-colonial Africa is pervaded by an enduring legacy of ex-colonial commercial configurations. Alongside these imperatives exists Pan-African movements, fostering their Africentric values and resistances against Western articulations of African history. Some indication of this struggle is evident in the following extract derived from Ligali's ethos statement:

> African history is the most suppressed history in the world. Of the history that we do have access to, much has been mutilated and manipulated to fit in with western perception of Africa...Academics have created a mythical Africa that has filtered through the psyche of Africans and non-Africans alike, forcing us to subscribe to a racial and imperialist view of our own culture, history and people. To this end, history and education are critical tools for the progression of African children and the re-education of African adults who have often been force fed a falsity that contributes to the repression of our true self. As well as educating and re-educating African and non-African people about the richness, diversity and social intellect of Africa her history, it is important that we learn from our history the ways in which we can aid the positive development and progression of the great Continent of Africa and her people throughout the world.

Ligali's ethos statement draws attention to a perplexing dialectic. It directly challenges the subordination of racialized representations, to the exigencies and cultural hegemony of an all pervasive Western panopticon. Incongruities arise partly because this Western vision is 'static' (Said 2003:239). There is only limited realization of history and little recourse to the development of cultural heritage through time. Instead the Western panopticon is reliant on the permanence of a mythologized Other. Edward Said (ibid:240) describes this perspective as a 'static system of synchronic essentialism'. The intense drama between Cadbury and the Ghanaian networks was configured in the UK press media as a battle over racism. But this interpretation does an injustice to a more troublesome problem presented by the 'universal chrono-politics' (Virillo 2005:109) of alternative trading networks, i.e., the fact that:

> The actors and tele-actors of the cybernetic telecommunication revolution, acting and interacting in real time, set a technical pace or tempo which now lords it over the properly historical importance of the local time of societies and countries. (ibid)

In traditional social theory space is defined as the context in which time sharing events and practices simultaneously unfold. Unparalleled advances in communication technologies have decoupled the contiguity of time-sharing in space. The space of micro-electronic based telecommunications collapses into 'timeless time'. Castells (2009:34) observes that in the network society space in social terms is now predominated by 'the space of flows', i.e., 'the technological and organizational possibility of practicing simultaneity without contiguity' (ibid). It is also evident that the space of flows is manifest in 'asynchronous interaction in chosen time, at a distance' (ibid). Asynchronocity is a feature of Cadbury's Zingolo music video. Available simultaneously on YouTube and to purchase on iTunes the advertisement as a moment in historical time was reconstituted, through technology, as an instantaneous, disembodied artefact that can be streamed 24/7 across the globe. This feature of the advertising campaign highlights the flattening out of time in network morphology. As Castells (2009:35) explains:

> In the network society, the emphasis on sequencing is reversed. The relationship to time is defined by the use of information and communication technologies in a relentless effort to annihilate time by negating sequencing: on the one hand, by compressing time...on the one hand, by blurring the sequencing of social practices, including past, present, and future in a random order.

It is my contention that the resistances directed at Cadbury's advertisement for its Fairtrade certified Dairy Milk confectionary, were misarticulated in terms of racism. An alternative explanation is that the advertisement's networked multi-media platform configured a space of flows that flattened out the sequential temporality of cultural history. And this disordering in the history of events rendered the diachronic complexity of Ghanaian cultural history 'simultaneous in the communication networks, thus installing society in structural ephemerality: being cancels becoming' (Castells 2009:35). By transforming cultural history into instantaneous globally disaggregated visual mirages, the media networked format of the advertisement effectively undermines any sense of cultural history as a basis of a collective political project. In this context, cultural political mobilization is reduced to the instantaneous (real time) democracy and 'social automatism' (Virillo 2005:109) of social networking internet sites. 'A reflex democracy, without collective reflexion?' (ibid).

Heterogeneous pattern of networking and allusive, ephemeral communications evident in the mobilization of enrolled Fair Trade agencies, became spectacularly prominent during the somewhat acrimonious takeover of Cadbury by Kraft in January–February 2010. On 19 January 2010 Cadbury plc accepted a revised final takeover offer from the board of Kraft Foods inc. The proposed takeover immediately sparked renewed concerns over the decline of the UK manufacturing sector. These fears were appropriately exacerbated by the vast debt incurred by Kraft as part of the takeover deal; an astonishing estimated increase 'from $10 billion in 2006 to $30 billion' (Parliamentary papers 2010). Kraft has an apparent history of aggressive cost reduction and the Cadbury's Union predicted that approximately 30,000 jobs would be jeopardized by the takeover (*Guardian* 2010). Contestation over the future of Cadbury quickly became a public campaign to preserve Cadbury's autonomy against the relentless onslaught of capitalist global monoculture. Media reports repeatedly traced the heritage of Cadbury to its Quaker origins in 1824. For example BBC News provided an abbreviated genealogy of Cadbury stating 'John Cadbury, a Quaker, opened a shop in Birmingham in 1824, selling tea, coffee and hot chocolate – as an alternative to alcohol' (BBC News 2010). The ethical values of Cadbury became a significant feature of the adjournment debate on 27 January 2010, in the House of Commons over Cadbury's future in light of the takeover bid by Kraft. During this parliamentary session the then MP for Birmingham, Selly Oak expressed much disappointment 'that the Cadbury board capitulated to the pressure from those hedge funds and other shareholders, who were making it known that they would be prepared to accept a higher bid from Kraft – in some cases a bid as low as 830p a share' (Parliamentary papers 2010). It was observed that, in this context of globalized market capitalism, 'The good will towards Cadbury from its employees and the wider population, as well as from small investors and some corporate shareholders, is apparently worthless' (ibid). Clearly Cadbury's accedence, to the American multinational Kraft, became a vehicle for the articulation of resistance to 'the light-touch regulation of market capitalism' (ibid). Indeed, in December 2009 a delegate of MPs and union representatives had met with Lord Mandelson 'to urge the Government to support the campaign to keep Cadbury a British company' (ibid). As an outcome of the meeting the MP for Birmingham, Selly Oak is noted to have stated that 'We are grateful to him for using the power of words, but nothing concrete came out of the meeting…' (ibid). On 2 February 2010, Kraft Foods completed its takeover of Cadbury. However, an intriguing twist leading up to this point involved a substantial cultural political battle over Cadbury's commitment to the Fairtrade Foundation. Some indication of the context of this contestation is evident in the following extract derived from the MP for Birmingham's speech to the House of Commons:

> As a result of the huge additional debt foisted on the business, as well as of the millions paid to bankers and accountants, Kraft is looking to make more than $675 million-worth of savings. I accept that some of that will come from so-called "synergies" within the business, but it will inevitably lead to corporate job losses. The question that my hon. Friend has raised is whether manufacturing jobs and jobs in research and development and innovation will be retained and will grow. Will Kraft retain the commitment to Fair Trade under Cadbury? (Parliamentary Papers 2010)

In this context of all consuming global market manoeuvring, political possibilities became expeditiously interconnected with Cadbury's existing commitment to sell Fairtrade labelled confectionary. Kraft has a long-stranding commitment with an alternative ethical trading network, the Rainforest Alliance. Kraft has previously described the Rainforest Alliance Certified programme as 'comprehensive and fits seamlessly with our strategy and priorities' (Kraft 2010). Given that this alternative ethical trading network is often organizationally distinguished from the Fairtrade foundation, the probability that Kraft might discontinue Cadbury's commitment to sustainable and ethical sourcing was an ominous possibility. At which point mobilization assumed a curiously networked politically engaged orchestration, in which the efficacy, political cooperation and organization, of competing ethical trade networks were compared. In this context of intensified network competition, the ability of Cadbury's Fair Trade advertising to have integrated diversified systems of global electronic media, provided the platform from which to galvanize the political encouragement and active participation of geographically dispersed individuals. While local experience of the Cadbury takeover was individualized and distant from the immediacy of the everyday life of most consumers. The politics of the Cadbury brand and its ethical allegiance to Fair Trade was inclusively played out in interactive, multi-media communication spaces. Of particular interest was the capacity of social-networking websites (culturally shaped and interlinked by previous Cadbury advertising campaigns), to enable the expression of self-determined resistance. Cadbury's advertising had effectively extended into the enclosure of networked digitalized communities. And this earlier presence in social networking websites was spectacularly exceeded by the velocity and scale of the online campaigns to 'Keep Cadbury Fairtrade'. Indeed, the boisterously entitled 'Kraft Must Keep Cadbury's Fairtrade Commitments' Facebook group, had attracted 3,615 members by February 2010. Following Castells' (2004:30) earlier observations, it is evident that 'the enclosure of communication in the space of flexible, interactive, electronic hypertext has a decisive effect on politics'. Castells further observes that 'it is in the media space that political battles of all kinds are fought, won, and lost' (ibid). Thus Kraft has been keen to convince sceptics that, despite its existing ethical trading obligation to the Rainforest alliance, it will honour Cadbury's commitment to the provision of Fairtrade labelled confectionary (Guardian 2010a).

After the acceleration of the immediacy of politics, and the installation of instantaneous political action, the fear of the incessant virtual reality of politics has unnecessarily become universal. Yes, conventional political boundaries are reversed in the geopolitical horizon of electronic premonitory advertising signs. But the informational multiplication of advertising channels marks a meteoric leap forward for global cultural politics. This is because; convergences in global advertising technologies are transforming political spaces into multi-faceted virtual arenas, which are facilitating social and cultural interaction between social movements across nation states and continents. This chapter has endeavoured to illuminate advertising technologies as a powerful material force and integral to the strategic operation of globally networked social movements.

Timely Reflections

Globalization refers to the intensification of worldwide processes integrating national economies through increasingly unfettered flows of commerce, and financial capital across national boundaries. The tendency for capitalist processes to converge in the production of a global market place is increasingly a consequence of the network society. Capitalism's historic post-1945 rapid decolonization, forced newly independent nations into a globally networked economic order in, which they were expected to adopt export-led trade as a primary vehicle of fiscal development. Thus capitalism has a legacy of global divisions of labour. Nevertheless, the deepening international connections of contemporary global processes, suggests that we are entering a new economic order driven by the powerful forces and the rapid diffusion of information technologies.

According to Castells a defining feature of global capitalism is that 'agents in this economy' are fundamentally dependent 'upon their capacity to generate, process and apply efficiently knowledge-based information' (2000:66). It is self-evident that information and knowledge have always been axiomatic to capitalist economies. But it is also evident that we are witnessing the evolution of an advanced technological paradigm configured around new formidable information technologies. The information-driven environment of global capitalism 'makes it possible for information itself to become the product of the production process' (2000:67). To this extent capital has achieved an unprecedented mobility. Unlike 'organized capitalism' with its synchronous flows of capital and labour circulating on a national scale, global capitalism is 'disorganized' (Lash and Urry 1994). Fragmented, flexible production, indomitable networks of financial flows now circulate on an international scale. In global capitalism, accumulation proceeds and profit is generated, 'increasingly in the global financial markets enacted by information networks in the timeless space of financial flows' (Castells 2000:472).

This involves the emergence of a new form of spatiality (space of flows) and the annihilation of organized capitalism's sequencing of historical time (rise of timeless time). Micro-electronic technological communication has brought into being a space of flows in, which actors can engage in communication processes simultaneously without territorial proximity. In the space of flows, capital can circulate regardless of the physical location of labour, its nodal points have untethered from the simultaneous practice of labour time. Under these conditions, the code of capital accumulation becomes 'the need of a constantly expanding market' and this chases capital 'over the whole surface of the globe. It must nestle everywhere, settle everywhere, establish connexions everywhere' (Marx and Engels 1986:83).

Given that the dominant logic of globally networked capitalism is the relentless annihilation of space by time, alternative projects for the restructuration of trade are by necessity enacted by 'locally rooted, globally networked' social movements (Castells 2009:49). Resistance to the unceasing degradation of the space of places, thus increasingly takes place through networked social movements. As Castells' (ibid) expresses it 'A central characteristic of the network society is that both the dynamics of domination and the resistance to domination rely on network formation and network strategies of offense and defense'. Thus alongside the growth of capitalist globalization has been an unprecedented advancement of alternative trading networks. These networks operate globally as connected nodal points, coordinating their activities through flows of information embedded in complex labyrinths of networks.

Because power, in globalized capitalism is configured around an opposition between the timeless time of the space of flows, versus the embodied times of 'living in the space of places', anti-globalization movements are 'global-local' networks struggling to resist the unceasingly rapacious material infra-structure of the network society (ibid:49). As Castells specifically expresses it:

> Resisting programming and disrupting switching in order to defend alternative values and interests are the forms of counterpower enacted by social movements and civil society – local, national, and global, with the difficulty that the networks of power are usually global, while the resistance of counterpower is usually local. How to reach the global from the local, through networking with other localities – how to 'grassroot' the space of flows – becomes the key strategic question for the social movements of our age. (Castells 2009:52)

Axiomatic to this conflict has been the use of information and communication technologies by social movements, 'aiming to reach their constituencies and target audiences through the decisive switch to multimedia communication networks' (ibid). To this end, advances in advertising information technology have become integral to geopolitical strategies intent on the global articulation of local crises of non-sustainable development. In their endeavour to resist the exclusive advantage of globally, commercially networked time-horizons, social movements have mobilized advertising media capabilities towards the possibility of living time 'in a *longue durée*, a cosmological perspective, seeing our lives as part of the evolution of our species, and feeling solidarity with future generations, and with our cosmological belonging…' (Castells 2009:35).

Conclusion
Towards a Transgressive Techno-Political Caesura

In autumn 2008 Benylin launched its 'Take a Benylin Day' campaign, which featured an intriguingly novel mix of creative wisdom and political fervour. Audiences were informed that, 'It's winter again, and with it comes all the coughing, sneezing and sniffles associated with the Season. But this year, BENYLIN® is here to take the guilt out of calling in sick when you need time off to rest and recover' (Benylin 2009). The television advertisement portrayed a woman waking up one morning sniffling and spluttering with a cold. As she valiantly struggles to get out of bed, a voice-over suggests 'What if today, you just worked at feeling better?' She is then acquainted with the restorative properties of Benylin's Cold and Flu medicine and counselled to rest and 'Take a Benylin Day'. The end scene features the woman taking a 'Benylin Day', as she lies propped up in bed merrily reading a book. The style of the advertisement is unspectacular in its visual imagery and yet one immediately senses the advertisement as colluding with a transgression of sacrilegious proportions. 'Take a Benylin Day' rhymes with the mischievous and fainéant colloquialism 'throw a sickie'. Indeed this associative meaning formed the basis of a maelstrom of pontificating within the Federation of Small Businesses (FSB). In January 2009 the FSB referred the 'Take a Benylin Day' campaign to the Advertising Standards Authority. The FSB was particularly concerned that the 'Benylin Day' campaign may 'encourage thousands to take time off for minor complaints' (FSB 2009). Benylin was also accused of accentuating the UK's financial meltdown by encouraging a culture of absenteeism that costs the UK economy billions each year. Although the £13 billion wildly quoted in the news media appears extravagant, there is clear evidence that Benylin intended to agitate current thinking around the long-hours culture in the UK. According to the Trade Union Congress some 3.6 million employees frequently work in excess of 48 hours per week (Fagan et al 2006:8). This long-hours culture is increasingly recognized as detrimental to social relationships, personal health and well-being. Research demonstrates that employees experience higher levels of job satisfaction 'when they can balance work with the rest of their lives' (ibid). Nevertheless the UK business community remains committed to a work intensive archetype that equates long-hours with economic growth. Unsurprisingly, the FSB's rancour was steeped in indignation at Benylin's apparent disregard of the broader economic imperatives, precipitated by the context of the recession that had beset British financial markets, and manufacturing industries.

Benylin's vigorous defence of the campaign provided for a fascinating instance in Henry Giroux's (1994) observation, that postmodern advertising has the propensity to paradoxically blur the modernist distinction between the 'politics of representation and the representation of politics' (as discussed in Part II of this book). Of significance is the fact that the brand was keen, to annex the 'Take a Benylin Day' theme to wider political campaigns calling for a fundamental attitudinal change in the UK's long-hours culture. Thus 'Take a Benylin Day' was positioned as a serious political engagement with the UK's excessive work hours. As Benylin expressed it:

> Remember the three Rs: rest, remedy, recover. If you're feeling unwell, don't spread your germs; take some time to rest and relieve your symptoms with the right remedy from BENYLIN®. (Benylin 2009)

Figure C.1 'Take a Benylin Day', part one
Source: Reproduced with kind permission of Benylin®.

Benylin's brand of representational politics was even more experientially intriguing when one entered the website that accompanied the 'Take a Benylin Day' television advertising campaign. One section of the website, entitled 'Join the Take a Benylin Day Debate', contained a clarion call for 'employers and employees alike to take a stand against cold and flu by staying at home, rather than going into work' (Benylin 2009). This exclamation was supported by statistical evidence suggesting that '73 per cent of bosses would prefer you to call in sick and get better than struggle into work' and in excess of '80% of people agree that going into work unwell affects productivity' (ibid). Quoting statistics linking productivity with healthcare was a frequent defense strategy used by the Benylin to riposte the business community's choler. According to a spokesperson for Benylin the 'stay home and rest' approach was endorsed by healthcare professionals and research published by the British Chambers of Commerce (*Telegraph* 2009).

The first wave of the 'Take a Benylin Day' campaign's circulation garnered some national and international interest. The story was taken up in the UK, by prominent news channels including Sky News, Channel Five and BBC News at Ten. Coverage of the campaign gained some momentum as audiences as far wide as Canada and the US were acquainted with the merits of taking a 'Benylin Day'. Nevertheless, coverage of the campaign grew exponentially with the FSB's denouncement of the campaign's communiqué. To 'Take a Benylin Day' rather than labour against adversity, ran up against an ethic of work integral to a Western commercial enterprise culture and its spirit of capitalism. But what really seemed to have irrevocably incensed the FSB's work ethic was the inclusion on, the Benylin website, of tips on out of office messages and scripts on how best to alert ones employer about the need for a 'Benylin Day'. Alongside this bricolage of tips and guides for taking a sickie, was included DVD reviews and popular culture paraphernalia. In accordance with my previous discussion of advertising technoscapes (see Part IV), it is my contention that the 'Take a Benylin Day's' curious electronically mediated assemblage of scripts, tips, home remedies and activities, are an extension of a persuasive shift in the politico-ethical foundations of Western capitalism. As Hopper (2007:72) has observed, '...this so called "push-button democracy" or electronic direct democracy provides new ways for...new voices to be heard, for minority and radical opinions to be articulated and for breaking free from the dominance of the public debate on the part of major political parties'. In this sense, digital advertising technologies are integral features of a major transformation in the spirit of capitalism. This is because advertising technologies are a powerful material force and an integral feature of 'the spirit of informationalism' (Castells 2010:215).

Figure C.2 'Take a Benylin Day', part two

Source: Reproduced with kind permission of Benylin®.

Innovations in advertising media have brought into being unprecedented technological convergences between different forms of mediated communication. The integration of advertising media with user generated horizontal networks of interactive communication (e.g., YouTube), have enabled activists to garner local support, for global political issues through the creation of online communities and transnational networks. For a generation of sociologists, such advances in advertising technologies provide a near-perfect analogy of Michel Foucault's principle of discipline. The incessant dedication to electronic performance monitoring and ubiquitous accumulation of coded information, evident in advertising research is often cited as typifying disciplinary modes of regulating activities in time/space (Goss 1995, Lyon 2002). There is a tendency in these accounts to read Foucault's conception of subjectivity 'as a product of controlling and dominating social bonds…of the person as simply responding to disciplinary power' (Ezzy 1997:428). Foucault's account of disciplinary technologies is (mis)read as hyper-rational tempo-spatial systems capable of 'electronically tagging', tracing, and regulating passive bodies within insidiously coercive 'information panopticons'.

Axiomatic to this techno-determinist reading of Foucault (1991a) is an absolutist conception of linear time/space (Knights and Odih 2002). Whereby, advertising technologies place the human subject in linguistic and semiotic systems which have the effect of dividing the subject according to the coding of disciplinary space. Some support for this supposition is evident in Foucault's account of the objective conditions which enable the efficient application of discipline to the body. The elementary portioning of subjects into spatial grids provides for an impressive economy of means in which 'Each individual has a place and each place has its individual' (quoted in Dreyfus and Rabinow 1982:155). And this breaking up and rearrangement of activities in space 'must also be understood as machinery for adding up and capitalizing time' (Foucault 1991a:157). It is this disciplinary time which authors observe to be imposed on advertising technologies, in its efforts to code and delineate the time/space paths of individual consumers. Nevertheless Foucault also observed that disciplinary technology 'has as its correlative an individuality that is not only analytical and "cellular", but also natural and "organic"' (1991a:156). Thus although advertising technologies are similar to the disciplinary modalities which effect changes on 'mute and docile bodies' one feature overrides such comparison, 'the modern subject is not mute; he must talk' (Dreyfus and Rabinow 1982:155). In short, a reading of advertising technologies as hyper-rationalist electronic panopticons designed to enact a monolithic regime of control fails to recognise the distinction between subjects being constituted through rather than by a variety of disciplinary technologies. Foucault argued that 'power is exercised not only subject to, but through and by means of conditions of possibility' (Gordon 1980:246). Consequently the seriation of activities in linear time is made possible by acting upon the existing actions of thinking subjects. Power is exercised upon free subjects who have the capacity to imbue each moment of time with social meaning. Thus Foucault's *Discipline and Punish* details modern subjectivity as constituted through technologies and techniques which operate in consequence of the cooperation of linear chronology and subjective social times. As he expresses it, 'The disciplinary methods reveal a linear time whose moments are integrated, one upon another, and which is orientated towards a terminal, stable point; in short, an 'evolutive time'. But it must be recalled that, at the same moment, the administrative and economic techniques of control reveal a social time of a serial, orientated, cumulative type: 'the discovery of an evolution in terms of "progress"' (Foucault 1991a:160).

Foucault's account of discipline is clearly not limited to the quantitative dimensions of abstract technological systems capable of mapping the activities of individuals according to the linear dimensions of clock-time. Rather social times involve the 'discovery of an evolution in terms of "genesis"' (ibid:160). Individuals have the ability to attribute meaning to duration and thus imbue the quantitative dimensions of abstract electronic surveillance systems with symbolic meaning. Thus, advertising technologies can be observed in Foucauldian terms as 'a new way of administering time and making it useful, by segmentation, seriation, synthesis and totalization' (ibid:160). Nevertheless this objectification of subjects in linear time relies on the co-existence of social times, which enable their subjectification. Without the spontaneous identification of subjects with the products of advertising practice, the motivations for consumers to buy products and services would require a more overt renunciation of freedom. Conversely, advertising incites, it induces, and it seduces our compliance. It achieves this through a complex dialectical 'macro- and a micro-physics of power' (ibid:160), in which advertising technologies exercise control by the seriation of time and the discovery of the genesis of subjectivity in the temporal continuum of social time. It is at this interface that 'power is articulated directly onto time…' (ibid:160).

Advertising media also coincides with the complex cultural codes and multiplicity of operating strategies that define network enterprises. For just like the 'spirit of informationalism' (Castells 2010:215) digital advertising technologies live within the accelerated 'speed of the opto-electronic circuits' that advance the informational networked flows of reflexive accumulation. Indeed, the ability of advertising technologies to connect 'the global from the local, through networking with other localities' (Castells 2009:52) in simultaneous timeframes, has intensified the pace and broadened the scope of cultural politics. 'In this globalitarian conjuncture, the "advertising space" is no longer to be found in the breaks between films or the TV slots between programmers; it is now the real space-time of all communication' (Virillo 2005:113).

References

Abernathy, F., Dunlop, J., Hammond, J.H. and Weil, D. (1999), *A Stitch in Time: Lean Retailing and the Transformation of Manufacturing: Lessons from the Apparel and Textile Industry*. New York: Oxford University Press.

Adam, B. (1990), *Time and Social Theory*. Cambridge: Polity Press.

Adam, B. (1992), Modern Times; The Technology Connection and its Implications for Social Theory, *Time and Society*, Vol. 1(2), pp. 175-91.

Adam, B. (1993), Within and Beyond the Time Economy of Employment Relations: Conceptual Issues Pertinent to Research on Time and Work, *Social Science Information*, Vol. 32, pp. 163-184.

Adam, B. (1995), *Timewatch*. Cambridge: Polity Press.

Adams, M. and Raisborough, J. (2008), What Can Sociology Say About Fairtrade?: Class, Reflexivity and Ethical Consumption, *Sociology*, Vol. 42, pp. 1165-1182.

Adorno, T. (1990/1941), On Popular Music, In *On Record: Rock, Pop and the Written Word*. Edited by Simon Frith and Andrew Goodwin. New York: Pantheon Books, pp. 301-314.

Advertising Archive (2006), *On Archive*. http://www.advertisingarchives.co.uk.

Ahola, H. (2000), Internet Marketing – Literature Review and Research Agenda. http://www.tekniikka.oamk.fi/netties/2000/papers/InternetMarketing.

Aleksandra, M. (2005), Not Everything is Always Black or White. http://www.aleksandramir.info/texts/fitzpatrick.html.

Allport, H. (1924), *Social Psychology*. Boston.

Allwood, J., Laursen, S., Rodriguez, C. and Bocken, N. (2006), *Well Dressed? The Present and Future Sustainability of Clothing and Textiles in the United Kingdom*. Cambridge: University of Cambridge Institute of Manufacturing.

Amin, A. (1995), *Post-Fordism; A Reader*. Cambridge: Blackwell.

Ancarani, F. and Shankar, V. (2003), Symbian: Customer Interaction through collaboration and Competition in a Convergent Industry. *Journal of Interactive Marketing*, Vol. 17, No. 1, pp. 56-76.

Andrejevic, M. (2003), Monitored Mobility in the Era of Mass Customization, *Space and Culture*, Vol. 6, No. 2 (May), pp. 132-150.

Annandale, E. (1998), *The Sociology of Health and Illness : A Critical Introduction*. Oxford: Polity.

Appadurai, A. (1996), *Modernity At Large: Cultural Dimensions Of Globalization* Minneapolis, Minn: University of Minnesota Press.

Aristotle (c.,350BC/1981), *The Politics*. Translated by Sinclair, T. Harmondsworth: Penguin Classics.

Auberbach, J. (2002), Art, Advertising and the Legacy of Empire, *Journal of Popular Culture*, Vol. 35, pp. 1-23.
Balakrishnan, R. (2002), *Gender Dynamics of Subcontracted Work in a Global Economy*. Connecticut: Kumarian Press.
Backhouse, R. (2002), *The Penguin History of Economics*. London: Penguin.
Banet-Weiser, S. (2007), *Kids Rule!: Nickelodeon and Consumer Citizenship*. Duke University.
Barnes, C., Mercer, G. and Shakespeare, T. (1999), *Exploring Disability: A Sociological Introduction*. Malden, Mass: Polity Press.
Barnes, S. (2002), Under the Skin: Short-Range Emebdded Wireless Technology. *International Journal of Information Management*, Vol. 22, pp. 165-179.
Barnett, A. (1969), A Revolutionary Student Movement. *New Left Review*, 1/53, January-February, pp. 43-53.
Barnett, C., Clocke, P., Clarke, N. and Malpass, A. (2005), Consuming Ethics: Articulating the Subjects and Spaces of Ethical Consumption, *Antipode*, Vol. 37, No. 1, January, pp. 23-45(23).
Bartels, R. (1986), *The History of Marketing Thought*. Coloumbus Horizons.
Barthes, R. (1977), *Image, Music, Text*. Essays selected and translated by Heath, S. London: Fontana Press.
Barthes, R. (1979), *The Effel Tower*. Translated by Howard, R. New York: Hill and Wang.
Barthes, R. (2000), *Mythologies*. London: Vintage.
Baudrillard, J. (1968/1996), *The System of Objects*. Translated by Benedict, J. London: Verso.
Baudrillard, J. (1975), *The Mirror of Production*. St Louis: Telos Press.
Baudrillard, J. (1981), *For a Critique of the Political Economy of the Sign*. Translated by Levin, C. St Louis: Telos.
Baudrillard, J. (1983), *Simulations*. Translated by Foss, P., Patton, P., Beitchman, P. New York: Semiotext(e) Inc.
Baudrillard, J. (1983a), *In the Shadow of the Silent Majorities... or the End of the Social and Other Essays*. Translated by Foss, P., Johnston J. and Patton, P. New York: Semiotext(e) Inc.
Baudrillard, J. (1984), The Structural Law of Value and the Order of Simulacra., in Fekete, J. (ed.), *The Structural Allegory; Reconstructive Encounters With The New French Thought*. Minneapolis: University of Minnesota Press pp. 54-73.
Baudrillard, J. (1985), The Ecstasy of Communication, in Foster, H. (ed.) *Postmodern Culture*. Wiltshire: Pluto, pp. 126-135.
Baudrillard, J. (1990), *Seduction*. Translated by Singer, B. New York: St Martin's Press.
Baudrillard, J. (1994), *Simulacra and Simulation*. Translated by Glaser, S. AnnAbor: University of Michigan Press.
Baudrillard, J. (2001), *Jean Baudrillard: Selected Writings*. Edited and Introduced by Mark Poster. Oxford: Polity Press.

Baudrillard, J. (2003), *The Consumer Society: Myths and Structures*. London: Sage.
Baudrillard, J. (2005), *The Intelligence of Evil*. Oxford: Berg.
Bauman, Z. (1988), *Freedom*, Milton Keynes University Press.
Bauman, Z. (1992), *Intimations of Postmodernity*. London: Routledge.
Bauman, Z. (2000), *Liquid Modernity*. Cambridge, Polity Press.
Bauman, Z. (2001), *Liquid Modernity*. Cambridge: Polity.
BBC (2006), M&S to Launch Fairtrade Range, http://news.bbc.co.uk/1/hi/business/4660410.stm.
BBC (2008), Quality Ranking Key to NHS Funds http://newsvote.bbc.co.uk.
BBC (2008a); Ad Breakdown's pick of 2008 http://news.bbc.co.uk/1/hi/magazine/7798837.stm.
BBC (2010), Cadbury Agrees Kraft Takeover Bid http://news.bbc.co.uk/1/hi/business/8467007.stm.
Beck, U. (1992), *Risk Society*. Towards a New Modernity. London: Sage.
Beck, U., Bonss, W. and Lau, C. (2003), The Theory of Reflexive Modernization. Problematic, Hypotheses and Research Programme, *Theory Culture and Society*, Vol. 20, No. 2, pp. 1-33.
Becker, G. (1965), A Theory of the Allocation of Time. *Economic Journal*. Vol. 75, September, pp. 493-517.
Becker, G. and Michael, R. (1973), On the New Theory of Consumer Behaviour. *Swedish Journal of Economics*. vol. 75, September, pp. 493-517.
Bell, D. (1976), *The Cultural Contradictions of Capitalism*. London: Heineman.
Bell, D. (1976), *The Coming of Post-Industrial Society*, New York, NY: Basic Books.
Bell, R., Kravitz, R. and Wilkes, M. (1999), Direct-to-Consumer Prescription Drug Advertising and the Public, *J Gen Intern Med*, November, Vol. 14, No. 11, pp. 651-657.
Benetton (1989), *Breastfeeding*, September 1989.
Benetton (1991), *New Born Baby*, September 1991, http://press.benettongroup.com/ben_en/about/campaigns/list/newborn_baby/?version=1.
Benetton (1992), *AIDS*, David Kirby February 1992, http://press.benettongroup.com/ben_en/about/campaigns/list/aids_david_kirby/?version=1.
Benetton (1993), *HIV Positive*, September 1993.
Benetton (1998), Benetton Sunflowers bloom in Autumn. Disabled youngsters in a German care institute stars of the new catalogue and international campaign, Benetton Institutional Campaigns – *The Sunflowers*, http://press.benettongroup.com/ben_en/releases/1998-09-11/.
Benetton (2003), *Fabrica and Colors Against Violence*, June 2003 Press Release, http://press.benettongroup.com/ben_en/releases/2003-06-04a/.
Benetton (2003), *Food For Life*, Press Release, http://press.benettongroup.com/ben_en/releases/2003-02-13/.
Benetton (2004a), *Fabrica 10 From Chaos to order and Back*, November 2004 Press Release http://press.benettongroup.com/ben_en/releases/2004-11-15/.

Benetton (2004b), Fabrica 10 x 10 a Global Phenomenon November 2004.
Benetton (2007b), *About Benetton* http://press.benettongroup.com/ben_en/about/.
Benetton (2008a), *About Benetton* http://press.benettongroup.com/ben_en/about/.
Benetton (2008b), *Index Complete Press Kit* http://press.benettongroup.com/ben_en/press_kit/en/complete/complete/press_kit.pdf?version=1.
Benhabib, S. (1992), *Situating the Subject*. London: Sage.
Benjamin, W. (1999), *Illuminations*. Translated by Harry Zorn. London: Pimlico.
Benylin (2009), *Take a Benylin Day* http://www.takeabenylinday.co.uk/.
Berger, J. (1972), *Ways of Seeing*. Bath: Penguin.
Berger, J. (2006), Contributions in Tribute to Ernesto 'Che' Guevara, in Sinclair, A. (2006), *Viva Che!: The Strange Death and Life of Che Guevara*. Gloucestershire: Sutton Publishing.
Berman, R. (1981), *Advertising and Social Change*. Beverly Hills: Sage.
Berry, M. (2006), *NHS Hospitals Set to Start Advertising to Attract Patients*, http://www.personneltoday.com/articles/article.aspx?liarticleid=38267&printerfriendly=true.
Best, S. and Kellner, D. (1991), *Postmodern Theory Critical Interrogations*. Hampshire: Macmillan.
Bettman, J. (1979), *An Information Processing Theory of Consumer Choice*. Addison and Wesley; Reading, MA.
Bheda, R. and Singla, A. (2003), Apparel Manufacturing: a Strategy for Productivity Improvement, *Journal of Fashion Marketing and Management*, Vol. 7, No. 1, pp. 12-22.
Binkley, S. (2009), The Bohemian Habitus: New Social Theory and Political Consumerism, in (ed.) Soper, K., *The Politics and Pleasures of Consuming Differently: Better Than Shopping*. Palgrave Macmillan.
Birmingham Post (2009), Complaints Over Cadbury Adverts Being Racist Rejected by Watchdog.
Bishop, P. (2000), Caught in the Cross-fire: Tibet, Media and Promotional Culture, *Media, Culture and Society*, Vol. 22, pp. 645-664.
Blair, M. (2003), Turning Viral Marketing into a Main Stream Proposition. http://www.ogilvy.com/viewpoint/pdf/v4_blair.pdf.
Blau, P. and Schoenherr, R. (1971), *The Structure of Organizations*. London: Basic Books.
Bloomfield, M. (1915), The New Profession of Handling Men, *Annals of the American Academy of Political and Social Science*. LXI, September.
Bluetooth (2006), *Bluetooth* http://www.bluetooth.com/Bluetooth/Learn/Technology.
BMA (2006), BMA Comment on Hospital Advertising http://web2.bma.org.uk/pressrel.nsf/wlu/SGOY-6VQG9W?OpenDocument&vw=wfmms.
Bonanno A. (1998), Liberal democracy in the global era: implications for the agro-food sector. *Agric. Hum. Val*. 15:223–42.
Boorstin, D. (1964), *The Image: A Guide to Pseudo Events in America*. New York.

Booth, P. and Whetstone, L. (2007), Half a Cheer for Fair Trade, *Economic Affairs*, Vol. 27, No. 2, pp. 29-36.

Bourke, L. (1991), *Women and Money*. London: Thorsons.

Bowlby, R. (1993), *Shopping with Freud*. London: Routledge.

Brandon, R. (2002), *How the Car Changed Life; Automobile*. London: Macmillan.

Braun, KA., Ellis, R. and Loftus, E.P. (2002), Make My Memory: How Advertising Can Change our Memories of the Past, *Psychology and Marketing*, Vol. 19(1), 1-23.

Braverman, H. (1974), *Labor and Monopoly Capital: The Degradation of Work in the Twentieth Century*. London: Monthly Review Press.

Brenton, P. and Hoppe, M. (2007), Clothing and Export Diversification: Still a Route to Growth for Low-Income Countries? *Policy Research Working Paper 4343*. September, The World Bank Poverty Reduction and Economic Management Network International Trade Department.

Brierley, S. (2002), *The Advertising Handbook*. London: Routledge.

Brooks, E. (2007), *Unraveling the Garment Industry: Transnational Organizing and Women's Work*. Minneapolis: MinnesotaPress.

Bruce, M., Daly, L. and Towers, N. (2004), Lean or Agile A Solution for Supply Chain Management in the Textiles and Clothing Industry? *International Journal of Operations and Production Management*, Vol. 24, No. 2, pp. 151-170.

Bruttini, A. (1982), Advertising and Socio-Economic Transformations in England 1720-1760. *Journal of Advertising History*, Vol. 5, pp. 8-26.

Burchell, G., Gordon, C. and Miller, P. (1991), *The Foucault Effect – Studies in Governmentality*. Hemel-Hempstead: Harvester.

Burrill, D. (2005), Out of the Box: Performance, Drama and Interactive Software, *Modern Drama*, Vol. 48, No. 3, pp. 492-512.

Cadbury (2008a), Wisp…Officially Back for Good, http://www.cadburyinvestors.com/cadbury_ir/press_releases/2008press/2008-08-05/.

Cadbury (2009), Our Sustainability Commitments. http://www.cadbury.com/ourcompany/ourstrategy/Pages/sustainabilitycommitments.aspx.

Cadbury (2009a), Purple Goes Green. http://www.cadbury.com/ourresponsibilities/purplegoesgreen/Pages/PurpleGoesGreen.aspx.

Cadbury (2009b), Cadbury Autumn 2009. http://www.cadbury.com/ourcompany/Documents/cadburycorporatefactsheet0809.pdf.

Cadbury (2009c), Fairtrade Cadbury. http://www.cadbury.com/ourresponsibilities/Fairtrade/Pages/Fairtrade.aspx.

Cadbury (2009d), Company Overview. http://www.cadbury.com/ourcompany/ouroverview/pages/ourcompany.aspx.

Cadbury (2009e), Cadbury Dairy Milk Commits to Going Fairtrade. http://www.cadbury.com/media/press/Pages/cdmFairtrade.aspx.

Cadbury (2009f), Fairtrade Towns http://cadburydairymilk.typepad.com/Fairtrade/2009/03/Fairtrade-towns.html.

Cadbury (2009g), Ghana Inspires Cadbury Dairy Milk's Innovative Advertising of Fairtrade. http://www.cadbury.com/media/press/Pages/GhanaInspiresCDMAFairtradeAd.aspx.

Cadbury (2009h), Ghana Inspires Cadbury Dairy Milk's Innovative Advertising of Fair Trade, 3rd October. http://www.cadbury.com/MEDIA/PRESS/Pages/GhanaInspiresCDMAFairtradeAd.aspx.

Cadbury (2009i), Todd Stitzer speaks at the Fairtrade Commercial Conference, 24 September 2009, http://www.cadburyinvestors.com/cadbury_ir/pressreleases/2009press/2009-09-24/.

Cadbury (2009j), Find out more about our Fairtrade Campaign Events and Tinny's UK Vist.

Cadbury (2009k), Ghana Inspires Cadbury Dairy Milk's Innovative Advertising of Fairtrade.

Calfee, J., Winston, C. and Stempski, R. (2002), Direct-to-consumer advertising and the demand for cholesterol-reducing drugs, *J Law Econ* XLV Vol. 2 No. 2, pp. 673–690.

Cammett, M. (2006), Development and the Changing Dynamics of Global Production: Global Value Chains and Local Clusters in Apparel Manufacturing, *Competition and Change*, Vol. 10, No. 1, March, pp. 23-48.

Campbell C. (1995), When the Meaning is Not the Message. A Critique of the Consumption as Communication Thesis. In (ed.) Nava, M., *Buy This Book*. Routledge.

Carlowe, J. (2009), Doctors Condemn NHS Comparison Website, *British Medical Journal*, http://www.bmj.com/cgi/content/extract/339/aug14_2/b3341.

Carr, W. and Hartnett, A. (2002), *Education and the Struggle for Democracy: The Politics of Education Ideas*. Buckingham: Open University Press.

Castells, M. (1996), *The Rise of the Network Society*. Oxford: Blackwell.

Castells, M. (1997), *The Power of Identity, The Information Age: Economy, Society and Culture*, Vol. II. Cambridge, MA; Oxford, UK: Blackwell.

Castells, M. (1998), *The Information Age; Economy, Society and Culture. Vol. II; End of Millennium*. Maiden, MA: Blackwell.

Castells, M. (2000), *The Rise of the Network Society*. Oxford: Blackwell.

Castells, M. (2001), *Internet Galaxy. Reflections on the Internet, Business and Society*. Oxford: OUP.

Castells, M. (2004), *The Network Society: A Cross-Cultural Perspective*. Cheltenham: Edward Elgar Publishing.

Castells, M. (2009), *Communication Power*. Oxford: Oxford University Press.

Castells, M. (2010), *The Rise of the Network Society*. Oxford: Blackwell.

Chanan, M. (2001), Alberto Korda; Ebullient Cuban Photographer whose Portrait of Che Guevara Became an Icon for a Generation of Protest, *The Guardian*, Monday 28 May 2001 02.03 BST http://www.guardian.co.uk/news/2001/may/28/guardianobituaries.cuba.

Channel 4 (2009), Interactive Applications, http://www.channel4.com/microsites/I/interactive_tv_sales/types.html.

Christerson, B. and Appelbaum, R. (1995), Global and Local Subcontracting: Space, Ethnicity and the Organization of Apparel Production, *World Development*, Vol. 23, No. 8, pp. 1363-1374.

Clammer, J. (1992), Aesthetics of the Self: Shopping and Social Being in Contemporary Urban Japan in Shields, R. (ed.), *Lifestyle Shopping: The Subject of Consumption*. London: Routledge.

Clarke, D. (2000), Space Knowledge and Consumption in Daniels, P., Bryson, J. et al (eds), *Knowledge, Space and Economy*. Routledge pp. 209-226.

Clarke, J. and Critcher, C. (1985), *The Devil Makes Work. Leisure in Capitalist Britain*. London: Macmillan.

Clarke, N., Barnett, C., Cloke, P. and Malpass, A. (2007), The Political Rationalities of Fair-Trade Consumption in the United Kingdom, *Politics and Society*, Vol. 35, pp. 583-604.

Cohen, G.A. (1978), *Karl Marx's Theory of History; A Defence*, Oxford: Clarendon Press.

Collins, J. (2003), *Threads. Gender, Labor and Power in the Global Apparel Industry*. Chicago: University of Chicago Press.

Collins, J. (2006), Redefining the Boundaries of Work: Apparel Workers and Community Unionism in the Global Economy, *Identities: Global Studies in Culture and Power*, Vol. 13, pp. 9-31.

Collins, J. and Quark, A. (2006), Globalizing Firms and Small Communities: The Apparel Industry's Changing Connection to Rural Labor Markets, *Rural Sociology*, Vol. 71, Issue 2, pp. 281-310.

Collin, R. (1980), *Weberian Sociological Theory*. Cambridge: Cambridge University Press.

Connor, S. (1992), *Postmodernist Culture: An Introduction to Theories of the Contemporary*. Oxford: Blackwell.

Conrad, P. (1992), Medicalization and Social Control, *Annual Review of Sociology* 18, pp. 209-32.

Conrad, P. and Leiter, V. (2004), Medicalization, Markets and Consumers, *Journal of Health and Social Behavior*, Vol. 45, Extra Issue: Health and Health Care in the United States: Origins and Dynamics, pp. 158-176.

Conservative Party, David Cameron (2010), Conservatives Draft Manifesto, Chapter One Our Reform Plan for the NHS, http://www.conservatives.com.

Cooper, R. and Law, J. (1995), Organization; Distal and Proximal Views, in Bocharach, S., Gaghardi, P. and Mundell, B. (eds) *Research in the Sociology of Organizations*, Greenwich, Conneticutt: JAI Press.

Corrigan, P. (1997), *The Sociology of Consumption*. London: Sage.

Cousins, M. and Hussain, A. (1984), *Michel Foucault*. London: Macmillian.

Cowan, J., Dembour, M. and Wilson, R. (2001), *Culture and Rights; Anthropological Perspectives*. Cambridge: Cambridge University Press.

Craig, R. (1991), Designing Ethnicity: The Ideology of Images, *Design Issues*, Vol. 7, No. 2 (Spring), pp. 34-42.

Cramption, J. (2003), Cartographic Rationality and the Politics of Geosurveillance and Security, *Cartography and Geographic Information Science*, Vol. 30, No. 2, pp. 135-148.

Crouch, C. (2003), Commercialisation or Citizenship. Education Policy and the Future of Public Services. Fabian Ideas 606.

Crouch, C. (2007). Neoinstitutionalism:Still no Intellectual Hegemony, *Regulation and Government*, Vol. 1, pp. 261-270.

Dalla Costa, M. and James, S. (1975), *The Power of Women and the Subversion of the Community*. Bristol: Falling Wall Press.

Daniel, B. (1976), *The Cultural Contradictions Of Capitalism*. London: Heinemann.

Daston, L. (1995), *Classical Probability in the Enlightenment*. New Jersey: Princeton University Press.

Davies, H.T.O. and Lampel, J. (1998), Trust in Performance Indicators? *Quality and Safety in Health Care*, Vol. 7, No. 3, 159-62.

Datamonitor (2004), *Skincare and Suncare in the UK to 2008*. London: Datamonitor.

Davidoff, L. (1976), The Rationalization of Housework, in Barker and Allen (eds) *Dependence and Exploitation in Work and Marriage*. London: Longman.

Davis, J. and Elliot, J. (2006), This is the Girl Band you can Buy, *The Sunday Times*, 9 April, p. 4.

Dean, M. (1994); *Critical and Effective Histories: Foucault's Methods and Historical Sociology*. Routledge: London

Debenhams (2009), Find Out More About Fairtrade, http://www.debenhams.com/webapp/wcs/stores/servlet/CategoryDisplay?identifier=Find%20out%20more%20about%20Fairtrade_7628&categoryId=65284&catalogId=10001&storeId=10001&top=N.

Debord, G. (2006), *The Society of the Spectacle*, New York: Zone Books.

DeCarlo, J. (2007), *Fair Trade*. Oxford: Oneworld Publications.

Defert, D. (1991), Popular Life and Insurance Technology, in Burchell, J., Gordon, C. and Miller, P. (eds), *The Foucault Effect-Studies in Governmentality*. pp. 211-33, Hemple Hempstead: Harvester.

Denzin, N. (1989), *Interpretive Interaction*. Newbury Park CA: Sage.

Derrida, J. (1973), *Speech and Phenomenon*. Evanston: Nother Western University Press.

Derrida, J. (1978), *Writing and Difference*. Translated by A. Bass. Chicago: University of Chicago Press.

Derrida, J. (1982), *Margins of Philosophy*. Translated by A. Bass. Chicago: University of Chicago Press.

Descartes, R. (1952), *Descartes Philosophical Writings* (edited and translated by N.K. Smith). London: Macmillian.

De-Winter, R. (2001), The Anti-Sweatshop Movement: Constructing Corporate Moral Agency in the Global Apparel Industry, *Ethics and International Affairs*, Vol. 2, Issue 15, pp. 99-116.

Dichter, E. (1964), *Handbook of Consumer Motivation*. NewYork: McGraw-Hill.

Dicken, P. (2003), *Global Shift: Transforming the Global Economy.* London: Paul Chapman Publishing.

Dicken, P. (2007), *Global Shift: Mapping the Changing Contours of the World Economy.* London: Sage.

Dickinson, R. and Carsky, M. (2005); The Consumer As Economic Voter. In R. Harrison, T. Newholm and D. Shaw (eds), *The Ethical Consumer* (pp. 25-36). London: Sage.

Dicks, B. (2003), *Culture on Display: The Production of Contemporary Visibility.* Maidenhead Berkshire: Open University Press.

Diggins, J. (1976), *The Bard of Savagery: Thorstein Veblen and Modern Social Theory*. Sussex: Harvester Press.

Diggins, J. (1978); *The Bard Of Savagery : Thorstein Veblen And Modern Social Theory*. Hassocks: Harvester Press.

Dill Scott, W. (1908), *The Psychology of Advertising. A simple Exposition of the Principles of Psychology in their Relation to Successful Advertising*. Boston: Small Maynard.

Dimbach, E. (2008), Weaving A Stronger Fabric: Organizing a Global Sweat-Free Apparel Production Agreement. *The Journal of Labor and Society*, Vol. 11, Issue, 1089-7011, pp. 237-254.

Dirks, T. (2006), *The Manchurian Candidate (1962)*. http://www.filmsite.org/manc.html.

Dirlik, A. (2002), Modernity as History: Post-Revolutionary China, Globalization and the Question of Modernity, *Social History*, Vol. 27, No. 1, pp. 16-39.

Dobres, C. (2004), Towards an interactive world? *Admap*, October, Issue 454, pp. 95-96.

DoH (1989), *Department of Health, Working for Patients White Pape*r, Session 88/89, Command Papers, Paper Number Cm 555, 20th Century House of Commons Sessional Papers, http://0-gateway.proquest.com.catalogue.ulrls.lon.ac.uk/openurl?url_ver=Z39.88-2004&res_dat=xri:hcpp&rft_dat=xri:hcpp:rec:1988-085198.

DoH (1990), Department of Health: National Health Service and Community Care Bill, Session 1989/90, Bills, Bill 1, 20th Century House of Commons Sessional Papers, http://0-gateway.proquest.com.catalogue.ulrls.lon.ac.uk/openurl?url_ver=Z39.88-2004&res_dat=xri:hcpp&rft_dat=xri:hcpp:rec:1989-086418.

DoH (1991), *Prime Minister. The Citizens Charter: Raising the Standard* White Paper. Session 1990/91, Command Papers, Paper Number Cm 1599, 20th Century House of Commons Sessional Papers., http://0-gateway.proquest.com.catalogue.ulrls.lon.ac.uk/openurl?url_ver=Z39.88-2004&res_dat=xri:hcpp&rft_dat=xri:hcpp:rec:1990-088356.

DoH (1997), *The New NHS Modern Dependable*. Department of Health 8 December, http://www.dh.gov.uk/en/Publicationsandstatistics/Publications/PublicationsPolicyAndGuidance/DH_4008869.

DoH (1998), *A First Class Service: Quality in the new NHS*, Department of Health, http://www.dh.gov.uk/en/Publicationsandstatistics/Publications/PublicationsPolicyAndGuidance/DH_4006902.

DoH (1999), *The NHS Performance Assessment Framework*, 1 March, http://www.dh.gov.uk/en/Publicationsandstatistics/Publications/PublicationsPolicyAndGuidance/DH_4009190.

DoH (2000), *The NHS Plan: A Plan for Investment, a Plan for Reform*, Command paper, 1 July, http://www.dh.gov.uk/en/Publicationsandstatistics/Publications/PublicationsPolicyAndGuidance/DH_4002960.

DoH (2004), *The NHS Improvement Plan. Putting People at the Heart of Public Services*. (Presented to parliament by the secretary of state for health, June 2004), Paper Number Cm 6268 http://www.artery.org.uk/files/ARTXXX0002/Documents/GeneralDocuments/NHS_Improvement_Plan.pdf.

DoH (2006), *Code of Practice for Promotion of NHS Services*, http://www.dh.gov.uk/en/Consultations/Closedconsultations/DH_063280.

DoH (2007), *NHS Performance Assessment Framework. Annual Report*, 8 February, http://www.dh.gov.uk/en/Publicationsandstatistics/Publications/AnnualReports/Browsable/DH_4992217.

DoH (2008), *Code of Practice for the Promotion of NHS-Funded Services*, http://www.dh.gov.uk/en/Publicationsandstatistics/Publications/PublicationsPolicyAndGuidance/DH_083556.

Dolan, C. (2007), Market Affections: Moral Encounters with Kenyan Fairtrade Flowers, *Ethnos*, Vol. 72, No. 2 pp. 239-361.

Dolan, C. (2008), In the Mists of Development: Fairtrade in Keynam Tea Fields., *Globalizations*, 1474 – 774X, Vol. 5, No. 2, pp. 305-318.

Douglas, J.D. (1970), *Understanding Everyday Life*, London: Routledge Kegan Paul.

Douglas, M. and Isherwood, B. (1978), *The World of Goods; Towards an Anthropology of Consumption*. London: Allen Lane.

Douglas, M. and Isherwood, B. (1979), *The World of Goods: Toward an Anthropology of Consumption*. New York: W.W. Norton.

Drapers (2008), Primark Closes on M&S market share, 28 March http://www.drapersonline.com/news/2008.

Dreyfus, H. and Rabinow, P. (1982), *Beyond Structuralism and Hermeneutics*. London: Harvester and Wheatsheaf.

Drèze and Zufrydeni from Drez, X. and Zufryden, F. (2000), Internet Advertising: The Medium is the Difference, *Consumption Markets and Culture*, Vol. 4(1), pp. 23-37.

Du Gay, P. (1996), *Consumption and Identity at Work*. London: Sage.

Dwyer, P. (2000), *Welfare Rights and Responsibilities; Contesting Social Citizenship*. Bristol: The Policy Press, pp. 49-69.

Dyer, G. (1993), *Advertising as Communication*. London: Routledge.

Dymock, E. (1993), *Rover: The First Ninety Years. One of Britain's Fine Cars 1904-1994*. London: G.T. Foulis and Co (Haynes Group).

Easton, G. and Araujo, L. (1994), Market Exchange, Social Structures and Time. *European Journal of Marketing*, Vol. 28, No. 3, pp. 72-84.

Eby, C. (1998), Veblen's Assault on Time, *Journal of Economic Issues*, Vol. XXXII, No. 3, September, pp. 680-707.

Elison, D. (2002), Socializing markets, not market socialism, in Panitch, L. and Leys, C. (eds), Socialist Register 2002: *Necessary and Unnecessary Utopias* pp. 67-85. Black Point, Nova Scotia: Fernwood Books.

Elliot, A. (2001), *Concepts of the Self*. Cambridge: Polity.

Elliot, B. (1962), *A History of English Advertising*. London: Business Publications LTD in associaton with B.T. Batsford Limited.

Elliot, R. (1999), Symbolic Meaning and Postmodern Consumer Culture, in Brownlie, D. et al (eds), *Rethinking Marketing, Towards Critical Marketing Accountings*. London: Sage.

Ellis, C. and Bochner, A.P. (2000). Autoethnography, Personal Narrative, Reflexivity: Researcher as Subject, in Denzin, N. and Lincoln, Y. (eds), *Handbook of qualitative research* (2nd edition) pp.733-768. Thousand Oaks: Sage.

EMCC (2004), *Sector Futures. Textiles and Clothing: A Dying Industry – or Not?* Dublin: European Monitoring Centre on Change.

Enthoven, A. (1988), Managed Competition of Alternative Delivery Systems, *Journal of Health Politics, Policy and Law*, Vol. 13, No. 2, pp. 305-321.

Ermarth, E. (1989), The Solitude of Women and Social Time, in Forman, F. and Sowton, C. (eds) *Taking Our Time Feminist Perspectives on Temporality*, pp. 37-46. Oxford: Pergamon Press.

Ermarth, E. (1992), *Sequel to History. Postmodernism and the Crisis of Representational Time*. Princeton N.J.; Princeton University Press.

Ermarth, E. (1995), Ph(r)ase Time: Chaos Theory and Postmodern Reports on Knowledge, *Time and Society*, Vol. 4, No. 1, pp. 91-111.

Esbenshade, J. (2004), *Monitoring Sweatshops: Workers, Consumers and the Global Apparel Industry*. Philadelphia: PA Temple University Press.

ETI (2009), Ethical Trading Initiative. Respect for Workers Worldwide, http://www.ethicaltrade.org/about-eti.

Evan, C. and Harrigan, J. (2005), Distance, Time and Specialization: Lean Retailing in General Equilibrium, *The American Economic Review*, Vol. 95, Issue 1, pp. 292-313.

Evans, R. (2005), *Thatcher and Thatcherism*. London: Routledge.

Ewald, F. (1991), Insurance and Risk in Burchell, J., Gordan, C. and Miller, P. (eds), *The Foucault Effect-Studies in Governmentality*. Hemple Hempstead: Harvester.

Ewen, S. (2001), *Captains of Consciousness: Advertising and the Social Roots of the Consumer Culture*. New York: Basic Books.

Ezzamel, M. (1994), Organizational Change and Accounting: Understanding the Budgeting System in its Organizational Context, *Organization Studies*. Vol. 15, No. 2, pp. 213-240.

Ezzy, D. (1997) Subjectivity and the Labour Process: Conceptualising 'good Work' *Sociology*, 31, 3 August, 427-444.

Fabian, J. (1983), *Time And The Other: How Anthropology Makes Its Object.* New York: Columbia University Press.

Fagan, C., Hegewisch, A. and Pillinger, J. (2006), Out of Time – Why Britain Needs a New Approach to Working-Time Flexibility. London: Trades Union Congress, www.tuc.org.uk.

Fairclough, N. (2001), The Discourse of New Labour: Critical Discourse Analysis, in (ed) Wetherell, M., Taylor, S., and Yates. S., *Discourse as Data*, London ; Thousand Oaks, CA: SAGE.

Fairtrade (2009), UK Government announces £12 million Investment for Fairtrade on 15th Anniversary of the Fairtrade Mark, http://www.Fairtrade.org.uk/press_office/press_releases_and_statements/october_2009/uk_government_announces_12_million_investment_for_Fairtrade_on_15th_anniversary_of_the_Fairtrade_mark.aspx.

Fairtrade Foundation (2008a), Awareness of Fairtrade Mark Leaps to 70%, http://www.Fairtrade.org.uk.

Fairtrade Foundation (2009), The Fairtrade Mark, http://www.Fairtrade.org.uk/what_is_Fairtrade/Fairtrade_certification_and_the_Fairtrade_mark/the_Fairtrade_mark.aspx.

Fairtrade Foundation (2009), Background, http://www.Fairtrade.org.uk.

Fairtrade Foundation (2009a), Fairtrade Labelling International History, http://www.Fairtrade.org.uk/what_is_Fairtrade/history.aspx.

Fairtrade Foundation (2009b), Fairtrade Standards, http://www.Fairtrade.org.uk/what_is_Fairtrade/Fairtrade_certification_and_the_Fairtrade_mark/Fairtrade_standards.aspx.

Fairtrade Foundation (2009c), The Fairtrade Minimum Price, http://www.Fairtrade.org.uk/what_is_Fairtrade/Fairtrade_certification_and_the_Fairtrade_mark/the_Fairtrade_minimum_price.aspx.

Fairtrade Foundation (2009d), Fairtrade Producer Certification and Auditing, http://www.Fairtrade.org.uk/what_is_Fairtrade/Fairtrade_certification_and_the_Fairtrade_mark/Fairtrade_producer_certification.aspx.

Fairtrade Foundation (2009e), Fairtrade Premium, http://www.Fairtrade.org.uk/what_is_Fairtrade/Fairtrade_certification_and_the_Fairtrade_mark/the_Fairtrade_premium.aspx.

Fairtrade Foundation (2009f), Fashion Industry Urged to Scale up Commitment to Fairtrade.

Fairtrade Foundation (2009g), Cotton, http://www.Fairtrade.net/cotton.html.

Fairtrade Foundation (2009h), Facts and Figures on Fairtrade.

Fairtrade Foundation (2009i), Composite Products.

Fairtrade Foundation (2009j), Cadbury Dairy Milk Commits to Going Fairtrade, http://www.Fairtrade.org.uk.

Fairtrade Foundation (2009k), Cadbury Dairy Milk commits to going Fairtrade http://www.cadbury.com/media/press/Pages/cdmFairtrade.aspx.

Falk, P. (1997), The Benetton-Toscani Effect: Testing the Limits of Conventional Advertising, in Nava, M., Blake, A., MacRury, I. and Richards, B. (eds), *Buy This Book: Studies in Advertising and Consumption*. London: Routledge.

Faulks, K. (1998), *Citizenship In Modern Britain*. Edinburgh: Edinburgh University Press.

Featherstone, M. (1991), *Consumer Culture and Postmodernism*. London: Sage.

Federation of Small Business (2009), Benylin, http://www.fsb.org.uk/default.aspx?id=23&loc=pressroom.

Fernandez-Kelly, P. (2007), The Global Assembly Line in the New Millennium: A Review Essay, *Signs: Journal of Women in Culture and Society*, Vol. 32, No. 2, pp. 509-521.

Fiore, A., Kim, J. and Lee, H. (2005), Effects of Image Interactivity Technology on Consumer Responses Toward Online Retailer, *Journal of Interactive Marketing*, Vol. 19, Issues 3, pp. 38-53.

Firat, A. (1994), Gender and Consumption; Transcending the Feminine?, in Costa, J. (ed.), *Gender Issues and Consumer Behaviour*. Thousand Oaks: London Sage.

Firat, A. and Venkatesh, A. (1993), Postmodernity: The Age of Marketing, *International Journal of Research in Marketing*, Vol. (10)3, pp. 227-250.

FiveG (2009), Men's Leisurewear http://www.steveredgrave.com/fiveg.html.

Flynn, L.T. (1999), Does direct to consumer advertising of prescription drugs benefit the public's health?–Yes, *American Council on Science and Health* 11 (1999), p. 4.

Foucault, M. (1970), *The Order of Things; an Archaeology of the Human Sciences*, London: Tavistock Publications.

Foucault, M. (1976), Questions a Michel Foucault sur la Géographie, *Hérodote*, Vol. 1, Issue 4, pp. 71-85.

Foucault, M. (1977), *Discipline and Punish.* Translated by Sheridan, A. London: Penguin.

Foucault, M. (1979), *History of Sexuality*, Vol. 1. London: Allen Lane.

Foucault, M. (1980), *Power/Knowledge, Selected Interviews and Other Writings 1972-1977* (ed.) Colin Gordon, Harvester: Hemel Hempstead.

Foucault, M. (1982), The Subject and Power, in Dreyfus, H. and Rabinow, P. (ed.), *Beyond Structuralism and Hermeneutics*. London: Harvester Wheatsheaf.

Foucault, M. (1982a), The Subject and Power, in Dreyfus, H.L. and Rabinow, R. (eds) *Michel Foucault: Beyond Structuralism and Hermeneutics*. Chicago, IL: University of Chicago Press.

Foucault, M. (1982b), Truth, Power, Self: an Interview, in Martin, L. et al (eds), *Technologies of the Self.* Amherst: University of Massachusetts press.

Foucault, M. (1983), Afterward: The Subject and Power, in Dreyfus, H. and Rabinow, P. (eds), *Michel Foucault: Beyond Structuralism and Hermeneutics*. Chicago: Chicago University.

Foucault, M. (1984), *The History of Sexuality, Vol. 3: The Care of the Self*, translated by Robert Hurley, New York: Pantheon.

Foucault, M. (1988), Technologies of the Self, in Martin, L., Gutman, H. and Hutton, P. (eds), *Technologies of the Self; A Seminar with Michel Foucault*, London: Tavistock Publication.
Foucault, M. (1988a), The Ethic of Care for the Self as a Practice of Freedom, translated by Gauthier, J.D., in *The Final Foucault*, ed. Bernauer, J. and Rasmussen, D. Cambridge, MA: MIT Press.
Foucault, M. (1990), *The Care of the Self; The History of Sexuality Vol. 3* London: Penguin Books.
Foucault, M. (1991a), *Discipline and Punish; The Birth of the Prison*. London: Penguin Books.
Foucault, M. (1991b), Governmentality in (eds) Burchell, G., Gordon, C. and Miller, P. *The Foucault Effect: Studies in Governmentality*. Hemel Hempstead: Harvester Wheatsheaf.
Foucault, M. (1991), On the Genealogy of Ethics: An Overview of Work in Progress, in Rabinow, P. (ed.), *The Foucault Reader: An Introduction to Foucault's Thought*. London: Penguin.
Foucault, M. (1992), *The Use of Pleasure, The History of Sexuality Volume 2*, London: Penguin.
Foucault, M. (1997), *The Order of Things*. London: Routledge.
Foucault, M. (1998), *The Will to Knowledge, The History of Sexuality Volume 1*, translated by Hurley, R. London: Penguin.
Foxall, G. (1986), The Role of Radical Behaviourism in the Explanation of Consumer Choice, *Advances in Consumer Choice*, Vol. 13, pp. 187-91.
Foxall, G. (1987), Consumer Choice in Behaviourism and Consumer Research; Theoretical Promise and Empirical Process, *International Journal of Research Marketing*, Vol. 4, pp. 111-29.
Foxall, G. (1990), *Consumer Psychology in Behavioural Perspective*. London: Routledge.
Foxall, G., Goldsmith, R. and Brown, S. (1998), *Consumer Psychology for Marketing*. International Thomson Business Press.
Frank, T. (1997), *The Conquest of Cool; Business Culture, Counterculture and the Rise of Hip Consumerism*. Chicago: University of Chicago Press.
Fraser, N. (2003), From Discipline to Flexibilization? Rereading Foucault in the Shadow of Globalization. *Constellations* Vol. 10, No. 2, pp. 160-171.
Freeman, J. (1977), The Publicity of the Empire Marketing Board 1926-1933, *Journal of Advertising History*, Vol. 1, pp. 12-14.
Freidberg, S. (2003), Cleaning up down south: supermarkets, ethical trade and African horticulture, *Social and Cultural Geography*, Vol. 4, No. 1, pp. 27-43.
Freundlieb, D. (1995), Foucault and the Study of Literature, *Poetics Today*, Vol. 16, No. 2, pp. 301-344.
Fridell, G. (2006), Fair Trade and Neoliberalism: Assessing Emerging Perspectives, *Latin American Perspectives*, November 2006, Vol. 33, pp. 8-28.
Friedman, M. (1962), *Capitalism and Freedom*. With the assistance of Rose D. Friedman. Chicago: University of Chicago Press.

Friedman, M. (2002), *Capitalism and Freedom*. London: University of Chicago Press.

Frow, J. (1997), *Time and Commodity Culture; Essays in Cultural Theory and Postmodernity*. Oxford.

Fuqua, Joy V. (2002), Ask Your Doctor About...': Direct-To-Consumer Prescription Drug Advertising And The Hiv/Aids Medical Marketplace, *Cultural Studies*, Vol. 16, No. 5, pp. 650-672.

Gabreil, Y. and Lang, T. (1995), *The Unmanageable Consumer. Contemporary Consumption and its Fragmentation*. London: Sage.

Galston, W. (1988), Liberal Virtues, *The American Political Science Review*, Vol. 82, No. 4, pp. 1277-1290.

Gamble, A. (1976), *Capitalism in Crisis*. Basingstoke: Macmillan.

Game, A. (1991), *Undoing the Social. Towards a Deconstructive Sociology*. Open University Press.

Gane, M. (2007), Baudrillard's Lucidity Pact, *Theory Culture and Society*, Vol. 24(5), pp. 127-133.

Gergen, K. (1991), *The Saturated Self*, New York: Basic Books.

Giddens, A. (1979), *Central Problems in Social Theory. In Action, Structure and Contradiction in Social Analysis.* London: Macmillian.

Giddens, A. (1981), *A Contemporary Critique of Historical Materialism, Vol. 1, Power Property and the State.* London: Macmillian.

Giddens, A. (1984), *The Constitution of Society*. Cambridge: Polity.

Giddens, A. (1988), *Capitalism and Modern Social Theory; An Analysis of the Writings of Marx Durkheim and Max Weber*. Cambridge: Cambridge University Press.

Giddens, A. (1990), *The Consequences of Modernity*. Cambridge: Polity.

Giddens, A. (1991), *Modernity and Self-Identity. Self and Society in the Late Modern Age*. Cambridge: Polity.

Giddens, A. (1992), *The Transformation of Intimacy: Sexuality, Love and Eroticism in Modern Societies.* Cambridge: Polity.

Giddens, A. (1993), *Modernity and Self Identity*. Cambridge: Polity.

Giddens, A. (1998), *The Third Way*. Cambridge: Polity.

Giddens, A. (1994), Living in a Post-traditional Society, in Beck, U., Giddens, A. and Lash, S. (eds), *Reflexive Modernisation: Politics, Tradition and Aesthetics in the Modern Social Order*. Cambridge: Polity Press 56-109.

Giddens, A. (1998), *Beyond Left and Right: The Future of Radical Politics*. Cambridge: Polity.

Giddens, A. (1998a), *The Third Way: The Renewal Of Social Democracy*. Cambridge: Polity Press.

Gigerenzer, G., Swijtink, Z., Porter, T., Daston, L., Beatty, J. and Kruger, L. (1999), *The Empire of Chance; How Probability Changed Science and Everyday Life*. Cambridge: Cambridge Press.

Gilroy, P. (1987), *'There Ain't No Black In The Union Jack': The Cultural Politics Of Race And Nation*. London: Routledge.

Girard, L. and Mulard, C. (2004), Fighting the Battle Against Age. *Guardian Weekly*. 10 Sepetmber, http://www.guardian.co.uk/guardianweekly/story/0,,1301015,00.html.

Giroux, H.A. (1993-1994), Consuming Social Change: The United Colors of Benetton, *Cultural Critique* Winter pp. 5-32.

Gitlin, T. (1989), Postmodernism: Roots and Politics, in Angus, I. and Jhally, S. (eds), *Cultural Politics in Contemporary America*. New York: Routledge.

Gittins, D. (1994), *The Family in Question; Changing Households and Familiar Ideologies*. Hampshire: Macmillan.

Gleick, J. (1998), *Chaos; the Amazing Science of the Unpredictable*. London: Vintage.

Glyn, A. (2007), *Capitalism Unleashed: Finance, Globalization, and Welfare*. Oxford: Oxford University Press.

Goldman, R. (1983-1984), Capitalist Development and the Development of Leisure, *Social Text*, Vol. 8 (Winter) pp. 84-103.

Goldman, R. (1987), Marketing Fragrances: Advertising and the Production of Comodity Signs, *Theory, Culture and Society*, Vol. 4, Issue 4, pp. 691-726.

Goldman, R. (1994), Contradictions in a Political Economy of Sign Value, *Current Perspectives in Social Theory*, Vol. 14, pp. 183-211.

Goldman, R. (1995), *Reading Ads Socially*. London: Routledge.

Goldman, R. (2003), *A Theoretical Sketch of the History of Commodity Signs*. http://www.lclark.edu/~goldman/contradictions/poleconsv4.html.

Goldman, R. and Wilson, J. (1977), The Rationalization of Leisure. *Politics and Society*, Vol. 7, pp. 157-88.

Gordon, C. (1980); *Michel Foucault: Power/Knowledge: Selected Interviews and Other Writings 1972-1977*. Hemel Hempstead: Harvester Press.

Gorz, A. (1976), *Division of Labour: The Labour process and Class Struggle in Modern Capitalism*. Hassocks: Harvester.

Gorz, A. (1983), *Ecology Politics*. London: Pluto Press.

Gorz, A. (1989), *Critique of Economic Reason*. London: Verso.

Gorz, A. (1994), *Capitalism, Socialism, Ecology*. London: Verso.

Gorz, A. (1999), *Reclaiming Work: Beyond The Wage-Based Society*. Cambridge, Polity Press.

Goss, J. (1995), 'We Know Who You Are and We Know Where You Live'; The Instrumental Rationality of Geodemographics, *Economic Geography*, Vol. 71, pp. 171-198.

Graham, P. (2000), Hypercapitalism; A Political Economy of Informational Idealism. *New Media and Society*. Vol. 2, pp. 131-156.

Gramsci, A. (1971), *Selections from the Prison Notebook Of Antonio Gramsci*. Edited and translated by Hoare, Q. and Smith, G. London: Lawrence and Wishart.

Guardian (2010), Cadbury's Board Agrees £12bn Sale to Kraft, http://www.guardian.co.uk/business/2010/jan/19/cadbury-board-agrees-kraft-sale.

Guardian (2010a), Kraft Pledges to Honour Cadbury's Fairtrade Sourcing Commitments, Carrell, S., (Scotland correspondent), Guardian.co.uk, Saturday 23 January 2010 01.25 GMT http://www.guardian.co.uk/business/2010/jan/23/kraft-cadbury-Fairtrade/print.

Guevara, C. (1996), *The Motorcycle Diaries*. Fourth Estate.

Gunter, B. and Furnham, A. (1992), *Consumer Profiles: An Introduction to Psychographics*. London: Routledge.

Hackley, C. (2002), The Panoptic Role of Advertisisng Agencies in the Production of Consumer Culture, *Consumption Markets and Cultures*, Vol. 5, Issues 3, pp. 211-229.

Hall, S. (1973), Encoding and Decoding in the Television Message, in Hall, S., Hobson, D., Lowe, A., Willis, P. (eds), *Culture, Media, Language*, London: Hutchinson.

Hall, S. (1988), *The Hard Road to Renewal: Thatcherism and the Crisis of the Left*. London: Verso.

Hall, S. (1987), The Politics of Representation, an Unpublished Lecture Delivered at the University of Minnesota, Minneapolis, April.

Hall, S. (1983), The problem of ideology-Marxism without guarantees. In B. Matthews (ed.), *Marx 100 Years On* (pp. 28-60). London: Lawrence and Wishart.

Hall, S. (1990), The Meaning of New Times, in (eds) Hall, S. and Jacques. M., *New Times: The Changing Face Of Politics In The 1990s*. London: Lawrence and Wishart.

Hall, S. and Jacques, H. (1989), *New Times*. London: Lawrence and Wishart.

Harper, J. (2000), 'Rich Media' Mixes, News, Ads and Entertainment, *Insights*, 7 August, p. 31.

Harris, C. (1983), *The Family and Industrial Society*, London: George Allen and Unwin.

Harrison,S. and Wistow, G. (1992), The purchaser/provider split in English health care. *Policy and Politics*, Vol. 20, No. 2. pp. 123-30.

Harvey, D. (1990), *The Condition of Postmodernity. An Inquiry into the Origins of Cultural Change*. Oxford: Basil Blackwell.

Harvey, D. (2005), *The Condition of Postmodernity*. Oxford: Blackwell.

Harvey, D. (2007), *A Brief History of Neoliberalism*. Oxford: Oxford University Press.

Hassard, J. (1990), *The Sociology of Time*. Basingstoke: Macmillian.

Hassard, J. (2001), Commodification, Construction and Compression: a Review of Time Metaphors in Organizational Analysis, *International Journal of Management Reviews*, Vol. 3, Issue 2, pp. 131-140.

Haug, W. (1986), *Critique of commodity aesthetics: appearance, sexuality and advertising in capitalist society*. Translated by Robert Bock. Minneapolis: University of Minnesota Press.

Havlena, B. (2005), The Complementary Role of TV and Online Advertising. *Admap*, October 465, pp. 47-49.

Hawking, S. and Mlodinow, L. (2005), *A Briefer History of Time*. London: Bantam Press.

Hayter, T. (1994), New Management Techniques. In Hayter, T. and Harvey, D. (eds), *The Factory and the City; The Story of the Cowley Automobile Workers in Oxford*. Mansell: London.

Heidegger, M. (1962), *Being and Time*, translated by J. Macquarrie and E. Robinson. Oxford: Blackwell.

Hellmund, M. (2001), *Convergence: WebTV versus Interactive Digital TV or Internet, TV and Humans*. www.mitbiz.de/gallery/publications/convergence.doc.

Hemingway, J. (1996), Emancipating Leisure: The Recovery of Freedom in Leisure, *Journal of Leisure Research*, Vol. 28, No. 1, pp. 27-43.

Hendra, C. (2003), The Next New New Thing: Brand Storytelling 24x7x365, http://www.ogilvy.com/viewpoint/pdf/v5_hendra.pdf.

Henley Centre (2001), *Tired of Feeling Pushed for Time?* Henley Centre.

Hilowitz, J. (1997), *Labelling Child Labour Products: A Preliminary Study*. ILO: Geneva.

Hirschman, E. (1987), Theoretical Perspectives of Time Use; Implications for Consumer Behaviour Research, *Research in Consumer Behaviour*, Vol. 2, pp. 55-81.

Hirst, P. and Thompson, G. (2002), *Globalisation in Question*. Cambridge: Polity.

Ho, L., Powell, C. and Volpp, L. (1996), (Dis)Assembling Rights of Women Workers Along the Global Assembly Line; Human Rights and the Garment Industry, *Harvard Civil Rights-Civil Liberties Law Review*, Vol. 31, Issue 2, pp. 383-414.

Hobbes, T. (1651:1968), *Leviathan*. London: Penguin.

Hocking, G. and Wilding, M. (2004), *Made at Home; British Homeworkers in Global Supply Chains*. Oxfam Briefing Paper 63.

Hodgson, G. (1995), Varieties of Capitalism from the Perspectives of Veblen and Marx, *Journal of Economic Issues*, Vol. XXIX No. 2, pp. 575-584.

Holbrook, M. (1986), Emotion in the Consumption Experience; Toward a New Model of the Human Consumer, in *The Role of Affect in Consumer Behaviour; Emerging Theories and Applications*, Peterson, R. (ed.), Lexington, MA: Heath.

Holloway, J. (1992), Crisis, Fetishism, Class Composition, in Bonefeld, W., Gunn, R. and Psychopedis, K. (eds), *Open Marxism*. London: Pluto.

Holstein, J. and Gubrium, J. (2000), *The Self We Live By; Narrative Identity in a Postmodern World*. Oxford: Oxford University Press.

Holton, R. (1992), *Economy and Society*. London: Routledge.

Hopper, P. (2007), *Understanding Cultural Globalisation*. Cambridge: Polity.

Howard, D.T. (1932), *The Psychology of Advertising by Walter Dill Scott*. London: Sir Isacc Pitman and Sons LTD.

Howard, J. and Sheth, J. (1969), *The Theory of Buyer Behaviour*. John Wiley and Sons; New York.

HSJ (2006), Public 'don't want NHS ads for services', http://www.hsj.co.uk/public-dont-want-nhs-ads-for-services/2787.article.

HSJ (2007), Marketing code is 'overly bureaucratic', http://www.hsj.co.uk/marketing-code-is-overly-bureaucratic/56287.article.

HSJ (2007), RCN wants 'teeth' behind advertising code, http://www.hsj.co.uk/rcn-wants-teeth-behind-advertising-code/56147.article.

Hudson, I. and Hudson, M. (2003), Removing the Veil?: Commodity Fetishism, Fair Trade, and the Environment, *Organization Environment*, Dec; Vol. 16: pp. 413-430.

Hudson, M. and Hudson, I. (2004), Justice, Sustainability, and the Fair Trade Movement: A Case Study of Coffee Production in Chiapas, *Social Justice*, Vol. 31, No. 3, pp. 130-146.

Hughes, A. and Wrigley, N. (2008), Global Production Networks, Ethical Campaigning and the Embeddednes of Responsible Governance, *Journal of Economic Governance*, Vol. 8, pp. 345-367.

Huh J. and Becker, L. (2002), Direct-to-Consumer Drug Advertising: Understanding its Consequences, paper presented to Midwest Association for Public Opinion Research, Chicago.

Hume, D. (1739/1967), *A Treatise Of Human Nature*; edited, with an analytical index, by L.A. Selby-Bigge. Oxford: Clarendon Press.

Husserl, E. (1928), *The Phenomenology of Internal Time-Consciousness* (ed.) M. Heidegger, translated by J. Churchill, Bloomington: Indiana University Press.

Independent (2009), Cadbury accused of racial stereotyping in chocolate advert, http://www.independent.co.uk/news/media/advertising/cadbury-accused-of-racial-stereotyping-in-chocolate-advert-1801020.html.

Ingold, T. (1993), The Temporality of Landscape. *World Archaeology*, Vol. 25, pp. 152-74.

Jackson, P. and Taylor, J. (1996). Geography and the cultural politics of advertising. *Progress in Human Geography*, 20(3), 356-371.

Jackson, P. and Thrift, N. (1995), Geographies of Consumption, in Miller, D. (ed.), *Acknowledging Consumption. A Review of New Studies*. London: Routledge.

Jacobs, M. (1998), *Sigmund Freud*. London: Sage.

Jameson, F. (1985), Postmodernism and consumer Society in Foster, H. (ed.) *Postmodern Culture*. Wiltshire: Pluto, pp. 111-126.

Jameson F. (1991), *Postmodernism, or, the Cultural Logic of Late Capitalism*. Durham: Duke University Press.

Jameson, F. (1992), *Postmodernism; or the Cultural Logic of Late Capitalism*. London: Verso.

Jameson, F. (2008), *Postmodernism, or The Cultural Logic of Late Capitalism*. London: Verso.

Jaramillo, D. (2006), Pills Gone Wild: Medium Specificity and the Regulation of Prescription Drug Advertising on Television, *Television New Media* 2006; 7; pp. 261-281.

Jenkins, A. (1994), Just-in-time 'Regimes' and Reductionism, *Sociology*, Vol. 28, No. 1, pp. 21-30.

Jensen, K.B. (1990), The Politics of Polysemy: Television News, Everyday Consciousness and Political Action, *Media, Culture and Society*, 12, 57-77.

Jhally, S. (1987), *The Codes of Advertising*. London: Routledge.

Johnson, I. (2002), Interactive TV Advertising; a Worldwide Perspective, *Admap*, June, 429, pp. 36-38.

Kannan, P., Chang, A. and Whinston, A. (2001), Wireless Commerce: Marketing Issues and Possibilities. Proceedings of the 34th Hawaii International Conference on System Sciences.

Kaphingst, K., Dejong, W., Rudd, R. and Daltroy, L. (2004), A Content Analysis of Direct-to-Consumer Television Prescription Drug Advertisements, *Journal of Health Communication*, Vol. 9, No. 6, January 2004, pp. 515-528.

Kates, S. and Shaw-Garlock, G. (1999), The Ever Entangling Web; A Study of Ideologies and Discourses in Advertising to Women. *Journal of Advertising*, Vol. XXVIII, No. 2, pp. 33-49.

King, A. (1998), A Critique of Baudrillard's Hyperreality; Towards a Sociology of Postmodernism, *Philosophy and Social Criticism*, Vol. 24, No. 6, pp. 47-66.

King, M. (2000), Make Love, Not Work; New Management Theory and the Social Self, *Radical History Review*, Vol. 76, pp. 15-24.

Klein, N. (2001), *No logo*. London;Flamingo.

Klein, N. (2002), *Fences and Windows: Dispatches from the Front Lines of the Globalization Debate*. NewYork: Picador.

Kleine, D. (2008), Negotiating Partnerships, Understanding Power: Doing Action Research on Chilean Fairtrade Wine Value Chains, *The Geographical Journal*, Vol. 174, No. 2, June, pp. 109-123.

Kline and Company (2004), Global Cosmetics and Toiletries, Kline http://www.klinegroup.com/reports/y559.asp.

Kline, S. and Leiss, W. (1978), Advertising Needs and Commodity Fetishism, *Canadian Journal of Political and Social Theory*, Vol. 2, pp. 5-21.

Knights, D. and Sturdy, A. (1997), Marketing the Soul: From the ideology of consumption to consumer subjectivity, in Knights, D. and Tinker, T. (eds), *Financial Service Institutions and Social Transformations: International Studies of a Sector in Transition*, London: Macmillan.

Knights, D. and McCabe, D. (1998a), 'A'int Misbehavin'?: Opportunities For Resistance within Bureaucratic and Quality Management Innovations', *Sociology*, Vol. 34, No. 3, pp. 421-437.

Knights, D. and Morgan, G. (1993), Organization Theory and Consumption in a Post-Modern Era, *Organization Studies*, Vol. 14, No. 2, pp. 211-234.

Knights, D. (1997), Governmentality and Financial Services Welfare Crisis and the Financial Self Disciplined Subject, in Morgan, G. and Knights, D. (eds) *Deregulation and Regulation in European Financial Services*. London: Palgrave.

Knights, D. and Odih, P. (2002), 'Big Brother is Watching You!', Call Centre Surveillance and the Time Disciplined Subject, in Crow, G. and Heath, S. (eds), *Social Conceptions of Time; Structure and Process in Work and Everyday Life* London: Palgrave Macmillan.

Knights, D. and Sturdy, A. (1997), Marketing the Soul: From the Ideology of Consumption to Consumer Subjectivity, In: Knights, D. and Tinker, T. (eds), *Financial institutions and social transformations: International Studies of a Sector*. London: Macmillan, pp. 158-188.

Knights, D. and Vurdubakis, T. (1993), Calculations of Risk: Towards an Understanding of Insurance as a Moral and Political Technology, *Accounting Organization and Society*, Vol. 19, No. 718, pp. 729-64.

Knights, D. with assistance of Tinker, T. (1988), Risk, Financial Self-discipline and Commodity Relations: An Analysis of the Growth and Development of Life Insurance in Contemporary Capitalism, *Advances in Public Interest Accounting*, Vol. 2, pp. 47-69.

Korthals, M. (2000), Taking Consumers Seriously: Two Concepts of Consumer Sovereignty. *Journal of Agricultural and Environmental Ethics*, Vol. 14, pp. 201-215.

Kraft (2010), Kenco Announces Major Expansion of Partnership with Rainforest Alliance http://www.kraftfoods.co.uk/kraft/page?siteid=kraft-prd&locale=ukenl&PagecRef=2526&Mid=2526.

Kraidy, M. and Geoddertz, T. (2003), Transnational Advertising and International Relations; US Press Discourses on the Benetton 'We on Death Row' Campaign, *Media, Culture and Society*, Vol. 25, pp. 147-165.

Krugman, H. (1966-1967), The Measurement of Advertising Involvement. *The Public Opinion Quarterly*, Vol. 30, No. 4 (Winter), pp. 583-596.

Kunde, J. (2000), *Corporate Religion; Building a Strong Company Through Personality and Corporate Soul.* London: Prentice Hall.

Lancet (2002), Europe on the brink of direct-to-consumer drug advertising, *The Lancet*, Vol. 359, No. 9319.

Lancet Editorial (2007); The Direct-to-Consumer Advertising Genie., *The Lancet*, Vol. 369, No. 9555, p.1, January 6th http://www.thelancet.com/journals/lancet/article/PIIS0140-6736(07)60001-4/fulltext.

Lane, R. (2000), *Jean Baudrillard.* London: Routledge.

Larrain, J. (1989), *Theories of Development: Capitalism, Colonialism and Dependency*. Cambridge: Polity.

Larsen, J., Allan, H., Bryan, K. and Smith, P. (2005), Overseas Nurses' Motivations For Working In The UK: Globalization and Life Politics, *Work, Employment and Society*, Vol. 19, No. 2, pp. 349-368.

Lash, S. and Urry, J. (1987), *The End of Organized Capitalism*. Cambridge: Polity.

Lash, S., and Urry, J. (1994), *Economies of Signs and Space*. London: Sage.

Lash, S. and Urry, J. (1999), *Economies Of Signs And Space*. London; Sage.

Latour, B. (1987), *Science In Action: How To Follow Scientists And Engineers Through Society*. Milton Keynes: Open University Press.

Latour, B. (2005), *Science in Action: How to Follow Scientists and Engineers Through Society*. Cambridge, MA: Harvard University Press.

Law M.R., Majumdar S.R. and Soumerai S.B. (2008), Effect of illicit direct to consumer advertising on use of etanercept, mometasone, and tegaserod in Canada: controlled longitudinal study, *British Medical Journal* 8 Sep 2;337:a1055.

Leclair, M. (2002), Fighting the Tide: Alternative Trade Organizations in the Era of Global Free Trade, *World Development*, Vol. 30, No. 6, pp. 949-958.

Lee, M. (1993), *Consumer Culture Reborn. The Cultural Politics of Consumption*. London: Routledge.

Lee, R. (2006), Reinventing Modernity: Reflexive Modenrization vs Liquid Modernity Vs Multiple Modernities, *European Journal of Social Theory*, Vol. 9, 355-368.

Lefebvre, H. (1991), *The Production of Space*, translated by D. Nicholson-Smith. Oxford: Basil Blackwell.

Leiss, W. (1983), The Icons of the Marketplace, *Theory, Culture and Society*, Vol. 1 (3), pp. 86-95.

Leiss, W., Kline, S. and Jhally, S. (1990), *Social Communication in Advertising*. London: Routledge.

Lerner, A. (1972:258), The Economics and Politics of Consumer Sovereignty, *The American Economic Review*, Vol. 62, No. 1/2 pp. 258-266.

Leslie, D. (1998), Consumer Subjectivity, Space and Advertising Research. *Environment and Planning*, Vol. 31, pp. 1443-1457.

Levacic, R. (1995), *Local Management of Schools: Analysis and Practice*. Milton Keynes: Open University Press.

Litchford, T. (2001), 'Mobile Commerce Helps Retailers Move Ahead', Microsoft (2000), SAP and Microsoft Join Forces to Bring Business Solutions to Pocket PCs, http://www.microsoft.com/presspass/press/2000/Apr00/SAPppcPR.mspx.

Locke, J. (1693/1964), *An Essay Concerning Human Understanding*. Woozley, A.D. (ed.), New York: Methuen.

Lockie, S. (2002), The Invisible Mouth; Mobilizing the Consumer in Food production Consumption Networks, *Sociologia Ruralis*, Vol. 42, No. 4, pp. 278-294.

Long (2009), US Pharmaceutical Market Trends: Tremendous Slowdown, Intelligent Market Solutions http://www.imshealth.com.

Lorraine, T. (1990), *Gender Identity and the Production of Meaning*. Oxford: Westview.

Loviny, C. (2006:78), *Cuba by Korda*. Melbourne: Ocean Press.

Low, W. and Davenport, E. (2005), Postcards from the Edge: Maintaining the 'Alternative' Character of Fair Trade, *Sustainable Development*, Vol. 13, pp. 143-153.

Lubove, R. (1981), Book Review of Zelizer, V. (1979), 'Morals and Markets; The Development of Life Insurance in the United'. *Journal of American History*, Vol. 67, No. 4, p. 938.

Luhmann, N. (1991), *Risk a Sociological Theory*, New York: Walter de Gruyter.

Lury, C. (2004), *Brands: The Logos Of The Global Economy*. New York: Routledge.

Lyon, D. (2002), Surveillance in Cyberspace: The Internet, Personal Data and Social Control, *Queen's Quarterly*, Vol. 109/3 (Fall), pp. 345-357.

Macaulay (1830), Mr Robert Montgomery's Poems and the Modern Practice of Puffin. *Edinburgh Review*, April pp. 194-210.

MacCannell, D. (1999), *The Tourist: A New Theory of the Leisure Class*, 2nd ed Berkley CA: University of California.

Macpherson, C.B. (1962), *The Political Theory of Possessive Individualism*. London: Clarendon Press.

Macpherson, C.B. (1983), *The Political Theory of Possessive Individualism*. Oxford: Oxford University Press.

Maddison, A. (1987), 'Growth and Slowdown in Advanced Capitalist Economics'; Techniques of Quantitative Assessment, *Journal of Economic Literature*, Vol. XXXV, June, Table 1, pp. 650.

Mail Online (2009), TV Advert For Cold Remedy Benylin Urges You 'To Throw A Sickie'...While Website Tells You How. http://www.dailymail.co.uk/news/article-1106226/Fury-TV-advert-cold-remedy-Benylin-urges-throw-sickie--website-tells-how.html.

MapInfo (2006), *MapInfo Corporation* www.mapinfo.co.uk/products/geo.cfm.

Marks and Spencer (2008), Press Releases, Fairtrade Fashionista Style At M&S!, 19 February http://corporate.marksandspencer.com/media/press_releases/planA/19022008_FairtradeFashionistaStyleAtMS.

Marks and Spencer (2009), Fairtrade Cotton.

Marks and Spencer (2009), The Plan A Way to Trade.

Marks and Spencer (2009a), M&S launches new 'Doing the Right Thing' campaign – Retailer underlines commitment to Plan A with marketing push, http://corporate.marksandspencer.com/media/press_releases/company/Doing_the_Right_Thing.

Marks and Spencer (2009b), Progress so Far.

Marshall, J. (1996), *Michel Foucault: Personal Autonomy and Education*. London: Kluwer Academic Publishers.

Marshall, T.H. (1950), *Citizenship and Social Class and other Essays*. London: Cambridge University Press.

Marshall, T.H. and Bottomore, T. (1992), *Citizenship and Social Class*. London: Pluto.

Marx, K. (1967), *Essential Writings of Karl Marx* (ed.), D. Caute. London: Panther.

Marx, K. (1971), *Critique of Political Economy.* Chicago: Charles Kerr Publishing.

Marx, K. (1973), *Grundrisse; Introduction to the Culture of the Critique of Political Economy*. London: Penguin Books.

Marx, K. (1973), *Marx's Grundrisse* (ed.), McLellan, D. London: Paladin.

Marx, K. (2003/1887), *Capital Vol. 1; A critical Analysis of Capitalist Production*, edited by Frederick Engels; translated from the third German edition by Samuel Moore and Edward Aveling. London: Lawrence and Wishart.

Marx, K. and Engels, F. (1985), *The Communist Manifesto*. London: Verso.

Marx, K. and Engels, F. (1986), *The Communist Maifesto*. Middlesex: Penguin.

Mason, R. (1995), Interpersonal Effects on Consumer Demand in Economic Theory and Marketing Thought 1890-1950, *Journal of Economic Issues*, Vol. XXIX, No. 3, pp. 871-881.

Mathew, I. (2005), *Review of 2005 Trends Presentations*, http://www.in-cosmetics.com/page.cfm/link=25.

Matthew, P. and McAllister, P. (1996), *The Commercialization of American Culture. New Advertising Control and Democracy*. London: Sage.

Maynard, J. (1936), *General Theory of Employment, Interest and Money.* London: Macmillan.

McCracken, G. (1990), Culture and Consumer Behaviour, *Journal of the Market Research Society*, Vol. 32(1), pp. 3-11.

McDougall, D. (2008), The Hidden Face of Primark Fashion, Sunday 22 June, *The Observer* and guardian.co.uk.

McFall, L. (2002), What About the Old Cultural Intermediaries? An Historical Review of Advertising Producers. *Cultural Studies*, Vol. 16(4), pp. 532-552.

McLuhan, M. (1997), *Understanding Media the Extension of Man*. London: Routledge.

McNay, L. (2007), *Foucault, A Critical Introduction*. Cambridge: Polity.

McRobbie, A. (2007), Top Girls? Young Women and the Post-Feminist Sexual Contract, *Cultural Studies*, Vol. 21, No. 4-5 July/September pp. 718-737.

McVeigh, K. (2007), Asda, Primark and Tesco Accused Over Clothing Factories, Monday, 16 July, *The Guardian*, guardian.co.uk.

Mead, G. (1967), *Mind, Self, and Society*. Chicago: The University of Chicago Press.

Meek, R. (1979), *Studies in the Labour theory of Value*. London: Lawrence and Wishart.

Meijer., C. (1998), Advertising Citizenship; an Essay on the Performative Power of Consumer Culture, *Media Culture and Society*, Vol, 20, pp. 235-249.

Mercantile and General (1991), *Financial Services are Women an Accessible Market*. Mercantile and General.

Michman, R. (1991), *Lifestyle Market Segmentation*. New York: Praeger.

Miller, D. (1998), *A Theory of Shopping*. Cambridge: Polity.

Miller, D. (2000), *Citizenship and National Identity*. Cambridge, Polity.

Miller, G. (1962), *Psychology: The Science of Mental Life*. Middlesex: Penguin.

Miller, P. and Rose, N. (1993), Governing Economic Life, in (eds) M. Game and T. Johnson, *Foucault New Domains*. London: Routledge.

Miller, P. and Rose, N. (1997), Mobilizing the Consumer. Assembling the Subject of Consumption, *Theory Culture and Society*, Vol. 14, No. 1 pp. 1-36.

Miller, P. and Rose, N. (2008), *Governing the Present: Administering Economic, Social and Personal Life*. Cambridge: Polity

Millward, B. (2008), Direct-To-Consumer Advertising Works, Millward Brown http://www.wpp.com/NR/rdonlyres/E21FD6F9-7F2C-4BC3-A795-AA92AB28A614/0/millwardbrown_direct_to_consumer_nov08.pdf.

Mintel (2004), *Skincare UK*. London: Mintel International Group Ltd Market Research and Consumer Intelligence.

Mintel (2005), *Women's Bodycare Products – UK: April 2005*. London: Mintel International Group Ltd Market Research and Consumer Intelligence.

Mintzes B, Barer ML, Kravitz RL, Kazanjian A, Bassett K, Lexchin J, Evans RG, Pan, R. and Marion SA. (2002), Influence of DTC pharmaceutical advertising and patients' requests on prescribing decisions: two site cross sectional survey, *British Medical Journal*, 324, pp. 278-279.

Mitchell, A. (2002), *Right Side Up; Building Brands in the Age of the Organized Consumer*. London: HarperCollins Business.

Moloney, S. (2007), Dancing with the Wind: A Methodological Approach to Researching Women's Spirituality Around Menstruation and Birth, *International Journal of Qualitative Methods* 6(1) March pp. 114-125.

Montgomery, J. (1968), *1900 the End of an Era*. London: George Allen and Unwin LTD.

Morley, D. and Robins, K. (1995), *Spaces of Identity Global Media, Electronic Landscapes and Cultural Boundaries*. London: Routledge.

Morris, B. (1965), Possessive Individualism and Political Realities, *Ethics*, Vol. 75, No. 3, pp. 207-214.

Morris, M. (2005), Interpretability and Social power, or Why Postmodern Advertising Works, *Media Culture Society*, Vol. 27, pp. 697-718.

Morse, M. (1990), An Ontology of Everyday Distraction. The Freeway, the Mall and Television. In (ed.) Mellencamp, P., *Logics of Television Essays in Cultural Criticism*. BFI Publishing.

Mort, F. (1988), Boys Own? Masculinity, Style and Popular Culture, in R. Chapman and J. Rutherford (eds) *Male Order: Unwrapping Masculinity*, London: Lawrence and Wishart.

Moynihan, R. (2002), Selling Sickness: The Pharmaceutical Industry and Disease. Mongering, *British Medical Journal* 324, pp. 886-91.

Mumford, L. (1955), The Monastery and the Clock, in *The Human Prospect*, Boston: Beacon Press.

Murray, A. (1998), *Who's Who in Mythology*. Middlesex: Senate Press.

Mutzel, S. (2009), Networks as Culturally Constituted Processes; A Comparison of Relational Sociology and Actor-Network Theory, *Current Sociology*, Vol. 57, pp. 871-887.

Needham, C. (2003), *Citizen-Consumers; New Labour's Marketplace Democracy*, A Catalyst Working Paper, London: Catalyst.

Negri, A. (2008), The Porcelain Workshop. For a New Grammar of Politics. Translated by Wedell, N., *Semiotext(e).*

Nicholls, A. and Opal, C. (2005), *Fair Trade: Market-Driven Ethical Consumption.* London: Sage.

O'Barr, W.M. (1994), *Culture and the Ad: Exploring Otherness in the World of Advertising.* Westview Press.

O'Connor, J. (1974), *The Corporations and the State: Essays in the Theory of Capitalism and Imperialism.* New York: Harper and Row.

O'Farrell, C. (1989), *Foucault Historian or Philosopher?* Hampshire: Macmillan.

O'Malley, P., Imagining Insurance: Risk, Thirft and Life Insurance in Britain, in Baker, T. and Simon, J., *Embracing Risk the Changing Culture of Insurance and Responsibility.* Chicago: The University of Chicago Press.

Odih, P. (1998), *Gendered Time and Financial Services Consumption.* PhD Thesis, UMIST, Manchester. United Kingdom.

Odih, P. (1999a), The Women's Market Marketing Fact or Apparition, *Consumption, Markets and Culture*, Vol. 3, No. 2, pp. 165-193.

Odih, P. (1999b), Gendered Time in the Age of Deconstruction. *Time and Society*, Vol. 8, No. 1, pp.9-39.

Odih, P. (2007), *Gender and Work in Capitalist Economies.* Berkshire: Open University Press.

Odih, P. (2007b), *Advertising in Modern and Postmodern Times*, London: Sage.

Ofcom (2006), Rules on the Amount and Distribution of Advertising. *Ofcom.* http://www.ofcom.org.uk/tv/ifi/codes/advertising/rules/.

Offe, C. and Ronge, V. (1984), Theses on the Theory of the State in Offe, C. (ed.), *Contradictions of the Welfare State.* London: Hutchinson.

Ogilvy, D. (1965), *Confessions of an Advertising Man.* London: Longmans.

Oppenheimer, J. (1997), Movements, Markets and the Mainstream: Gay Activism and Assimilation in the Age of Aids., in Oppenheimer, J. and Reckitt, H. (eds), *Acting on AIDS Sex, Drugs and Politics*, London: Serpents Tail.

Osaka Senken Ltd. (2005), Thailand: textile Exports Grow Favorably, http://www.allbusiness.com/asia/912399-1.html.

Overbeek, H. (2001), *Restructuring Hegemony in the Global Political Economy: The Rise of Transnational Neo-Liberalism in the 1980s.* London: Routledge.

Overbeek, H. and van der Pijl, K. (2001), Restructuring Capital and Restructuring Hegemony: Neo-liberalism and the Unmaking of the Post-war Order, in (ed) Overbeek, H., *Restructuring Hegemony in the Global Political Economy: The Rise Of Transnational Neo-Liberalism in the 1980s*, London: Routledge.

Ovid (1904), *Metamorphoses*, XV, translated by A. Golding. Carbondal: University of Southern Illinois.

Oxfam (2004), *Made at Home*, Oxfam Briefing Paper 63, May, pp. 1-37 www.oxfam.org.uk.

Pangsapa, P. (2007), *Textures of Struggle: The Emergence of Resisting Among Garment Workers in Thailand*. Ithaca, NY: Cornell University Press.

Parker, M. and Slaughter, J. (1988), *Choosing Sides: Unions and the Team Concept: A Labor Notes Book*. Boston: South End Press.

Parliamentary Papers (2010), Commons Hansard: Future of Cadbury http://news.parliament.uk/2010/01/mps-debate-the-future-of-cadbury/.

Pawley, M., Winstone, D. and Bentley, P. (1991), *UK Financial Institutions and Markets*. Hampshire: Macmillan.

Pearson (2007), *Financial Times launches new brand advertising campaign*, 23 April 2007, http://www.pearson.com/index.cfm?pageid=144&pressid=2248.

Peterson, J. and Lewis, M. (1999), *The Elgar Companion to Feminist Economics*. Cheltenham: Edward Elgar.

Pietrykowski, B. (1999), Beyond the Fordist/Post-Fordist Dichotomy: Working Through the Second Industrial Divide. *Review of Social Economy*, Vol. 57, No. 2, pp. 177-98.

Pigou, C. (1925), *Memorials of Alfred Marshall*. London: Macmillan.

Piore, M. and Sable, C. (1984), *The Second Industrial Divide; Possibilities for Prosperity*. New York: Basic Books.

Pollard, S. (1965), The Adaptation of the Labour Force, in Pollard, S. (ed.), *The Genesis of Modern Management*. Edward Arnold Ltd London.

Poole, R. (1985), Morality, Masculinity and the Market, *Radical Philosophy*, No. 39, Spring Princeton, NJ: Princeton University Press.

Pope, D. (1983), *The Making of Modern Advertising*. New York Basic Books.

Porter, D. (1999), *Health, Civilisation and the State; A History of Public Health from Ancient to Modern Times*. London: Routledge, pp. 195-279.

Poster, M. (1995), *The Second Media Age*. Cambridge.

Poster, M. (1998), *Jean Baudrillard Selected Writings*. Cambridge: Polity.

Postma, P. (1999), *The New Marketing Era; marketing to the Imagination in a Technology-Driven World*. NewYork: McGraw-Hill.

Powell, M. (2000), Analysing the 'new' British NHS, *International Journal of Health Planning and Management*, 15, pp. 89-101.

Preston, G. (1971), *Advertising*. London: Batsford.

Primark (2008a), Primark, www.primark.co.uk.

Primark (2008b), Primark Supplier Code of Conduct, http://www.primark.co.uk/suppliers.shtml.

Primark (2008c), Primark Stores – Statement on Ethical Trading. 16 June.

Primark (2008d), Primark Background, http://www.primark.co.uk/background.shtml.

Proctor, S., Proctor, T. and Papasolomou-Doukakis, I. (2002), A Post-modern Perspective on Advertisements and their Analysis, *Journal of Marketing Communications*, Vol. 8, pp. 31-44.

Puntoni, S., Schroeder, J. and Ritson, M. (2006), Polysemy in Advertising, ERIM Report Series Reference No., ERS-2006-043 MKT.

Qualter, T. (1991), *Advertising and Democracy in the Mass Age*. Macmillian.

Quinones, R. (1972), *The Renaissance Discovery of Time*. Cambridge: Harvard University Press.

Rabinow, P. (1991), *The Foucault Reader; An Introduction to Foucault's Thought*. London: Penguin.

Raney, A., Arpan, L., Pashupati, K. and Brill, D. (2003), At the Movies, on the Web; An Investigation of the Effects of Entertaining and Interactive Web Content on Site and Brand Evaluations., *Journal of Interactive Marketing*, Vol. 17, No. 4, pp. 38-53.

Redgrave, S (2009), Fairtrade Clothing, http://www.steveredgrave.com/fiveg.html.

Rifkin, J. (1996), *The End of Work: The Decline of the Global Labour Force and the Dawn of the Post-Market Era*. New York: Tarcher Putman.

Rivoli, P. (2005), *The Travels of a T-Shirt in the Global Economy: An Economist Examines the Markets, Power and Politics of World Trade*. Hoboken: John Wiley and Sons.

Roberts, K. (1976), *Contemporary Society and the Growth of Leisure*. London: Longman.

Robins, K. and Webster, F. (1999), *Times Of The Technoculture: From the Information Society to the Virtual Life*. London: Routledge.

Robinson, J. (2005), Time Heals all Dotcom Wounds. *The Observer*. Published by *Guardian Unlimited* http://media.guardian.co.uk/newmedia/story/0,,1604501,00.html.

Rodaway, P. (1996), Exploring the Subject in Hyper-Reality, in Pile, S. and Thrift, N. (eds), *Mapping the Subject*. Routledge.

Rojek, C. (1998), *Decentring Leisure*. London: Sage.

Rosaldo, R. (1989), *Culture and Truth*. Boston: Beacon P.

Rosaldo, R. (1993), *Culture and Truth: The Remaking of Social Analysis*. London: Routledge.

Rosaldo, Z.M. (1980), *Knowledge and Passion: Ilongot Notions of Self and Social Life*. New York: Cambridge University Press.

Rose, M. (1975), *Industrial Behaviour; Theoretical Development Science Taylor*. England: Middlesex.

Rose, N. (1988), Calculable Minds and Manageable Individuals, *History of the Human Sciences*, vol. 1, pp. 179-200.

Rose, N. (1989), *Governing the Soul – The Shaping of the Private Self*. London: Routledge.

Rosen, E. (2002), *Making Sweatshops: The Globalization of the US Apparel Industry*. Berkeley: University of California Press.

Rousseau, J.J. (1762/1968), *The Social Contract*. London: Penguin Books.
Ryan, M. (1988), Postmodern Politics, *Theory Culture and Society*, Vol. 5, Issues, 2-3, pp. 559-76.
Said, E. (2003), *Orientalism*, London: Penguin.
Sampson, H. (1874), *A History of Advertising; From the Earliest Times*. London: Chatto and Windus Piccadilly.
Sandvoss, C. (2004), One-Dimensional Fan; Toward an Aesthetic of Fan Texts, *American Behavioral Scientist*, Vol. 48, No. 7, 822-839.
Sarup, M., (1996), *Identity, Culture and the Postmodern World*. Edinburgh: Edinburgh University Press.
Sarup, M. (1998), *Identity Culture and the Postmodern World*. Edinburgh University Press.
Sayer, A. (2002), (De)commodifiedcation, Consumer Culture, and Moral Economy, *Environment and Planning D, Society and Space*, Vol. 21, 341-357.
Sayer, D. (1989), *Readings from Karl Marx*. London: Routledge.
Schudson, M. (2007), Citizens, Consumers and the Good Society, *The Annals of the American Academy of Political and Social Science*, Vol. 611, pp. 236-249.
Schulman, S. (1997), Niche Marketing to People with AIDS., in Oppenheimer, J. and Reckitt, H. (eds), *Acting on AIDS Sex, Drugs and Politics*, London: Serpents Tail.
SConHR. (1998), Purchaser Efficiency Index, *Select Committee on Health Report*, 2 November, http://www.publications.parliament.uk/pa/cm199798/cmselect/cmhealth/959/959m10.htm.
Scott, D.W. (1908), *The Psychology of Advertising. A simple Exposition of the Principles of Psychology in their Relation to Successful Advertising*. Boston: Small Maynard.
Seccombe, W. (1973), The Housewife and Her Labour Under Capitalism, *New Left Review* 83, January-February pp. 3-24 http://www.newleftreview.net/IssueI82.asp?Article=01.
Shakespeare, T. (1999), Art and Lies? Representations of Disability on Film, in Corker, M. and French, S. (eds), *Disability Discourse*, Buckingham: Open University Press.
Shapiro, M. (1994), Images of Planetary Danger: Luciano Benetton's Ecumenical Fantasy, *Alternatives* 19 No. 4, pp. 433-54.
Sheppard, D. (1983), *Bias to the Poor*. London: Hodder and Stoughton.
Sheridan, A. (1994), *Michel Foucault. The Will to Truth*. London: Routledge.
Sherman, C. and Price, G. (2001), The Invisible Web; Uncovering Information Sources Search Engines Can't See. *Information Today*, Inc: Medford New Jersey.
Sheth, J. and Gardner, M. (1986), History of Marketing Thought: An Update, in Sheth, J. and Garrett, D. (eds), *Marketing Theory: Classic and Contemporary Readings*. Cincinnati: South-Western Publishing Co.
Shields, R. (1992), *Lifestyle Shopping. The Subject of Consumption*. London: Routledge.

Siebers, T. (2001), Disability in Theory: From Social Constructionism to the New Realism of the Body, *American Literary History*, Vol. 13, No. 4 (Winter), pp. 737-754.

Simons, J. (1995), *Foucault and the Political*. London: Routledge.

Sinclair, A. (2006), *Viva Che!; The Strange Death and Life of Che Guevara*. Gloucestershire: Sutton Publishing.

Slater, D. (1998), Work/Leisure. In Jenks, C. (ed.), *Core Sociological Dichotomies*. London: Sage.

SMART (2005), *Market Segmentation*. SMART: Strategic Marketing and Research Techniques, http://www.s-m-a-r-t.com/index.htm.

Smith, P. (1995), On the Unintended Consequences of Publishing Performance Data in the Public Sector., *International Journal of Public Administration*, Vol. 18, No. 2 and 3, pp. 277-310.

Sobchack, V. (1991), *Screening Space*. NewYork: Ungar.

Somers, M. (1992), Narrativity, Narrative Identity and Social Action: Rethinking English Working-Class Formation. *Social Science History*, Vol. 16, No. 4, pp. 591-630.

Spencer, G. (1996), Microcybernetics as the Meta-Technology of Pure Control, in Sardar, Z. and Ravetz, J. (eds), *Cyberfutures*. London: Pluto pp. 42-61.

Springer, C. (1996), *Electronic Eros. Bodies and Desire in the Postindustrial Age*. London: Athlone.

Spybey, T., (1996), *Globalisation And World Society*. Cambridge: Polity Press.

Stalson, J. (1942), *Marketing Life Insurance. Its History in America*. Cambridge: Harvard University.

Stern, J. and Stern, M. (1978); *Auto Ads*. New York: Random House.

Steuer, J. (1992), Defining Virtual Reality: Dimensions Determining Telepresence. *Journal of Communications*, Vol. 42, Issue 4, pp. 73-93.

Steuer, J. (1992), Defining Virtual Reality: Dimensions Determining Telepresence, *Journal of Communications*, Vol. 42, Issue 4, pp. 73-93.

Stitzer, T. (2009), Leadership in Adversity: Brands Built to Endure, IGD Convention, Royal Lancaster Hotel, London.

Stitzer, T. (2009a), *Tipping the Balance through Principled Capitalism*, HTS Speech to the Fartrade Commercial Conference Kensington Town Hall, London, 24 September 2006.

Strong, C. (1997), The Problem of Translating Fair Trade Principles into Consumer Purchase Behaviour, *Market Intelligence and Planning*, Vol. 15, No. 1, pp. 32-37.

Stuart, R. (1889), Letters from the Lake Poets to Daniel Stuart. London. *The History of the Times*, Vol. 1 n.d.

Swinfen-Green, J. (2002), Broadband: the Advertising Opportunity. *Admap*, March 2002, pp. 43-46.

Taaffee, P. (2008), 1968: Year of Revolution, *Socialism Today*, Socialist Party magazine, http://www.socialismtoday.org/118/revolution.html.

Tagg, J. (1989), *The Cultural Politics of Postmodernism*. Binghamton: State University of New York at Binghamton.

Taplin, I. (1996), Rethinking Flexibility: The Case of the Apparel Industry, *Review of Social Economy*, Vol. LIV No. 2, Summer pp. 191-220.

Taylor, F. (1911), *The Principles of Scientific Management*. Harper and Brothers New York.

Taylor, F. (1947), *Scientific Management: Comprising Shop Management, The Principles Of Scientific Management And Testimony Before The Special House Committee.* New York: Harper.

Telegraph (2009), Benylin advert 'advises workers to throw a sickie', http://www.telegraph.co.uk/health/healthnews/4128040/Benylin-advert-advises-workers-to-throw-a-sickie.html.

Textiles Intelligence (2008), World Textile and Apparel Trade and Production Trends, http://www.textileintelligence.com/tistoi.

Thatcher, M. (1993), The Downing Street Years, Hammersmith: HarperCollins.

The Independent (2009), Cadbury Accused of Racial Stereotyping in chocolate advert.

Thomas, J. (1996), *Time, Culture and Identity; An Interpretive Archaeology*; London: Routledge.

Thompson, E.P. (1967), Time Work Discipline and Industrial Capitalism, *Past and Present*, No. 38, pp. 56-97.

Thrift, N. (1991), For a New Regional Geography 2, *Progress in Human Geography* Vol. 15, No. 4, pp. 456-465.

Tinic, S. (1997), United Colors and United Meanings: Benetton and the Commodification of Social Issues, *Journal of Communication*, 47(3), Summer, pp. 3-25.

Trentmann, F. (2005), *Knowing Consumers – Histories, Identities, Practices: an Introduction.* Birkbeck ePrints: An open access repository of the research output of Birkbeck College, http://eprints.bbk.ac.uk/276/1/Binder1.pdf.

Tribe, M. (1993), *Postmodern Time*, http://mural.uv.es/alulla/defin.html.

TUC (2006), Patients don't want NHS ads for services, survey shows, Trade Union Congress, Press release issued 20 Nov 2006, http://www.tuc.org.uk/publicsector/tuc-12670-f0.cfm.

Turkle, S. (1995), *Life on the Screen: Identity in the Age of the Internet*. New York: Simon and Schuster.

Turner, E. (1952), *The Shocking History of Advertising*. London: Michael Joseph.

Underhill, G. (1998), *Industrial Crisis and the Open Economy. Politics, Global Trade and the Textile industry in the Advanced Economies*. Hampshire: Macmillan Press.

Unison (2006), Patients Don't Want NHS Adverts, http://www.unison.org.uk/news/news_view.asp?did=2955.

Unison (2007), UNISON Response to DH Consultation Document: 'Code of Practice on Promotion of NHS Services', February, http://www.unison.org.uk/file/A5021.1.pdf.

Urry, J. (1990), *The Tourist Gaze*. London: Sage.
Urry, J. (1995), *Consuming Places*. London: Routledge.
Urry, J. (2005), The Complexities of the Global. *Theory Culture and Society*, V, 22(5) pp. 235-254.
Van Dijk. J. (1999), The One-Dimensional Network Society of Manuel Castells, *New Media and Society*, Vol. 1, Issue 1.
Varul, M. (2009), Ethical Selving in Cultural Contexts: Fairtrade Consumption as an Everyday Ethical Practice in the UK and Germany, *International Journal of Consumer Studies*, Vol. 33, pp. 183-189.
Veblen, T. (1899/1994), *The Theory of the Leisure Class*. New York: Modern Library.
Veblen, T. (1919) *The Place of Science in Modern Civilization and Other Essays*. New York: Huebsch. Reprinted with a new introduction by W.J. Samuels. New Brunswick: Transaction.
Veblen, T. (1934), *Essays on Our Changing Order*, L. Ardzrooni (ed.). New York: Viking Press.
Venkatesh, A., Meamber, L. and Firat, F. (1998), Cyberspace as the Next Marketing Frontier(?) – Questions and Issues, in. Brown, S. and Turley, D. (eds), *Consumer Research: Postcards From the Edge*. Routledge.
Virillo, P. (1991), *The Lost Dimension*. New York: Semiotext(e).
Virillo, P. (2005), *The Information Bomb*. London: Verso.
Virual, M. (2008), *Fair Trade Consumerism as an Everyday Ethical Practice – A Comparative Perspective*.
Wai-ling Chan, J. (2006), Chinese Women Workers Organize in the Export Zone, *New Labor Forum*, Vol. 15, Issue 1, pp. 19-27.
Watson, J. (1980), *Asian And African Systems Of Slavery*. Oxford: Blackwell.
Watson, M. (2007), Trade Justice and Individual Consumption Choices: Adam Smith's Spectator Theory and the Moral Constitution of the Fair Trade Consumer, *European Journal of International Relations*, Vol. 13, No. 2, pp. 263-288.
Wayne, M. (2003), *Marxism and Media Studies*. London: Pluto.
Wearing, B. and Wearing, S. (1992), Identity and the Commodification of Leisure, *Leisure Studies*, V. 11, pp. 3-18.
Webb, T. (2006), The Blurred Vision of 3G. *The Independent on Sunday*. 12 February pp. 6-7.
Weedon, C. (1992), *Feminist Practice and Post-Structuralist Theory*. Oxford: Blackwell.
Weissman, J., Blumenthal, D., Silk, A., Newman, M., Zapert, K., Leitman, R. and Feibelmann, S. (2004), Physicians report on patient encounters involving direct-to-consumer advertising, *Health Aff*, W4–219.
Wells, M. (2000), After 40 Years And Millions Of Posters, Che's Photographer sues for copyright, http://www.guardian.co.uk/world/2000/aug/07/cuba.mattwells.
Wendell, S. (1996), *The Rejected Body; Feminist Philosophical Reflections on Disbaility*. New York: Routledge.

Wexler, P. (1990), Citizenship in the Semiotic Society, in Turner, B. (ed.), *Theories of Modernity and Postmodernity*, pp. 164-176. London: Sage.

Wheale, N. (1995), *The Postmodern Arts: An Introductory Reader*. London: Routledge.

White House (2009), How Health Insurance Reform Will Strengthen America's Small Business, The White House, Office of the Press Secretary, 3 October 2009, www.whitehouse.gov/the_press_office.

Whitrow, G.J. (1989), *Time in History*. Oxford: Oxford University Press.

Whitty, G. and Power, S. (2000), Marketisation and Privatization in Mass Education Systems, *International Journal of Educational Development*, Vol., 20, pp. 93-107.

Whysall, P. (2004), What Can We Learn From Retailers' New Releases? A 'Stakeholder Engagement' Perspective, *International Review of Retail, Distribution and Consumer Research*, Vol. 14, No. 1, pp. 31-45.

Wigand, R. (1996), Electronic Commerce: Definition, Theory and Context, *The Information Society*, Vol. 13, pp. 1-16.

Wilkes, M., Bell, R. and Kravitz, R. (2000), Direct-to-Consumer Prescription Drug Advertising: Trends Impact, And Implication, *Health Affairs*, Vol. 19, No.2, pp. 110-128.

Williams, R. (1980), Advertising; the Magic System, in *Problems in Materialism and Culture*, London: Verso.

Williams, R. (1997), Advertising the Magic System, in During, S. (ed.), *The Cultural Studies Reader*. pp. 320-339, London: Routledge.

Williamson, J. (1978/2000), *Decoding Advertisements*. London: Marion Boyars Publishers.

Wills, P. (2003), *The Ethnographic Imagination*. Cambridge: Polity.

Winship, J. (1980), Sexuality for Sale, in Hall, S. et al (eds), *Culture, Media and Language*. London: Hutchinson and Co.

Winship, J. (1993), Adworlds, *Media, Culture and Society*, Vol. 15, No. 1, pp. 137-141.

Winship, J. (2000), Women Outdoors: Advertising, Controversy and Disputing Feminism in the 1990s, *International Journal of Cultural Studies,* April, Vol. 3, pp. 27-55.

Woloshin, S., Schwartz, L., Tremmel, J. and Welch, H. (2001), Direct-to-consumer Advertisements for Prescription Drugs; What are Americans Being Sold?, *The Lancet*, Vol. 358, No. 9288, pp. 1141-1146.

Wright, L. and Heaton, S. (2006), Fair Trade Marketing: An Exploration Through Qualitative Research, *Journal of Strategic Marketing*, Vol. 14, No. 4, pp. 411-426.

ZenithOptimedia (2005), Ad Growth Stable with Healthy Hotspots, http://www.zenithoptimedia.com/gff/pdf/Adspend%20December%2005.pdf.

ZenithOptimedia (2006), Press Release: World Cup to Boost Adspend Growth in 2006.

Index

For Product Safety Concerns and Information please contact our EU representative GPSR@taylorandfrancis.com
Taylor & Francis Verlag GmbH, Kaufingerstraße 24, 80331 München, Germany

www.ingramcontent.com/pod-product-compliance
Ingram Content Group UK Ltd.
Pitfield, Milton Keynes, MK11 3LW, UK
UKHW022014180926
475701UK00003B/358
9780367602727